The Christian Counselor's Commentary

Hebrews
James
I & II Peter
Jude

Jay E. Adams

MID-AMERICA
INSTITUTE FOR NOUTHETIC STUDIES

Institute for Nouthetic Studies, a ministry of Mid-America Baptist Theological Seminary, 5640 Airline Road, Arlington, TN 38002
mabts.edu / nouthetic.org / INSBookstore.com

Hebrews, James, I & II Peter, Jude:
The Christian Counselor's Commentary
by Jay E. Adams

ISBN: 978-1-949737-51-6 (Paper)
ISBN: 978-1-949737-53-0 (eBook)
ISBN: 978-1-949737-52-3 (Hard Cover)
Old ISBN: 978-1-889032-01-8

Editor: Donn R. Arms

Library of Congress Cataloging-in-Publication Data
Names: Adams, Jay E., 1929-2020
Title: *Hebrews, James I & II Peter, Jude:*
The Christian Counselor's Commentary
by Jay E. Adams
Description: Arlington, TN: Institute for Nouthetic Studies, 2023
Identifiers: ISBN 978-1-949737-51-6 (paper) | OCLC: 36124174
Classification: LCC BS2341.2 .A35 | DDC 227.87

Published in the United States of America

Contents

Contents

Introduction to Hebrews

Hebrews is unlike the rest of the New Testament books in that no one knows who wrote it. There has been speculation (if I were to guess I'd say Jude—yet that is no more than a guess), but in the end, the writer remains unknown. What is known, however, is the *telos* (or purpose) for writing. As the name of the book indicates it was written to Jews (Hebrews). They had begun to suffer some persecution, but no one had suffered physically yet. Probably the persecution extended to ostracism, verbal abuse and possibly the loss of jobs and income. Beyond that it did not go. Yet, some of those whom the writer is addressing were reconsidering whether they should remain in the Christian faith or return to Judaism. If this was to be the outcome of their new beliefs, then they weren't so sure—! The letter speaks to this matter. Not only is it dangerous to think of going back (cf. chapters 2,6,10), but foolish. Why foolish? Because Christianity is so much ***better*** than Judaism. Better is the key word of the epistle. Largely, the argument of the letter is an extended attempt to prove this thesis to doubting Jews.

Well, then, of what value is Hebrews to Christian counselors? In addition to the many valuable subsets of interests found in the letter, the overall themes and arguments are highly pertinent. You see counselees who doubt their faith. There is material for them in the letter. Others wonder about the treatment they are accorded for adhering to their faith. Still others are troubled about loss and wonder if something else might not be better. All of these are themes useful for counselors to pursue. So if that is true, without further comment let's move right into the letter itself.

CHAPTER 1

1 It was in a number of stages and in a variety of ways that God spoke to our fathers in the past by the prophets.

2 But in these last days He has spoken to us by His Son, Whom He appointed Heir of everything, and through Whom He made the ages.

In the Books that we call the Old Testament, the writer observes, **God spoke to the fathers...by the prophets** at different periods and in varying manners. Not all revelation came at once. It came, rather, **in stages**. It was progressive and what appeared later was built on what was given earlier. It neither contradicted nor replaced previous revelation. Some came by means of dreams and visions, some by direct address and the rest by the Holy Spirit speaking in and through prophets. That was wonderful—God deigned to speak and reveal His will and something of His purposes to sinful, rebellious human beings. That He did so was pure grace. Nothing compelled Him to do it. Of His own free will, He determined to reveal His nature, His holy will and His plan of salvation through a Savior Who, in time, would come to redeem His people.

Counselors must never forget the wonder and importance of the Old Testament revelation. It was from God, tells us much about Him, about ourselves and about our world that we could know in no other way. Many counselors, unfortunately, fail to use the Old Testament as fully as they should. Ask yourself, from time to time, "How well do I use the Old Testament in counseling?" Obviously the Proverbs, Psalms, Genesis and Ecclesiastes are books to which you ought to refer regularly. But what of others? Thumb around in your Old Testament from time to time and notice how much there is for the counselor in Isaiah and Jeremiah, Job and Malachi for instance. Remember **God spoke** to man through these books.

But as wonderful as the Old Testament writings are, there is a revelation that tells of something that far surpasses anything found in the Old Testament—something far ***better***—a revelation that came through God's **Son**! In the **last days** of the Old Testament period, He **spoke** once again. This time, however, what He said came not in the form of types and shadows, of dreams and visions, but in reality and fulfillment of that which all the prophets of former times predicted. And it was no longer an anticipation of the forgiveness of sins, looking forward to the Messiah Who would appear as God's Lamb, but now a solid reality founded on His sacrifice of

3 He is the radiance of His glory and the perfect representation of God's very being. He sustains everything by His powerful word. And when He had accomplished the cleansing of sins, He sat down at the right hand of the Majesty in the heights.

Himself on the cross of Calvary.

This Son of God was not merely man, but as the God-man He was **appointed Heir of everything.** Think of that Christian when you are about to lose everything through boycotting by those who resent your turning to Christ for salvation; here you may lose everything that you ever had, but in eternity you will enter into the inheritance of all that *He* has—everything that there is! Counselees suffering loss for their faith can take heart from these words. You are aligning yourself with a Savior Who is so superabundantly rich, it would take all the ages to come to count His wealth.

And He is not a Person Who is stuck in time and space (though as man, He was a truly historical figure). In His deity Jesus is the One Who made the ages. Time itself is the product of His creative work. He knows just when everything should happen—indeed, He is in sovereign control of how time and the events that occur in time progress. Nothing can slip between His fingers. There is nothing that is out of His providence. Persecution, loss, whatever may transpire—all of it is working through time to bring about His eternal purposes. You are part of that plan and are an integral element in demonstrating the eternal glory of God. Rejoice! Take heart, troubled counselee.

Now in order to show how great the One in Whom the reader has placed his faith is, the writer of the letter says **He is the radiance of His glory and the perfect representation of God's very being.** Counselees sometimes ask, "Why is it that God doesn't reveal *Himself* to us?" Your answer: He has done so. If you want to know what God is like, look at Jesus Christ. Everything you could ever want to know about God is revealed in the words, works, life and person of His beloved Son. Others would prefer a physical representation of God in the form of an idol. But God has forbidden making and bowing down to idols. Why? Because no idol could properly represent God to us. And no idol is necessary; Jesus Christ is the **perfect representation of God's very being** (v. 3). Look to Him and bow the knee.

God's Son **sustains everything by His powerful word.** As God spoke and there was light, so now by the mere command of His Son the

4 He became as much superior to the angels as the name He has inherited is more excellent than theirs.
5 To which of the angels did God ever say,

---

universe remains intact. With such phenomenal power manifest in His very word, why would anyone—counselor or counselee—for even a moment doubt the outcome of his faith? Yet counselees do, all the time. Why is that? Many times the doubts and the fears that permeate counselees stem from the fact that they have forgotten all that the Bible teaches about God and Christ. How important, then, to keep everyone's eyes and hearts focused on Him, on what He is and on what He is able to do throughout the counseling hour. If you focus on the counselee in all his weakness or even on yourself with your many limitations, where will hope and strength come from? But when the focus rightly is placed on God the Father, Son and Spirit there is all the hope that there is in creation—and more!

But where is the remarkable Person Who **sustains everything by His powerful word**? He is seated **at the right hand of the majesty in the heights**. He is in the position of power, authority and glory, seated next to the Father Himself. Why was humanity exalted to such a position? Because it was in and through humanity the eternal Son of God **accomplished the cleansing of sins**. That is to say, He died for those whom the Father gave Him, bearing the punishment for all their sins and iniquities so that they might be cleansed from them, nevermore to be held accountable for them. That is why He came. And by analyzing what He did in accomplishing the cleansing of sins, you can learn all about God—His wrath, His justice, but also His mercy and His forgiveness.

And because of what He did, Jesus was raised to the **right hand** of God. In Christ, humanity reigns over the universe! No wonder then that the writer points out **He became as much superior to the angels as the name He has inherited is more excellent than theirs**. He has been named "Lord" (cf. Philippians 2:11). Already the writer is beginning to show how the Lord Jesus is **superior to** and **more excellent** than the highest beings in the universe. Can you walk away from such a Person when you recognize that? And should you do so, can you do it with impunity? Those are two good questions to put to doubting, wavering counselees.

To establish his point the writer cites several Old Testament passages that support his contention, asking **To which of the angels did God ever**

You are My Son;
today I have begotten you?

And again:

I will be a Father to Him
and He will be a Son to Me?

6 Then again, when He brings His Firstborn into the world, He says,
All of God's angels must worship Him.

7 Now referring to the angels He says,
He makes His angels winds
and His servants a flame of fire.

8 But referring to the Son
Your throne, O God, is forever and ever,
and the rod of Your empire is the rod of uprightness.

9 **You have loved righteousness and You hate lawlessness;**
therefore God, Your God, has anointed You
with the oil of gladness beyond Your companions.

10 And:
You, Lord, laid the earth's foundations at the beginning,
and the heavens are the works of Your hands.

---

say... And again... Then again... These verses from the Old Testament say that Jesus is God's Son (God never said that to an angel); that He will be His **Father** and that Jesus will be **His Son** (or that), and that the **angels** must **worship Him** (now think of that!). Truly Jesus is the unique Son of God, and if worthy of the angel's worship, surely He is worthy of yours.

Continuing, he contrasts what God has said of the angels with what He said about His Son: The angels are like **the winds, God's servants** who are like **a flame of fire** (with destructive power to be feared: cf. II Thessalonians 1:7-9). But in speaking of His Son, God has declared (cf. Psalm 2) that He is seated (as the God-man) on a throne, ruling with power to execute **righteousness** in **gladness beyond [His] companions** (other human beings). But that isn't all. Referring to His eternal might and glory, He says **You laid the earth's foundations at the beginning, and the heavens are the work of Your hands.** And even though all the creation will be melted down and destroyed, He, not being a part of creation, will remain (vv. 10-12). The implication? If you want to be on the eternal, winning side, stick with Him! And in this chapter, one more thrust—God will put all things **under His feet**. Angels, on the other hand are but **ministering spirits sent off to serve for the benefit of those who are going to inherit salvation** (that is, God's elect). If these things are true (and

11 **They will be destroyed but You remain;**
they will all grow old like a garment
12 **and You will roll them up like a robe.**
Like a garment they will be changed,
but You are the same
and Your years will not come to an end.
13 Now, to which of the angels has He said at any time,
Sit at My right hand
till I put Your enemies under Your feet like a footstool?
14 Aren't they all ministering spirits sent off to serve for the benefit of those who are going to inherit salvation?

---

they most certainly are) why turn away? Of what moment is the temporary pain and suffering that one must endure here when compared with all that there is in Jesus Christ? In counseling, it is always important to sound this note of victory and glory, since the notes of defeat and misery have been ringing loudly in the heart and the minds of many counselees.

CHAPTER 2

1 So then, we must pay all the more attention to what we have heard so that we won't drift away from it.

The description of Jesus Christ with which the Book of Hebrews opens is magnificent (reminding one somewhat of that which is painted for us in Colossians). And the very fact that it is this description of the Savior-God that the writer puts up front ought to tell you something: he wants to set up Jesus Christ in contrast with Judaism. He is what makes Christianity "better." It doesn't matter what the problem is that your counselee presents; learn to set Jesus Christ over against it. When you do, the seeming significance of it will pale beside Him. This is true of both negative things and positive. Don't only set Jesus over against suffering and pain (as the One Who makes this endurable) but over against every attraction toward which one might be drawn away. With the writer of Hebrews, make *Him* appear so attractive that nothing else can compare with Him. Nothing can, can it? That is often the very best way to begin counseling—especially when you are aware of something else that seems to have a hold on your counselee.

The writer draws a conclusion: **So then, we must pay all the more attention to what we have heard so that we won't drift away from it.** Here is the first inkling of the problem that he is addressing: some were inclined to drift from the faith. We shall hear more of it especially in chapters 6 and 10. But in this place, the defection is not considered so much a deliberate thing but a careless one—drifting. The word is used of drifting with the tide (cf. our present-day expression, "to go with the flow") Drifting, perhaps, is the most common way in which people depart from the Church. How many show up less and less to Christian gatherings until, one day, you realize that they have stopped coming altogether. An alert eldership will not allow this to go unnoticed. They will do something about it. And counselors who find that some counselees, while claiming to be believers, rarely (if ever) attend church must not neglect the problem either. One way of determining how frequently one attends church is from the P.D.I. (the Personal Data Inventory; see *The Christian Counselor's Manual* for a sample). Counselors may not look lightly on drifting. Whenever you encounter it (and it is quite frequently met in Christian counseling) you must warn about the problem of drifting. The writer of this letter

2 If the word spoken through angels was certain, and every transgression and disobedience received its full punishment,
3 how can we escape if we neglect such a great salvation? It was at the outset declared by the Lord, and it was confirmed to us by those who heard Him.

---

does not allow his readers to drift without issuing a warning; neither should you.

What do you tell drifters? To **pay all the more attention to what [they] have heard.** That point is clear; there can be no ifs, ands or buts about it. When they do, in the manner that we have described in the previous chapter (focusing on the superiority of Christ over everyone and everything else), if genuine believers, they will correct the drift. But he says **all the more attention**. All the more than *what*? All the more than the Old Testament revelation, as marvelous as it was. They must pay attention to the apostolic word even more than to earlier revelations. By doing so, they will find Christ far more clearly portrayed in all His magnificence as the God-man. This revelation, given to and by the apostles, is full and complete. It is all that one needs for life and godliness. So it must be heeded. Drifters are those who do not pay adequate attention to the Bible. I am sure that long ago I would have drifted from a vital interest in the Christian faith if I had not been committed to the study of the Bible. Wouldn't you, counselor? Surely, along with me, you have noticed time and again that counselors who do not use the Scriptures in their counseling drift more and more away from the biblical revelation into man-centered ideas. If you want to stop drift, therefore, says our writer, direct people to the Scriptures (the present depository of the apostolic word that they **heard**).

In verses 2 and 3 there is a rhetorical question to which the answer is, "No way." One cannot **escape**. Let's see why. In the Old Testament, God's message to His people came **through angels** (Galatians 3:19). And if that revelation was accompanied by the **full punishment** of **every transgression and disobedience**, then surely this more wonderful and fuller revelation should be all the more so. Therefore, take heed! When God does something this fine for His own, He expects them to appreciate it. If they fail to do so, the heavenly Father will punish them as disobedient children. If they are reprobates, they will receive all the more severe punishment in eternity for having rejected the message clearly proclaimed to them.

And the words of angels were **certain** ("firm"). The threats given

4 God also testified to it by signs, wonders, all sorts of miracles and gifts from the Holy Spirit, distributed as He wished.

---

then were not in vain; nor will those accompanying the newer, greater revelation in God's Son be any less so (cf. 3:17). A **salvation** as **great** as the one proclaimed concerning Christ may not be neglected with impunity. The term translated **neglect** is worth considering. It means "to lose care [concern] for." That word accords very nicely with the idea of **drift.** Both characterizations of one who is defecting indicate a gradual, perhaps even at first indiscernible, movement away from the faith. Salvation, for some reason or other, has lost its charm. The person who is drifting, neglecting God's salvation, has lost the wonder of it. The most exciting word ever spoken no longer excites. One cannot help but think of the ground mentioned in Matthew 13:19-21. These people are exactly like those mentioned in the parable—a little persecution and they become disenchanted with what, at first, seemed to them to be the greatest thing in the world.

This **salvation** was first preached by the **Lord** Himself while here on the earth. Then, it **was confirmed to** the writer and his readers by the disciples (now apostles) **who heard Him**. But that is not all: **God also testified to it**. How could one want a stronger threefold cord of testimony? It is a cord that cannot be broken. Is there any reason, then, for doubting that there is severe punishment coming to those who have heard and rejected this testimony? Persons who show such disregard and neglect will not **escape**! There are very many counselees who, because of the difficulties in which they find themselves, have begun to drift. If you fudge, and fail to warn them, you will be an unfaithful servant of Christ and a poor watchman on the city wall.

But how did God lend His attestation to the message and work of salvation? By **signs, wonders, all sorts of miracles and gifts from the Holy Spirit, distributed as He wished.** God sovereignly stepped into the course of human history (as He does no longer) making known that the work and words of His Son were not merely another historical event;, they were *the* event of all events for all time. The amazing and powerful works that God performed through and accompanying the ministry of Jesus Christ were given as signs. That is, they were indications that God was stamping His seal of approval on Christ's ministry. (Cf. comments on Acts 2:22, II Corinthians 12:12 etc.) If God went to such great lengths to attest His ministry of salvation, woe to those who neglect His saving Word and drift away from the message! There is a strong warning here.

5 Now it wasn't to angels that He subjected the coming world, about which we are speaking.
6 And somebody at some place has testified:
What is man that You remember him
or a son of man that You should take care of him?
7 **You made him for a short time lower than the angels;**
You crowned him with glory and honor
8 **and subjected everything beneath his feet.**
And, in subjecting "Everything" to him, He didn't leave anything that isn't subject to him. Of course, at the present time we don't see everything subject to him.

You must deal with persons who think that signs and wonders are prevalent today and that since they don't have the ability to perform them they must not be saved. To understand what this passage has to say about them, therefore, is important to the counselor. They are not signs of salvation; they are signs attesting the *message* of salvation and those who brought it. It is, therefore, necessary for you to be able to handle this matter. If you have questions about this read the discussion of this in the pertinent passages listed above (see also comments on Ephesians 2:20).

Verse 5 assumes a very important fact: **the coming world** will be **subjected** to human beings. Think of that. Not only are we to judge angels, but the entire rulership of the world to come will be under the control of God's saints. What is the problem, then, with those who want to turn back? With those who are drifting? Simply this: either they do not fully realize the glories of the future of the Christian (that is the point the writer is laboring to make clear) or they have so fixed their attention on the present world that they have forgotten God's promises about the world to come. Or both. Your task is to remind them.

In support of what he is saying he quotes Psalm 8:4-6 in order to discuss the past, present and future of man. Man was created in a state below the angels (v. 7); a state that will last for a **short time.** Why then, if man is so unimportant in the universe, should God be so concerned about him as to send His Son to die for Him (that is the import of the question in v. 6)? Not because of anything in the man himself. He was originally created on a lower level than the angels which are not stronger in might and greater in glory. And of course, man sank even lower into sin. The answer to the question lies not in man or his high state—the opposite is true—but in God's great condescending mercy and grace. It is not because man is great, but because God is.

9 But we do see Jesus, Who for a short time was made lower than the angels, crowned with glory and honor because He suffered death, so that by God's grace He might taste death for all sorts of people.
10 It was fitting that He, for Whom and by Whom everything exists, in leading many sons to glory, should make the Leader of their salvation perfect through suffering.

Yet though man is a lowly creature and wretched sinner, God has determined to exalt him through His Son (v. 8). He will be crowned as ruler of the world to come, with everything placed in subjection to him. What mercy and grace that is! And the writer notes, by "**Everything**" he means just that—***everything***. Nothing in the created order will be excepted. Remind your counselees of that. When they whine and complain, when they doubt and they waffle, when they get frustrated and depressed—remind them!

But as he points out, that is all in the future. The greatness of the Christian's glory is certain, but it is not yet a realized fact: **at the present time we don't see everything subject to him.** Yet, mankind, in Jesus (Who became man that He might redeem us), **Who for a short time was made lower then the angels, crowned with glory and honor,** has been exalted to that position. Why? **Because He suffered death, so that by God's grace He might taste death for all sorts of people.** He is the Forerunner of all that is to come for the believer. It is not yet true of us, but all that will be true for us is already true for Him.

And this is **fitting** (v. 10) because **He, for Whom and by Whom everything exists, in leading many sons to glory, should make the Leader of their salvation perfect through suffering.** There are several things to note in this verse. First, why it was fitting for Jesus to be made perfect (i.e., "complete"). He was **leading many Sons [of God] to glory** (the state of the world to come). As the **Leader** it is altogether appropriate that the honor and the glory should come first to Him. The leader goes first. He was the One Who will bring them into glory since He is the One by Whom they receive salvation. Next, note that He is made **perfect**. Wasn't Jesus always perfect, from birth? Yes, of course, in moral terms. But there were things that He must accomplish as the Leader of (the One Who leads into) salvation. These He achieved (completed) through suffering the penal, substitutionary death of the cross. Then *as Leader of the Sons of God* He was complete. He was the **perfect** Leader. Nothing more needed to be done or could be done to bring about the salvation of those

11 Both the One Who sanctifies and those who are being sanctified are all from One. That is why He isn't ashamed to call them "Brothers" when He says,
12 **I will announce Your name to My brothers;**
In the midst of the church I will sing a hymn to You.

---

for whom He died.

He and we (the **Sanctifier and those who are being sanctified**) come from One: Adam. That is to say, we are both truly human. Because of that fact—that Jesus became truly human—He is not **ashamed to call [us] "Brothers."** We are fellow humans; brothers according to heritage. Here is the initial use of the word **sanctified** in the Book of Hebrews. While in Christian theology, the word means progress in putting off the old way of life and in putting on the new one, the writer uses the word differently. He means one who has been set apart by God for Himself.

The Christian is already fully sanctified *in God's sight*. That does not mean that he is so in his actual state. But because it is so, he may realize that God views him as he does His Son; perfectly holy and righteous. He is set aside from others in Christ, Who is the Sanctifier (the One Who sets apart for Himself). Because that is true, there is no remorse or self agonizing that one should engage in over longs periods of time. He should recognize his status before God and the fact that God sees him as perfect. God, through Christ, has set him apart for Himself; he is God's. He belongs to Him. He is really and truly God's own. Let him rejoice over that fact and not waste time that ought to be spent serving God moaning over his sins and wondering whether he is a child of God. That is not to say that he should not regret sinning against his loving Father in the heavens; he should. Nor does it mean that there is no need for repentance; there is. He must be sorry for displeasing His Father, and he must seek His forgiveness. But it is family forgiveness of which we are speaking; not judicial forgiveness (the latter was dealt with once and for all; that is why the believer can be said to be "set apart" to God in Christ. Judicially, he is so.). Many counselees have these things confused. They fail to distinguish between judicial forgiveness and Fatherly forgiveness; between once-for-all sanctification (how one is counted to be) and progressive sanctification (what is going on day by day in life now). To help them get this straight is not only a freeing experience but a necessary one.

Support for the fact that Jesus counts believers as brothers (fellow human beings is what he means by the term here) is found in the Old Tes-

13 And again,

I will put My trust in Him.

And once more,

Here I am and the children whom God gave to Me.

14 So then, since the children have had blood and flesh in common, He likewise shared these things with them, so that by His death He might destroy the one who has the power of death, that is, the devil,

---

tament passages he now quotes (vv. 12,13; see Psalm 22:22). He is so much one of us, sharing **blood and flesh** with us (v. 14), that He announces God's Name to those He calls His **brothers** and, like us, as man puts His **trust in Him** while, gathering together in common worship of the Father **in the midst of the church [congregation]**, He sings praises to God. He, as Leader of those who will follow Him to glory, declares **Here I am and the children whom God gave Me.** He is with us, as one of us, to redeem us.

If Jesus was God with us (Immanuel), then He knows us through and through. Every counselee should rejoice in this fact. Jesus, Who suffered in the flesh, knows your sorrows and pains. He is not aloof; He was here among us *as one of us*. No Christian can rightly say, "Nobody knows the trouble I've seen." He must continue, "Nobody knows but Jesus." Yes, He does. And cares. But more of that at a later place.

Working out his point more fully, the writer says **So then, since the children have blood and flesh in common, He likewise shared these things with them, so that by His death He might destroy the one who has the power of death, that is, the devil** (v. 14). How important it is for dying, suffering, fearful saints to learn this fact! Think of it: the devil, the one who formerly held the **power of death** has been destroyed. That is to say, his power has been destroyed. As the one who could always hold over us the fact that at death we must face the Judge of all the earth as unforgiven sinners, he could bring icy fear to our hearts. But no longer. Christ has died to forgive us and acquit us from God's judgment on our sins.

But is the devil destroyed? The word used in the original means to "render inoperative, to make ineffective." It is true that He goes about as a roaring lion, but it is also true that he may be resisted (I Peter 5:8,9). There is no way in which the devil can dupe or injure a Christian against his will. Indeed, contrary to all of the quite erroneous ideas floated about among some Christians, he cannot even **touch** him (I John 5:18). It is harmful for Christians to buy into views of Satan that make one fear him. The Christian is perfectly safe so long as he is doing God's will. The devil

15 and deliver those who, by fear of death, were subjected to slavery throughout their entire lifetime.
16 Now, of course, it wasn't for angels that He undertook this; rather, He undertook it for Abraham's seed.
17 That is why He had to become like His brothers in every way, so that He might become a merciful and faithful High Priest in what is related to God, to make propitiation for the people's sins.

---

cannot *make* Christians do or think anything even though some seem to teach such errors. He is a defeated foe. Sure, if one aligns himself with his ways he can do harm, but there is no need to do so. And any trouble into which one falls by way of the devil's temptation is the result of his own failure. He no more needs to succumb to the devil's temptation than Christ did. Nor is it possible for the devil to possess (or oppress) a believer. In the Lord Jesus Christ he has all that is necessary to resist the devil. Inform, teach and comfort fearful Christians with these facts in counseling.

What the evil one once was able to do—to bring fear into the heart of the unforgiven sinner—he can do no longer once that sinner is forgiven. He can no longer subject him to **slavery [to fear] throughout [his] entire lifetime.** That power has been taken away by the blood of Christ's cross. Believers are **delivered** from the **fear of death.** How is that? Read I Corinthians 15:54-57 and see comments on that passage. The fearful counselee must be confronted with the joyful news of verses 14 and 15. You, as his counselor, must never allow him to continue in fear of death. There is no excuse when there are words like these in the Bible. Point him also to the first chapter of Philippians where Paul, as one who knew about the great victory of Christ over Satan, responds to death as every believer ought to. Any continued fear stems either from lack of faith in the Scriptures or from lack of salvation in the counselee who might think that he is a Christian when he is not. Either way, you must deal with the problem of faith: faith in Christ as Savior or stronger faith.

Continuing his comparison of Christ and the Christian with angels, he writes, **Now, of course, it wasn't for angels that He undertook this; rather, He undertook it for Abraham's seed.** That is for all believers, Jew and Gentile alike (who have become children of Abraham by faith. See full discussions of that point in Romans and in Galatians). But especially, note that Christ died only for those who are the true seed of Abraham.

Since He was doing so, **He had to become like His brothers in**

18 Because He Himself was tempted in His suffering, He is able to help those who are being tempted.

---

every way, so that He might become a merciful and faithful High priest in what is related to God, to make propitiation for His people's sins. Had He been anything less, or anything more (above), Jesus' sacrifice would not have been acceptable. He had to be a man like us.

Propitiation is the smoothing of the wrinkled brow of God. It is an appeasing of His wrath. It is the rendering of satisfaction for sins. God cannot allow sin to go unpunished. The debt of sin had to be paid. Christ, as a merciful High Priest (He did what He did out of mercy, not out of necessity) sacrificed Himself on the cross to do so. Counselees who fear may be told that God is no longer angry with the wrath of a magistrate over their sins. Many do not realize this fact. Nor do they see the cross as mercy poured out on them. Set them straight.

Then comes verse 18, the climax of what has been said. Every counselor must have this verse at his fingertips, ready to use. Christ was **tempted in His suffering.** That is why **He is able to help those who are being tempted.** The very fact that He does help is enough. But the writer goes farther: He was tempted in suffering. There were those who cried "come down off the cross." There was the agony in the garden of Gethsemane where He contemplated becoming the scapegoat upon whom the sins of His people were cast, who would be sent away into the wilderness bearing the shame. There was the temptation when hungry in the desert, when the devil offered an easy way out of suffering. But He faced them all successfully. Tell that to your suffering counselee who thinks there is no help for him. Jesus says He will help. And He knows how to—because He suffered from temptation too. Indeed, He suffered greater temptation than anyone; His temptation was to the zenith. Yours is far less intense. Tell Him about all your trials and temptations; He is a merciful High Priest Who understands and cares. Counselor, armed with this verse as well as those about the destruction of the devil, you have all you need to successfully enable your counselee to face every and any temptation.

CHAPTER 3

1 The result of which, holy brothers, is that you who share in a heavenly calling must regard Jesus as the Apostle and High Priest of our confession.

The third chapter of the Book of Hebrews begins by making a logical transition from what has already been said about Jesus to what that should mean to the reader. He says **You who share in a heavenly calling must regard Jesus as the Apostle and High priest of our confession.** Now there is a heavily loaded statement if there ever was one. What, exactly, does he mean?

Well, he begins by pointing out that the readers who believe in Christ **share in a heavenly calling**. They **share**, as he has been telling us for quite some time, in the present but especially in the future glories of Christ, the One Who is willing to be called **brother** and Who is now **crowned with glory and honor, sitting at the Father's right hand**. Being joint heirs, considered by God to be as set apart as He is, believers share in all that has been accorded Him because of His work of redemption. Those are the wondrous truths that he has already been emphasizing throughout the first two chapters. As important as they are for counselors, however, there is more.

The idea in reemphasizing these things is to set them over against the former life in which, ultimately, there was nothing more than the fear of death that dogged one's steps. Rather than look forward to death (and **after that—the judgment**), which as the ultimate end **subjected [him] to slavery throughout [his] entire lifetime**, the Christian now has the glories of the world to come toward which to live. Life has a very different outcome. And it is this new life, with its new outcome that some are thinking of abandoning? For the old life of fear and slavery? Does that make any kind of sense?

The fear of death is something that every counselor must realize motivates many (if not in some unconscious sense *all*) of the basic decisions of unbelievers. And you must remember, when one becomes a Christian he does not automatically leave behind his old patterns of thought and action; quite to the contrary. Indeed, it is these with which the Christian counselor must deal. So, the question at many points in counseling must be: "Don, what do you think is behind that sort of attitude (or decision, etc.)? Could it be a fear of death, or the ultimate outcome that follows death? Were you thinking [acting] like someone who must 'get it all here' because there is no certainty about your future?" Or perhaps, "Were you acting like death is the worst thing that could happen to you?" If, indeed, you discover that he is still acting out of the slavery that such fear engenders, you will be wise to turn to this passage and develop the themes set forth here that have to do with the new outlook believers may enjoy. One's entire outlook on life ought to change so that he can face death and beyond with joy and expectation.

To do so, the counselee should **regard Jesus as the Apostle and High Priest of [his] confession.** He once confessed Jesus as such. When he declared his faith in Jesus Christ as Savior and was baptized into the church, in effect, he **confessed** that Jesus is his Apostle and High Priest. That Jesus is the **High Priest** of forgiven sinners, Who offered Himself as a pleasing sacrifice for their sins is understandable. But what does it mean that He is our **Apostle**? In the Book of Hebrews there are terms used to describe the work of Christ that we find nowhere else. We have already encountered him as **Leader** of many sons to glory. And here, He is designated as the One Whom believers confess as (declare that they believe Him to be their) Apostle. What is an apostle? The word comes from the Greek as a transliteration. It is *apostolos*. The apostle was one who was "sent off" on a mission. He went forth, representing someone else with a message to proclaim. Of course, Jesus did precisely that; He came preaching that "the empire from the heavens is at hand." The message of the **great salvation** that God had prepared for those who would confess Him as their own was **at the outset declared by the Lord** (i.e., the Lord Jesus; cf. 2:3). Thus, He was the first apostle (as He is the first in all good things of God). This, of course, makes it doubly serious when one turns his back on the message of salvation: he rejects not only the message, but also the One Who brought it as God's faithful Apostle. The warning in the concept of Jesus as Apostle is implicit, but powerful; one rejects not only Paul or Peter, etc., but Jesus as well when he drifts from the Word.

And to drift from the **heavenly calling** (v. 1) is madness. Having described the call to eternal life so fully, and so gloriously, what can we say of the one who still turns his back on it? Only that we must question his very salvation: was it real? There will be more about this as the writer of Hebrews returns to the warning theme over and over again. In a very real sense, the book is but one long warning, coupled with a powerful appeal to heed it. It is a plea to consider what one is leaving for what he is returning to. That idea of *considering* is built into the first verse as well. I

2 He was faithful to the One Who appointed Him, just as Moses also was in all His house.

---

have translated it as **regard**. The word means to give such careful consideration of something that you come to regard it for what it truly is. That is precisely what the writer wants his readers to do. He is confident that when such full consideration is given so as to come to regard Christ for what He truly is (High priest and Apostle of their confession) they will not want to turn back.

With Hebrews, we have emphasized all along the need to see Jesus for what He is. That is the message to counselors. Most problems involving fear (a very powerful emotion), hesitancy, cowardice or timidity may be overcome by bringing counselees into a full appreciation of Who Christ is. That means filling in their weak and sometimes not quite adequate understanding of the **confession** of faith that they made when they trusted Him. But counselor, how do *you* regard Christ? You aren't sure? Well, ask yourself, "What is my view of death?" That should clue you in.

But now, moving on to verse 2, let us see where the writer wishes to turn next. He is still talking about Jesus. Here he describes Him as the One Who is **faithful** to God Who **appointed Him, just as Moses was also in all his house.** No one can deny the faithfulness of Christ as the Apostle and High priest Who fulfilled His mission, going even to the cross to do so. He is *like* Moses (the one they were pitting over against Christ in their thinking)—not in contrast to him (except that he is **greater** than Moses; v. 3). The two should not be contrasted as leaders of two opposed systems. They differ only in the fact that the latter system, proclaimed and brought about by Jesus Christ, is greater than the former one brought about by Moses. But in other respects, the two men and the two systems are alike. Indeed, one foreshadowed the other. Both were **appointed** by God. It is wrong to pit them over against each other as opposing systems.

Counselees will attempt to pit various churches, beliefs, ideas over against each other in order to avoid doing the will of God or in order to justify sin. You may often be able to point out that the beliefs or churches are not fundamentally opposed to one another (whenever this is true), but that one is simply a better, clearer expression of what the other person wants to say as well. While human viewpoints are not inspired as the Old Testament law and the New Testament gospel are, but do contain errors and contradictions, nevertheless, there are many respects in which what I

3 Yet He has been considered worthy of greater honor than Moses; just as much so as the builder of a house has honor above the house.

---

have just said is true. Take the following example. Mildred wants to go on gossiping about her neighbors, even though it is clear that gossip is a sin (mentioned frequently in Scripture as such). She insists that what she is doing is not gossip; "I am only telling the truth," she explains. "What you say may be the truth," you reply, "but is it necessary?" To her, gossip means only telling lies, whereas to biblical writers it is telling anything about another (true or false) that it is not necessary to tell. You explain this to her. She responds, "But, my friend said that I was to expose sin whenever I saw it." You tell her that is correct, "but the teacher that she heard may have forgotten to emphasize the additional fact that such an exposure of sin must begin with an exposure of it *to the one sinning* (Matthew 18:15ff.). Your friend was right so far as he went, but what he said was not all that must be said on the subject. He and I are both telling you that it is necessary to expose sin, but there is a biblically correct way of doing so that involves no gossip." You can see how you can link yourself with what is right and true while still rejecting what is wrong, can't you? Certainly, Mildred's friend wanted the right thing, even if he failed to present the proper ways and means of bringing it about. Mildred, on the other hand, wishing to continue her sinful practice, may have even distorted what the friend said. Regardless, you can side with what is right in the advice, while pointing out the greater truth that the Bible sets forth about ways and means of exposing sin.

Though Moses was faithful in what he did for **all** the **house** of Israel, Jesus **has been considered worthy of greater honor than Moses.** Why is that? Because He, as God, was the One Who conceived and constructed the entire system in which Moses carried out his mission. This is the point of the explanation he now gives in saying that Jesus is greater—**just as much so as the builder of a house has honor above the house** that he builds. The former is greater in power and intelligence: he can design and erect a house, but the house (glorious as it is) cannot do so. The writer has slipped back and forth between the two meanings of **house**. He begins by thinking of the family or people of Israel (the house of Israel) but then, as illustrative of his point, thinks next of the literal meaning of house as a building. The Hebrews had no word for "family"; they used the word house to convey this concept. For them the term house is a warm one; it meant family. You might even say, contrary to our expression, for a

4 Every house, of course, is built by somebody, but God is the builder of everything.
5 So, on the one hand, Moses was faithful in His whole house as a servant, testifying to things that would be disclosed in the future;
6 on the other hand, Christ was faithful over His house as a Son. And we are His house if we hold firmly to the confidence and pride that we have in our hope.

Hebrew a house *is* a home.

The upshot of the discussion so far, then, is that Jesus is greater than Moses, though both the Mosaic message and the Christian message, which are complementary rather than disjunctive, are the product of the Same Person—Jesus Himself (as God). God is the Builder of everything (v. 4), he says, observing that everything must have its source (as every house must have its builder). But in comparing the two systems, one must understand that Moses was faithful **as a servant** while Christ was faithful **as a Son** (vv. 5,6). There is, of course, a great difference between the two. And as the two are contrasted *as Greater and lesser*, so to is what they offer to the Christian. That is the point of the writer's discussion: why accept the lesser when you can have the greater?

So often, the choice before a counselee is just that. For various reasons, that may largely have to do with fear, he is willing to accept the lesser in place of the greater. Only in the final analysis, as we shall see in this very Book, such a choice is not really for the lesser instead of the greater; it is for the wrong as over against the right. Indeed, hints of this are already surfacing: **testifying to things that would be disclosed in the future** (v. 5). There was not really a choice between Moses and Jesus. Although what Moses offered in the past was acceptable, it was no longer so. And Moses himself **testified** that this would be the case. He looked forward to and wrote about things that would happen in days to come, things that one must accept if he were to accept Moses. Moses predicted by word and type and shadow all that has now happened in Jesus Christ. The lesser predicted the greater which has now come. In order to be faithful to the teachings and practices of Moses one would find it necessary to abandon Moses's system for that which replaced it.

You must often make clear to your counselee that "in order to be faithful to what you are claiming is the basis for your actions, you must now do something different. You may no longer follow old ideas and ways that once may have been right, and that, in principle may still be right, but that in the present no longer hold. The new wine may not be poured into old wineskins." What am I talking about? For one thing, take a situation where, before knowing otherwise, one thinks that playing Old Maids (to use a facetious example) is a sin (I hope no reader thinks that it *is* for the sake of my example!). What is proper for a Christian in that state? It is proper *not* to play. Indeed, if he does so, thinking that it might be sinful or that it *is* sinful, he sins. That is what Romans 14:23 teaches. He sins, not because the *act* of playing Old Maids is sinful but because his attitude is. How is that? Well, if he went ahead and did something that he thought was (or might be) sinful, even if it wasn't, his attitude was sinful. He was willing (for whatever reason—embarrassment, or whatever) to sin against God.

But now he has come to see that playing Old Maids is not sin. There is no longer any excuse he can offer for not doing whatever he once thought was wrong. Now, he has been enlightened and understands clearly that it is not. Indeed, to use such an excuse is in effect a lie. With Old Maids there is no problem (who has to play?), but in other situations clearly there could be a problem. The point is that, in good conscience, he may no longer plead to be excused as he once could. Why not take the time to think of a dozen circumstances in counseling where you have known counselees to beg off from a responsibility for reasons that no longer hold, and that since they do not hold, were wrong for him to offer as reasons? Well, let's return to the passage.

The new Israel is Christ's **house** (v. 6). That is, those who **hold firmly to the confidence and pride that we have in our hope.** Again, the note of faithfulness to the end is sounded. Of course, the teaching "once saved, always saved" is correct; but it is incomplete. The biblical doctrine is best summed up in the teaching of the "perseverance of the saints" which says that those who endure to the end will be saved. That is the point of the warnings in this book—if persons who say that they are saved do not endure, their **confession** of faith, not being **firm**, can only be viewed as false. There is little reason, the writer says, to think of the one who fails to endure to the end as genuine if he loses his **confidence and pride [in his Savior].** The Christian **hope** is such that one ought to speak proudly about it. He ought not to hide it or talk about it apologetically; He has the greatest hope mankind has ever known; why shouldn't he boast and be able to speak confidently about it? The drifter, the one who shrinks back at the earliest sight of opposition or persecution evidences either the lack of genuine faith or the need for growth in faith. Keep these things in mind as you counsel fearful saints (or those who only purport to be saints).

7 So then, as the Holy Spirit says,
Today, if you hear His voice,
8 **don't harden your hearts as in the revolt during the day of testing in the desert,**
9 **where your fathers tried and proved Me and saw My works for forty years.**
10 **As a result I became very angry with that generation and I said, "Their hearts are always going astray; they haven't known My ways."**
11 **As I swore in My wrath,**
"They will never enter into My rest."

Now from verse 7 on, the warning becomes sharp and clear. And it translates into a strong exhortation as well. In the words of the Psalmist (which, incidentally, he calls the words of the Holy Spirit) the writer makes it plain that those who harden their hearts (the drifting is now conceived not as an unconscious neglect, as he earlier had characterized it, but what that may become—full-blown apostasy) will experience the angry sentence of God upon them: **They will never enter into My rest.** This rest, as he is going to make clear, is the eternal rest of salvation, a rest from striving to be saved by one's own works.

The writer quotes the Psalmist, who explains that turning from God is a matter of **hearts...going astray**. Hardened hearts and hearts that go astray are the problem. Heart in the Bible does not mean emotion (that is spoken of as bowels), but the interior aspects of a person—the inner man, what one genuinely is and thinks. Heart is never contrasted with the head (as we sometimes do in Western thought) but always with the mouth, the hands, the lips, or some other aspect of the outer person. So here the writer, following the Psalmist, puts his finger on the cause of the difficulty: those who turn back, who desert Christ have never truly known Him; they made an outer profession of faith, were baptized, lived and talked as though they were Christians and took a place among God's people, but as soon a trouble arose, it became clear that their hearts were not with Him. Trial and trouble—those very things that constitute the core of most counseling cases—may bring out the fact that the counselee is, in fact, not a genuine believer. If he **hardens** his heart against other Christians, the truth and the Lord Himself, he must not be allowed to continue in the church (church discipline must be applied). If his **heart** continually leads him to **go astray** (into sin) with no change or growth of lifestyle, but only a continual following of some way other than God's, again, he must

12 Watch out, brothers, so that there won't be in any of you an evil, unbelieving heart that would turn you away from the living God.
13 Instead, encourage one another every day, as long as we can still call it "today," so that none of you will become hardened by sin's deceiving ways.

---

be disciplined and put out of the church. These, as the writer observes, are evidences of **an evil, unbelieving heart** that turns people **away from the living God** (v. 12). He warns, **Watch out**, so that you won't fail to enter into God's rest. The purport of the words **Watch out, brothers** is not that a brother in Christ can fall from grace and be lost, but that those (all of whom we rightly *call* **brothers** until they deny their profession of faith) who might have deceived themselves into thinking they were for real when they were not, might realize it and believe before it is too late. And genuine brothers in the faith must be careful not to be influenced wrongly by such persons.

Instead, those who are genuine Christians must **encourage** them (and all who believe) to stand steadfast in the faith as trial and persecution dawns. It is important to warn those who are not yet **hardened by sin's deceiving ways.** That is to say, we (counselors included) must be on the outlook for the telltale signs of **unbelief** among professing Christians. Sin has a way of **deceiving** people into thinking they are Christians when they are not. That he is not talking about people who were once Christians but have lost their salvation is apparent from the fact that he says they were deceived; they never were for real.

Whenever there is the likelihood of a counselee not being a true Christian, you must also give warning. While you have no right to try to discern the reality or unreality of one's inner convictions, you may warn whenever you see signs of what *may* be an indication of **an evil heart of unbelief**. To fail to do so is to fail the counselee. But if you cannot pronounce that he is ingenuine, you can institute the process of church discipline by which his membership in the church is bound or loosed (retained or not; see Matthew 18:18). It is up to the church to make the decision whether he belongs within its midst or not; it is not your prerogative as an individual counselor.

And this encouragement to examine one's heart to see if he is really in the faith should take place while there is time, **every day, as long as we can still call it 'today'** (v. 13). There is an imperative that has to do with time; perhaps for someone there will be no tomorrow in *this* world. Once

14 (We have become sharers of Christ if, indeed, we hold firmly till the end to the assurance that we had at the beginning.)
15 It is just as in what is said,
Today if you hear His voice,
don't harden your hearts as in the revolt.

---

more, the writer of Hebrews explains the salient fact that we know who is a **sharer of Christ** by the fact that he will **hold firmly till the end to the assurance that [he] had at the beginning.** That is to say, though at times he may waver, he will never turn away from Christ; he will endure to the end. Perseverance is in belief and in action. He continues to firmly believe that Christ has saved him from sin and will lead him to glory. That **assurance** remains. While there may be doubts from time to time, he always returns to that faith.

There is no such thing as belief in Christ to which assurance is not attached. It is not that belief comes and then, perhaps sometime long after, assurance may appear. No. There is assurance **at the beginning.** If one believes in Christ, what does he believe? He believes that Jesus died to save him from the penalty for his sins—hell. If he believes, he believes *that.* That means he *believes* Christ has forgiven him and will take him to be with Himself at death or at His second coming. Belief in Christ, then, is concomitant with **assurance**. Persons without assurance must be checked out for three possibilities. First, do they lack assurance because they are not saved? Secondly, do they lack it because they have been taught wrongly about it—that they must wait and pray for it? Or thirdly, are they confused about salvation, thinking that people may be saved and lost and saved and lost? Take them back to the **beginning** of their Christian lives to recall the blessed assurance (if there is no reason to suspect it was ingenuine) that they had then. That is what they should retain to the end. And if they lack it now, but have no good reason to do so, help them by encouraging them to read and understand Scripture aright. In one way or another, you will find that the reason why their assurance is weak is that their Scriptural understanding is equally weak or faulty.

In verse 15 and following, the implications of the fearful warning first found in the Psalms and now reechoed by the writer are worked out. (If fear motivates, this ought to do so!) Quoting a part of the passage spelled out in full in the verses above, he asks, **Who were they who revolted when they heard?** He is still interested in the message heard (cf. 2:1-4). His answer: it was **all who left Egypt under Moses' leadership**.

16 Who were they who revolted when they heard? Wasn't it all those who left Egypt under Moses' leadership?
17 With whom was He angry for forty years? Wasn't it with those who sinned, whose corpses fell in the desert?
18 To whom did He swear that they would never enter into His rest, it if wasn't to those who disobeyed?
19 So we see that they weren't able to enter in because of unbelief.

As Paul pointed out in I Corinthians 10, it is not enough to be baptized into (united with) Moses as a part of the people (see comments on that passage); it is equally necessary to possess the inner reality of union with him. **All** is a key word there and here alike. Paul observes, as this writer implies, that all accompanied Moses and went through the same temporal experiences that he did, but with **most of them** God was displeased. And as here observed, their **corpses fell in the desert.** They never did enter into the promised land.

The same will be true of those with whom He is displeased because of **an evil heart of unbelief:** they will never enter into the greater rest from sins in which they will be made perfect and enjoy the blessings of glory forever. What was it that hindered? **They weren't able to enter in because of *unbelief*** (v. 19). The problem of unbelief has serious moral implications that no counselor may neglect or simply pass over. In counseling, everyday he deals with the very essence of the issues involved: faith and practice and how they interrelate. He, therefore, must not only be conversant with all aspects of the matter (about many of which Hebrews will provide significant information), but also have the courage to speak straightforwardly whenever he suspects that warnings may be necessary. While he assumes as a matter of course that all who have made a profession of faith are genuine (he too may at that point call them **brothers**), there may come a time when he must call this into question and even, if necessary, (when his patient encouragement is rejected) bring the matter before the church. Counseling is not easy, often not very pleasant, but always essential.

CHAPTER 4

1 Therefore, since the promise of entering into His rest still remains, let us be concerned that none of you might seem to have come short of it.

In the fourth chapter of Hebrews the writer continues the thought of entering into God's rest. Only now, he works out the biblical understanding of what God meant by that rest about which He spoke in Psalm 95:11. He infers from the verse that some were not allowed to enter into the rest that others could, saying: **the promise of entering into His rest still remains.** On the basis of that fact, he expresses his deep **concern** (Greek, "fear"): **that some of you might seem to have come short of it.** Clearly, he wants all those who are reading to enter into the rest. Yet some of them **seem** to be like the Israelites in the desert who **came short of** entering into it.

That must be the concern of every counselor. If your counseling focuses only on the matter that is presented by the counselee, and if there is a seeming possibility that he may not truly be a Christian, yet you do not raise the question to warn him, you have failed in the most important matter that a counselor could deal with. The writer of Hebrews is interested in God's **promises**. There is strong force in this word; it permeates the Book. In fact, there are more references to His promises in Hebrews than in any other New Testament book. What God has promised His people is so great, he would have none of those he addresses miss those promises. Stressing God's great promises in Christ is a principal means for motivating counselees that should be acknowledged and used by every biblical counselor. Why not underline every occurrence of the word "promise" in the Book of Hebrews for study and future reference?

The word translated **concerned** probably is what the grammarians call an ingressive aorist. That means it should have the impact of saying "Let us *begin to* be concerned." If there has been all too little concern of this sort on your part (or on the part of the counselee) it is time to *begin to* be concerned. As you will see, throughout the chapter he is not speaking of the rest from the slavery of Egypt and from the wilderness wanderings that the possession of the promised land afforded. Clearly, those who **entered in** received that. Rather, he thinks not only of the land of Palestine, but of that greater land of glory (as he earlier called the place of abode for believers in the **world to come**). The Israelite promise of the

2 Indeed, the good news came to us just as it did to them; nevertheless, the word that they heard was of no benefit to them because it wasn't mixed with faith by those who heard it.

---

land was but a type of the promise that they (and we, he says) still have of entering into the *eternal* land of glory. He is about to explicate the matter.

He points out that the gospel (**good news**) **came to us just as it did to them.** Interestingly, today, to some we have to observe the opposite. They doubt that the people of the Old Testament had the gospel. We have to assure them that in the Old and New Testaments alike the good news was clear to all the people of God; that all who were saved in either era were saved by faith in the Messiah who was to (or had) come. The good news they heard was that as there is an earthly promised land so too there is a heavenly one. True believers, in that day, looked not only for the earthly but, principally, for the heavenly one (cf. 11:10,39,40). And they knew that the promised land here was but the type of the one in the coming age.

But those who heard, *and did not believe*, received **no benefit** from hearing God's message (**word**) of salvation (v. 2). Why? Because it **wasn't mixed with faith by those who heard it.** Just as when a chemical process takes place by the mixture of two or more elements, but nothing happens apart from that mixture, so too the failure of the Israelites to bring faith into conjunction with the message of eternal life meant that there was no saving **benefit** derived. It is not enough to hear; one must believe what he hears. And as James so clearly says, that faith must lead to action.

The idea that education alone will solve problems seems to be one of the foolish notions of our time. Politicians seem to think that if you throw money at these problems in order to "educate" drug addicts, mothers who bear children illegitimately, etc., you will solve these difficulties. Before World War II, Germany was one of (if not *the)* best educated countries in the world. Yet those highly educated persons followed Adolph Hitler. Education, knowing facts, often only makes criminals shrewder criminals, sex offenders smoother in their approaches and drug pushers more able to avoid the law. Education, apart from change in the person educated, may only exacerbate problems.

One thing is sure, it will not **benefit** persons. That is what the writer of Hebrews is pointing out. The Israelites had all the knowledge necessary to enter into both of the promised lands (the earthly and the heavenly).

3 Now we who believe do enter into that rest, as He said: **As I swore in My wrath, "They will never enter into My rest,"** even though His works had been completed from the foundation of the world.

But they failed to do so *because their knowledge of God's promise was not mixed with their faith.* So too if one fails to enter into the promised heavenly rest of God today, Hebrews says, it is because he will not trust God's Word.

Counselees may be taught all they need to know to extricate themselves from their problems. But teaching—as important as it is (and one may never minimize the Word of God)—is not enough. They must exercise faith that leads to action as well. But on the other hand, it is not the Word and action alone either. There must be belief. Faith means trusting God. It means that one relies on what God has said in such a way that he expects His promises to be fulfilled. And, faith is not exhibited in a spirit of "Oh well, I might as well try what the Bible says; nothing else has worked so far." No, a purely pragmatic approach is not faith. It is but skepticism in despair. One must believe that God will do what He promised. Counselors must often challenge those whom they counsel with this fact. They can expect little or nothing if their attitude is like the one expressed above. They must cast themselves on the promises of God trustingly; relying on what He says as "gospel." It is!

If counselees attempt to follow the commands of the Bible, but fail to achieve the desired end, you may be wise to investigate whether or not the action taken was done in **faith**. James 1:6 and 7 is still in the Bible. By merely hearing, one attached to a good Bible-believing, Bible-teaching church of the Lord Jesus Christ, does not automatically receive saving benefits. There are external, restraining benefits to be sure, but the heart is unaffected if the message is not **mixed with faith.** The Jews of Christ's time were of the belief that being a part of the chosen people was sufficient: they were "children of Abraham." And you will meet modern-day persons, purporting to be Christians because they belong to such-and-such a church, who are no more so than they. The point made in verse 2, then, is of great significance and should be sounded often in counseling rooms.

On the contrary, the writer says, **Now we who believe do enter into that rest**. The heavenly rest is for those who have faith. That, he insists, is the point of the passage quoted from the Psalm. But he continues, **even though His works had been completed from the foundation of the world.** Even though what? That they had heard and had known that from

4 He has spoken somewhere about the seventh day this way: **And God rested on the seventh day from all His works.**
5 Again, in this place: **They will never enter into My rest.**
6 Since, then, it remains for some to enter into it, and those who previously had the good news announced to them didn't enter because of disobedience,
7 He again marks out a certain day, "Today," saying after so long a time by David, as He said before, Today if you hear His voice, don't harden your hearts.

---

the beginning of civilization the facts about God's rest from His works as a type of the heavenly rest. "You also have known about this long enough," is what he seems to be saying; "this is no recent idea I am presenting. You are Hebrews who have had the Old Testament that tells you these things from the beginning." Nor was it because the heavenly rest of God was not available to the Israelites; it had been since the completion of creation. And they knew this—as you do too.

It is time now and then for you to chide counselees like those to whom the writer was addressing his letter. They must be reminded that whatever you are telling them has been made known to them and, therefore, been available to them for as long as they have been among their fellow-members of Christ's church. Often those who know better will excuse continuing in their sin claiming that what you are saying is a new idea when all the while you, as well as they, know that they have heard it from way back. The question to ask is, "When, if ever, are you going to trust God's Word and do as He commands?"

In verses 4 and 5, the writer further substantiates what he has to say by means of two quotations (the first from Genesis 2:2 and the second a repeat of the verse from the Psalm with which he has already been working). Verse 6 begins a sentence in which he sums up what he has said already, preparing for a further application of it. "It is true [he says, in effect] that this rest of which I speak is still available and that some will still enter into it. Those who heard and disbelieved failed to enter. To them (and to you) God makes the following appeal: **Today if you hear His voice, don't harden your hearts**." That, counselor, will often be your appeal as well. You will find yourself urging hesitant, discouraged, doubtful counselees in similar words. Here it has to do with believing the gospel that leads to forgiveness of sins; in your case, it may also include urging those who have heard God's **voice** concerning other matters to heed it. The danger is, that having heard, having been around the truth so

8 You see, if Joshua had given them rest, He wouldn't have spoken later on about another day.
9 So then, there remains a Sabbath rest for God's people
10 (once a person enters into His rest, he stops working, just as God stopped working).
11 Therefore, let us make every effort to enter into that rest so that nobody will fall by the same pattern of disobedience.

---

often and not having heeded it, one's heart can become hardened. Warn of that danger too.

The writer further explains that it is not about the rest of the promised land but of **another day** that he has been speaking. It is the day following eternal judgment that leads to eternal life in the heavenly country that he has in mind. Joshua's rest doesn't fit the exhortation by David because at that later time when David was writing, they had already entered the earthly rest. Therefore, it must have been about another period (**day**) that David wrote (v. 8). So (v. 9) there remains (to this day) a **Sabbath keeping** (or Sabbath rest that comes from observing this other Sabbath **day** through faith). And when you enter your rest (on that day), like God Who did so, you too will rest from your works (v. 10). All the hard times, the trials and the difficulties occasioned by sin and the curse will be over. There will be rest from such things. That does not mean inactivity—God is still very active. But it does mean rest from sin and misery. A difficult fact to convey to your counselee from this passage I'll admit! Perhaps the best way to put it is something like this: "This will not go on forever. If you have truly trusted Christ as Savior, there will come a time when trials will cease, misery will be over and you will have rest from all these problems you are now enduring. That is what God's promise means when he speaks of entering into His rest (the one He Himself experiences and will share with those who are truly saved by faith)." Perhaps a comparison with II Thessalonians 1:7 would help consolidate the idea of the coming, eternal rest.

Because these facts are true, he goes on to say, you should **make every effort** [or possibly, "you should hurry"] **to enter into that rest.** Otherwise he warns that some of you, like the Israelites who fell in the desert (3:17), **will fall by the same pattern of disobedience.** The pattern is a pattern of delay and negligence that marked their failure to heed God's Word when they heard. Warn counselees that God will not forever put up with their indolence. They must do as He says—**today.** Look for patterns and point them out as you observe them. Incidentally, somewhere

12 God's Word is alive and active, sharper than any two-edged sword, penetrating deeply enough to cut open soul and spirit and joints and marrow; it can judge the desires and thoughts of the heart.

---

it would be advisable to make a list of all the patterns you discover in the Bible and in the counselees to whom you minister. When you see a pattern occurring in a counselee, then if you have noted also those biblical portions to deal with them, you will know where to turn for help.

We come now to a very important passage concerning the Word that it seems some were neglecting—or failing to heed. To help them understand what it is that they are doing, the writer describes some of the characteristics of God's Word. In order to do so, he likens it to the **two-edged (mouthed) sword** of the Roman soldier. Such a sword could cut (devour or eat up the enemy like a mouth) when swung in either direction. Unlike a human word, God's Word has such power that it could be said to be **alive and active, sharper than any two-edged sword.** That is quite a description of the Word they had heard and which some, it seems, were possibly neglecting to heed in faith. How could they if once they recognized it for what it is?! The Word does not **benefit** those who fail to mix faith with it, but that does not mean that it has no effect (cf. Isaiah 55:11). It is sent forth to save those who believe and to condemn those who do not. It will have one of those two effects; it will not return to God void.

One of its active effects is its ability to **penetrate deep**ly (v. 12). It has, therefore, the ability to disclose the most secret and closely hidden sins of the human heart. It does so by laying open the very innards of a person. It lays bare what is going on in his **soul and spirit**, the very physical **joints and marrow** and—the point of the previous two examples—**the desires and thoughts of the heart**. He does not say that the Word divides ***between*** soul and spirit, joints and marrow (they are not attached) or desires and thoughts of the heart. But what he says is that it can cut open for viewing each of the six items in the three couplets. It lays bare what one thinks and wants as it reveals to him what his sins are in order to bring him to repentance. People do not like the revealing nature of the Scriptures, and will often attempt to avoid all contact with it. That is one reason why they do not heed it. That is why as soon as you mention Scripture there are those who shut down and those who say "I don't want to hear about it!" God's Word does reveal sin. And if counselees are to change, they must often be brought to conviction of their sins by the powerful application of biblical truth to their words, thoughts and actions.

13 Before Him no creature can hide, but all are naked and laid open to the eyes of Him to Whom we must give an account.

That is why the dead, insipid words of men that some counselors seem to value in counseling above the living, active Word of the living God cannot change people at a level of depth. Why would you prefer them over the powerful Word of God?

People will attempt to do so, but the writer of Hebrews says, **Before Him no creature can hide, but all are naked and laid open to the eyes of Him to Whom we must give an account.** Friends, and even we ourselves, may be deceived about our sincerity, but that is not true of God. He knows your counselee (and you) inside out. The fact that God's Word can lay one **open and naked before His eyes** is important for every counselor to realize. You, counselor, cannot do that. But if your counseling relies on and is filled with God's Word you will find that in the most unusual ways, at times, people will be convicted by what they hear. That does not mean that you should minister the Word in a slipshod fashion, expecting the Spirit to do what you should, but it does mean that His Word is so powerful and active that hearing it often convicts those who hear of things you never thought were problems. Just yesterday, when preaching from a passage in which I was emphasizing one legitimate meaning, someone afterwards came up to me and said (good-naturedly), "Pastor, you stepped on my toes this morning!" I responded, "Well, they must have been protruding where they shouldn't have." After these pleasantries, she went on to explain what she meant. The passage read and exposited had had an impact that I never thought about, even though she was right about applying it to her situation. The Word of God was actively cutting through her defenses, laying her bare and convicting her of changes that she needed to make. If that can happen, how much more can be done to convict when the Bible is *directly* applied to a counselee in a proper manner?

If God knows us and can reveal something of the wickedness of our hearts to us, then we ought to remember that it cannot and will not escape His notice. All sin will be dealt with later on if not now: He is the one **to Whom we must give an account**. We cannot get away with our sin forever. It is impossible to avoid God's righteous judgment. If we fail to heed His Word as it actively penetrates to the secret places of our lives, then we shall hear His pronouncement about that sin in the day of judgment when we **must give an account**.

14 Since, then, we have a great High Priest Who has gone through the heavens—Jesus, God's Son—let us hold to our confession.

With these words, the writer concludes this section of the letter. *Chapter 5* should have begun with what is called verse 14 of chapter 4 in our Bibles (there were no chapters or verses in the original autographs). Therefore, in the next chapter, we shall begin with 4:14.

The warning theme emerges again and again. It takes many forms. The writer of Hebrews comes at it from every angle. As a biblical counselor, you must understand how much of this letter is devoted to the same thing. He is not yet finished warning. Indeed, he will come back to the matter explicitly over and over till the end. But in doing so, note the fact that it is not just warning that he gives; rather, he makes his case by this repeated reference to those things that they had heard and it could be assumed they knew. Their problem was not knowledge; it was neglect and hardening of their hearts. And he attempts to remedy this situation by highlighting those things that they knew, but to which they had not attached the significance that they should. These truths were understood as facts—i.e., academically—but were not taken to heart in such a way as to motivate to belief and action. Much of what you will be doing as a Christian counselor will be similar to this. You will not always have to instruct. But you will have to go over old material, not merely in a repetitive form but in order to point out the implications of facts for life. It is in this area that what you do is most important. And while the active Word of God can bring conviction when you least realize it, more often than not you will find that it is in its implications, applications and implementations that the Spirit causes the light bulb to go on. Often, the exhortation that he needed—surely the writer of Hebrews was an exhorter if he was anything—was never heard by the counselee. Let that not be so of your counseling. If exhortation, including application, etc., were not needed, then much (most?) of Hebrews was written in vain.

The writer had mentioned that Jesus is the great Apostle and High Priest of our confession (3:1) and that as a merciful and faithful High Priest He made propitiation for His people's sins (2:17). He now returns to the subject of Jesus as **High Priest**. He is unlike other high priests on earth; He has **gone through the heavens.** The confession of Him as such, therefore, must be **held on to** at all costs (v. 14). In returning to the presence of the Father, Jesus, the God-man, was now **seated on His right hand in power and glory**. To return to this position as God (and now as

15 We don't have a high priest who isn't able to sympathize with our weaknesses, but One Who has been tempted in every way that we are, yet without sin.

---

man as well) He had to pass **through the heavens.** Paul speaks of being caught up into the third heaven (II Corinthians 12:2). Presumably from the way in which the word **heavens** is used elsewhere (almost always in the plural), He passed through the air (where the birds of the heavens fly) and through space (where the stars and the planets may be found) into Paradise where the throne of God beyond the former two heavens is. To say much more about this is impossible from our meager knowledge. Yet, to say more is not necessary. The point is made by the writer that He is a remarkable High Priest, like earthly priests in some respects and unlike them in others. Those likenesses and unlikenesses is what he will explore next.

This **great High Priest** is great because He is **God's Son**. He is great because He has passed through the created heavens into the very presence of God and can intercede for us as no other priest could. He is great because He has experienced the **weaknesses** of human nature and has been **tempted** as we are, yet **without sinning**. He is able to **sympathize** with us, even though He is greater than we are, because He became one of us. Clearly stated in these three verses is the superiority of Jesus to all others. Since that is so, the writer urges us to **hold to our confession** (v. 14; see 3:1). There are times when there is little else for a counselor to urge than "hold to your confession of Jesus." This is true particularly in times of temptation—times when one is ready to throw everything to the winds. All you may be able to do is to point him to Jesus and reiterate these facts about Him, urging him to **hold** fast on the basis of them.

Although Jesus is great—greater than any other high priest—His exaltation to the throne of God did not exempt Him from temptation. He was **tempted**, He suffered and He experienced our **weaknesses**. Unlike the charge against the politicians who are ensconced "within the beltway," Jesus is above us, but not beyond knowing all we endure. He can sympathize with us because He became one of us (v. 15). But there must be more than sympathy. People can say, "I feel your pain," and whether sincere or not in uttering those words, if they stop with sympathy, little is accomplished. Some forms of counseling, like some forms of government, leave everything at that point. *Something more than sympathy* is needed—help. And that is precisely what Jesus offers to those who are

16 So then, let us come close to the throne of grace with boldness, that we may receive mercy and find help just when we need it.

---

tempted to drift (v. 16). The answer is not to drift away when under trial but to draw near (**come close to the throne of grace with boldness**). Continually, the invitation to **come close** may be heard throughout the letter (cf. 7:25; 10:1,22; 11:6; 12:18,22). This repeated call emphasizes both the need to do so and the sincerity of the One Who issues the invitation. Who is it? God, the Spirit, is speaking through the writer of this letter. We must never forget that fact (the letter itself will make that point more than once before we complete the exposition of it). The One Who has become one of us, Who is able to sympathize with us, is the One who recognizes what we as human beings **need**. He urges us not to hesitate, but to draw near with **boldness (confidence) that we may receive mercy and find help just when we need it.**

Too many counselees in need try to go it alone. He, just at the right time (lit., at the appropriate season) not only provides what we **need**, but gives it to us *just* when we need it (not before or after, but just at the right time). We may think that we need it sooner than He knows we do, but faith trusts Him to give **mercy** for our sins and failures and **help** for our trials and troubles *precisely* when it is needed. Call on your counselees to approach Him for help and to wait patiently to see how and when He provides it.

If your counselee fails to receive what he requests from the throne which is the source of help (grace), you may explain this to him as follows:

> First, let me remind you that God says you must come near to Him and ask boldly (confidently). If you asked in any other manner, why should you expect Him to respond? If there was no confidence, but only doubt or even fear in asking, why should you expect anything from him (cf. James 1:7)? But then, secondly, it is possible that you *did* draw near confidently expecting mercy and help. Good. But what He gave you in response may have been what you *truly* need, not what you *thought* you needed. Real trust says "Thank You" even when you do not receive what you want. Thirdly, notice that He supplies what we need just when we need it. His timing and yours may not coincide. Indeed He may not provide the help *before* the height of the trial, but only *in the midst of* it. He may even use the trial as the means of providing help in some way or other.

Tell him, "The key thing here is confident trust. If you have that, you will see your true needs met—in time (*His* time)." What more could a counselee want?

CHAPTER 5

1 Now every high priest among men is appointed to represent men in matters related to God so that he may offer gifts and sacrifices for sins.
2 He is able to act gently toward the ignorant and wayward since he himself is inextricably involved in weakness.

If you have been reading along in these chapters successively you will recall that at the end of the previous chapter, we pointed out that the section we were discussing closed with verse 13 and that the new one that will concern us for some time opens with verse 14.

These three introductory verses, chapter 4:14-16, begin what is the longest section of the Book. They pick up after the interlude that follows 2:17,18. What is to come in this section, then, is important to the writer. And it should be of extreme importance to counselors as well. So please go back and begin there if you are just joining the discussion.

High priests, the writer reminds us, are **appointed to represent men in matters related to God.** Jesus Christ, our High Priest, therefore, is our representative before the throne of Grace. Who could want a better priest to intercede for him? Here is a priest, unlike others, Who does not need to offer sacrifices for Himself as they did. He was perfect. Jesus, Who offered the once-for-all sacrifice *of* Himself, offered it exclusively for His people, not *for* Himself. Yet because He became one of us, suffered among us and understands us, He too is **able to act gently toward the ignorant and wayward** who come needing forgiveness and knowledge. There are counselors, unlike their great High Priest (being themselves sinners), who show far less compassion to their counselees than this High Priest. It is not the part of counselors to berate counselees for their ignorance or their waywardness. Surely, they must point out their sin and call them to repentance. But to do so in a harsh, superior fashion hardly becomes them because of their own sin. If He Who committed no sin refuses to act that way, how can you? There is a fine line here, always observed in the Bible, between condoning sin (something no one ever has the right to do) and treating the sinner with gentleness. Have you cultivated the attitude of the Lord in this matter? The word used here is current in Greek philosophy for the maintenance of a right attitude in the indulgence of feelings. It implied control over one's feelings, especially over the manifestation of anger. There are times when one wishes he could get a point across to a counselee who seems to be especially thickheaded by

3 But because of this he is obligated to offer sacrifice for his own sins as well as for those of the people.
4 Now a person doesn't take this honor upon himself, but, on the contrary, he is called by God just as Aaron was.

---

screaming at him. But he may not. On other occasions, he would like to take him by the shoulders and try to shake some sense into him. It is all such attitudes that the **gentle** counselor will forebear.

When a high priest was **appointed** it was his task to represent men before God. He was an intermediary. Jesus opened the way to God so that we can come to the throne of grace (4:16) freely through Himself. And we can know that we have access because He Who represents us before Him is perfect and altogether acceptable to the One Who appointed Him. That the high priest, though moderate in his attitude toward sinners, did not condone sin is clear from the fact that his very office obligated him to **offer gifts and sacrifices for sins**. In doing so, he found it necessary to make a point of the sins committed in ignorance and in waywardness. That was the purpose of his work. By the nature of his office, he was **appointed** to make an issue of **sins**. It is neither possible nor right, then, for a counselor to bypass the sins of his counselees. But, while making a point of them, he must direct them to the great High Priest in Whom they may find forgiveness; all the while treating them with gentleness. It is not gentle or moderate to fail to call their transgressions sin. Neither the high priest on the Day of Atonement did so, nor did Jesus Who died for our sins. Indeed, the whole purpose of a high priest, as the writer of Hebrews observes, is to **offer gifts and sacrifices** ***for sins*** **on behalf of those he represents** before God. That Jesus is our Representative is one of the marvelous aspects of the plan of salvation.

The previous facts are mentioned to introduce the idea of Christ as the better High Priest. But now note verse 4: **a person doesn't take this honor upon himself, but, on the contrary, he is called by God just as Aaron was.** He is going to extrapolate on this statement by indicating that even Jesus **didn't exalt Himself, but, rather, was appointed by** God when said to Him, **You are My Son; I have begotten You today.** It is time that this point be made with force. People should not simply take on the task of counseling on their own authority. They should be duly **appointed** by lawful authorities of the church of Jesus Christ. In working with His people in this day, as well as in the Old Testament era, God **appointed** officers and ordained them to His work. He expects all such

5 So too, Christ didn't exalt Himself to become a High Priest, but, rather, He was appointed by the One Who said to Him, **You are My Son; I have begotten You today.**

---

things to be done decently and in order. One of the major problems of our time has been the extremes to which the liberation of the laity has gone. There once was an overbearing prelacy in the church; that was wrong, failing to recognize the priesthood of all believers. But now there has been a swing to the opposite extreme in which the authority of the church of Christ, particularly as it is wielded by those who have been appointed by God to rule and minister in His Name in the church, has been ignored or (even) deprecated. Since the task of helping people with their problems is essentially a pastoral one, it belongs to those appointed to the pastoral office to do such work as a life calling. It is a part of their office in Christ's church. It is not, therefore, proper for one who has never been ordained to the work to **take this honor upon himself** (v. 4). Yet that is precisely what has happened. All sorts of unauthorized persons have appointed themselves to the work of counseling as a life calling. They have no calling from God, no confirmation of it from the church and bear no responsibility to anyone but to themselves. It is a lawless situation. And to boot, it is some of these very persons who are setting the pace for what the task of counseling should look like in the church. People with money to do so have captured the airwaves, are publishing the books, are holding the seminars, are producing the videotapes and are teaching in seminaries *with no divine appointment through the church.* That is a tragic affair.

And it has had tragic effects. Every error that is taught by pagan psychologists and psychiatrists is now taught by one or more of these members of a self-appointed caste among the people of God. There has been more error and heresy inculcated in the last 50 years by such persons among the churches that stand for the gospel and the Bible in other areas than there has been by all the false cults put together. People know and resist the teachings of the cults; they don't recognize the error that is propagated among them by the false teachers who represent themselves as researchers. They have brought error into the church by the back door. And it has so weakened the church that in an all-out spiritual war most Christians would prove to be so adversely affected by it that they could not stand. Indeed, unwittingly, some would stand with the enemy! The church has been inundated by false doctrine as a result of this unlawful intrusion of unauthorized, self-appointed persons.

6 Similarly He says in another place: **You are a Priest forever according to Melchizedek's order.**

7 During the days when He was here in flesh, He offered specific requests and prayers for help with audible cries and tears to the One Who was able to save Him from death, and He was heard because of His reverence.

If you are among them counselor, think about your situation. If you want to do things God's way; if you are biblical in your form of counseling, then apply for ministerial or elder status and authorization by the church. Stop acting like a loose cannon, accountable to no one but yourself. No longer should you take upon yourself the office of instructing and ministering to God's people about living. If you truly have the calling, knowledge and ability then seek the confirmation and appointment (ordination) of the church of Jesus Christ (I Timothy 3:1).

Psalm 2:7 is quoted in verse 5 to validate the divine appointment of Christ (as also is the quotation from Psalm 110:4) in the next verse. It seems that to **beget**, in such contexts, was a ritual for expressing the appointment, by one who held an office, of another who was assuming it. Obviously, in 1:5 it is used of the coronation of the Son as He is inducted into office as King. (Cf. Acts 13:33 where He is raised to reign and the Pyramid texts of the Near East in which the formula was used. Cf. also Romans 1:4.) If even Christ had to be duly appointed to His office, then why shouldn't you?

Christ was a better High Priest in that He had no sins for which to offer sacrifice as other high priests did. He was a sinless priest on the throne. Yet those facts did not exempt Him from suffering. **During the days when He was here in flesh** [human nature] He too agonized over sin and its consequences (v. 7). The misery that He experienced however was substitutionary; He suffered for the sins of His people. In the Garden of Gethsemane, anticipating the cross where because of the vicarious sacrifice of Himself, in which the Father for the three hours of atoning sacrifice turned His back on Him as the Sin-bearer, **He offered specific requests and prayers for help with audible cries and tears to the One Who was able to save Him from death, and He was heard because of His reverence.** There was nothing short of agony in the garden, as this seventh verse indicates. That was not because Jesus was afraid, nor because He, unlike others, could not bear the physical pain that the cross involved. No. You must neither think of nor portray Him that way. It was the fact that He Who knew no sin was to be made sin for others that led to the agony in the garden (cf., especially, Luke 22:44). The cup of death for sinners—the baptism with which He must be baptized—was a horrible thing for a holy, undefiled man to contemplate. And to be punished by suffering their hell for them on the cross, was more than He wanted to undergo. That accounts for the prayers that were offered up in agony of soul.

Obviously, your counselees, who have so much less to bear, may be helped by recognizing how much Jesus suffered for them. Moreover, they should note that the writer records the fact that His prayers were heard because of the reverent fear with which He prayed. How was He answered? Did He not die contrary to His prayer? Yes He died, but the prayer was not merely to let the cup pass from Him, **if possible**. He went on to pray, **Yet don't do what I want, but what You want** (Mark 14:36). That was the ultimate prayer—and it was **heard**. The point that counselees must be helped to understand is that we may not merely pray for what we want; we always must pray in the same spirit that Christ did, asking that regardless of what we want may the Father's will be done. By praying thus, not only will one be heard, but the best possible answer will be given. And that best possible answer may not be what one desires. Jesus' desire was not granted; had it been, you would be lost and headed to hell. Thank God that the dependent prayer was refused, and the fundamental prayer was answered! That is the spirit that the counselee must be helped to acquire. He, like His Lord, must recognize that the difficult way, the way that He does not wish to go, in the long run may be the very best way. And whether using the words or not, every prayer must be uttered with the understanding that if that is not the will of God—so be it. Many times what we want very much would be the worst for us and for others if granted.

Note the reason why He was heard: **He was heard because of His reverence.** The word translated **reverence** means "to take hold cautiously, carefully, respectfully." That is how he treated the matter at hand. It is another way of strongly emphasizing that He would not blunder or bluster into demanding what He wanted in prayer, but that in praying He was careful to put the Father's will above His own. Some of the prayers uttered by faith healers, and also by some who have the idea that prayer is a means of telling God what to do, lack that quality. It is important, to explain to a counselee that though he may agonize in prayer, he must always be careful never to *demand* that his will be done. Requests must be made to God in reverent fear and cautiously. There is a fine balance here:

8 Even though He was a Son, He learned obedience from what He suffered;
9 and having been perfected, He became the Origin of eternal salvation to those who obey Him,

---

great desire and feeling expressed, yet care and caution exercised.

In His training for the divine priesthood, Jesus **learned obedience from what He suffered** (v. 8). And, **even though He was a Son**, He was subjected to suffering. The willingness to reject His own desire to see the cup pass, and to put His Father's will above His own human wishes, completed His obedience in this world. He had obeyed the Father in all ways prior to this, but never before had He found it necessary to face such a trial. In learning how difficult it is to obey in the face of the ultimate suffering anyone could ever face, He became a sympathetic High Priest Who is able to sympathize with you and your counselee. To spell out once again for a counselee exactly what it was that Jesus endured on the cross and how difficult even He found obedience should greatly encourage him. It is not wrong to desire to escape those things that are unpleasant, so long as we do not draw back from them when they occur. Jesus obeyed; so too must your counselee.

One of the reasons for suffering, you may point out to a counselee, is to teach him greater **obedience** to the will of God. It may be to qualify him for some other work that he must later do (cf. II Corinthians 1). And counselor, you yourself may have undergone almost unendurable trials for the very same purpose; God in His providence, through obedience in the face of your "cup" of sorrow, was preparing you for a ministry of comfort, encouragement and counsel to others. Thus He became the **perfect** High Priest (v. 9). The word **perfected** means "to reach or attain a goal." Through suffering He realized the purpose for which it was given.

It is interesting to note also that obedience may be **learned.** If a counselee protests that he is having difficulty obeying God's commandments, assure him that it is possible for him to do so. He may *learn* to do so—and that such learning will probably come through suffering. So, if he prays for ability to obey, he may expect suffering.

And to those who **obey** Him by exercising faith (v. 9) He is the cause (author or origin) of their **eternal salvation**. His learning of obedience, fitted Him to become the Originator of their redemption through the offering of Himself on the cross. And having done so, God **introduced Him as High Priest, according to Melchizedek's order,** in the passage quoted

10 and He was introduced by God as High Priest according to Melchizedek's order.

11 We have a lot to say about this, but it is hard to explain since you have become dull of hearing.

12 Indeed, because of the length of time that has expired you ought to be teachers, yet you need somebody to teach you the elementary principles of God's revelation once again. You need milk, not solid food.

---

above (v. 6). That is the title that God, Himself, gave to Him.

The writer had more to say about these matters than he found himself able to say since his readers **had become dull of hearing** (v. 11). It is important to recognize the depth of understanding that a counselee may (or may not have). Here, they were **dull of hearing** not because they had not heard, but because they failed to take advantage of what they had heard. Indeed, at a previous time they had been much more responsive to God's Word. But now they had ***become*** dull. It is altogether possible for those who once were keen Christians to slack off. So much so that (as he does in the next chapter) it might be wise to ask them to consider whether their original profession of faith was genuine. There are many fellow-travelers who purport to be Christians but are not really so.

You will encounter counselees who once had what seemed to be a vital Christian life. When you see what they are like as they come to you for counseling, you *also* may wonder whether or not their profession of faith was real. In this case, the writer seems to hold forth the possibility that both facts may be true; some may have *become* dull of hearing while others may never have been converted in the first place. In order to cover both possibilities he speaks both ways—talking to each sort of reader. Here, he chides them for their dullness. By now, he says, **you ought to be teachers**. Yet instead, **you need somebody to teach you the elementary principles of God's revelation once again.** Once having learned, it is possible to forget, to forget so thoroughly that you must start all over again.

That is the message for counselors (and counselees like these whom he counsels). You may not presuppose more knowledge in counselees who have been drifting for some time than they actually possess. They may tell you about how long they have been Christians, how much they learned under Dr. so-and-so's teaching when they were members of the church he pastored, etc. But test them out; discover how much they know *now*. It is always better to err in supposing less knowledge than a counselee may have than the opposite. It never hurts to repeat. You may say

13 The truth is that everybody who feeds on milk is inexperienced with the righteous Word; he is still a baby.
14 Solid food is for mature people, for those whose perceptual faculties have been trained by practice to distinguish good from evil.

---

what he has heard before in a fresh and sharper way and he may have only had a superficial understanding (or a misunderstanding) in the first place.

There was no excuse for their dullness. They had been taught and had been part of the church for many years. The word dullness has the meaning of something slow to push, dawdling or (as I have discovered in one contemporary Greek text) even the idea of going into a coma. From eagerness to hear, they had gone to dullness in their hearing. Christianity had lost its zest; they were simply Christians by default. Such persons ought to be shamed as the writer does here when he calls them little babies incapable of chewing **solid food** and needing **milk** once more. A baby with a bottle is cute; an adult with one looks silly. The writer is trying to awaken them out of their dullness. It is probable that, from time to time, you too will find it necessary to use language and figures of speech calculated to prick the conscience of your counselees. Here, you find good warrant for doing so. When you must motivate those dull in hearing you may discover that it is the only means that will work. Remember, it is biblical to do so. And it is the kindest way to go.

How is it that they reverted to childlike faith? He explains in the last two verses of this chapter: they had neglected the Scriptures (God's **righteous Word**). They had reverted to the pabulum stage in which they found themselves when they were first converted. They were "fed up" with the substantial diet that they once enjoyed. Now, they were back to the point of their first experience with Christianity. There are those who decry any solid food as "mere doctrine" or something of the sort. They will talk about the few things that all Christians have in common as all that is important. "Don't bother me with doctrine," is the theme they sing. And they can become very self-righteous in doing so. "After all," they may piously intone, "we should be above all the detailed and intricate matters which separate Christians, that I once thought were important." Don't let them snow you. They are covering up their failure to grow and their unacceptable lifestyle. What has actually happened is that they have failed to learn and **practice** God's **Word** in meeting the more mature issues of Christianity. The problem that led to dullness is a lack of **experience** with Scripture. In many cases the failure to learn a method of study, or the abandonment of regular study may be at the heart of the problem. You cannot put into daily practice those things that you don't (or don't know how to) understand. God's **Word** is the answer to dullness. It alone will create the eagerness, provide the knowledge and encourage the effort necessary to grow spiritually. Spiritual growth is growth that is brought about by the Holy Spirit using His Word (cf. John 17:17).

There is a lack of discernment in persons like these. Because they do not know the Scriptures as they should, because they therefore cannot put them into practice, their Christian lives atrophy. They do not know how to **distinguish good from evil**. That is a sorry state. They become suckers for anything that may sound good, even outright heresy. Because they have not trained their **perceptual faculties** to discern what is true and what is false, what is good and what is evil, they become involved in all sorts of things that further deteriorate their Christianity. The **training** of which he speaks is the regular experience in the study and the application of the Bible that he mentions in verse 13. For more on the matters mentioned here, see especially my books *A Call to Discernment*, which deals with this passage and others in much more depth, and *What to Do on Thursday,* which is a book that teaches how to use the Bible in a practical way to meet problems that arise in the course of life.

This chapter has been a fruitful one for you if you have savored it from its various aspects. The writer is concerned about these people; you can readily see that. In the next chapter that concern emerges in a very strong way. As you read it, ask yourself, "does your concern reach such proportions?"

CHAPTER 6

1 So then, leaving the elementary teachings about Christ, we must advance toward maturity, not again laying a foundation of repentance from dead works and of faith toward God,

---

Even though up until now the readers were unable to receive the more mature teaching that the writer wished to give them (see 5:11), nonetheless, he will not let them remain where they were. He wants them to **advance toward maturity**. The *reason* they were sluggish (or dull of hearing) was inexcusable; assuming now that he has stirred them sufficiently, he will do what heretofore he has been unable to do (v. 3). He will do so, that is, **if God permits**. He seems uncertain about the tactic and wishes God either to confirm or frustrate it by making it possible or not. It is not only about prayer that a counselor must be tentative, asking that God's will be done. It is also about many aspects of his counseling as a whole. For His own wise and sovereign purposes, even when you have done all you can, God may not permit progress **toward maturity** in your counselee. After having examined all that you can to be sure that his failure is not due to some lack on your part, you may walk away with the same attitude that this writer had: "I will do what I should, and leave the results to God." That is difficult to do, I recognize. It is always hard, after expending time and effort with a counselee, to see those expenditures end in failure. But you must not be like the physician who because he hates to fail goes to extraordinary lengths to save a patient who will die anyway. You must remember, results depend on God; not on you. You minister the Word; God gives the growth (I Corinthians 3:7). And it is difficult because as a counselor, you often wonder, "Is there something more (different) that I could have done? The answer to all such inquiries is to do your best, seek forgiveness where you fail and then leave the rest to God. The **elementary teachings** he wishes to leave behind are not about Judaism (as some think) but, as he plainly says, **about Christ.** They are teachings that they learned when they first made their profession of faith. Some of these teachings may have been best understood as they were pitted against apostate Judaism with its doctrines of works and self-righteousness, but (essentially) it is positively set forth doctrines that he has in mind. It is not enough to dwell forever and a day on what one *first* learned. Some churches never seem to go beyond the gospel; while the gospel ought always to condition everything else, there *is* more to Christianity. He wants progress; he wants them to bite into some **solid** teaching about their faith so that they may mature in it. And it is exactly that which you, as a counselor, must endeavor to help your counselees do. Whatever else you attempt, at the end of counseling sessions you must always seek to leave him a more **mature** Christian than at the beginning. As I have just said, God may not permit. But the goal ought to be there regardless. Have you counseled in the past with this goal clearly in view? If not, you must begin to think about the matter. Ask yourself questions like these: "For this counselee, of what does maturing consist? Where is this counselee lacking in an understanding of the faith? How well does he apply what he understands to everyday living? What stands in the way of his growth in the faith?" Size up the situation as early in the counseling process as possible so that your sights may be trained throughout on the particular growth factors that are involved in each counseling case.

What were these **elementary teachings** that they were to **leave** behind? He speaks of **foundational** truths like **repentance from dead works,** of **faith toward God,** of **teaching about baptisms,** of **laying on of hands,** of **the resurrection from the dead and of eternal judgment.** Let's see if we can elucidate these for you.

First, **repentance from dead works.** These works are mentioned again in 9:14. There he speaks of the cleansing of the **conscience** from dead works. It is apparent that they are works that do not clear the conscience of guilt. Indeed, they seem to produce more guilt, since the conscience must be cleansed of (or possibly, *because* of) these works. The **dead works** are the same as those that people attempt to offer to God for their eternal salvation. They are **dead** because they were not produced by the Spirit of life. Being dead, they accomplish nothing. They are the complement of James' **dead faith** (James 2:26). They also include the **works of the flesh** (cf. Galatians 5). Even the best of these works is sinful because unbelievers **cannot please God** (Romans 8:8). As a matter of fact, to trust in one's own works to commend him to God, while rejecting the work of Christ, is heinous in God's sight (Romans 10:3). It is *the* most egregious error mentioned in the Bible. Self-righteousness fails to clear the conscience because it cannot cleanse from sin. This teaching was **foundational** thinking for Jews who came to Christ; they had been *taught* to trust their own works. Nothing less need be said to counselees who do the same than that to think that way is to revert to a sinful, pre-conversion mentality. It is always possible to confront a self-righteous counselee with the rejoinder, "But Mary, what you are offering here is unacceptable; it is what God's Word calls 'dead works.'" Keep grace uppermost in all you say in counseling.

And what must you urge in contrast to the dead works of a counselee? Repentance toward God and faith in our Lord Jesus Christ. **Repentance** is sometimes misunderstood. It means "thinking again; rethinking; a change of mind." About what do counselees (as well as unbelievers) need to change their minds? Fundamentally, about offering God anything that is solely the product of their own efforts in order to please Him. By definition, all such works are **dead**. Those works that are the fruit of the Spirit alone are *alive*; they are a sweet smelling savor to God. They are done by the counselee, but only at the instigation and instruction of, and empowering by, the Holy Spirit. In other words, *works that God Himself does not work through him* are **dead**. That, essentially, is what one must rethink. He must come to the conclusion that he has nothing in and of himself to give to God. That all that is worthwhile is of grace—even the things that he does that *do* please Him. He must recognize that these are the fruit of the regenerating Spirit dwelling within. The efforts he puts forth must be blessed by the Lord Jesus, done for His honor and performed by the strength and wisdom of His Spirit. In short, he is to turn from self to the Savior for even those things that he does to honor and obey God. *He* does them, but only by the wisdom and the strength that the Spirit supplies. Repentance is a change continually necessary in every believer, in which he more and more learns to see God as God (in all dimensions of that fact) and man as man. The notion that we can "do it on our own" is deeply embedded in all of us and must be rooted out. Look for it in every counselee. You will find that there is all too much of it in every one of them. And you will discover that you, too, may be prone to fall into such thinking. In such cases, repentance is warranted not only for the counselee, but also for his counselor!

The next item on his list is **faith toward God.** Nothing could be more foundational than this. One is saved not by works, but by faith. He must believe the gospel. He must trust in God rather than in himself. Of course, faith is the corollary of grace. There will be much more teaching about faith—especially as it relates to Christian living (the concern of the counselor as counselor)—in chapter 11.

Thirdly, he writes concerning **teaching about baptisms.** Even though in 9:10 the writer is going to mention the sprinklings of the law as *baptismois* ("baptisms" required by the Old testament law), it is not those that he has in mind here. In this place he is concerned with **elementary teachings about *Christ.*** Probably, since the word is in the plural, he is

2 of teaching about baptisms, of laying on of hands, of the resurrection of the dead and of eternal judgment.

---

referring to the baptisms of John the Baptist and those of Christ which succeeded those required by the Old Testament law. To Jews, who had known the preaching and baptizing ministry of John, the relation of the baptizing ministries of the apostles must have posed questions that needed immediate answers. In Acts 19, we read about Jews who had received John's baptism and knew of nothing more. They had to be instructed about both baptisms at the beginning of their newfound faith. This letter is written to Jews who have left Judaism for Christianity. Obviously they would need similar instruction. The matter would be **foundational** to converted Jews.

Next comes teaching concerning **the laying on of hands**. Hands were laid on someone as a means and/or symbol of imparting something to him. Among those things imparted at this time were the gifts of the Spirit and even the Spirit Himself (Acts 19:6). In addition, hands were laid on someone who was receiving the office of elder or deacon. Thereby, the rights and duties of these offices symbolically were imparted to him (Acts 13:3). Such matters would be pertinent to the founding of new congregations.

Then there is **the resurrection of the dead**. This probably refers to the resurrection of human beings at the last judgment (the next, and last foundational matter mentioned). That human beings will be raised bodily was guaranteed by the resurrection of Jesus Christ Himself. For more on the absolutely foundational character of this teaching, see remarks in the commentary on I Corinthians 15.

Finally, he refers to the **eternal judgment**—i.e., the eternal state in heaven or hell of all according to how they are apportioned as sheep or goats by the Lord Jesus Who will judge the living and the dead. While one is *saved* through faith by God's grace, he is *judged* by works, which are the fruit of true faith.

All these, he says, are foundational doctrines. Unfortunately, you will find counselees who do not know much about them; if you asked them to give you a thumbnail sketch of what is meant by each, they might get one or two right. There is such ignorance in the modern church about fundamental truth (not to speak of more sophisticated teaching) that it is appalling. But note well, these doctrines are laid down as a **foundation**. One does not keep laying the foundation over and over again. The founda-

3 This is exactly what we are going to do, if indeed, God permits.

---

tion exists to build upon. That is what these readers of Hebrews should have been doing; and it is what your counselees must do as well. Don't let them go on foolishly exploring basics; help them mature in their faith. And take no excuses for the failure to do so. The writer here doesn't. He is going to go on anyway (v. 3), in spite of their dullness. They may not be babied any longer; they must grow up. He will stretch them. That is what you must do for your counselees. It is most informative that, though he says he couldn't teach them all *he* wanted, nevertheless, he intends to teach them more than *they* wanted. He will not allow their faith to atrophy any longer.

How is that? Well, he knows it is this failure to leave **the elementary teachings about Christ** and to **advance toward maturity** that occasioned their **dullness**. If he caters to this spirit he cannot help them. They must be stretched as far as they can be. People who fail to advance in their faith soon find that it becomes dull to them. After all, how much of the same thing and nothing more—wonderful as it may be—can one take, for how long? One can become surfeited with truth if no new truth is added to it. You are wrong if you cater to dullness. Whenever you recognize it, the answer to dullness is to challenge the counselee to move toward maturity.

The failure to advance toward maturity (that is, to move ever closer to the goal of becoming like Jesus Christ) may lead to a condition where it is difficult to distinguish between a genuine Christian and one who is not. Many profess faith; not all truly believe. Because of this, the writer goes on to describe the state of the fellow-travelling professor whose faith is false. As some of his readers might need to examine themselves to see if they are in the faith (cf. II Corinthians 13:5), so too some whom you counsel may need to do the same. It is a fearful warning that he issues in the next few verses, one from which you might learn something about how to speak to counselees who are dull of hearing. Certainly on my own I wouldn't ever have told a counselee anything of the sort, but apparently because the Spirit moved the writer to do so, it is necessary for dull, professed Christians to hear it. Perhaps the very best way to issue the warning is simply (but powerfully) to read the very words of this passage.

One ancillary reason he wants them to go on toward maturity, doubtless, is because this will separate the true from the false. Those who truly know Christ will respond; those who don't cannot. And in recognizing

4 We will do this because it is impossible to renew again to repentance those who have once been enlightened, who have tasted of the heavenly gift and have become sharers of the Holy Spirit,

---

these facts, some may actually come to saving faith. After all, as he will show, it is a fearful thing, for one, having once made a profession of faith later to reject it. Why is that and what does that mean? In verses 4 through 9, he explains. We must now take up those purposely frightening verses.

The connection between verse 4 and what precedes is simply this: the writer is saying "Go on to maturity or you will be in danger of apostasizing. If you don't follow me in this, you are probably not a Christian after all." Let's see how he develops this severe warning.

If you drift back into Judaism, you repudiate your Christian faith, and—of greater importance—you repudiate Christ Himself. If you do so **it is impossible to renew [you] again to repentance.** This then is a tricky and important matter to pursue. But be careful that you do not confuse counselees into thinking that there is no hope for them. That is exactly the opposite of what the writer has in mind. He does not want true Christians who read this to think their situation is **impossible**. No, quite to the contrary. He wants them to advance toward maturity, thus proving to him and to themselves that they are genuine, though erring and sinful (see v. 9). But if an unbeliever apostatizes by repudiating the gospel, there is nothing more that one can do for *him*.

"But," you say, "He was repentant. It speaks of **'renewing'** him to **repentance**. If he didn't have it, it cannot be renewed." You might think that this is the case at first blush. But in the writer's thinking, it is otherwise. See verse 9 where he makes it clear that he is not talking about believers; of believers he expects **better things...that are true *of those who have salvation.*** Clearly then, he envisions the behavior of those who engage in such disreputable activities as those described in verses 4 through 6 as becoming involved in things that are true only of those who *do not* have salvation. The entire argument runs this way: If you have had all the benefits of association with the people of God as a member of the outer body of the church but at length determine that this is not for you and leave, there is nothing more to say to you. You have not only known the truth of God, but you have seen evidence of the work of God's Spirit among your fellow-members of the church. You know both intellectually and experientially all that one could be told or shown. There is no more. And having heard and seen, if you reject Jesus Christ, walking out on Him

5 and have tasted the goodness of God's Word and the miracles of the coming age,

---

as it were, there is no way to **renew** you to **repentance**. That is, there is no place for another profession of faith, a renewing of the supposed repentance that you claimed.

What your counselees need to know is that association with God's people can be a great blessing, but it can also be a curse. How is that? You can receive so many good things, experience so many blessings, be protected from so many harmful influences, that you may well think (wrongly) that you have truly repented. And just because everyone else thinks you are genuine, don't let that deceive you. You must know down deep within that your repentance and faith are real, and you must show it in your lifestyle.

What are the benefits that one may receive from association with the people of God, though he is not a genuine believer? **Enlightenment** is the first mentioned. How important that is—to hear and know the truth about man, God and the world. An unbeliever, attending the fellowship of God's people and listening to solid preaching will learn much truth. Even though he cannot know this truth savingly until he trusts Christ as Savior (I Corinthians 2), he may learn many things. This is a blessing; it will help him think straighter than if he went on ignorant of it. It may steer him from greater iniquity. Yet it may be a curse; if having heard all he rejects Christ, what more is there to show or tell him?

Next, we read of **tasting of the heavenly gift** and becoming **sharers of the Holy Spirit**. To see the evidences of the Holy Spirit at work all around you, to see lives changed, prayers answered, people saved is to taste and share in what is happening among God's people as the Holy Spirit moves in their midst. Again in a similar way, that can be both a blessing and a curse.

Lastly, to **taste the goodness of God's Word and the miracles of the coming age** is a great privilege. If preaching of the Bible and the working of the miracles that were prevalent in the apostolic age does not convince him of the truth of Christianity, what else remains?

What we have here is a person who has had every advantage, and yet refuses to believe. Indeed, at length, because of his lack of faith, he leaves the people of God, drifts back into apostate Judaism and *by that act* **crucifies God's Son all over again and publicly disgraces Him** (v. 6). The renunciation of Christ and the gospel that is inherent in leaving the church

6 if they fall away, because they themselves crucify God's Son all over again and publicly disgrace Him.
7 Now ground that drinks up the rain that frequently waters it and bears vegetation that is useful to those who farm it receives God's blessing,
8 but ground that bears thorns and thistles is worthless, and is close to being cursed and finally burned.

---

and returning to Judaism, the writer makes clear, is equivalent to standing with the crowd who cried "Crucify him!" After having taken a stand for Christ by public baptism into His church, to leave and return to Judaism is a public act akin to blaspheming Him. Thus to do these things is a serious matter. One cannot act that way with impunity. Tell fearful, sluggish counselees that this is so (or at least read them this passage). To fail to warn against such defection, when he has expressed thoughts that indicate he is contemplating it, is to do a great injustice to the false professor. It leaves him in a fearful state of affairs if he does not sincerely repent before it is too late to recoup. Returning to any false religion is tantamount to rejecting Christ and crucifying Him all over again.

How do we know for sure that he is speaking of those who have made a false profession of faith? Well, elsewhere in Scripture it is clear that persons once saved cannot again be lost. See, for instance, comments on I Peter 1:3-5. But even more so, look at verses 7 through 9 in the chapter before us. The writer draws a very clear picture of the difference between a regenerate and an unregenerate person. All the blessings of God, like rain, fall upon both as they associate among the people of God in His church. One field drinks it up and bears useful vegetation. Another, receiving the very same rain, bears only thorns and thistles. All the blessings of God produce nothing. Why the difference between the two results of the same showers? The difference lies in the ground. The first represents the truly regenerate person who benefits from the blessings of God and produces fruit. The second represents the effect of all those showers of benefits mentioned in verses 4 and 5 that rain upon an unregenerate person who falsely professes faith in Christ. The blessings from God were the same; the results were the opposite.

Well, it looks as if he thought that the bulk of the membership in the church was composed of such unregenerate, false professors (and he knew that what he wrote might seem so to the reader). He didn't. Listen to verse 9: **Even though we speak this way, dear friends, we are convinced of better things about you—things that are true of those who have salva-**

9 Even though we speak this way, dear friends, we have been convinced of better things about you—things that are true of those who have salvation.
10 We say this because God isn't unjust so that He forgets your work and the love that you showed for His name by serving His saints in the past and at present.

---

tion. Obviously he must mean he thinks that the majority of them are saved. He speaks here of the congregation *as a whole*; not of individuals, some of whom he did suspect were unsaved. Otherwise, there would have been no point to the warnings here or throughout the rest of the Book of Hebrews. It is right to warn then, because no one can read another's heart.

What is his evidence for the confidence that he expresses in verse 9? Consider verse 10: **We say this because God isn't unjust so that He forgets your work and the love that you showed for His Name by serving His saints in the past and at present.** Plainly there were some live works that were the basis for his affirmation. There were works (not dead works, but Spirit-wrought works) that they had done. And he mentions at least one in particular: honoring God's Name by serving His saints in love. The **and** may also mean "even" so that what follows it is explanatory of that which precedes.

If there is no evidence of saving faith at work in the life of your counselee, you had better warn him as the writer did above. But, regardless of how pitifully weak such evidence may be, if there is any genuine fruit at all, then the Spirit has been at work, and there is good reason to think he is regenerate. Where there is an effect, there must be an adequate cause. Love for God's people (the **saints**) shown in continued service (**in the past and at the present**) for them was one very good evidence of salvation. Unbelievers cannot continue in loving service of that sort. To observe this may be reassuring. What this loving service was in particular (if some specific ministry was actually in view) we do not know. But whatever it may have been, it brought glory to the Name of God. Now, says the writer, in the spirit of what you all have done *collectively* in the past I want you to do *individually* in the future. Let's see what he has in mind.

We want each one of you to show the same eagerness to the very end with regard to the full assurance of hope, he says. He has praised them for the diligent care with which they ministered to other believers. Now he wants to see the very same diligence in maintaining a **full** and

11 Now we want each one of you to show the same eagerness to the very end with regard to the full assurance of hope,

---

unwavering **assurance** about the Christian **hope** present in each one of them. And he wants it to remain until **the very end** (i.e., until they go to be with the Lord). They were weak and doubtful. They vacillated between Christianity and the Judaism they had left behind. Consequently, they were weak, their assurance was incomplete; they were vulnerable. This was an unacceptable state of affairs.

This verse is a wonderful resource for dealing with fearful, uncertain and wavering Christians whose assurance of salvation (to say the most) is incomplete. They are up and down; they lead lives of doubt and fear with periods of certainty and joy interspersed. That, you need to tell them, is an unacceptable condition in which to live. It is not the abundant life of which Jesus spoke. It is not the steady condition of hope that here is enjoined on these readers. They lack maturity. What God wants is for you to show **eagerness** to develop and maintain to the very end a **full assurance of** the Christian **hope.** And since he addresses **each one** of them, it is clear that this is something that *every* believer may and ought to attain. If there is no eagerness, no desire to attain it, there is something wrong with the goals and objectives of your counselee. You need to probe to discover what it is that has frustrated this very normal and natural desire. It may be that he has tried and failed often and has simply given up hope of assurance. Perhaps he is holding on to some sinful pattern that he thinks casts doubt on his salvation. It may be erroneous teaching that he has bought into, saying that a saved person may be lost. Conceivably, you may discover that he is uncertain about almost everything, and that assurance of his salvation (because it is so important to him) seems to stand out. But he may have developed patterns that make decision-making an agonizing thing. He has never learned to plan according to biblical principles, act in accordance with these plans, then say "Lord, nevertheless not my will but Yours be done" and leave it there. He is always looking back, wondering whether that was the right decision that he made yesterday, three weeks ago, etc. In such cases as those just mentioned, more is needed than merely exhorting him to **eagerness**. What he needs is a total revamping of his working philosophy of life. He must learn what faith means in daily living. Faith in God's Word and faith in His providence in working out answers to the prayer mentioned above. Perhaps a study of Matthew 6 would be of help.

12 so that you won't become dull but imitators of those who through faith and patience inherit the promises.

At any rate, counselees must be made aware of the fact that **full assurance of hope** is not unusual but the norm. It is not natural for a child to go about wondering who his father is. Under normal circumstances, a child grows up in a home understanding from the outset who is what in the household. And he never doubts it. Why? Because there is no reason to doubt. He trusts the word of his father and mother. Why should a child of God not trust the word of his heavenly Father all the more?

In verse 12, he notes that failure to maintain a **full assurance of hope** is an additional cause of **dullness** (cf. 5:11). And the two neatly intersect. Previously he said that the lack of experience and training one has in using the Scriptures so that one is able to discern between good and evil was at the root of dullness. That is so. And when one fails to use the Bible as he has described that will lead to vacillation, a wavelike existence of doubt and fear with a focus on self rather than on Jesus Christ and others about whom one should concern himself. Few things can be more dulling to one's spiritual life than a lack of assurance. The only way that some put to rest the fear involved in never knowing if you were to die today whether you'd be with God or not, is to try to put the matter out of mind. Though it is doubtful whether that can be done in an effective way, nonetheless, when attempted (and to some extent achieved) that leads to dullness with reference to everything else the Word says. Consequently, the Christian soon puts down the Scriptures, focuses on something else and his spiritual life begins to atrophy.

So what is the answer? Don't allow that to happen. Help your counselee to become eager to attain to a full assurance of hope. It is your task, counselor to do two things then. First, you must show how abnormal uncertainty of hope is for the believer. One of the key words used by the reformers (especially Calvin) was "certainty." That was something Rome could not offer, but what the Scriptures, ministered by the reformers, could! Secondly, having held out hope of hope, you must help counselees attain that hope. These are two things that often must precede other issues. After all, if one is unsure of his salvation, it is likely that he will be **dull** with reference to other biblical matters as well.

In the second half of verse 12 there is another factor that will be helpful in counseling vacillating counselees. Point them to the **faith and practice** of others who **inherit the promises**, and call on them to **imitate** what

13 When God made a promise to Abraham, since He didn't have anybody greater to swear by, He swore by Himself

---

they see in their lives. While it is true that your counselee may be helped by observing and imitating those around him, the principal concern here seems to be to imitate *biblical* examples such as those that will be mentioned in the eleventh chapter. After all, you *know* they made it! You can never be quite sure of a contemporary who has not yet died and about whom there is no divine revelation telling you that he went to be with Christ. So once again you are directed to the Scriptures. Fortunately, in harmony with his own advice, the writer will list a body of persons whose faith and assurance counselees may imitate. That every counselee will imitate someone is a given. Remember that. Check out who is (or has been in the past) his ideal. Has he imitated (in this matter) a poor example of assurance or Bible study or faith? Here may be the source of many of his problems. On the matter of **imitation** see comments on I Corinthians 11:1 in this series.

He is now going to show, in detail, how Abraham was able to reach a full assurance of hope (v. 13ff.). **Abraham** had **an anchor for his soul** (v. 19) that enabled him to achieve and maintain a full assurance of hope. What was it? Verses 13 through 20 tell us. God's **promise**, sealed by an **oath** did it. And according to verse 18, we too have the same anchor. This anchor allows one to remain steadfast regardless of the tides of life. It enables him to become firm in hope and assurance because it keeps him from drifting. That is precisely what many of your counselees need. But the anchor-promise, sealed with an oath, again requires understanding of and faith in the teachings of the Bible, because it is there, alone, that one may learn of it.

First let us note, God took an **oath** about the **promise made to Abraham**. He has promised him a land (not only the land of Canaan, which was only a type and shadow of the eternal land in which he would find true rest from sin and its consequences—see chapters 4 and 11) and a seed. In a human oath, one calls on someone superior to witness to what he says; supremely, he calls on God. On whom could God call? There is no one greater than He. So **He swore by Himself**. The structure of the words quoted from the Old Testament in verse 14 is the structure of an oath. Indeed, it *is* the oath by which God swore. Verse 15 says that **Abraham waited patiently** for God to fulfill His promise. As we shall see in chapter 11, to do so required faith. And we shall see also that though the

14 in these words, **I will surely bless you and bless you and multiply you and multiply you.**
15 So, because Abraham waited patiently, he got what was promised.
16 Human beings swear by somebody who is greater, and the oath as confirmation ends all arguments.
17 So when God determined to show the heirs of the promise more forcefully the unchangeable nature of His purpose, He did it by interposing an oath between them and Himself.

---

type of the promise (the earthly land) eventually was given to him, to that extent fulfilling the promise, the antitype (the heavenly rest) was received only at death. Part of one's trust in the promises of God means waiting until God is pleased to grant what He has promised. But there was no lack of assurance about God's promise of eternal life because God swore He would bless and multiply Abraham's seed. This He did in the people who entered the earthly land of promise; this He still is engaged in doing as He redeems the present-day seed of Abraham and takes them into heavenly rest. From this, a counselee may learn at least two things. One, is that God may not fulfill all of His promises right away, and secondly, that He may fulfill some of them only at death. Many counselees want what they want right now and, what they want is *all* that they hope to receive. Yet it may not be all that they should seek. They are not satisfied with Abraham to wait patiently for the fulfillment of God's sworn promise. Many of the problems that counselees have are a matter of lack of patience, which in turn, is a matter of the lack of faith. Check these out.

In verses 16 and following the writer explains the difference between a human oath and the one that God took. But he also shows the purpose of an oath is nonetheless the same: **and the oath as confirmation ends all arguments**. That is the point. When a counselee stubbornly argues for more than God will give him by way of confirmation of salvation (God clearly promises that whoever believes is saved), he is virtually saying that God's oath is worthless. That is a serious matter. Assurance has been provided for those who accept the Bible by faith. Does God say that all who believe on the Lord Jesus Christ will be saved—or not? That is the only issue. If God's says it, and that is the intent of the greater aspects of His oath to Abraham (see Galatians 3), then that settles the matter for all who trust God's Word.

The taking of an oath is a **forceful** way to give assurance, he says (v. 17). Moreover, it confirms the fact that the promise is for good (he writes of its **unchangeable nature**). There must be two witnesses, so **by two**

18 The result was that by two unchangeable things, in which it is impossible for God to lie, we who have fled for protection might have strong encouragement to lay hold of the hope set before us.
19 We have this hope as a safe and secure anchor for the soul; it is one that enters into the place on the inner side of the curtain
20 where Jesus has entered as a Forerunner on our behalf by becoming an eternal High Priest after the order of Melchizedek.

---

unchangeable things, in which it is impossible for God to lie, He acted so as to provide **strong encouragement** to those who **have fled for protection by Him** from sin and its consequences. What more could one want? God said it, and He cannot lie; that is one witness. God swore to it; and He cannot lie; that is the other. How could He more certainly affirm anything?

Thus, the believer has **this hope as a safe and secure anchor for the soul**. There is no excuse for drift. If he trusts firmly in God's Word, given by Him and certified by His oath, how can he doubt his salvation? The promise is secure. And it becomes an anchor to make one firm. The anchor grips the ark of the covenant where the blood on the Day of Atonement was sprinkled. It goes right through the curtain that separated the holy place from the most holy place into the latter. As High Priest in the heavenly sanctuary, that is where Jesus has entered to atone for our sins. He is the Forerunner. We too now have access to the mercy seat over which the shekinah glory shone as a sign of the visible presence of God through the torn veil. If Jesus is there, and is our High Priest, then all is safe and secure, because He cannot fail us.

Counselor, I recognize that this chapter is bittersweet. There is much here in the severe warning given that is unpleasant to have to talk about. Yet, if you are to be faithful to God and to those who come for counsel, you must do so. Warnings are never easy, but they are important. On the other hand, the chapter is filled with assurance and hope. In bringing those two virtues to the attention of counselees, you will find your task more pleasant.

CHAPTER 7

1 Now this Melchizedek, king of Salem, priest of the Most High God, met Abraham when he returned from the defeat of the kings and blessed him,

---

At this point we come to a long chapter in the Book. It is somewhat intricate in that it discusses in detail the relationship of the Melchizedek priesthood to the Aaronic, and what that means in relationship to Christ and Christianity. Moreover, the discussion arises from the careful analysis of a very meager amount of information about Melchizedek recorded in Genesis 14:18-20 and Psalm 110:4. Let's take a look at it to determine what it holds for the Christian counselor.

Melchizedek was **king of Salem** (most think this was the city later named Jeru*salem*). He was also a **priest of the Most High God** (v. 1). Already, one can see a distinction between him and other priests: he was both a priest and a king. That was unusual. Christ is both and prophet as well. He **met Abraham when he returned from the defeat of the kings and blessed him** (see Genesis 14)**.** The Jews, the children of Abraham, were thinking of returning to Judaism. But Judaism had only an Aaronic priesthood. Abraham, on the other hand, submitted to a greater priest, Melchizedek. David had predicted Another after the order of Melchizedek; why would they not follow their great forefather and serve Him?

When God is called **the Most High God**, that is not because there are other gods. The meaning is that above all beings and all things He is God. When the nations pose their so-called Gods, He is greater than any of their imagined gods. In short, *He* is God! Counselees sometimes need to be reminded of the fact that God *is* **Most High**. Too often they put themselves, others or things above God. That is their fundamental problem that, in turn, leads to many others. Once more, they ought to be taught to understand that to put anything or anyone above God, in any way, is pure idolatry. Look for idolatrous strains in a counselee's life. Ask, "What does she mean to you?" Oh, pastor, everything! "Really?" Yes, I don't think I could live without her. "Then God is not enough? Does she mean more to you than He?" That sort of exchange may prove profitable in many situations. What you want to know by your questions is whether in the counselee's thinking God is ***Most* High**.

To **bless** another means to ask God to do good things for him. As a

2 and Abraham divided a tenth part of all the spoils with him. First, his name means "king of righteousness"; then he is also king of Salem, which means "king of peace."
3 Without father or mother or ancestral lineage, without a beginning of days or end of life, but like God's Son, he remains a priest perpetually.

---

minister of the Word, you who are preachers are required to bless others. You ought to do so. It means that you will assert your authority and your position as you pronounce a blessing on them. Do you ever do so in a counseling session? I don't mean in some sentimental way, saying, "Blessings on you brother," but as His representative, in full understanding that you are calling on God to do good to a counselee. You do not dispense blessings as you might hand out cookies; you do not have them in your possession to give. But like Melchizedek, you do have the right and duty to *minister* such blessings to others by asking God to shower His goodness on them. Rather than the cavalier "Blessings on you brother," mentioned above, you might solemnly stand with arms outstretched and say, "In the Name of Jesus Christ I call on God to bless you."

And showing his respect for the authority and position of Melchizedek, Abraham gave a tithe of all his spoils to him. It is not wrong for those to whom you minister to return something of what they have received. Indeed, that is a constantly mentioned duty. But here it is mentioned to show the relative position of the founder of the Hebrew people to Melchizedek; Abraham, thereby, acknowledged the priesthood of Melchizedek. Why then would *they* reject it?

The name **Melchizedek** means **King of Righteousness**. And he was also the **king of Salem**, which means **King of Peace** (v. 2). These two characteristics were clearly true of the Savior in the fullest sense. He was all that Melchizedek was—in perfection. In verse 3 we read how there is no lineage given for Melchizedek; he simply appears and disappears on the biblical scene. There is no indication of when he was born or when he died. So far as the record goes, then, both his order and he, himself, seem to have no end; on the record he **is a priest perpetually**. His priesthood, as a result, was not ancestral in nature; it was not passed down from his forbearers. He was a **priest of the Most High God.** That is to say, he received his priesthood *directly* from God, not through some intermediary. In that respect, Christ is also like Melchizedek.

The greatness of Melchizedek is emphasized by the writer to contrast the priesthood that was his with the priesthood of Aaron, to which they

4 See how great he was. Abraham, a patriarch, gave a tenth of the spoils to this man.
5 Levi's sons, who receive the priestly office, are commanded by the law to take tithes from the people (that is, their own brothers) even though they are Abraham's descendants.
6 But this man, who didn't have their ancestral lineage, took tithes from Abraham and blessed him who had the promises!
7 Now it is beyond all dispute that the lesser is blessed by the greater.
8 Here tithes are received by dying men; there, by one of whom it is witnessed that he lives.
9 So, one might even say that Levi, who received tithes, paid tithes through Abraham,
10 since he was still in his forefather's loins when Melchizedek met him.

---

were thinking of returning. Even a **patriarch gave a tenth of the spoils to this man.** Thereby he recognized the greatness of the position that God had granted to him. Unlike **Levi's sons, who receive the priestly office** and **are commanded by the law to take tithes from the people (...their own brothers),** Melchizedek took tithes from ***Abraham*** (who is more than a mere "brother," but rather the **one who had the promises** given to him (vv. 5,6). What's the point? Simply this: **it is beyond all dispute that the lesser is blessed by the greater.** Not that he was any greater than **Abraham** in his person, but because of his office, Abraham—the father of the Jews—had to acknowledge his greater place in God's Kingdom. That is the import of all so far as the writer sums it up in verse 7.

At the time of writing, the temple priests **received** tithes; but they were **dying men**. Of Melchizedek, nothing is said about his death. He is simply one who, when he received tithes from Abraham, was living. He passed nothing on to any ancestry because he had to die; rather, he would pass it on to One alone Who would *never* die: Jesus Christ. As a matter of fact verses 9 and 10 point out that **one might even say that Levi, who received tithes, paid tithes through Abraham.** How could that be? Well, he **was still in his forefather's loins when Melchizedek met him.** In every way the writer is indicating how much greater Melchizedek (and as he will say, the greater Melchizedek) was than the Aaronic priests. In one more way, he is showing how far superior Jesus is and how much greater Christianity is. The hermeneutics in use here are most revealing. Not only does the writer use the evident meaning of a passage as he argues, but draws logical, sometimes very tight, intricate implications from them. You may wonder at some of the inferences in these commen-

11 Now, then, if perfection could have been attained through the Levitical priesthood (it was the law), why would there still be a need for another priest to be appointed after Melchizedek's order rather than to be named after Aaron's order?
12 When there is a change of priesthood, there also must be a change of law.
13 The One about Whom these things are said belonged to a different tribe, from which nobody has ever attended to the altar.
14 Now it is perfectly clear that our Lord arose from the tribe of Judah, and with reference to that tribe Moses said nothing about priests.

---

taries that I have made from passages that we are studying. On the basis of the writer's authoritative example it is valid to do so. I am studying the New Testament with you, not to preach it (I am not merely delivering God's message) but to understand it and to make inferences that are valid, though they may not necessarily be the prime intention of the passage. If I were preaching from these passages, I would do so quite differently.

Beginning with verse 11, the writer now launches a devastating comparison between the Levitical and the Melchizedek priesthood. He begins by showing how **if perfection could have been attained through the Levitical priesthood** [which the law required], there would be no need for **another priest to be appointed after Melchizedek's order,** yet that's what the Psalmist predicted (v. 17). Perfection (a *complete* cleansing from sin) could not be attained from Levitical animal sacrifices. Otherwise, there would be **no need for the psalmist to promise the advent of another priest**. And since there was to be **a change** of the Levitical **priesthood** that was set up by **the law** given to Moses, there would of necessity also be **a change of law.** In his effort to show how much better the New Covenant is, he is beginning to demonstrate the imperfections of the Old which consisted of types and shadows and not the reality. The old was good for its purpose, but its purpose was to point to the New Covenant reality. Clearly since the latter came, the former is no longer necessary. The sacrificial system of the Old Covenant law has been done away with because the Savior of which it spoke has come.

The Messiah, Whose coming was predicted in the Psalm, **belonged to a different tribe, from which nobody has ever attended the altar** (v. 13); Jesus was not from the tribe of Levi, but from Judah. Moses, in the law, said nothing about priests of the Aaronic order coming from Judah (v. 14). And, because Jesus is said to be of the Melchizedek order, it is **all the more evident** that there was the necessity for another order of priests.

15 This becomes even more evident when another Priest like Melchizedek arises,
16 Who has become such, not according to a commandment that requires fleshly qualifications, but rather according to the power of an indestructible life.
17 It is witnessed of him, **You are a Priest forever according to Melchizedek's order.**
18 On the one hand, a former commandment is set aside because of its weakness and uselessness

---

The Aaronic order did not provide for such a Priest. This greater order was not populated by those who qualified according to tribal ancestry (i.e., according to **fleshly qualifications**) but rather, according to **the power of an indestructible life** (vv. 15,16). It is He, about Whom the Psalmist wrote in Psalm 110 (v. 17). The only qualification mentioned in the Psalm is that He is a priest **forever**. That is, He must possess **indestructible life.** That could be true of only One—the God-man, Jesus Christ. **In Him *was* life!**

The former commandment (to ordain priests according to tribal qualifications into the Aaronic order) **was set aside because of its weakness and uselessness.** That command, along with the sacrificial system accompanying it, could never take away sins (as the author will say clearly at a later point). It was **weak** in that it was not the saving reality, but merely foreshadowed it. It was now **useless** because the reality that it foreshadowed had appeared. No one hugs and kisses the picture of her loved one any longer when he, himself, appears on the scene. The picture was fine in its place; it served its purpose so long as he was not there in person. But now it is useless as a reminder of one who has actually appeared on the scene. **The law didn't make anything perfect**. Containing but types and shadows, it was incomplete. It looked forward to its completion in the coming of the One it typified. Now that the **better hope is introduced by which we come close to God** (Jesus has opened the way to God through His death and resurrection), who would want to go back to the old way of coming to God through sinful, earthly priests? That is the argument in a nutshell.

Counselees who complain that God is unreal to them; who think God is distant and not accessible, might be given the assignment of looking up all the places where (in this Book) the Christian is said to be able **to come close to God.** Set him to work with his concordance. Don't give him the verses (as I am not giving them to you) so that he will have to search them

19 (the law didn't make anything perfect); on the other hand, a better hope is introduced by which we come close to God.

20 And it wasn't without an oath! On the one hand, they became priests without any oath-taking,

21 but on the other hand, He became one by oath-taking when God said to Him,

> **The Lord swore,**
> **and will not change His mind,**
> **"You are a Priest forever."**

22 By so much more, then, has Jesus become the guarantee of a better covenant.

---

out for himself. Two things might happen: first, he may obtain the satisfaction of having done some Bible study for himself; second, he may find that the contexts in which the phrase is found teach wonderful truths that he needs to hear. If God seems distant, perhaps that is because the one to whom He seems to be afar off needs to heed the exhortation to **come close.** It is not God's fault if *that* is the problem. Somehow, *he* has wandered from God. *How* is the question to explore in counseling. He has the **better hope** of direct access to the holy of holies and the throne of grace. Why hasn't he been using that privilege? When you discover the answer to that question and have remedied the problem you will have helped him immeasurably.

And this new order **wasn't without an oath!** as he repeats (v. 20). That is to say, the promise that you may have such access to God is absolutely sure. You can count on it as surely as if you were able to hold God to an oath.

The Aaronic priests, **on the other hand, became priests without any oath-taking** (v. 20); Jesus **became one by oath-taking** according to the Psalm (v. 21). Since that is true, he says, the **better covenant** has a **better guarantee** of blessing and ability to complete what God promised than the old one did (v. 22). Counselor, if you find counselees who wonder whether the promises of the Bible are dependable, perhaps this is the passage to which to refer them. What more could he say? How many more times must he repeat it? He is assuring the reader that what one has in Christ is utterly dependable.

Now under the old system, **there were a lot of those priests, because death kept them from continuing in office.** That is because none of them had an **indestructible life**. Since Jesus does, **He holds His priesthood permanently, because He remains forever** (vv. 23,24). And

23 There were a lot of those priests, because death kept them from continuing in office,
24 but He holds His priesthood permanently, because He remains forever.
25 It is this fact, indeed, that makes Him able to save completely those who come close to God through Him, because He always lives to intercede for them.
26 Now, of course, such a High Priest was suited to us; One Who is holy, innocent, unstained, set apart from sinners and Who has become more exalted than the heavens.

---

because of this, He is **able to save completely those who come close to God through Him, because He always lives to make intercession** (v. 25). He is not only the One Who gave His life for His own, but the One Who also represents them before God in the heavens throughout eternity. His priesthood is, then, all-encompassing. Any and everything necessary is achieved by Him because He is *always* there to see to it.

Is that what you need to help counselees? Is it that sort of priest that *you* need counselee? Well the writer of Hebrews thought so: **such a High Priest was suited to us; One Who is holy, innocent, unstained, set apart from sinners and Who has become more exalted than the heavens.** I'd say that's a pretty fine High Priest! Wouldn't you? If we need one who is suited to poor, helpless sinners, He fits the bill—*perfectly*. He is all the things we are not. And He is above all created things. He is with God the Father, our man at God's right hand. The counselee who needs something may, therefore, come boldly to the throne of grace to find help in time of need. He is there to see that he not only has access to that throne, but that the helpless, needy sinner is heard. An answer—the very best one possible—will be given to all those who come close to God in the ways He has invited them to.

And this High Priest **doesn't have to offer daily sacrifices...first for His own sins, then for the sins of the people** because He has no sins for which to atone. That means that He is heard in His own right, that He cannot fail to offer His sacrifice properly and that you may have every assurance about what He has done for you. And further **He offered a sacrifice for their sins once for all when He offered up Himself** (vv. 26,27). The writer is going to make a very large point of the once-for-all sacrifice of Christ later on. For now note simply this: a once-for-all sacrifice means that God is satisfied. The task is completed at last. There is nothing more that needs to be done or can be done to enhance redemption. God, in Christ, has done it all. Any counselee, who thinks he can do otherwise

27 He doesn't have to offer daily sacrifices like the other high priests, first for His own sins, then for the sins of the people. He offered a sacrifice for their sins once for all when He offered up Himself.
28 The law appoints as high priests men who have weakness, but the oath-taking that came after the law appoints a Son Who has been perfected forever.

---

needs to be told otherwise. There are counselees who want to offer their own works in addition to the work of Christ. No way! That is the message of the last verse.

Finally in this chapter the writer says, **The law appoints as high priests men who have weaknesses, but the oath-taking that came after the law appoints a Son Who has been perfected forever.** This is a powerful summary of all that he has said throughout the chapter. And once more, it rings the changes on the fact that in this High Priest, there is a filial relationship to the Father; He is God's Son. That is the only ancestry that counts!

Counselor, what a magnificent tribute to Jesus Christ the writer of this Book has offered! Do you see it? Can you convey it to your counselee? Why not do so? Anything less that he offers as a possible way of life can be compared and contrasted with Christianity, as the writer does, and you will find that Jesus Christ always comes out on top.

CHAPTER 8

1 Now the main point of what has been said is this: we have such a High Priest! He sat down at the right hand of the throne of the Majesty in the heavens,

---

The eighth chapter opens with a clarification of what the writer has been saying about Christ and the two priesthoods: **Now the main point of what has been said is this: we have such a High Priest!** The words **main point** have been translated "crowning point" or the "head point." He has been speaking of the advantages of a **perpetually-living priest**, a **holy**, sinless priest and a priest **more exalted than the heavens.** Now, he says, the discussion about such a priest has not just been for the sake of curiosity or interest or speculation; no, exactly not that. The point of it all is the **we have such a High Priest!** "Why," then, is the implication, "would you want to go back the priesthood you left behind when the one in which Jesus ministers to you is so much **better**?" The argument for a Jew, to whom the entire sacrificial system was such a vital part of his life, should have been most persuasive. Think of all that it meant to him to have such a priest. To us today, the impact is less, unless we put ourselves back into his shoes (or should I say sandals?).

The idea of understanding a passage in its historical-cultural setting is important to the interpreter of the Bible. Passages such as these mean little to the untrained Christian. It is your task as an interpreter of Scripture who cares to use the Bible with impact on your counselees, to so interpret passages. You should make God's Word come alive, so that *all* of the Bible becomes useful in counseling. Here, if you can picture for a counselee the burdensome, wearying system that foreshadowed the coming of Christ, with all its inadequacies and inabilities to really do anything more, if you can picture the Jew spending his last penny to take a trip to Palestine from some far distant land in order to spend an exorbitant amount on sacrifices that could do nothing more than picture what he didn't yet have, then you possibly can make hay out of the passage for your counselee. Otherwise, possibly the whole argument will have no **main point** for him. The counselee who complains about his lot today, who gripes about having to go to church and give money for the support of the Lord's work is the one who needs to understand something of the contrast. The counselee who wonders why Christianity isn't a tangible,

2 a Minister of the sanctuary and the true tabernacle that the Lord, not human beings, set up.

---

physical religion, why he has to look forward to everything with anticipation rather than have it here and now, is also the one upon whom you might impress what physical religion involves, also what it would mean to have only physical blessings with their merely temporal orientation.

We have such a High Priest! Make those words come alive for your counselee, and the passage will have meaning and impact. While it is true that some biblical passages are more immediately applicable to the problems of counselees, *all* of the Bible, regardless of how fully cultural in nature passages may be, when handled properly, can be used in counseling. And indeed, there are some problems that cannot be dealt with in any other way than by use of one of those passages. Your task, then, is to understand and use as much of the Bible as possible. Don't limit yourself to those Bible portions with which you have become familiar. You will be cheating your counselees if you don't attempt to understand as much of Scripture as you can, and learn how to use all you learn with impact.

The High Priest of which the writer speaks **sat down at the right hand of the throne of the Majesty in the heavens.** That means all authority, all power are His *and* available to all of those with whom He identifies Himself. If your friend was the King of the land, would you turn away from him in your need? Certainly not! Then why turn from Christ when in trouble—He is the *King* of kings? This throne, about which Hebrews has so much to say, is also the throne of *grace* to which you may turn for help in time of need (cf. 4:16). Here then is another encouraging word for discouraged counselees! Hebrews has words of exhortation, encouragement and comfort. Don't fail to locate and use them just because these purposes may not be immediately apparent.

Jesus is now described as **a minister of the sanctuary and the true tabernacle that the Lord, not human beings, set up.** Is there truly a heavenly temple, etc.? Clearly, heaven is a *place*, not merely a condition. But, heaven is described in language that would be understandable to those who read. These descriptions are not to be taken literally. How do you know that? Well, the various descriptions do not correspond to one another. In Revelation, for instance, the heavenly city that comes down to earth is pictured as a cube. Elsewhere it is called Paradise, etc. It seems evident, therefore, that because the actuality is far greater than contemporary words and concepts can convey, more than one description is used to

3 Every high priest is appointed to offer both gifts and sacrifices, from which fact arises the necessity of this Priest's having something to offer.
4 So, then, if He were on earth, He wouldn't be a priest, since there are priests who offer such gifts according to the law.

---

give us *some* idea of what it is like. Here, when discussing the temple and the sacrificial service, the ideal of sacrifice and intercession is set forth. You can be sure that though we cannot imagine what a priest on the throne of God in heaven is truly like, we can get ideas about it from that description. Again, who would turn from Someone like that? That is the **main point**.

Now he goes on to extrapolate on the work of our High Priest in this heavenly temple, all the while comparing and contrasting the **true** [meaning the reality, the substance that casts the shadow] **tabernacle** with the earthly shadow of it. In verse 3 he speaks of the earthly high priest: he is **appointed to offer gifts and sacrifices, from which fact arises the necessity of this Priest's having something to offer.** Since that is the work of a High Priest, then, Jesus is said to engage in this work. What is it that He offers? He will tell us at length in the next chapter. But for now, we must be content to observe that Jesus is a Priest that is not on earth; if He were, **He wouldn't be a High Priest.** Why? Because a high priest had to be appointed and had to serve **according to the law**. And the law did not allow those who came from the tribe of Judah, as Jesus did, to be priests.

It is instructive to see how important it is to the writer to show how God does everything in harmony with His own requirements. Again and again this point emerges. Along with it is a repetition of the word **appoint**, which also emphasizes the *official* way in which God's requirements are met in an orderly manner. I don't want to run it into the ground, but in the light of this strong emphasis of the Bible, how can anyone without warrant from God, confirmed by ordination to the work, take on himself the task of counseling others? Clearly, the life calling of changing lives belongs to the minister of the Word (see again II Timothy 3:15 and my book, *How to Help People Change,* with reference to the words "man of God" that appear in the passage). Unless one has been **appointed** (ordained) by God through His church to that work, he has no warrant.

Verse five sets forth the relationship of the heavenly temple and ministry to the earthly one. The former is the reality (the substance) of which the latter is the **shadow** (or **copy**). What he is showing throughout this

5 They serve a copy and a shadow of the heavenly things. This is evident from the warning Moses was given when he was about to complete the tabernacle: **See to it that you make everything according to the pattern shown to you on the mountain.**

---

chapter and the one that follows is that the Hebrews have left nothing behind when they left the earthly for the heavenly. They have everything they ever had—only of a far better sort. Indeed, the difference is between that which is *real* and lasting and that which is only a copy and ephemeral. It is the difference between that which is imperfect and that which is perfection itself.

He proves that the earthly tabernacle and ministry is only a shadow of the everlasting reality by quoting Exodus 25:40; see also Acts 7:44. And as he does so, he points out that the words of God to Moses contain a **warning: See to it that you make everything according to the pattern shown to you on the mountain.** He was not to deviate from that pattern in any detail. When it comes to doing the work of God, He *will* have His way; we dare not innovate. Not only should integrationist counselors take heed to this warning, but it is a point to emphasize at times with counselees who will offer what they think are better solutions to problems than those that the Scriptures set forth. Tell them that when God has spoken about *how something is to be done* there may be no deviation from that instruction. I am not referring to those situations in which God commands, but does not choose to tell one how to obey the command. That is different; in such instances He expects you to use the principles of prudence and wisdom within the general parameters that He *does* set forth. And in such cases, it is possible that more than one way of fulfilling a given commandment may be acceptable. Here, because He wanted the tabernacle to speak of Jesus Christ, He spelled out the particulars in minute detail. Moses *dare not* innovate. Whenever God gives detailed methodology we must follow it to the nth degree whether we can immediately understand the reason for this or not. The passage before us is a fine example of a warning that you will often find it necessary to issue to a counselee.

Let's take an example of that. "You say that you think it is foolish for a person to speak to others who are caught in sin and attempt to restore them as Galatians 6 says?" Yes, pastor, that's what I think. "Why do you say so?" Well, because I don't know how to do it and, therefore, I might do more harm than good. Not only that; if somebody gets himself entan-

6 But now the ministry that He has received is as superior to theirs as the covenant of which He is the Mediator is better than the former one, because it has been enacted on the basis of better promises.

7 Now if that first covenant had been faultless, there wouldn't have been any reason to seek a place for a second.

---

gled in a mess of his own making, then why shouldn't he get himself out? Why should I get involved? "Ah, but not only does God tell you to do so—it *is* a command, you see—but He *tells* you how: see verses 1 through 5." Or take the person who says, "But you know, pastor, I would forgive him once, perhaps twice—but three times? Never!" Well, the particulars of this matter are clearly commanded by Christ (see Luke 17:3ff.), so you must warn that to go his own way rather than to follow God's is rebellion against God. It is nothing less than saying "I am smarter and wiser than God". Warn from this passage that whenever God says "Do this or that, and do it My way," He means business and it is dangerous to do otherwise. God does not command His people to do things in vain (Isaiah 55:11).

But not only is the ministry that Christ **received superior to theirs** but also **the covenant of which He is the Mediator is better than the former one because it has been enacted on the basis of better promises** (v. 6). Here in this transition verse, the writer begins to compare and contrast the old and the new covenants. As **Mediator**, Jesus is the One Who stands between God and His people. As Mediator, He sacrificed Himself for their salvation. And as Mediator, He now intercedes for them before the throne of Grace to which He bids them come boldly (confidently). Death alone brings a testament (the other translation of "covenant") into effect (as he will observe in 9:15). That is why a Mediator was needed. No sinful man could stand between a holy God and other sinful men. Priests on earth failed to do so in any efficacious manner. But Christ, by the sacrifice of Himself, effected redemption and made atonement for the sins of all His people, thus propitiating God.

Here is how he reasons: **If the first covenant had been faultless there wouldn't have been any reason to seek a place for a second** (v. 7). So then, not only does the second covenant stand on the foundation of **better promises**, but unlike the first, the second alone is **faultless**. What were the better promises and how was the first covenant flawed? The promises are not better in substance, says Lenski, but only in that there is "nothing standing in the way of fulfilling every one of them for us in this

8 But He finds fault with them when He says,
See, the days are coming, says the Lord,
when I will complete a new covenant
with Israel's house and Judah's house.

---

life and in the life to come." And he points out that, "we no longer need to wait for the Mediator as Abraham had to wait."

But I think that this somewhat misses the point. The old covenant is not that which was given to Abraham. It is that which was given to Moses. The promises to Abraham are the very promises given to us. Abraham was promised that salvation through Jesus Christ and that in Him all the nations of the earth would be blessed. The blessings of Abraham have come upon us today. It is the old covenant law that was added 430 years later that is here contrasted with the new. Its promises, in keeping with the physical, material nature of the temple and its services, were physical, temporal in nature. But the promises to us in the New Covenant that was made by the shedding of Christ's blood (as He said at the institution of His supper) are spiritual and eternal.

One thing that runs through this entire section is the contrast between the physical and the nonphysical. The average counselee is looking for the former (that, in most cases, is what motivated him to come for counseling) and thinks that it is superior to the latter (which notion was precisely what these readers were toying with). They are wrong. Use this epistle, and especially the sections like these that contrast the two, to demonstrate to them that they have it all backwards. For a great elucidation of the message, read them excerpts from C.S. Lewis' novel, *The Great Divorce,* in which this truth is powerfully made.

But what of the flawed nature of the first covenant? He says that the only reason there is for instituting a new covenant is because the first was flawed (v. 7). The fault lies not in the purpose or in the nature of the covenant itself; after all, it was given by God. It fulfilled its purpose, which never was to save anyone. It was given to convict people of the need for a Savior to Whom it pointed. And it served that purpose well. But it was not faultless when viewed from the perspective of what it could do to forgive sins and redeem men. It simply could not do that. A New Covenant therefore was needed. The people were at fault in that they could not fulfill the terms even of such a covenant as the Old one was (cf., Romans 7:7-12). If the **first** could do the job, it would have been foolish to **seek** to establish a **second** covenant in the **place** of the first (v. 7).

9 **It won't be like the covenant that I made with their fathers**
in the day when I took them by the hand
to lead them out of the land of Egypt,
because they didn't continue to keep My covenant,
and I left them alone, says the Lord.
10 **But this is the covenant that I will contract with Israel's house**
after those days, says the Lord:
I will put My laws into their minds
and I will write them on their hearts,
and I will be their God
and they will be My people.

But as the writer observes from Jeremiah 31, Jeremiah himself **finds fault with them** [the recipients of the first covenant]. To prove this, in verses 8 through 12 he quotes at length Jeremiah 31:31-34. It is not important to deal with every word of the prophecy, but (for our purposes) to see what it says and to apply it to the process of biblical counseling. What does Jeremiah predict about the New Covenant? The **completion** or consummation of the New Covenant which would take place in **days** to come, he says, would be made with the church, the new people of God (Israel recombined with Judah as Abraham's seed; something that never happened literally). This covenant would be different (v. 9), unlike the covenant **made with their fathers in the day when I took them by the hand to lead them out of the land of Egypt.** Clearly, here you see that the old covenant was the covenant made at Sinai; not the covenant with Abraham. What was wrong with that covenant? How does the New avoid the same fault? What was wrong, God says through Jeremiah, is that **they didn't continue to keep My covenant.** As we said before, the old covenant was flawed because it could not save. And the evidence of this was that they did not remain in the covenant (v. 9). Because of that, God eventually **left them alone.** That is a terrible judgment. Better for God to reprimand, rebuke and punish painfully than for Him to abandon one. He did so because of the hardness of their hearts. Rather than seeing the physical and material aspects of their covenant as pictures pointing to the coming of Jesus Christ, they trusted in them to save them from sin. That was to substitute the shadow for the reality; it was to kiss the picture rather than the loved one whom it represents.

But the New Covenant would be different in that, being spiritual, it would consist of inner change and belief. People would **worship in Spirit and in truth** (John 4:21,22). How would this come to pass? God Himself

11 **A citizen won't teach his neighbor or**
each one his brother, saying, "Know the Lord,"
because all will know Me,
from the least to the greatest of them;
12 **I will be merciful toward their unrighteous deeds**
and I won't remember their sins ever again.

---

would see to it. Notice the words "I" and "My" that dominate the tenth to twelfth verses of this chapter. But how did He accomplish it? Through a Mediator Who was one of us. He shared our weaknesses. He endured our pain. He suffered for our sins.

Through His Spirit, Whom God sent into our hearts (Romans 5:5), He has made His worship an interior thing. Apart from the two sacraments and the outer discipline of the church, all aspects of the New Covenant are internal. A community in which few know and believe will no longer be the rule. The widespread ignorance that prevailed in Israel of old will be replaced by correspondingly widespread knowledge in the church: **all will know Me**. Thus the few will not find it necessary to teach the many concerning what the faith is all about. Here is the superior nature of a spiritual covenant. Old Testament times were times of incomplete revelation. In the New, revelation was brought to perfection in God's Son. In former times a prophet would speak. Then what he said had to be taught to all the people. That would take time and often not everyone would hear. But in the New, an event surrounding a Person occurred. All who enter the New Covenant know about Jesus and His death and resurrection. They understand the message of salvation by grace through faith. That is the very basis for adult entrance into the Covenant community. Thus the revelation that came through a Son in these last days (1:2) is known to all. Entrance was *by means of understanding.*

This covenant contained a clear message of forgiveness: **I will be merciful toward their unrighteous deeds and I won't remember their sins ever again.** Let's consider the idea of God not remembering. Can God forget? Of course not. He knows all things past, present, future. And He knows all aspects of all things comprehensively. The very thought of God forgetting is not only ludicrous but repugnant. But the passage does not say that God *forgets*. What He promises is not to **remember**. What is the difference? One that you must learn as of the greatest importance to the matter of forgiveness as you must so often discuss it with counselees since their forgiveness of one another is to be like that of God toward us

13 By speaking about a "new" covenant, He has made the first obsolete. And whatever is becoming obsolete and aging is ready to disappear.

(Ephesians 4:32). When God says He will not remember, He means that He will not remember sin *against* us. He will no longer hold it against us; He will not judge us for it. He will not bring it up for remembrance. He buries it once for all. Not remembering is an active thing; something anyone may do. Forgetting is passive; it is something that cannot be *done*. It simply happens. It is involuntary. For details about this aspect of biblical forgiveness and others as well, see my book, *From Forgiven to Forgiving*.

Finally (v. 13) the point is made that the old covenant is **obsolete,** is **aging** and **is ready to disappear.** When I read this I cannot help but think of automobiles. There comes a time to obtain a new one. As I write in 1995, the 1980 models are **aging**; those from the 70's have become **obsolete**; most of those from years prior to that have **disappeared**. It was something like that which the writer had in mind. He had watched as the Old Covenant had begun to become old and was about to disappear, only to be superseded by the New.

Notice the interesting way in which he presents his argument. He has argued for the superiority of the New Covenant in so many ways in order to persuade the reader not to turn back to Judaism. Now in a clincher of an argument, he claims that the old will not last much longer; it was ready to disappear. He was thinking of the Destruction of Jerusalem that would occur a few short years off in 70 AD. Who wants to sign on to a sinking ship? When you are arguing your case for some action that you wish a counselee either to take or not to take, be sure that you use an abundance of arguments from the Bible. Some people seem to think that it is pious only to use one: "It will be to God's glory to do (or stop doing) so-and-so." While doubtless that is the ultimate motivation that we would like to drive every counselee exclusively, if you read the Bible you will see that it is not the only one that the writers use. While never veering from this motive as the fundamental and highest motive, they nevertheless use a multiplicity of other arguments that appeal to lesser motives as well. If it is right for the authors of the inspired pages to do this, surely it is right (and wise) for you to emulate them in it. As a gracious God, Who in so many ways condescends to our frailties, He has deemed this not only permissible and realistic, but to be encouraged. Don't try to be more pious than Paul!

CHAPTER 9

1 Now, indeed, the first had regulations for worship and a sanctuary of a worldly sort.
2 The first tabernacle, called the "Holy Place," was furnished with the lampstand, the table and the presentation bread.
3 Beyond the second curtain was a tabernacle called "The Holy of Holies"
4 that had the golden altar of incense and the ark of the covenant that was covered on all sides with gold (in which were a golden pot containing manna, Aaron's rod that budded and the tablets of the covenant).
5 Above it were the cherubim of glory overshadowing the mercy seat. But it isn't possible to speak in detail about these things at this time.

This long 28-verse chapter contains the heart of the contrast between the Old and the New covenant worship. In it are some of the most important points that the Book of Hebrews makes about the salvation that we have in Christ. Every counselor should both know what is in the chapter and also how to use these materials in counseling to the best effect.

The writer begins by saying that the **first** covenant **had regulations for worship and a sanctuary of a worldly sort.** The words **worldly sort** do not refer to anything sinful. He does not use the term here to indicate what John in His first epistle calls **worldly** (I John 2:15-17). Rather, the reference is to that which is earthly, a part of the present, tangible world, *in contrast to* that which is heavenly in the unseen world and world to come (2:5; 6:5). And in this earthly, physically oriented covenant, there were regulations regarding worship that God Himself initiated. Some of these consisted of the ways in which the tabernacle (and later temple) were arranged and furnished: **the "Holy Place," was furnished with the lampstand, the table and the presentation bread. Beyond the second curtain** [which separated the holy place from the holy of holies] **was a tabernacle called the "Holy of Holies" that had the golden altar of incense and the ark of the covenant that was covered on all sides with gold (in which were a golden pot containing manna, Aaron's rod that budded and the tablets of the covenant). Above it were the cherubim of glory overshadowing the mercy seat** (vv. 2-5[a]). This is a reminder of how the worship of the Old Covenant had to do with all sorts of material, physical, "worldly" items. There is no point to going over each of these items, what it might have represented, etc., because that is not the writer's

6 So the first tabernacle was furnished with these things and the priests regularly enter the first tabernacle to accomplish their ministries.
7 But into the second only the high priest enters, and that once, and once only, each year; and not without blood, which he offers on behalf of himself and the people's sins of ignorance.

---

concern. What he is showing is that this worship was decidedly earthly. He indeed reins himself in, refraining from going into **detail** at this time (v. 5^b). Verse 6 is but a summary statement. What can a counselor make of this description? Well, because the buildings in which worship is offered today are also made up of earthly objects or furnishings, people often become enamored with stain glass windows, property, etc. And because of an overemphasis on the material aspect of some building or its furnishings, they make these things all-important. As a result, they bicker and quarrel over these matters in every sort of way. Counselees, having difficulties of that nature, need to be shown that our worship is not **worldly**. These things are all right in their place, but they have no place in the essential worship of the New Testament church. God has decreed nothing about buildings, the types of furnishings we should use in worship, where they must be placed or in what ways they should be used. Anything material that we have as congregations is merely for convenience and comfort. Apart from the elements used in the sacraments, the worship in which we engage requires nothing **worldly**; indeed it is entirely spiritual. To understand this, and to inculcate this understanding into the thought and practice of some counselee who finds himself in bitter conflict with another over the type of piano the church should buy, the color of the drape behind the pulpit (or whether there should be one) etc., can be a vital part of good counseling. These things are all good in their place, but their place is quite secondary.

Having described the furnishings of the tabernacle (temple), the writer goes on the describe the worship and ministry carried on in it: **But into the second** [holy of holies] **only the high priest enters, and that once, and once only, each year; and not without blood, which he offers on behalf of himself and the people's sins of ignorance** (v. 7). He is speaking of the Day of Atonement. This was the great Day of the Jewish year. What does he make of the facts so far presented? In verses 8 and 9 he begins to relate these facts to the argument he is mounting: **By this the Holy Spirit is showing that the way into the Holy of Holies hadn't yet been cleared as long as the first tabernacle was still standing. This**

8 By this the Holy Spirit is showing that the way into the Holy of Holies hadn't yet been cleared as long as the first tabernacle was still standing.
9 This is a parable for the present time that shows that both the gifts and the sacrifices that are being offered aren't able to perfect the conscience of the worshiper.

---

is a parable for the present time that shows that both the gifts and the sacrifices that are being offered aren't able to perfect the conscience of the worshipper. Here, before considering his argument, note two facts: first, sacrifices were still being offered in Jerusalem (the letter, therefore, was written prior to 70 AD); second, the way in which he speaks of Scripture is that as one reads it he is hearing the Holy Spirit speak. Of the utmost importance is the fact that God, the Holy Spirit, does not address us in prayer (as many suppose) or by promptings or checks in the spirit as others seem (with no biblical warrant) to think, but strictly by means of the Bible. It is imperative to help confused Christians who have been taught loose doctrine about revelation and guidance that these are unbiblical concepts. Many Christians are confused and frustrated as the result of following such teachings. Straighten them out. Show them that the Spirit speaks through the Bible, the Book that He inspired (see also 10:15,17). Perhaps this is one of the most important things you could do for him.

But now to the use the writer makes of the facts he has presented from the Old Testament. He says that the Holy Spirit, who (through Moses) wrote the facts he is summarizing, was showing that so long as the temple stood, with its veil (or curtain) separating the holy place from the most holy one, the true, final redemption of men had not yet taken place. He calls that fact a **parable**. That is, it has meaning beyond its use in the worldly temple ministry. That meaning is that, because of his sins, God stood aloof from man and could be approached only by the high priest once a year. And then only to make atonement by the blood sprinkled on the mercy seat atop the ark of the covenant and beneath the wings of the covering cherubim. That was where the shekinah glory appeared as a symbol of God's presence. But as he says, the fact that this offering had to be made yearly indicates that **the sacrifices that are being offered aren't able to perfect the conscience of the worshipper.** How is that? Well, the yearly offering showed that the previous offerings did not really do away with sins. Otherwise there would be no need of further offerings. The **consciences of the worshippers** were not eased once and for all by what he did because they had to be eased again and again year after year. He

10 They have regulations that have to do with the flesh, depending only on foods and drinks and different kinds of baptisms, set up until the time of correction.

---

will contrast them with the once-for-all offering of Christ which relieves the conscience of the believer for good.

How do counselees need to apply such thinking to their lives? Those who come with consciences that are burdened with guilt, who are trying to relieve themselves of that guilt by **worldly** means, will find that they do not work. The prescriptions of the psychiatrists and psychologists who, in one way or another, attempt to deal with guilt do not work. Indeed, you will discover that they all require one to observe rituals and methods devised by these men over and over again. Take the twelve-step methodology (now applied, it seems, to everything except your cat). In it the "worshipper" has to tell himself he is addicted every day of his life until he dies. Every day, he must go through the ritual steps outline by his counselor. There is no once-for-all freeing from sin, either in terms of its guilt or power. Biblical counseling says something quite different (cf. I Corinthians 6:9-11). One may not only be forgiven once-for-all, but may shake off the shackles of his sin and replace them with the bonds of Christ's loving service. That is quite a different message to give hurting, sinful counselees. It is every bit as distinct from the world's way of dealing with sin as the **worldly** way of worship is from the worship of Jesus Christ.

The writer continues (v. 10): **They have regulations that have to do with the flesh, depending on foods and drinks and different kinds of baptisms, set up until the time of correction.** Clearly, this earthly, worldly system was temporary: it was **set up until the time of correction**. What is that talking about? Well, plainly, the **time of correction** is the New Testament era, since it was at the beginning of it that temple worship was brought to a close. But in what sense is the present era a **time of correction**, and what does that have to do with us?

Well, the parabolic period of worship was not the final one; it was but a forecasting of the future when this would all be replaced by the reality itself. It is that replacement of the shadow with the reality that is the **correction** [or setting things straight]. Things were, so to speak, out of line until Christ came. After all, the whole world was subject to Satan. God operated by means of and through one little outpost in this foreign territory—the nation of Israel. The great promise to Abraham that in his Seed all the nations of the earth would be blessed was not yet a reality. The gospel was not preached in all the world. The evil one was the "god of this world." And the sins of God's people had not yet been finally atoned for. All was awaiting the **time of correction** when the Savior would appear and set things straight. Now that He had come, the old system, appropriate for a time when all was askew, would be done away with.

Again the writer is filling in his major argument that the old is obsolete (why go back to it?) with further observations and facts. Counselors should learn from the way in which God acts. He does not do everything at once. Some counselors seem to think that they can. But it is often not possible to achieve things except in stages, *the earlier of which may be temporary and not final*. Indeed, these early stages, being simply approaches to, but not accomplishments of his purposes, may need to be *corrected*. On the micro level, think about each session in counseling. Often I have said to a counselee, "Now you must understand that we are not able to deal with the problem of communication this week as we hope to be able to in weeks to come. We have had to spend our time this week ferreting out your communication problem. So this week, make every effort not to get into an argument. Walk on eggs. We'll do better than that in subsequent weeks, but for now do so. If a problem arises about which you are unable to reach a solution, instead of fighting about it, write it out on a pad that you place in a prominent place, and bring it in next time. Then we will work on how to solve it God's way from God's Word. That won't be necessary when you learn how to solve problems on your own in days to come, but *for now* it will get us started until you learn something *better*." If you expect all change to come "yesterday," you are wrong. It doesn't happen that way. While promising something better (as the Old Covenant did) you may have to take preliminary, temporary measures until the time is appropriate to **correct** matters once and for all. The forms must be erected and kept in place until the concrete can be poured and hardens.

All the sacrificial ritual was temporary. The regulations about the kinds of animal sacrifices to be offered (**flesh**), the other **foods and drinks** that were required and the various **kinds of baptisms** (the sprinklings of various elements that will be mentioned presently) were all until the **time of correction**. To hang on to them afterward would be like continuing to "walk on eggs" after the reasons for doing so no longer existed; like using the note pad after items no longer need to be brought to the counselor.

In verse 11 he makes the point he has in mind: **when Christ made His presence known as High Priest of the good things that have come,**

11 But when Christ made His presence known as High Priest of the good things that have come, He went through the greater and more perfect tabernacle (the one not made with hands, that is, the one that is not a part of this material creation).
12 He didn't enter by means of the blood of goats and calves, but He entered the Holy of Holies once and for all by means of His own blood, having obtained an eternal redemption.
13 Now if the sprinkling of polluted persons with the blood of goats and bulls and heifers' ashes sanctifies in such a way that the flesh is cleansed,

---

He went through the greater and more perfect tabernacle (the one not made with hands, that is, the one that is not a part of this material creation). Again, Jesus is the High Priest of the **good things that have come** with the correction and replacement of the temporary things. The New Covenant is as much better as is the communication of the husband and wife who, having learned how to communicate properly in a biblical fashion, no longer have to "walk on eggs" or use the notepad. Why would they want to continue the former temporary measures? How foolish to consider returning to them when, instead of temporary, makeshift measures, they have entered into the **good things** that proper communication brings into their marriage? Those good things are now effected by Christ, Who **made His presence known** as **He went through the greater and more perfect tabernacle** which men did not manufacture, but is the heavenly temple made by God.

And His offering for the sins of His people was not the temporary shadowy **blood of goats and calves,** but **His own blood** offered **once for all**, thereby obtaining for them eternal **redemption** (v. 12). Christ appeared, He **entered the Holy of Holie**s and **He obtained** an **eternal redemption**. That is a succinct summary of His work as the Mediatorial Savior. Now the Old Covenant baptisms, by which people were **sprinkled** in order to cleanse them from outer **pollution** (cf. I Peter 3:21), were baptisms that required the sprinkling of water and the blood and ashes of *animals* (v. 13; cf. Numbers 19). If that sort of sprinkling **cleansed the flesh, how much more so does the blood of Christ cleanse our consciences from dead works?** The old ordinance was physical and serves but a physical purpose. The work of Christ was spiritual and achieved what physical rituals could not—the **cleansing of the conscience from dead works**. This was accomplished **by means of the eternal Spirit** as He **offered Himself unblemished to God.** What does all of that mean?

As the offering and the means are greater, so is the effect; the former

14 how much more so does the blood of Christ, Who by means of the eternal Spirit offered Himself unblemished to God, cleanse our consciences from dead works so that we can serve the living God.

---

were only worldly, earthly, material offerings brought on the Day of Atonement and throughout the year, while the latter were spiritual. The former could not cleanse **consciences** (v. 9), the latter does. By means of the offering of His blood (dying for guilty sinners) Jesus achieved an **eternal redemption** (lit., ransoming). His blood was the ransom price required to free us from eternal punishment, the desert of our sin.

The blood of Christ frees the New Covenant saint from **dead works.** These are the self righteous works of the flesh that men who reject the death of Christ have the temerity to offer to God. When a counselee says, "But I'm not as bad as so-and-so. I go to church; I give to the needy, etc., etc.," tell him, "Sorry, those are all 'dead works.'" They are **dead** in that they have no life before God; they are **dead** because to trust them for salvation is to trust a way that seems right to a man, but is the way of death (Proverbs 14:12). Ask him, "What is a Christian doing trying to offer dead works to God? Don't you know that the only offering God accepts is the offering of His Son's blood?"

But how is it that the **eternal Spirit** is the **means** by which Christ **offered Himself unblemished to God** (v. 14)? What does that mean? The Holy Spirit, Who came upon Christ at His baptism, and guided, empowered and motivated His ministry was the One Who also led Him into the sacrifice of Himself. The cross was an act of all the Persons of the Trinity. Jesus had walked a perfect life and ministry before God and man by means of the Spirit. So too, the Spirit did not depart from Him when contemplating and accomplishing the work of redemption.

Well counselor, your counselee has been freed from the guilt and the power of dead works. Why? So that he may **serve the living God.** *Dead* works do not befit the *living* God. There is a striking contrast here between the two. Your counselee is free now to serve God with a good conscience under the power of the same Spirit Who enabled Jesus to live an **unblemished** life that was worthy to offer to God. So too, God wants you to live that sort of life. If the eternal Spirit could so strengthen and empower the Lord to serve God in living works, He can also do the same for your counselee. There is no longer any excuse for **dead works** (compare comments on 6:1). When he was an unbeliever, that is all he had to offer God in service. It was like bringing a mangled, dirty, blemished

15 So, because of this, He is the Mediator of a new covenant, so that
those who are called may receive the eternal inheritance that was promised,
now that there has occurred a death that redeems them from the transgressions committed during the first covenant.[a]
16 Where there is a will the death of the testator must be proven,
17 since a will has effect only at his death; it has no force when the testator is still alive.
18 From this consideration arises the fact that not even the first covenant
was inaugurated without blood.
19 When Moses had declared every commandment of the law to all the
people, he took the blood of calves and goats, with water and scarlet wool
and hyssop, and sprinkled both the book itself and all the people, saying,

---

offering to Him. Self-righteousness is as filthy rags (to change the simile). But now, because the Spirit dwells within, there is hope to serve God through offerings of genuine praise and fruit energized by the Spirit (cf. Galatians 5).

In the verses immediately following, the writer will interplay the two meanings of the word that, so far, we have been translating "covenant." The word *diatheke* can mean either "will" (in the sense of a *testament*) or "covenant" (in the sense of an *agreement*[1]). As the **Mediator of a new covenant** Christ has secured for His own (those whom He **calls**) the **eternal inheritance that was promised** (see 3:1). But an inheritance comes only at the death of the one leaving behind the inheritance at death. He does so by means of a will. Christ has died. We are, therefore, His rightful heirs. He has willed the eternal inheritance of life eternal to us. This death of Christ, then, not only redeems the elect from the sins that under the first covenant could never be cleansed by the blood of bulls and goats, but it also means that they have come into their inheritance.

Verse 16 makes the point that **the death of the testator** is a necessary fact that must be **proven** before the will is executed. Verse 17 clarifies: the **will has no force when the testator is still alive**. And, even the first covenant was not inaugurated apart from blood (that is, death). **Moses**, at its institution, shed the **blood of calves and goats with water and wool** and dipping hyssop into the liquids, **sprinkled both the book itself and all the people.** That was the **blood of the covenant** (v. 20). He

1. In the case of a *diatheke* made with God, the covenant is unilateral. Both the imposition of the covenant and its terms are laid down by God Himself. God's covenants are gracious.

20 **This is the blood of the covenant that God ordered you to keep.**
21 He sprinkled the tabernacle and all the vessels of worship in the same way.
22 Now according to the law almost everything is cleansed by blood; and without bloodshedding there is no forgiveness of sins.
23 So then, it was necessary for the copies of the heavenly things to be cleansed by these ceremonies, but the heavenly things themselves had to have better sacrifices than these.
24 Christ hasn't entered a handmade sanctuary that is a picture of the true one, but rather into heaven itself, so that at this time He could appear in God's presence on our behalf.
25 Nor did He go in order to offer Himself repeatedly, as the high priest enters the Holy of Holies every year, bringing blood that isn't his own

---

also **sprinkled the tabernacle and all the vessels of worship in the same way**. Indeed, the law required **almost everything** to be sprinkled (cleansed) by **blood** (vv. 20-22). It is clear then that those who have never been sprinkled by the precious blood of Jesus Christ are not cleansed from their sins: **without bloodshedding there is no forgiveness of sins.** What the law did outwardly, by type and shadow, the death of Christ did inwardly as a reality.

The cleansing of the heavenly sanctuary means, as Bruce and Milligan say, that the consciences of God's people had to be cleansed. The people of God are His house (temple; see Ephesians 2:22). In this regard, see I Peter 1:2,19,22ff. Nothing but the blood of Christ could thus cleanse men. The church is conceived of as the original, as God has constructed it, of which the earthly copies are but vague sketches. This is the church of the firstborn in heaven (cf. 12:22-24). That sanctuary has God alone as its builder and maker. Christ, **on behalf of** your counselee has appeared in heaven before the Father (v. 24). Think of that! Help the counselee to marvel in the love and concern that He has exhibited on his behalf. There is no place for all the gripes and whines and complaints that so often are found in the counseling room when one contemplates Christ interceding for all things necessary *for him* before the Father.

And Jesus didn't enter the heavenly sanctuary often to offer sacrifice, like the earthly **high priest**, but **once, and once only, at the end of the ages to set aside sin by sacrificing Himself** once for all (v. 26). If He were like the earthly high priest, He would die on the cross yearly. What a monstrous thought! No, **just as it is appointed for people to die only once, and after that they face judgment, so too Christ, Who was**

26 (otherwise He would have to have suffered repeatedly from the foundation of the world). But now He has appeared once, and once only, at the
end of the ages to set aside sin by sacrificing Himself.
27 Just as it is appointed for people to die only once, and after that they
face judgment,
28 so too Christ, Who was offered only once to bear the sins of many, will
appear a second time, not to deal with sin again, but to give salvation to
those who are waiting for Him.

---

offered only once to bear the sins of many, will appear a second time, not to deal with sin again, but to give salvation to those who are waiting for Him. There is much here. The meaning of what is said is apparent and needs no exposition. But what is in it for counselors? Much.

First, people are **appointed once to die, and after that they face judgment**. Many counselees, stubborn or sloppy, because of their refusal to do as Christ commands, need to be alerted to the fact that, before they know it, they will be in God's presence—to face judgment. While no true believer will be sent to hell, he will be judged on the basis of his works. This judgment will have to do with his eternal reward (or lack of it). What is most important in the long run? Some matter of only earthly consequence, or one's eternal status before God? That is the choice that many counselees should be made to face. Only then can they gain a true perspective on time and eternity. Not enough is made of the judgment in counseling. Don't let that failure be true of you.

Secondly, Christ will return. He dealt with sins His first time; He will not do that again. There is no necessity to do so, since His first coming was sufficient for the purpose for which He came: **to bear the sins of many** (not for all, but for all those "whom the Father had given Him"). God's purpose in Christ's death is not frustrated. All for Whom He died will be saved. There is no way that it could be otherwise. If He truly *bore* the sins of **many**, then those **many** no longer may be held liable for their sin. Either He actually *did* satisfy God or He did not. To say that Christ died for every and all persons ever born is to say that He did not; that His death was not really efficacious. Something more must be added to make it do so. That is heresy, a denial of grace. Help your counselee to appreciate the fact that Christ really did pay the price for his sins on the cross.

Lastly, the fullness of the salvation that He purchased will become a reality at His second coming. There is a movement in some circles today to deny that Jesus Christ will return again; that He came back in the destruction of Jerusalem, and that all passages that refer to the coming of

Christ have been fulfilled. True, 70 AD was a judgment-coming of Christ, and a more significant event than many realize. Moreover, it is true that *some* of the passages that have been referred to the second coming really have to do with the Destruction of Jerusalem, but not all do. This passage clearly refers to a second coming of Jesus to earth.

The present chapter is powerful. It is one that refutes the idea of many offerings, such as those of the Roman Catholic Church, in which Jesus is said to be sacrificed thousands of times daily on Roman altars. If that were true, His death could never take away sins. In the next chapter, the writer will spell this out even more clearly.

CHAPTER 10

1 Now the law has only a shadow of the good things to come, not the reality itself, so it can't possibly make perfect those who come near by offering the same sacrifices continually year after year.
2 Otherwise, wouldn't they have stopped offering them? If the worshipers had been cleansed once for all, they wouldn't have a conscience about sins any longer.

With the close of this chapter, the writer of Hebrews will conclude the discussion of the two priesthoods. But that will not happen before many significant facts have been set forth. Those we shall now consider.

He begins by saying that **the law has only a shadow of the good things to come, not the reality itself**. When he speaks of the **good things to come**, he refers to those that were to come with the dawn of the New Covenant, not at some date yet future to us today. That is clear because the law, as he has been telling us at some length, foreshadowed the New Covenant that was inaugurated by Christ (see also 9:11). Christ, and His death, are the **reality** of which the law's rituals were a **shadow**. While it could not **make perfect those who come near by offering the same sacrifices continually year after year,** his whole point is that *Christ did just that*. The **good things** we now enjoy are, of course, but a foretaste of the wonders of the world to come. We are now only beginning to experience the goodness of God's marvelous grace. That is not because it has not been poured out on us in abundance, but because of the limitations brought about by our sin and because we still live in a sin-cursed world. But according to the sixth chapter, we already have much (cf. 6:4,5).

There was one thing wrong with the sacrifices of the old sacrificial system: They involved doing the same thing, over and over again. There was no progress. There was nothing definitive accomplished. What was done was temporary and had to be repeated continually. That, as I said before, is a lot like the twelve-step addiction programs that are so big today. If the writer of Hebrews were commenting on them, he surely would have said much the same thing about them as he does here about the sacrifices of the Old Covenant. The difference, however, would be that the latter were instituted by God as a temporary thing and the psychological programs today have no divine sanction whatsoever.

If the worshipper could have been made **perfect** in God's sight by Levitical sacrifices, then as he notes in verse 2 he would have **stopped**

3 But, on the contrary, by these sacrifices sins are remembered year after year,

---

offering them. But the **consciences** of the worshippers could never be **cleansed** by animal sacrifices, let along freed from guilt so as to have no need to **remember sins year after year** (v. 3). It is important to consider that issue. What is this once-for-all cleansing of consciences from the guilt of sin that Christ did perfect by the unique sacrifice of Himself? That matter is of great importance to your counselee and to you. You must think straight about this or you will not be able to help counselees as you ought.

There is a balance to be achieved here. You can go overboard in one direction or the other. On the one side, the work of Christ was definitive—those who believe in Him are not only considered perfect in the sight of God, but some day actually will be made perfect in heaven. That means that all their sins, past, present and future were paid for by Christ when He died on the cross. No longer need any Christian have a conscience problem in which he fears the possibility of being condemned by God for his sins. Christ was judged in his place. His conscience is freed from guilt; it is **cleansed**. Now, that is important for many counselees who are not certain about these matters. By showing them how that is the crux of the issue that the writer is joining here by comparing the inability of the old sacrifices to produce such assurance and the absolute certainty that one may have in Christ, you can bring great relief to them.

Yet on the other hand, being freed from guilt, having one's conscience relieved, does not mean that one may sin as he pleases. If truly saved, he will not want to. Out of gratitude to the Lord he will desire to please Him by obeying His commands. And they are not grievous. He will be much concerned to honor his Father by living righteously, and will relieve his conscience *whenever he recognizes that he fails to do so* by repentance toward God *as a Father*, not as a *Judge*. He will seek and receive family forgiveness. To maintain this biblical balance is essential, and is of the essence of good counseling. Be sure when you emphasize the one side that you do not fail (at least) to mention the other as well.

A believer in Christ may "forget" his sins; he does not have to carry a load of guilt over what he has done in the past. That is the problem with the old covenant sacrifices: **by these sacrifices sins are remembered year after year** (v. 3). The superiority of the sacrifice of Christ is that one need no longer do so. That means that while never forgetting the grace of

4 because it isn't possible for the blood of bulls and goats to take away
sin.

5 Consequently, when He came into the world, He said,

You didn't want sacrifice and offering;
You prepared a body for Me.
6 **You weren't pleased with burnt offerings and sin offerings.**
7 **Then I said, "See, I have come to do Your will, O God**
In the roll of the book it has been written about Me."

8 He says above, "**You didn't want, and weren't pleased with, sacrifices and burnt offerings and sin offerings,**" which are offered according to the law.

9 Then He said, "**See, I have come to do Your will.**" He takes away the first order to set up the second.

God that saved such a wretched sinner as he, the apostle Paul no longer suffered the pain and guilt associated with his wicked deeds as an unsaved, pharisaical murderer. He never failed to remember the pit from which the Savior dug him; but he did not go about with a conscience burdened down by shame and guilt. He was forgiven! He was joyful over it. And like the woman who was forgiven much and therefore loved much, he devoted his life to the loving service of Jesus Christ. That is the spirit to inculcate in counselees.

It isn't possible for the blood of bulls and goats to take away sin is what verse 4 says. So since that is true, Jesus had to come. But in doing so, He had to become one of us—a second Adam, representing all that were "in" Him (see Romans 5). But to become one of us, in speaking to God, He says, **You prepared a body for Me** (quoting LXX**).** That had to be. Since it was as a true man he had to die for men, he must share our physical as well as spiritual existence (yet without sin). And addressing the Father again, He had this to say, **See, I have come to do Your will, O God.** Since God **wasn't pleased** with **offerings** of the Old Testament system (vv. 5,6), it was essential for another kind of offering to be made by the One Whom Old Testament prophets said would come (v. 7^{b}). And it is clear, as the writer observes, that these declarations of the Son amount to taking **away the first order to set up the second.** Another proof is added to show that the old covenant is done and over with as far as God is concerned, and that it is, therefore, foolish even to consider returning to it.

The **will** of God that Christ came to do, sets us apart **through the offering of the body of Jesus Christ once, and once only** (v. 10). To know that one has been made a saint (a set apart one) is of supreme

10 It is by that will we have been set apart through the offering of the body of Jesus Christ once, and once only.

---

importance. Sainthood is not something conferred on someone after his death by the church. It is a fact, forensically and actually true, of all who are saved here and now. To be set apart from sin to righteousness, from the service of the evil one to the service of God is a marvelous fact. It is one that every counselee must be taught, if he does not already know it. "You are a saint; try to live like one this week as you call on the Holy Spirit to help you live as He tells you in His Word," is a kind of statement that ought to help. Remind counselees of their sainthood. Now that does not mean in actuality they are "saintly." But in God's sight they are considered perfect in Christ. And they are set apart in actuality more and more as they follow the Bible's teachings and apply them to everyday life. It might not be bad in greeting a counselee, who is not living as he ought, with the words, "Hello, saint Tom," or "Hello saint Mary." That ought to make him think. Surely, to do so would elicit a reply from which you could make relevant comments about the matter. As you say it, have a small smile on your lips, indicating that you are serious, but not apart from trying to get a point across.

Throughout this section there is a discussion of the **cleansing** of the **conscience**. It is important for a Christian counselor to understand what the conscience is. The Greek term *suneidesis*, means "to know together with." The English word conscience comes through the Latin term that corresponds exactly to the Greek; it means the same. The idea behind the terms that are used is that when we think or do something, we know what we are up to. That is, if I plan to do evil, I know what I am doing; indeed, all along I am evaluating myself and my plan. Whenever I carry out that plan, again, I know what I am doing and I evaluate my actions. It is not that I act instinctively; rather I think and act in full awareness as the result of my own evaluative processes. The **conscience**, though spoken of as a noun, is not an organ of the body; it is not a black box within. Rather, it is a *capacity*. It is the capacity to judge one's own thoughts, attitudes and actions. Whatever I am about, I have an audience—myself! And in accordance with what one's particular standards are, he judges himself. His thoughts are not simply observed; they are evaluated. Paul pictures the conscience as a courtroom. The conscience is where a trial takes place. But the conscience also is the judge, the witness, the prosecution and the defense (Romans 15). The conscience has witnessed what I am thinking

11 Every priest stands daily ministering, again and again offering the same sacrifices that can never take away sins.

---

or doing. It testifies. The two attorneys debate with one another about the evidence adduced—whether I am guilty or not. The judge decides the case. All this goes on inside the Christian—and the judgment is made according to the law written on his heart. A bad conscience is when he has evaluated himself as sinning in thought, word or deed. Until he confesses his sin and is forgiven, he will feel bad. The "judge" sentences him to experience bad feeling in order to drive him to repentance. When he repents and rights all wrongs, he has a clear (or cleansed) conscience. A seared conscience is one that has been ignored so often and/or one that has been browbeaten so frequently by rationalizations and excuses, that its ability to alert the individual to sin has been badly compromised. Many today have seared their consciences by blameshifting, excuse-making, simple avoidance and refusal to heed it, etc. The conscience is a blessing from God that enables us to evaluate ourselves along with the thought, word or action. That means it has been placed in us as a capacity to alert us to and correct us when doing wrong. It does not, however, come pre-packaged with a set of evaluative principles or laws. Therefore, it is often risky to "let your conscience be your guide." The Standard by which the conscience rightly evaluates a thought, word or deed correctly is the Word of God, the Scriptures. When one's knowledge of the Bible is weak, his conscience also will be weak. As a result, he may be the "weaker brother" of I Corinthians or Romans. When encountering this situation, one must help a counselee to learn better than he has thus far. Otherwise, his conscience will either condemn him wrongly or excuse him wrongly.

Moving on now to verse 11 we read, **Every priest stands daily ministering, again and again offering the same sacrifices that can never take away sins.** This was, of course, a description of the temple services which were still in place in the writer's day. But today, this could be every bit as easily a description of the Roman Catholic priest. Indeed, whenever dealing with a Christian who may be enamored with Catholicism, thinking he might consider uniting with that church, among others, you will want to mention this verse. The argument used here is precisely the one you should use with him: if Roman priests must stand daily offering sacrifices, then what they do does not really take away sins. And the death of Christ on the cross was futile.

Jesus however did not die in vain: **He, after offering for all time a**

12 But He, after offering for all time a single sacrifice for sins, sat down at God's right hand,
13 waiting from that time on until His enemies are placed beneath His feet as a footstool.
14 By a single offering He has perfected for all time those who are being set apart.
15 Indeed, the Holy Spirit also testifies the same thing to us. After saying,
16 **This is the covenant that I will contract with them**
after those days, says the Lord:
I will put My laws on their hearts
and write them on their minds,
17 then He adds,
I won't remember their sins and their unrighteous deeds ever again.

---

single sacrifice for sins, sat down at God's right hand, waiting from that time on until His enemies are placed beneath His feet as a footstool (vv. 12,13). No contrast could be more starkly opposite. The Jewish priest *stood*; Jesus *sat down*. The former was not finished; he had to offer the same sacrifice again and again. Jesus by a single sacrifice did the job once for all. That is why he sat down—His work was done and over with. He had nothing more to do until the future when the last enemy would be destroyed.

To be able to set forth truth over against error, you can learn a lot from this writer. Not only are his contrasts sharp, certain and clear; he also works them out in full so that no one can misunderstand his meaning. That is precisely what he is now about to do in the next verses.

In verse 14, he writes: **By a single offering He has perfected for all time those who are being set apart.** So far as God is concerned, the offering of Christ's sacrifice of Himself was sufficient. Nothing more need be or could be added to it. When He said "It is finished," he was saying "I have completed redemption." By that one offering Jesus **for all time** redeemed His own. That is a bedrock proposition upon which to rest all counseling: those that He is sanctifying (making more like Himself) in God's sight He already has perfected. Forgiven, cleansed and **perfected:** that is what Christ's death has done for us. We have been "perfected" or "completed." That is to say, believers are *completely* restored to a proper relationship with God. This is true because of Christ; they themselves are far from being complete. They are still **being set apart**.

Again in verses 15 and 17, the Holy Spirit is said to speak through

18 Now where there is forgiveness of these, there is no longer any offering for sins.
19 So then, brothers, since we have confidence to enter the Holy of Holies with the blood of Jesus,
20 by a new and living way that He inaugurated for us, through the curtain (that is, through His flesh),
21 and since we have a great Priest over God's house,
22 let us come close to God with a true heart in full assurance of faith, having our hearts sprinkled to rid us of an evil conscience and our bodies washed by clean water.

---

the words of the Bible, two quotations from which are given. These verses are cited in order to give Scriptural support to what he has been teaching: **the Holy Spirit also testifies *the same thing* to us.** Part of the New Covenant is God's promise "**I won't remember their sins and their unrighteous deeds ever again.**" Then he comments (v. 18), **Now where there is forgiveness of these, there is no longer any offering for sins.** Why would there be? If because of the offering of Christ, once for all, sins have been forever forgiven, there is no need for any further offering. The logic is impeccable. The argument is forceful. The application is clear: "You'd be a fool, reader, to return to that which is uncertain, imperfect, partial, shadowy and incomplete."

We come now to verses 19 through 22. These verses contain the practical upshot of all that has gone before (though, as the writer is wont to do, he repeats some of what he has already said; if you want to learn about *repetition*, study Hebrews).

Two summary statements lead to a conclusion; **since we have confidence...since we have a great Priest over God's house...Let us come close to God with a true heart in full assurance of faith, having our hearts sprinkled to rid us of an evil conscience and our bodies washed with clean water.** Since, by His torn **flesh (represented by the torn curtain that hung before the Holy of Holies)**, Christ has **inaugurated a new and living way** of access to God, and since He is our **great Priest over God's house,** the writer bids his readers to **come close to God.** And as they do, they may come in **full assurance of faith**—that is, with the certainty that they are saved and do have access to God through Jesus Christ. How can *sinners* approach God with that kind of faith? Often counselees ask questions akin to that one. The answer is, we do not come as sinners at all. Our **hearts are sprinkled to rid us of an evil conscience**. That is, the blood of Jesus Christ has made us clean of all sin in

23 Let us hold firmly to the hope that we confess without swaying,
24 and let us give thought to ways of stimulating one another to love and fine deeds.

God's sight, and it should do so in our sight as well—we need no longer approach God as one who has guilt on his conscience, condemned and dejected. No, we may come as those whose **hearts** have been cleansed by faith (I Peter 1:2; Acts 15:9). It is the **pure in heart** who see God. They may enter into the Holy of Holies stepping into the very presence of God—a place that only the high priest could go, and that, only once a year. Now every believer has access to the heavenly sanctuary through Jesus Christ—as frequently as he **has need**.

The inner sprinkling, by which one's heart is cleansed corresponds to the outer cleansing of the body, **washed by clean water.** The sprinkling of clean water in baptism is the act of reception into the visible church that symbolizes the inner sprinkling that incorporates him into the invisible church. The great High Priest is thus placed **over** us as **God's house**. These were unheard of privileges to a Jew who knew only the Levitical system. How could he fail to marvel and wish to retain his place in that house of God when he considered how much more there is for him in Christianity?

So having made this powerful point, the writer says, **Let us hold firmly to the hope we confess without swaying.** There is an exhortation for your counselee. Many sway back and forth with the winds of falsehood, persecution, doubt and unbelief that blow against them. Hebrews is written to make pillars out of such frail reeds. If you have swaying counselees, then Hebrews is your book to help firm them up. God's ideal—and He has done everything possible to achieve it (as the Book shows)—is for every Christian to be absolutely certain of the **hope** of eternal life **that he confessed** when he stepped forth to receive the sprinkling of baptism. It is not wrong to remind him of his profession of faith, and that he stood before God and others and made a confession of his belief in the Lord Jesus Christ for eternal salvation. The writer does just that. One of the purposes of baptism is to put an emblem on those that are God's own. To be reminded of his profession of faith in baptism, therefore, is a salutary thing.

The writer knows that we can not "go it alone," especially in times of persecution or trial. So he calls on each member of the congregation(s) to **give thought to ways of stimulating** [lit., "irritating"] **one another to**

25 We must not abandon our practice of meeting together, as some are in the habit of doing, but rather, we must encourage each other, and all the more as you see the day drawing near.

---

love and fine deeds (v. 24). One factor that contributes to the firming up one's hope is the encouragement that others give. That is why we must **not abandon the practice of meeting together** (v. 25). Mutual stimulation of believers is important. When one sees another doing what he should do, he can recognize its practicality. When he is sad there are others who will weep with him as he weeps. When he needs encouragement, there are many who can share with him their experiences of the comfort they received from the Bible (cf. II Cor 1). On and on we could go, speaking of how we may **stimulate one another to love and fine deeds**. It is doubtful that, unless there are extraordinary circumstances, for which God sends extraordinary grace, one will firmly maintain his faith apart from the stimulation he receives from being a vital part of a vital congregation.

Counselors, you can never emphasize strongly enough that your counselees belong under the care and discipline of such a congregation. If a counselee does not belong, one of your principal tasks is to convince him of the necessity to unite with the church. If he belongs, but fails to attend or is reticent to mingle and associate with its other members, encourage him to do so. If the church fails to be a stimulating body, get him to urge them to become such by seeking it from them. If they fail to do so, he may need to change congregational membership.

And there is nothing more important for a counselee than for him, himself, to stimulate others to **love and fine deeds**. "But I don't know how to do that," he may protest. Well listen again to the opening words of verse 24: **and let us give thought to ways to stimulate...**It is his task to give time and thought to discovering ways to do it. That is an assignment you can give him: "This week, make a list of at least 30 ways that you can stimulate other Christians to love and fine deeds. Bring it in next week." When he does, you will certainly find several of his suggestions that you could help show him how to implement. Then the following week(s) send him back to start doing it. When a counselee becomes less wrapped up in himself and his problems, but takes concern for helping to stimulate others to love and fine deeds, you will find that he will suffer less, acquire clearer insight into his own circumstances and be better able to cope with those problems. When a counselee focuses only on himself, that tends to create wrong attitudes. One way to turn his focus outward is to urge this verse on him in some practicable way.

Some of the members of this congregation were in the habit of missing the regular gatherings of the people of God (v. 25). No wonder they were becoming discouraged and were in danger of drifting. And when absenting one's self in this manner becomes a **habit** as it did with them, it is time for the members of the congregation to **consider ways of stimulating** *him* to return. And note whether it be the congregation or the counselee who is stimulating others to love and to good works, to do so properly takes **thought.** That is, one must invest time and energy in doing so. Such stimulation ordinarily does not take place by simply frequenting gatherings of God's people (as enervating as that may be in some instances). It will take more than that. It will take determined effort to do so on the part of those who do the stimulating. That means that you, counselor, in stimulating your counselees to love and to fine deeds, will also have to give thought beforehand, take time to do so and often develop well thought through plans for bringing it off. Now there may be ways that you have thought about before in helping others that may be adapted to a present case, or (at times) even used as they stand. But before using canned approaches, be sure that those that you employ *do fit the present situation exactly.* Don't take short cuts; people's lives are too important to handle in that manner.

And the fact that they **saw the day drawing near** was not a reason for letting up, but, rather, an incentive for intensified **encouragement** of one another (v. 25[b]). But did the second coming come in their lifetime? No, of course it didn't. One must distinguish between the two days that the early Christians anticipated. One was the second coming which could not come until many things happened first. The other was the predicted coming of Christ to judge Jerusalem (in 70 AD). There can be no doubt that this is the day that is in view, and not the second coming of Christ to earth, from the fact that they were ***seeing*** (or about to see; probably they were looking at the early signs of it just as he writes) **the day drawing near.** Obviously, they did not see the second coming either then or later on in their lifetime. For us, who live this side of 70 AD, and who are anticipating only the second coming of Jesus Christ, the principle still holds: the closer we come to the end (of our lives, of the present order of things, or whatever) the more necessary it is to be engaged in the activities mentioned in verses 22 through 25. Nearness to an event that will make a gigantic difference in one's life does not relieve him of responsibilities. Indeed, if these Christians were about to endure serious sufferings (they

26 If we deliberately go on sinning after receiving the full knowledge of the truth, there no longer remains a sacrifice for sins,
27 but only a fearful anticipation of judgment and **the fury of fire that is going to consume God's adversaries**.
28 Somebody who has violated Moses' law dies without mercy on the testimony of two or three witnesses.
29 How much worse do you think the punishment will be for anybody who tramples on God's Son, who has considered the covenantal blood that set him apart unclean, and who insults the Spirit of grace?

---

had not yet suffered physical injury; possibly only ostracism) they would need stimulation, the gatherings of God's people, encouragement, etc. If they were having trouble handling the meager difficulties that they were experiencing, what would it be like when the real test came? Tell counselees that present trials often offer them a valuable opportunity to tool up for the real tests that are around the corner. Success in meeting this one is God's way of preparing you for the future.

Now the writer pens the second strong warning (we met the first in chapter 6). It runs from verse 26 through 31. Again it must be read in light of the entire epistle (especially in light of 6:9). People who take this section alone, out of the context of the rest of the letter, often teach very erroneous doctrines from it that were never intended. Remember, we have seen how the writer thinks most of his readers are genuine Christians who are **dull of hearing.** Though he acknowledges that there may be some bad ground that will produce thorns and thistles, he conceives of (at least) the majority as good ground from which much good fruit may be harvested. That is why he writes. But he is also warning any in the midst who have participated in Christian activities, and who may have deceived others (and perhaps themselves) of their faith, that they should take a hard look to see if they truly are in the faith.

Here he says **If we deliberately go on sinning after receiving the full knowledge of the truth, there no longer remains a sacrifice for sins.** There is nothing more to do for those who do. Christ has done all that can be done, and if they reject that, such persons are without hope. They have heard it all. Their problem is not ignorance. In the full light of the **truth**, they reject Christ and commit the unpardonable sin (**insult the Spirit of grace**; cf. Matthew 12:25). Obviously these are people who, in the end, demonstrate their unbelief. Indeed, in insulting the Spirit of grace they must be doing what the Pharisees did: they attributed the work of the Spirit to the devil. This is full-fledged apostasy we are dealing with here.

30 We know Him Who said, "**Vengeance is Mine; I will repay.**" And
again, "**The Lord will judge His people.**"
31 It is a fearful experience to fall into the hands of the living God!
32 Now remember the former days when, after you were enlightened,
you endured great battles with suffering,

They **trample on God's Son**, he says. That is not mere sin; it is sin that involves the rejection of all that is essential to the faith. They **consider the covenantal blood that set him apart unclean**. Here is the indication that they attributed the work of the *Holy* Spirit to an *unclean* spirit (the essence of the unpardonable sin).

Counselees, fearful that they might lose their salvation must not only be told that God wants and expects them to reach a **full assurance of the faith**, but that this passage, that many fear so much, refers not to persons who are concerned about whether or not they are genuine Christians, but to those who have trampled the gospel under foot. This is apostasy that is described here.

What will happen to these apostates? A number of frightening statements are made about them: they may expect **a fearful anticipation of judgment and the fury of fire that is going to consume God's adversaries.** That is to say, right here and now (not only when they actually suffer it) they will be haunted by the fear of hell. This **fearful anticipation**, of course, will melt into reality one day at death. Moreover, those who **violated Moses' law died without mercy**. If that was true of the lesser covenant, what do you think God will do to those who violate the greater one? Their **punishment** will be **much worse** (v. 29). God **will judge His people**. He will determine who among those who profess faith, and thus become a part of the visible church, are genuine. And those who are not (in addition to the apostates) will be sent to hell. People may make jokes about hell, but soon they will find that **it is a fearful experience to fall into the hands of the living God**! (for judgment) as verse 31 says.

One more argument remains in this section: "in former times you were doing so well. Now, after having suffered for the faith successfully, don't turn away under additional persecution." He calls on them to **remember** those days. Possibly he refers to Acts 8 when speaking of **the former days when, after you were first enlightened, you endured great battles with suffering, by being exposed to reproaches and afflictions and by becoming sharers with those who are treated that way.** If then, when so young in the faith, you endured, why not now? You

33 by being exposed to reproaches and afflictions and by becoming sharers with those who are treated that way.
34 Indeed, you had compassion on those in bonds and you accepted the seizure of your possessions with joy, knowing that you have a better possession that is left.
35 So then, don't throw away your confidence, which carries with it a great reward.
36 You have need of endurance so that, having done God's will, you may obtain the promise.

---

not only handled the **seizure of your possessions with joy**, but you **had compassion on those in bonds.** Why, then, would you throw all that to the winds now that you are once more suffering for your faith? Remember how you fought and *won* those **battles with suffering** (he doesn't treat the endurance of suffering lightly; it is truly a **battle** to be fought). Don't quit fighting. Don't give up the war, surrendering to the enemy against whom you once fought so valiantly. Remember how you used to think? You said, "I have **better possessions** awaiting me in heaven when I enter into my eternal inheritance." Think once again the way you thought then and you will not drift away.

If you know that in the past your counselee has endured suffering successfully *remind* him. The points to make in doing so are twofold: First, why waste all your previous effort by giving in now? Do you want it to have been in vain? Second, you *know* how to endure successfully, because you did. If, therefore, you give in now you will not be able to offer a justifiable reason, only excuses. That is the tack to take. So he exhorts them, **don't throw away your confidence, which carries with it great reward** (another incentive). What he is saying is that you have already amassed reward; continue in your confidence in Christ and your reward will be great. Previously, I have intimated that the Bible writers use every sort of legitimate motivation. Here **reward** is set forth as a motive for continuing as they had in the past during persecution. Reward may not be the highest motive for faithfulness, but it must be legitimate (contrary to those who think they must be more pious than the biblical writers) or the Scripture's authors, writing inspired letters under the direction of the Spirit, would never use it.

So he says, **You have need of endurance so that, having done God's will, you may obtain the promise.** Here he seems to be warning again. Any who do not **endure** are not genuine; and they will not **obtain the promise** that God made to Abraham and to all his children. Then he

37 **It is just a short time**
before the coming One will come
and won't delay.
38 **But My righteous one will live by faith,**
and if he draws back,
I won't be pleased with him.
39 But we don't belong to the group that draws back into destruction, but rather to the group that has faith that leads to the preservation of their souls.

---

quotes Habakkuk 2:3, giving comfort over the fact that the persecution to be endured will be for **just a short time** and **the coming One will come and won't delay.** God will wipe out the persecutors (see the early part of my exposition of the Book of Revelation in *The Time is at Hand* for more about the nearness of the judgment of God on apostate Judaism). And then, after quoting the great text of the reformation, he goes on to quote the following words: **if he draws back, I won't be pleased with him** (vv. 37,38). Another warning. Always, God's method is incentive/warning; incentive/ warning. That is also the way to counsel.

In the conclusion of this drawn-out discussion that has covered several chapters, he says, **But we don't belong to the group that draws back into destruction, but rather to the group that has faith that leads to the preservation of their souls**. This, following such severe warning as we have been considering is the verse that brings it all back into focus again. As he indicated in chapter 6, after that severe warning, so too here, he assures his listeners that he thinks better things of them (cf. 6:9). **Enduring** to the end, note, is what pleases God. Every war-weary counselee must be urged to endure. Counseling may take time, obstacles to overcome may be many, defeats on the way to victory may take place, but what God wants is those who endure and thus **preserve their souls.**

The chapter has so much varied material that the wise counselor may learn to use, I advise you to spend at least several weeks digesting all that it has in greater detail than we could go into here. You will be rewarded by doing so; and soon your counselees will notice the difference in your counseling.

Chapter 11

1 Now faith is a solidly grounded certainty about what we hope for, a conviction about the reality of things we don't see.

We come now to what is probably the best known chapter in the Book. But before examining it for what it holds for counselors, let's ask why this list of Old Testament heroes appears. First, we must see in it encouragement. Doubtless, the examples were given in order to show that the saints of the past were able to endure suffering and persecution *by faith*. But more than this, notice it was not through ceremonies and ritual, not through animal sacrifices that they obtained favor with God, but through **faith**, the very same factor that is at the heart of the call to follow Jesus Christ. To turn back to Judaism is not to turn back to these men and women, but to turn one's back on them. To desert Christ is to desert those whose names are listed here. Again, the chapter is a call to be sure your name is included on the list with them. These written examples show the reader how he must respond in the face of trouble.

But what do we see in each example that he gives? Clearly this: by faith, they all put the unseen world first. Things in this world, including safety and life itself, meant nothing in comparison to that toward which they were looking. None of them received the fulfillment of the promise for which they were waiting—the heavenly life with God. These people, who had nothing more than God's promises, were able to face all sorts of trials because they believed. They acted as though what they were promised were already present—so certain were they that God's Word would/could not fail. That, as the writer will say, is the crux of the matter; it is what faith is all about. And as I have been saying from the outset, unless you maintain an atmosphere of eternity in the counseling room, your counseling will not succeed. Your counselee must perceive that you are certain that the unseen world, and the promises of God that pertain to it, are as real to *you* as if they were already in your hand. Any counselor who counsels abstractly misses the point of his faith. He must counsel from a faith-standpoint. He must be a committed person in whom at all times the counselee must see genuine belief in what he is saying.

Having just quoted Habakkuk 10:38,39, at the conclusion of chapter 10, in which the emphasis is on faith, the writer then goes on to enumerate many of the **elders** of Old Testament times whose lives counted for God

2 By it our elders received a good testimony.

---

because of their faith. We must now look at them.

At the outset the writer gives a definition of **faith**. While it is not a "scientific" definition (according to our standards), it is his definition which is highly satisfactory for his purposes and to his understanding of what a definition should be [he was not operating by our standards!]. What is faith? The answer is given in verse 1: **Now faith is a solidly grounded certainty about what we hope for, a conviction about the reality of things we don't see.** Quibble all you want about whether or not these words constitute a definition, they are [to me at least] a magnificent statement of what faith is all about. What is the writer saying? He says that **faith** makes that which we cannot now see, but that we hope to receive in the future, as sure and certain as if we could see it. He says that **faith** enables us to understand that the unseen world, with all its wonders about which God has hinted here and there in the Scriptures, is as real to us, although we have never been there, as if we had. Saving faith makes the promises of God come alive.

If counselees, face to face with present problems against which their noses are tightly pressed, need anything, it is the perspective on life and eternity, this world and the next that such faith yields. Faith, perhaps, is the greatest need of most counselees. Therefore, this chapter, rightly understood and properly used, should be of great help in counseling. By it, counselees may be bolstered against despair, disillusionment and dejection. If it does anything, the chapter is designed to pry their noses away from such a tight fix on the present. It translates them into the future; never with an other worldly vacuity, but with a biblical realism that enables them to view present difficulties in light of the future.

The **elders** mentioned in verse 2 are the persons whose names are immortalized in this chapter (as well as those who might have been included, but were not; cf. vv. 32-39). Of them he says that they **received a good testimony**. From whom? He probably means from the Holy Spirit as he represents Him moving the writers of the Scriptures to pen words that were equally His as well as theirs (see 10:15 where a Biblical quotation is referred to as the Holy Spirit's **testimony**).

Now remember, this list is not used moralistically. It is not that the Holy Spirit, speaking through the writer of Hebrews, praises these elders for their great deeds, etc. His concern is to show how in all sorts of diffi-

3 By faith we understand that the universe was framed together by God's Word, so that what we see wasn't made from things that are apparent to us.

---

cult circumstances, **faith** (a God-given quality as Ephesians 2:8 makes clear) will see one through. But it is not faith in the abstract; nor is it faith in faith. During World War II, a poster of a soldier on the battlefield administering plasma to a wounded comrade appeared everywhere. The legend that it carried was KEEP THE FAITH. But apart from the emotion that it evoked, it was meaningless. What faith? In whom or in what? How? All these questions remained unanswered—even though they were most pertinent. The hortatory legend was like a Rorschach test into which one projects his own meaning. That is not the faith in Hebrews 11. The **faith** here held out is faith in Jesus Christ as Savior and Lord and the promises that (in Him) God has given His people for this life and the life to come. Never talk about faith without mentioning its object. Faith, by itself, is meaningless.

Well, what can faith do? The writer answers this question in verse 3: **By faith we understand that the universe was framed together by God's Word, so that what we see wasn't made from things that are apparent to us.** Faith begins with an acknowledgment of God as the Creator of all things. And that creation is said to be *ex nihilo*; that is to say, **not from [out of] the things that are apparent to us** [preexistent material], but out of God's fiat (He called it into existence by His mere Word). That is a marvelous summary of the early chapters of Genesis. In other words, faith believes the Scriptures for what they say about God and what He has done. The faith that these persons had was centered in the truths of the Bible.

In the final analysis, if a counselee continues to gripe, complain and reject all comfort that is offered, you must draw the line with him: "Do you really believe what the Bible says or not (That is the question to ask.)?" Hold him to it by turning to this passage and by reading what faith accomplished for those who trusted God. Many of the problems that people have is a simple lack of faith. Eclectic counselors tend to complicate matters by searching for hidden meanings and causes. But perhaps more often than we think, the basic problem a counselee has is lack of faith in God's Word. Let me emphasize that fact. Always test the possibility when nothing else seems to work (and frequently, long before you reach that point). Ask, "Do you really believe that God will do as He said in the passage I just read? If so, then let's begin to trust Him to deal with this prob-

4 By faith Abel offered a sacrifice that was superior to Cain's, by which he received the testimony that he was righteous, God giving testimony about his gifts. And by it, though he has died, he still speaks.

5 By faith Enoch was removed to another place, so that he didn't face death; **and he wasn't found because God removed him**.

---

lem as He has promised and stop fretting." In the list that follows, you will discover some of the ways in which faith on the part of a counselee could make all the difference in his situation and in the progress of counseling.

Now to the list itself. First comes **Abel** who **offered a sacrifice that was superior to Cain's**. By this he **received the testimony that he was righteous.** How? As we said before, the testimony to him (as to all the elders) was by **God,** Who **testified** about **his gifts.** Unlike his brother **Cain's** gifts, **Abel** brought the firstlings and of the fat [best] ones of his flock. He put God first and gave Him his best. That was what faith led to. "How often," it might be profitable to ask a particular counselee who may bear the marks of Cain rather than Abel, "do you put God first in your life and give Him the best of your money, your property, your energy, your thought and your time?" Specifically ask yourself (and sometimes ask him too) "How would putting God first in the problem at hand change things for the better? How would giving God the best in this circumstance solve some aspect of the problem?" Faith, believing that God really wants to be put first and wants the best from His children, makes the difference.

And it is interesting that the writer observes, **though he has died, he still speaks.** This seems to be a reference to Genesis 4:10 in which Cain is told that the voice of his brother's blood is crying to God from the ground (cf. the same idea in Revelation 6:9ff.). See also 12:24. At that place I intend to say more on this point. Here it is enough to note that Abel's God testified to the genuineness of his faith as his blood cried out for vindication. Abel's gifts and the cry of his blood for justice both testify to his faith. Ask a counselee, "At the close of your days will there be anything to which others may point that testifies to your faith?" If not, then either you don't have genuine faith (in which case you should believe and be saved) or, if a believer, you had better start exercising faith. Faith, as James said, is seen in works.

Then there is **Enoch** (v. 5). He is such an extraordinary person, one might expect the writer to say something very special about him. But no, all we read (as in every other instance) is **By faith Enoch....** It was because of his faith, in a time when it seemed very few others had faith,

6 Before the removal he had received the testimony that he was well-pleasing to God. But without faith it is impossible to please Him, because whoever comes to God must believe that He exists and that He rewards those who seek Him.

Enoch **was removed to another place, so that he didn't face death; and he wasn't found because God removed him.** Why? Because **Before the removal he had received testimony** [from God] **that he was well-pleasing to God.** Once again, it is something about the man that gives evidence of his faith; here, that seems to be, his righteous life. To be **well-pleasing to God** means to do those things that please Him (that is what the phrase "he walked with God" in Genesis 5:22 means). This lifestyle was evidence of his **faith**.

How does one become **well-pleasing to God**? That is a question that many counselees (in one form or another) may ask. The writer tells us: **without faith it is impossible to please Him** (cf. Romans 8:8). It is faith that leads to the well-pleasing walk with God that should be the goal of every Christian and the goal of all counseling. Notice, unbelievers cannot please God. There is nothing they can do to win God's smile of approval. Apart from Jesus Christ, and His redeeming sacrifice, they are utterly unable to do anything that pleases God. This, many eclectic counselors will not accept. I once had a long, curious discussion of this very point at a college in which the psychology department maintained that the unbeliever can love God and one's neighbor in ways of which God approves. Hebrews is a stout testimony to the contrary. Because there is so little understanding of Scripture and so little emphasis on theology among the eclectics in Christian schools, they are confused about the matter and, consequently, teaching error, confuse many others. Every successful biblical counselor knows Scripture and theology. This is the *sine qua non* of true Christian counseling. It is also the reason why I am spending long hours in what could be the remaining years of my life writing these commentaries to uncover and anchor counseling principles and practices firmly in the Bible.

"Why must one have faith in order to **please God**?" The writer continues: **because whoever comes to God must believe He exists and that He rewards those who seek Him.** If you seek God's help, you must, of course, believe that He exists and that He is beneficent to those who do so. Apart from that, the entire business of calling on a god—any old god (if, indeed, there is such) is in vain. Prayers like, "O god, if there is a god..."

7 By faith Noah, having been warned about things that could not yet be seen, because he was devout prepared an ark that led to the salvation of his household and that condemned the world. And he became an heir of the righteousness that is according to faith.

---

do not cut ice with Him. One must believe in Him (that is, the God of the Scriptures) or He will not respond. The God of the Bible is Trinitarian; it is not enough to believe in some vague sort of deity who is not (John 2:23). When counseling, be sure that the one whom you counsel, who says that he is Christian, understands the fundamentals of the Christian faith. Many who use the label think, "If you're not a Jew or a Mohammedan or an atheist, you must be a Christian." That, of course, is inadequate.

Noah, having been warned about things that could not yet be seen, because he was devout prepared an ark that led to the salvation of his household and that condemned the world. Once more, faith rests on God's Word. God warned Noah of the coming flood, and Noah believed Him. He stood up against the unbelief and the jeers of those who did not for 120 years! And your counselee "can't take any more of the verbal abuse he receives at home?" Nonsense. Your counselee simply doesn't have faith as Noah did. When God said that the flood would come, though nothing like it had ever occurred before, Noah *believed* God. That is the crucial thing. When you work with a counselee of the sort just mentioned, who is all wrapped up in problems of "low self esteem" (see my Book on the subject, *The Biblical View of Self Esteem, Self Love and Self Worth* for more help), don't try to bolster his self-concept. Rather work on his relationship to God and His Word. There is a lack of faith in what God says about him and about Himself. Noah was **devout**. That is to say, in Noah there was a godly fear that motivated him to believe and to act as he did. He was a man of faith, whose faith was more than theoretical; it was practical. And it energized and fortified him. That is what your counselee needs. How to get it? By studying, trusting and acting on God's Word. That is what makes Christians devout. That is what strengthens them to withstand the objections of the world. That is what energizes them to work long and hard in His service. That is the faith of which this chapter speaks.

By that faith Noah **condemned the world.** That phrase probably does not refer to his preaching (II Peter 2:5) but to the contrast of his life of faith with their lives of unbelief. When others see and hear the results

8 By faith Abraham, when he was called, obeyed by going out to a place that he was to receive for an inheritance; and he went out not having the faintest idea about where he was going.

---

of faith, they often react negatively (cf. N.E.B.). Frequently that is the ruling motivation behind their scoffing. They mock the messenger, never knowing that it is the One from Whom the message came that they were really mocking. You cannot maltreat God's servants without that behavior becoming a reflection on the One Whom they represent.

And like the rest of those still awaiting the ultimate promise of heaven, Noah **became an heir of the righteousness that is according to faith.** Just as his faith condemned the world, that same faith made him heir of the righteousness that comes by faith (v. 7; see Genesis 6:9, LXX). The world was pronounced "guilty," while Noah was pronounced "righteous." This is certainly the forensic righteousness of which Habakkuk, and Paul after him, spoke. Noah was also heir [of salvation] *because of* the righteousness that comes through faith. Both facts seem to be implied in the unusual phrase **became an heir of the righteousness that is according to faith**.

We move next to a consideration of Abraham and Sarah. There are problems here. Two difficulties protrude: one with reference to Sarah's unbelief (evidenced by her laughter); and the other textual (which *seems* to indicate that it is not Sarah's faith that is under discussion but Abraham's). The solution that Hughes gives is probably correct. The idea being that by faith Sarah received power to found a posterity. The faith discussed throughout is Abraham's. That is to say, *his* faith led to the overcoming of her inability to bear children.

At any rate, it is important to examine Abraham's faith, a discussion of which continues from verse 8 through verse 19, the most substantive discussion in the entire chapter. His faith is evidenced in several ways. First, when called, he obeyed (v. 8); then he traveled **not having the faintest idea about where he was going**, simply following God's directions; thirdly, his faith enabled him to conceive a posterity though he and his wife were of an advanced age; lastly, he was willing to offer up his son Isaac, through whom God determined to fulfill the promise, having faith that **God was even able to raise him from the dead** (v. 19). Truly Abraham was a man whose faith led to consequences. At every point in his life that is indicated, he was operating not on what was practical (as a man might determine) or on what others had to say, but solely on the basis of

9 By faith he traveled in the promised land as a foreigner, living in tents with Isaac and Jacob, who were heirs together with him of the same promise.

---

the Word of God about things that could not be verified. He was *par excellence* a man of faith.

No wonder then that it is during the discussion of his faith that the great words spoken here about the men of faith appear which describe not only Abraham, but those who are mentioned in the remainder of the chapter (vv. 13-16). But first to Abraham. He obeyed God's call to leave Ur of the Chaldees (v. 9). But he had no idea where God wanted him to go. He was faced with *the unknown and the unseen*. These are the very elements that frighten many counselees. They fear entering into anything until they have in front of their noses tangible evidence of what they are contemplating. But of course that is the spirit of the age in which we live. If it can't be perceived by the senses, and it can't be counted, they are leery of it. It is one of the wiles of the devil to make us think that modernity is always better than the traditional. But it isn't always so. If the clock is too fast, then we should set it back. The contemporary emphasis on the tangible is evidence of a culture in which faith plays little or no part—except for faith in the tangible. But it is the unseen and the unknown that motivated Abraham. The choice that many counselees have to make is precisely about that issue: will they choose the present, perceptible reality which takes no faith to perceive over the unseen and (as of yet) little known promises of God, which *do* take faith to accept. That choice is what lurks in the background of many who seem to lag behind in doing what the Scriptures command. When confronted with reluctant believers, it is often worth asking, "Are you afraid to trust your life into the hands of God?" Or, "Is your problem that you are hesitant to launch out into that which is unknown and unseen?" Or, "It's tough, isn't it, to act simply on the basis of what God promises? It sorta' means climbing out on a limb doesn't it?" People seem to appreciate it when you phrase for them what they have been sensing and express the difficulties for them in terms they can receive as their own. It also indicates that you understand how hard faith is. Well, you can turn to this passage and show what it meant to Abraham. Here is a man who staked everything on God's Word. His entire life was a life in which he was utterly dependent on what God said. But he **obeyed** (v. 9). And God blessed. That is the point.

In all four of the instances mentioned above, faith was the foremost

10 He did this because he was looking forward to the city that has foundations, that had God for its Architect and Builder.
11 By faith also Sarah herself received the ability to conceive children, even though she was beyond the age to do so, because she considered Him Who promised trustworthy.
12 And as a result, from one man—a man who was a good as dead—there came a multitude of descendants **like the stars of the sky, as innumerable as the grains of sand at the seashore**.

---

factor. The average counselee has little faith. He may even be saying (in one way or another) "I believe; help me about my unbelief." That is how many are—they believe for salvation, they are sure that much the Bible says is true, but they are loathe to take steps that will expose them to embarrassment, failure or suffering. Only faith can impel such persons forward. You cannot instill faith within them. Tell them that. They must prayerfully read the Bible in greater depth concerning the men of faith, like Abraham, to see how they were enabled by God's Spirit to exercise faith and what the consequences were. Moreover, they should look at contemporary examples of those whose faith they admire (cf. 13:7; we shall say more about this when we reach that passage).

For now let's look a bit more closely at the commentary on Abraham (and others) that we find in the midst of the discussion of how God worked through his faith that is found in verses 10 and 13 through 16. These verses are perhaps the most helpful in the chapter.

In verse 10, we read **He did this because he was looking forward to the city that has foundations, that had God for its Architect and Builder.** What a powerful concept is embedded in those words! When a counselee gets beyond the statements about Abraham's faith, to see what it consisted of makes all the difference in his understanding of faith. Faith is not some hope-against-hope vagary. It is not vaporized reality. It is specific and concrete. God, presumably, gave to Abraham information about the heavenly city and country to which he would travel *after having found the earthly promised land.* We don't read a lot about THAT in the Genesis account, but by the Spirit moving him to pen these words, the writer of Hebrews lets us look inside the mind of Abraham to see what was going on. It was not that Abraham had no idea where he was going in this life or in the next. No, exactly not that! Because he knew what the *ultimate* destination was he was able to operate so trustingly on the short term. He knew what eternity held; because of that he could go anywhere and do anything God required of him in this life. That is the heart of the matter of faith.

13 These all died in faith without receiving the things that were promised; but they did see them from a distance, and welcomed them. And they confessed that they were strangers and travelers on the earth.
14 Now those who say such things are making it clear that they seek a homeland.

Faith is **a solidly grounded certainty of what we hope for** [read *expect*], **a conviction about the reality of things we don't see.** Because the eternal question was settled, the earthly one didn't have to be. The insight of the writer of Hebrews at this point is important to counselors. Because Abraham knew where he was headed [eternally] he didn't need to know where he was going tomorrow or the next day. Wherever the earthly route took him, it didn't matter because he knew that God was mapping out a road to the eternal city. It was not the land of Palestine that mattered (except as its acquisition affected the history of the people of which he would become the Father), it was the **heavenly country, the city** in that **homeland** of which Palestine, and [eventually] the city of Jerusalem, were but a shadow and type that counted (see vv. 10,14,16). What counselees often need to discuss, rather than the present problems that they are focusing upon, is the ultimate destination to which the course through those problems will take them. If that is clear, and they believe in the eventual fulfillment of God's promises to them, they can more readily conform to the will of God, expressed in His Word. What causes the lag in going forward into the unseen and the unknown, purely because God's Word tells them to, is the shortsightedness of their faith. When faith like that of verse 1 motivates, action like that in verses 8 and 9 ensues. So concentrate on the future *in order to* bring about action in the present.

The city **made without hands, that has foundations** and **had God for its Architect and Builder**, **in the heavenly country** is that about which you ought to speak when helping counselees to lift their eyes above the present circumstances. Look at what is said in verse 13. They were so certain of the **heavenly inheritance** of the **city** in the **land** of **God** that it says that though **these all died in faith without receiving the things that were promised**, nevertheless, they were so convinced of them that **they did see them from a distance, and welcomed them. And they confessed that they were strangers and travelers on the earth.** Until one has that much certainty about the promises of heavenly things, he will feel perfectly at home on earth, rather than consider himself a pilgrim or stranger. Another way of saying what was said in the previous paragraph

15 If they had been remembering that land that they left, they would have had opportunity to return.
16 But, the fact is, they desire a better (that is, a heavenly) country. Therefore, God isn't ashamed to be called their God. Indeed, He has prepared a city for them!
17 By faith, when he was tested, Abraham offered up Isaac; the one who had received the promises offered up his only son,
18 about whom it was said, **"Your descendants will come through Isaac."**
19 He reasoned that God was even able to raise him from the dead; from which—figuratively speaking—he did receive him back.

---

is that until a counselee "sees" the realities of the eternal life to come, if only **from a distance**, and 'welcomes' them (like travelers who see a city toward which they have been traveling in the distance, and shout for joy, "There it is"), they will not strike out as they should for Christ. The earthly trek is a journey to eternity. And for the Christian, it should be a journey toward his **homeland** (v. 14). Perhaps because so much contemporary writing and preaching in Christian circles, along with the psychologist's and psychiatrist's nearly sole emphasis on this world, the sense of being a traveler and stranger on earth had all but dissipated. People who feel more at home here than they ought to will never take the risks that faith in the future promises of God energizes. When it comes to doing things God's way—the way of faith, not the way of sight—they hesitate. So what is the upshot of this discussion? Simply this: if there is nothing more to your counseling than solutions to present problems involving present ways and means, you will probably not succeed in moving fearful counselees with little faith off the dime. Keep the eternal dimension burning bright and lively in all your talk. That will make the difference.

The writer makes the point that Abraham (and others) might have retreated when the going got tough—as some of his readers contemplated doing, but **the fact is, they desire a better (that is a heavenly) country** (vv. 15,16). His point? Don't be a fool and do otherwise. To put it simply, motivating faith in counselees means they truly believe that God **has prepared a city for them** (v. 16[b]).

Verse 17 indicates that God sometimes **tests** those whom He uses. Abraham passed the test because he **reasoned that God was even able to raise him** [Isaac] **from the dead** (v. 19). The mental processes of Abraham worked this way: "God has promised that He will make a great nation out of the descendants of Isaac. Now He tells me to sacrifice him.

20 By faith Isaac also blessed Jacob and Esau regarding things to come.
21 By faith Jacob, when dying, blessed each of the sons of Joseph and worshiped while leaning on the top of his staff.
22 By faith Joseph, at the end of his life, spoke of the exodus of Israel's sons and gave instructions about his bones.
23 By faith Moses, when he was born, was hidden three months by his parents, because they saw that he was a delightful child, and they weren't afraid of the king's decree.
24 By faith Moses, when he had grown up, refused to be called the son of Pharaoh's daughter,
25 choosing instead to be mistreated along with God's people rather than to enjoy the short-lived pleasures of sin.
26 He considered the reproach of Christ greater riches than the treasures of Egypt. This was because he was looking ahead to the reward.

His promise can't be wrong, so this seeming contradiction to it is *just that*—a *seeming* contradiction. There is no contradiction at all. So if I sacrifice him, that means God will still honor His promise, even if it takes raising Isaac from the dead!" Today, when discussing the command to sacrifice Isaac, preachers tend to focus on the so-called "psychological" side of it; they talk about how hard it must have been for Abraham to do such a thing, because it was the son whom he loved. That of course is a part of the story. But in doing so they also tend to forget the matter with which this verse is concerned: Abraham's solid faith in God's promise. It was so solid, that not for a moment did he question it. Rather, he began to consider how it might be that God would keep the promise and even hit on a solution: resurrection from the dead. It is that sort of faith that this chapter is commending to the reader.

Isaac, Jacob and Joseph are included in the list (vv. 20-22) because they too were men of faith. But little is said of them (it seems obvious that the writer is emphasizing the better known instances of faith). So next he turns to the story of Moses (vv. 23-29).

Moses' parents trusted that God would preserve Moses when they took the action of hiding him and, sure enough, God honored their faith. Their faith enabled them to disobey the **king's decree** without fear (v. 23). But Moses, himself, was also a man of faith. When power and wealth were his for the taking, instead he **refused to be called the son of Pharaoh's daughter, choosing instead to be mistreated along with God's people rather than to enjoy the short-lived pleasures of sin** (vv. 24,25). How is that? Well, we are told in verse 26 that **He considered the**

27 By faith he left Egypt, unafraid of the king's anger; he endured because he "saw" the One Who is unseen.

28 By faith he kept the Passover and sprinkled the blood so that the destroyer of the firstborn wouldn't touch them.

29 By faith they went through the Red Sea as if it were dry land; but when the Egyptians tried it, they were drowned.

30 By faith Jericho's walls fell after they had been encircled for seven days.

31 By faith Rahab the prostitute didn't die with those who disobeyed because she received the spies in peace.

32 Now what more can I say? Time would fail me to speak about Gideon, Barak, Samson, Jephthah, about David and Samuel and the prophets,

33 who by faith conquered kingdoms, brought about justice, obtained promises, shut lions' mouths,

34 put out raging fires, escaped the sword's edge, gained strength from weakness, became mighty in war, put foreign armies to flight,

35 and about women who received their dead back by resurrection. Yet, others were tortured, refusing to be delivered, so that they might obtain a better resurrection;

36 some received jeers and lashings, and others were chained and imprisoned.

---

reproach of Christ greater riches than the treasures of Egypt. This was because he was looking ahead to the reward. Moses, and men of faith like him, all have sense enough to weigh the short term over against the long term. That is what the writer is saying. And having done so, Moses concluded that all the temporary treasures of Egypt (the greatest in the then known world) could not begin to measure up to **the reward** God had laid up for him in eternity. He was even able to **endure** the **king's anger unafraid** by **looking ahead to the reward**, and by "seeing" **the One Who is unseen.** That is to say it was all so real to him that he was able to picture what was ahead as vividly as if it were present to him. Neither preaching nor counseling about today enables people to do that. Work on helping counselees to gain strength and courage to make good decisions here based on what is coming in the future (cf. II Corinthians 4:16-18).

Verses 28 and 29 relate Moses' faith in observing the commands of God and in performing tasks He led him to do. Without mentioning Joshua, his deeds at Jericho are recounted as an example of faith. Even Rahab, who had so little knowledge (but believed) is held forth as an

37 They were stoned, they were sawed in half, they were murdered by the sword, they went about in sheepskins and goatskins, destitute, afflicted, ill-treated.
38 They were people of whom the world wasn't worthy! They wandered over deserts and mountains, and lived in caves and holes in the ground.
39 These all received good testimony because of their faith; yet they didn't receive what was promised
40 because God had something better in sight for us. So then they couldn't be made perfect without us.

---

example of what faith can do (v. 30). Then in verses 32 through 37, person after person is ticked off as having faith that led to proper conduct in face of trial and affliction. The thing to see in this listing is that all possessed faith alike (and like faith), yet some were delivered from danger and death while others suffered both. Having faith does not guarantee that one will escape persecution—often of even the most severe sort. What faith does, however, is enable one to triumph over it. To be able to endure it and overcome it. Neither the martyr nor the confessor (the one whose faith was every bit as evident but who was not persecuted or put to death because of it) is considered superior. Faith says, "God, whatever You have for me to do is OK with me. I will die for You or live for You." For some the latter is more difficult than the former. Either way, faith commits itself into the hands of God for His use—whatever that may be.

Now the conclusion of the matter (vv. 38-40). These people are compared with the unsaved world, of whom the writer says, it **wasn't worthy.** God gave them all a **good testimony because of their faith** (v. 39). And there was one characteristic that was true of all of them: **yet, they didn't receive what was promised.** Why? Why was it that they didn't in their day enter into all that had been promised? In the concluding verse he explains: **God had something better in sight for us. So they couldn't be made perfect** [complete] **without us.** The final consummation of all things, including the resurrection of the immortalized and glorified body by which one may dwell in the eternal city in that heavenly country has not yet occurred. The reason? Because God had others—from among the gentiles, in particular—who throughout the New Testament era would be gathered into the church. Until the last one of His elect is brought to faith, the completion (restoration) of all things could not fully take place. Now much has been accomplished, but the church is still operating within the present, earthly order of things. The city from God in the newly former heavens and earth, in which righteousness is at home, yet awaits (even us).

Whew! What a chapter. Don't read it today and forget it. It is so very practical for counseling purposes. How many counselees (counselors, for that matter!) have the sort of faith about which it speaks? Yet that is precisely what is needed. Strengthen your own faith, counselor by reflecting every day on the promises of the country and the city to come. Make sure that in the background of everything you see today, you see also the outlines of the heavenly city that lie on the horizon **at a distance**. That will help you make those decisions that are proper in your own life and will give you insight into and perspective on the affairs of others whom you counsel. Without that heavenly background against which present difficulties loom, the present is neither understandable not endurable.

CHAPTER 12

1 Therefore, since we are surrounded by such a great cloud of witnesses, we must put off every weight and the sin that is so readily found all around us, and we must run the race that has been set before us with perseverance,

---

When a new chapter begins with the word **therefore**, you know that there should have been no chapter heading dividing it from the previous one. It is important, then, in interpreting any chapter when that happens to link it to what has preceded. To begin by saying **therefore, since we are surrounded by such a great cloud of witnesses...** requires us to ask who those witnesses are. Unquestionably, they are the many individuals mentioned as having the faith that we, today, also must have in order to please God. How are they witnesses? Do they actually look from heaven to see what we are doing? Probably that is not what is meant (although that is not an impossibility). Since he is about to picture the Christian life as a race, it would seem that in order to complete the picture he places them in the stands at the stadium watching the race. As a way of urging us by their example and attendance on our running to emulate their faith, the picture drawn is quite effective. Those who have successfully completed their race now view ours, cheering us on. In other words, instead of saying, "be like them," he says that by means of this striking and memorable picture.

How should we run so as to win the race (in this race, *all* who run well win!)? He explains **we must put off every weight and the sin that is so readily found all around us, and we must run the race that has been set before us with perseverance.** Two things are mentioned in verse The first, lay aside everything that encumbers you. The second, don't give up; persevere.

Consider the first. Encumbrances may be of two sorts: **weights** and **sins**. While some translate the **and** "even," making the word **sins** epexegetical of **weight** (so that the sentence would read "every weight, *even* the sin") it is more likely that the writer viewed more than sins as possible encumbrances. I take it that he refers not only to those sins that are everywhere around us, but also to perfectly legitimate activities (at the proper time) that may not be proper under certain circumstances *so that, if indulged in,* they too *become* sin. Counselees must recognize that stressing family, business, recreation and the like, at proper times and in proper ways, is acceptable to God. But when these interfere with living the

Christian life as one should, they become **weights** we must lay aside. When a child takes up inordinate amounts of a parent's time, especially in a home school context where the danger is perhaps most likely to occur, so that the parent is only home-centered and refuses to do anything if it doesn't contribute to the enhancement of his home and his children, he has put those children on a pedestal that neither honors God nor is good for the children. On the other hand, if a man puts his business before his family, then business becomes a **weight.** Properly conducted, business is a blessing to the church, one's family and the life that the businessman leads; but like anything else, it can *become* a curse. The same can be said for the great American religion—entertainment (TV, video and sports). Anything good can be perverted. Even going to church can become a **weight**. The person who tears up her family or who avoids her husband and her responsibilities by running off to church meetings every night in the week has made church a **weight**. As a counselor, it is your task to point out this fact to your counselees, to warn them of the dangers, to contradict them when they protest unreasonably and to help them to get their lives in order. To help them better recognize the problem, have them draw up a list of possible and potential **weights** to discuss at the next counseling session. Many counselees are totally unaware that the biblical admonition to lay aside weights pertains to proper and right things that may become wrong. That is an important principle, therefore, to inculcate.

That **sin is so readily found all around us**, as the writer says, makes it important for you to help counselees to avoid the monastic reaction to it. Some try to avoid sin by living a detached, isolated lifestyle. The result is that they try to weave a sort of Christian cocoon around themselves and their children. Even if it were possible (which this verse clearly indicates it is not), it would be wrong to do so. The ascetic is faulted in two ways: he cannot escape sin (he carries it in himself *wherever* he goes) and to attempt the escape is a violation of the second great commandment in favor of the first. Jesus never opposed the two commandments; only one with a deficient and self-centered interest could ever do that. One *must* love his neighbor to love God since God gave both commands.

So then, what is the answer to the problem of **sin that is so readily found all around us**? The answer is both learning and teaching your children to be in the world but not of it. Since the readily available temptations to sin confront us everywhere, the answer is to learn how to pick one's way through the mine fields without exploding them. That is the counselor's task—to teach others how to do so. The example of the Lord's temptation is helpful. Not only did the Spirit drive Him into the desert **to**

2 looking off to Jesus the Author and Completer of our faith, Who, for the joy that had been set before Him, endured the cross, despising the shame, and is seated at the right hand of God's throne.

---

be tempted of the devil (Matthew 4:4), but He then motivated Him to call upon the truths of the Scriptures to enable Him to resist and withstand the temptations that were offered. As the Bible teaches, if we **resist** the devil, he will flee from us (I Peter 5:9). That, not monasticism (even of a Protestant sort) is the answer to the problem of temptation from the sin that is found all around us.

Perseverance is important to running a race. Every runner, at some time or other, contemplates giving up. But, if he can make it through that next lap—then the next—and the next, the first thing you know he will cross the finish line. In doing anything that requires time and effort, it is necessary to develop the quality of **perseverance**. More people with good intentions fail because of the lack of this essential quality than, perhaps, from any other failing. It is not that many Christians are ignorant of what they should do, it is simply that they have bad habits of procrastination and (when they finally do begin) of quitting before achieving success. Counselors will find that this is both a primary and a complicating problem. Not only does it cause the difficulties that a counselee may encounter, but it becomes a hindrance to the development of good, new patterns that you are attempting to develop in those whom you counsel. Apart from disciplined perseverance (doing something regularly, consistently, without giving up) your counselee will not replace the old, sinful patterns with the new righteous ones that God requires. So by staying with him, encouraging him as a spectator in the stands cheers on his favorite runner, you must help him learn the virtue of **perseverance**. Many stubborn counselees, properly brought to repentance and then taught to transform the former stubbornness into perseverance, will learn to do so before those who are seemingly more easy going.

As one runs, he must have an objective before him. In verse 2, that objective is to reach Jesus. One is to run, **looking off to Jesus.** He is to keep his eyes fixed on Him as he runs. In no other way will he run successfully (for the Christian, success is always pleasing God, whether that pleases others or not). When a counselee begins to look at the other runners in the race, or at himself or at the crowd in the stands, he will fall behind. There is no surer way to trip up than to take one's eyes off of Jesus. There He stands at the finish line, beckoning you on. He has run the

3 Consider Him Who endured such opposition from sinners against Himself, so that you won't get tired and give up—

---

race before you, so he knows the obstacles you must overcome. He knows how difficult it is. He knows what you are going through. But as the **Author and the Completer of your faith**, He also knows how much you can stand, what is best for you and what you need to cross the finish line. He will see that you complete your race (not merely begin it). He will see you through to the end. To those counselees who from time to time wonder whether the Lord has abandoned them, this great epithet applied to Christ should be most reassuring: He is not only the **Author** but also the **Completer** of the believer's faith. He does not merely get you started on the Christian life, but is there throughout, enabling you to run until the race is complete.

How tough was the race for Him? Tougher than for you. The course He ran went by the way of the cross. What sustained Him? **The joy that was set before Him.** He saw His seed, and rejoiced (cf. Isaiah 53:11) He was bringing many sons to glory. He could see what lay on the other side of the cross. While the word translated "for" (*anti*) may also be translated "instead of," that translation in this place is not appropriate. Here he is talking about the exaltation to the Father's right hand as well as the great number of believers who would be exalted with Him. It is that which spurred Him on. Your counselee can **endure** whatever God has for him and he too can learn to **despise the shame** that often is the lot of those who espouse the gospel if he, like His Lord, continues to think of the **joy that has been set before him** in Christ. Never allow counseling sessions to drift away from the joys of knowing and, someday seeing, the Lord Jesus Christ.

It is not natural even for redeemed sinners to think that way. It therefore takes deliberate thought to fix one's mind on Jesus when struggling with various difficulties that he encounters day by day. That is why the writer urges your counselee to **Consider Him Who endured such opposition from sinners against Himself, so that you won't get tired and give up.** As a matter of fact, like these Hebrew believers, it could be said of most of those who are reading these pages that **in your struggle against sin you haven't yet had to resist to the point of shedding your blood.** The Lord Jesus did shed His blood, however. That is why it is important to take thought about His race, His struggle against sin. To **consider Him** and what He **endured** at the hands of sinful men will help your

4 in your struggle against sin you haven't yet had to resist to the point of shedding your blood.

---

counselee to endure. But this consideration means hard, thorough thought. It is not speaking of some halfhearted review of the life and death of Christ. What it means is to think of him going through the same things you are enduring, and then multiply their intensity any number of times. Think of the **shame** that was involved in the holy, harmless, undefiled Savior becoming sin for you. You will never know all that meant for Him. But try to understand as fully as you can. Think of Him, betrayed by one of the twelve when you are betrayed. Think of Him in pain of soul as well as body on the cross, knowing that His people had turned their backs on Him. And on, and on and on. If two things do not happen as a counselee **considers Him**, namely, that he is strengthened by Christ's example and that he is grateful for His love and mercy, then the "consideration" leaves much to be desired.

Verse 4 is a point to make with your counselee. With rare exceptions, those who are reading this book and counseling others will be able to say, **in your struggle against sin you haven't yet had to resist to the point of shedding your blood.** When all he gives you are complaints and whining, that is the time to mention the fact. Not only did Christ suffer to the **point of shedding His blood**, but hundreds of thousands throughout the years who faithfully served Him have done so as well. What is he complaining about? He has it so easy. That is often the bottom line for those whose complaints concern nothing more than mere inconveniences. In this coddled age in which we live, it is almost ludicrous to hear some of the things that counselees bring into counseling sessions. When compared with shedding one's blood for the faith, what is it to be made fun of? How can you even speak of slights, gossip and innuendoes in the same breath? Why would anyone who recognizes that he has not yet had to suffer physically for Christ even think of complaining about the way other Christians have treated him? The thought, as the writer intended it to be, *is* ludicrous. Here were people who had suffered even more than most believers today (cf. 10:32-34), and yet, his point is that they didn't even know what suffering is in comparison with some of those who suffered for their faith listed in the previous chapter. There are times when all you can say to a counselee, is "cut it out; your whining hardly becomes a servant of the suffering Savior!" Now I know that it is often hard to draw the line between those who need encouragement and those who need rebuke.

5 Now, have you forgotten the encouragement that reasons with you as sons?—

> **My son, don't think lightly of the Lord's discipline, and don't give up when He corrects you.**

6 **The Lord disciplines those whom He loves, and whips every son that He receives.**

7 You have to persevere through these things in order to become disciplined. God is treating you like sons. What son is there that a father doesn't discipline?

When in doubt, it is probably wise to err (if need be) on the side of compassion. But surely there is a time when some counselees must be faced with the absurdity of their attitudes and behavior.

The writer asks his readers **have you forgotten the encouragement that reasons with you as sons?**—and then he quotes Proverbs 3:11,12 (see also Revelation 3:19). The Hebrews to whom this letter was sent had not endured serious persecution; what persecution they had suffered was but **chastisement.** Chastisement is not intended to kill or harm; it is intended to alter behavior. Therefore, it is but the **encouragement** of a loving Father toward His erring children. All of which the writer explains is the Lord's way of exercising discipline for their good.

You don't **discipline** the kid up the street when you see him doing wrong. Why not? Well, he isn't your child. But you *do* discipline your own children—out of love—for their own good *because you love them.* **The Lord disciplines those whom He loves, and whips every son that He receives** as a son. That is why one may never **think lightly of the Lord's discipline** or **give up when He corrects** (v. 6). The point needs to be made often to sinning counselees. They need the Lord's discipline. If they will not discipline themselves they must expect the Lord to do it (see comments on I Corinthians 11:31,32).

What is **discipline** like? The first fact observed about it is that it often lasts for a while: **You have to persevere through these things in order to become disciplined** (v. 7[a]). In other words, the good effects of discipline occur only when one perseveres until the completion of the process. It is possible to **give up** instead of reaping the benefits of the full force of the disciplinary process (v. 5). That was what these Christians were contemplating. "Things are beginning to get tough," they were saying; "why don't we go back to our former lives where we had no such problems?" Many counselees come with that very thought in mind. Like the writer, therefore, it is your task to convince them to persevere **through**

8 But if you are without discipline, in which all have had a share, then you are illegitimate children and not sons.
9 Furthermore, we have had fathers of our physical bodies who disciplined us and we respected them; shouldn't we much more submit to the Father of our spirits and live?
10 They disciplined us for a short time according to their thinking about what was best, but He disciplines us for our benefit, so that we may share in His holiness.

---

these things. How will you do it? By showing them that it is the loving hand of a heavenly Father that is guiding the course of their lives. By observing the benefits of discipline: **it yields the peaceful fruit of righteousness to those who have been trained by it** (v. 11[b]). And by making it clear that if one fails to suffer discipline, he is not a true child of God but is **illegitimate** (v. 8). Every true son is disciplined by his father (Oh that that were still true in the age after Spock!), the reader says. Discipline is a sign of legitimacy. God doesn't always remove His children from trouble—never promise a counselee that He will. Often He wants to sustain him in trouble for his own good. Discipline molds, purifies, chips away at rough edges, strengthens, etc.

Earthly fathers did their best to discipline us (though they may not always have been right in their attempts), and **we respected them** (something counselees need to be taught today—respect by children is shown to those who attempt to discipline fairly, not to those who fail to discipline). Why **shouldn't we much more submit to the Father of our spirits and live** (v. 9)? God's discipline is always fair and correct (v. 10) and it is **for our benefit**. Why does He discipline? **So that we may share in His holiness.** To be holy as God is holy means many changes in our lives. The means that brings about godly change is disciplined training in righteousness (see comments on II Timothy 3:16,17). God is realistic about discipline: **Of course, all discipline seems painful rather than pleasant for the moment, but later on it yields the peaceful fruit of righteousness.** Nobody said that discipline would be pleasant; it isn't. But righteousness, the pleasant result of such discipline, is like a fruit into which you bite and discover that it tastes like peace! While undergoing discipline, there is pain. People tell us today that discipline should never cause pain. If it doesn't, according to this passage, then it is not true discipline. Counselees, who have adopted modern methods of disciplining their children must be taught what God says about discipline. It is crucial. Here is an inspired dissertation on discipline, its nature and effects; discipline as

11 Of course, all discipline seems painful rather than pleasant for the moment, but later on it yields the peaceful fruit of righteousness to those who have been trained by it.
12 So then, lift your listless hands and strengthen your weak knees
13 and make straight paths for your feet, so that your lame ankles may not be twisted, but rather healed.

---

practiced by God Himself. This is the place to turn to instruct counselees about matters of discipline, not to some psychological theories about child rearing. You will find that it is much more effective and, of prime importance, that it pleases God. Psychology fails because it has no divine instruction to which to refer. It flails about today denouncing discipline; tomorrow advocating it. Here is the steady, certain Word of the living God on the subject. As you read, you will find help. And what you read, at many points, trashes many of ideas of modern psychology that are to the contrary. If you want **peace**, that will come from **righteousness**. And **righteousness** is the result of proper **discipline** (v. 11). But remember, it takes **perseverance** (v. 7) in order to become **trained by it** (v. 11[b]).

Alluding to Isaiah 35:3 and Proverbs 4:26, in the next two verses the writer urges the reader to "Get with it." Stop sitting there as if the world has come to an end. Straighten up and fly right! **Lift those listless hand and strengthen your weak knees.** There is a race to be run. You'll never do that successfully if you sit on the sidelines thinking how bad things are. If you have a **lame ankle** from the race, then be sure to run on the **path** which is **straight** and level rather than wander off the course God laid out and really hurt your **ankle** by **twisting** it on some uneven turf. There is a place in counseling for acting like a cheerleader! In fact, you may even find yourself shouting (or nearly so) words of encouragement. When a teammate makes a bad play, fellow teammates do not berate him, but, rather, encourage him to "get in there and get 'em this time." That is in effect what verses 12 and 13 are all about. They are a call to go back to running the race.

Now as one begins to take his place once again on the race track, there are certain rules that he should keep in mind so as to run well. The first is **Pursue peace with everybody.** It is not the Christian's calling to be a troublemaker (though plenty of them are—perhaps even some of your counselees!). Rather he is to be a **peacemaker** and thus be called God's (the Peacemaker's) son (Matthew 5:9). Many counselees come fighting. They are ready to fight other members of their church, the pastor,

14 Pursue peace with everybody, and sanctification, without which nobody will see the Lord.

---

their bosses, husbands or wives, etc. One of the most important things you can do as a counselor is to remind counselees of this verse (see also comments on Romans 12:18 for additional help). Often their attitudes will not allow progress on any front until they have been shaped by repentance leading to a desire to bring peace. It is so interesting how many counselees scream for peace—for themselves—but care little about bringing peace into the lives of others. The word **pursue** is a powerful word meaning to hunt down until one finds his quarry. In other words, seeking peace may not merely be the expression of a wish ("It would be nice to be on speaking terms with him/her"), but must be an earnest quest in which one is determined *at all costs* to reach the goal of peace. That means, even at the cost of personal loss, embarrassment, time, energy, granting forgiveness, etc. Of course, when I say "at all costs," I mean all that the Bible allows or encourages.

It doesn't matter who it is that the counselee has difficulty with (whether it is a believer or an unbeliever) he is to **pursue peace with *everybody***. That means that it is always his duty to endeavor to develop a peaceful relationship with everyone—no matter who that person may be or what he has done. He may not beg off saying, "But he's not a believer." It may not be possible to achieve peace with every unbeliever, but if that is not possible, that must be because of the unbeliever. The Christian must be sure that from his side of the relationship he has done everything possible to bring about peaceful relations.

And he is to pursue **sanctification, without which nobody will see the Lord**. Sanctification is a progressive setting apart of the Christian more and more to Christ and less and less to sin. No one will see God unless, as he seeks to **pursue peace** toward *men*, he also **pursues sanctification** toward *God*. Here are the two great commandments to love God and neighbor put in terms of life pursuits. Anyone who does not want to be more clean and holy, like his heavenly Father, is not a true son of God (Matthew 5:8). If there is absolutely no progress in becoming sanctified, the counselee with whom you are working either is doing the wrong things, and needs to change his endeavors, or he is not a believer after all.

Here is another rule for running the Christian race: **Take care (lit., the care of an overseer) that nobody falls away from God's grace, that a root of bitterness doesn't sprout to cause trouble and become the**

15 Take care that nobody falls away from God's grace, that a root of bitterness doesn't sprout to cause trouble and become the way of polluting many,
16 that there isn't any sexually immoral or godless person like Esau, who for a single meal sold his birthright.
17 You know, of course, that afterward when he wanted to inherit the blessing he was rejected. He found no opportunity to change his mind, even though he sought it with tears.

---

way of polluting many (v. 15). How powerful this warning is. Many who mean well **fall away** from truth and stop running the course because of the influence of the bitter attitudes of others. On the other hand, the person himself, dropping by the side of the race course may himself become sour grapes. This attitude on his part may **pollute many** others. There is danger here. How often, those who fail in their own lives, denounce the whole process as if it were not worth doing. They become bitter and resentful of those who are succeeding. So they find fault, take potshots at the church in general and at individuals in it in particular. They are able to find fault, because, if you look closely enough, you will discover faults in everyone. But by this faultfinding that grows out of resentment toward others, they can destroy a congregation. That is why it is necessary to oversee matters as carefully as a shepherd oversees his flock. When resentment is being expressed even in small measure (as a sprout), it must be countered before it springs up and grows into a plant that spreads and propagates itself throughout the whole. This talk of "root problems" that some think they get from this passage is a misunderstanding by those who do little true exegesis and who, instead, make out of a word something it was never intended to convey. They then build a doctrine, principle or system of counseling on it. The root here is a root growing up in a church that has the potential of destroying it. Counselor, be sure to be on the watch for bitterness and resentment—a prime counseling problem. See Ephesians 4:31,32 as well.

This **care** and oversight is to extend to another problem: also look out for **any sexually immoral or godless person like Esau, who for a single meal sold his birthright.** Sexually immoral persons act first, and like Esau (v. 17) think afterwards; after the damage is done. That is why it is important to guard against any sexually explicit language or suggestive talk in counseling. Especially, refuse to participate in or sponsor "confession" groups, in which not only gossip and slander, but also sexual titillation may occur.

18 Now you haven't come to a mountain that can be touched, one that blazes with fire, to darkness, gloom and a whirlwind,
19 to the sound of a trumpet, or to the sound of a voice that made it hearers beg that no further word be spoken to them.
20 They couldn't bear the command, **If even an animal touches the mountain, it must be stoned.**
21 Indeed, so terrifying was the sight that Moses said, **"I am trembling with fear."**

When it is discovered in a congregation or in a counselee, you must do all you can to put it down. Few attitudes spread as rapidly as bitterness. The warning here about **a single meal** is important. Esau's action was stupid—to sell a birthright, with all it entailed, for one bowl of red bean soup! Why would he? Because he was a man driven to satisfy his appetite. Like an animal, filling his belly was more important than anything else, even though it was selling the hour to buy the minute. A sexually driven person is also like that. He will cry about it afterwards, after he has gotten the girl pregnant; when it is too late to do anything about it. But **there is no opportunity to change his mind** (v. 17). The damage is done; it is too late. Protect your congregation from such persons. Protect individuals involved from counselees in whom you detect a desire-driven sexual orientation.

The rest of the chapter compares and contrasts Mt. Sinai (v. 18) and the covenant given to Moses there with Mount Zion in heaven and the covenant that Jesus brought by means of His blood (v. 22ff.). It is a striking contrast. We haven't **come to a mountain that can be touched** (that is, to a physical mountain), **one that blazes with fire, to darkness, gloom and a whirlwind, to the sound of a trumpet, or to the sound of a voice that made its hearers beg that no further word be spoken to them.** What is he describing as he ticks off these facts about Mount Sinai and the giving of the law? Just this: **so terrifying was the sight that Moses said, "I am trembling with fear."** It *was* a fearful experience. Why was the giving of the law so terrifying? Because the law could not save; it could only show us our sin and demonstrate how fearful a thing it is to sin against a God with such power and wrath. The idea? In effect, the writer is asking, "Do you want to go back to *that*?" It cannot save you; it can only condemn you.

No!, he says, that is not what we have **come to** as believers of the New Covenant. Instead, **we have come to Mount Zion, to the city of the living God** (the one that the heroes of faith were longing to see), **to the**

22 No! You, instead, have come to Mount Zion, to the city of the living
God, to the heavenly Jerusalem and to myriads of angels,
23 to the festal gathering and church of the firstborn who are enrolled in
heaven, to God, the Judge of all, to the spirits of just persons who have
been made perfect,
24 to Jesus, the Mediator of a newly established covenant, and to the
sprinkled blood that has a better message to tell then did Abel's blood.
25 See to it that you don't refuse to hear the One Who speaks. If they
didn't escape when they refused to listen to the one who warned them on
earth, how much less will we if we turn away from the One Who warns us
from the heavens?

---

heavenly Jerusalem and to myriads of angels (v. 22)**.** Well, is that also a fearful experience; one we should dread? Absolutely not! Precisely the opposite is true. We have come to **the festal gathering and the church of the firstborn who are enrolled in heaven, to God, the Judge of all, to the spirits of just persons who have been made perfect, to Jesus the Mediator of a newly established covenant, and to the sprinkled blood that has a better message to tell than did Abel's blood** (vv. 23,24)**.** Everything there is wonderful, joyful—even festal**.** There is nothing about this picture to fear. There is no need to tremble, except with anticipation. There is no need to draw away or beg for no more. There is, instead, every reason to approach, desire to enter into the holy city of God, and to participate fully in all that is taking place. But **God** is there, described as **Judge**. That is very true. But **Jesus,** your **Mediator** of the **covenant**, whose **sprinkled blood** is mentioned, is also there. And safe for all time, there is the heavenly church, occupying the heavenly city of God, awaiting the resurrection of their bodies, but whose **spirits** have already been **made perfect** (free from all sin). The **blood** of Jesus has a better message than Abel's. **Abel's blood** cried out for punishment, vengeance. It was a forecast of what the sinful nature of man would bring about through intrigue, war and murder of every sort. Jesus' **blood proclaims** salvation for all who will come to Him. That is a **better message**.

Verse 25 is a warning and a call to remain steadfast: **See to it that you don't refuse to hear the One Who speaks. If they didn't escape when they refused to listen to the one who warned them on earth, how much less will we if we turn away from the One Who warns us from the heaven?** While there is nothing to fear *if* one remains true to the Lord Jesus, if he does not, there is much to fear. Indeed, he has more to fear than the Old Covenant saint at Mount Sinai. To reject an earthly message

26 At that time His voice shook the earth, but now He has promised, **Once more I will shake not only the earth, but heaven too!**
27 Now, "once more" indicates the removal of what is shaken (created things, that is), so that what can't be shaken may remain.
28 Therefore, let us be thankful that we have received an unshakable empire, and let us serve God in a manner that pleases Him with reverence and awe.
29 Our God is a consuming fire!

---

from God was serious; to reject the glorious message from the heavens about Christ is far more so. To the extent that Mount Zion offers such a marvelous contrast, just so much more fearful it is for one so enlightened to turn his back on it (cf. chapters 6,10).

In verse 26, he returns to the giving of the law at Sinai: **At that time His voice shook the earth.** Now, the contrast: **but now He has promised Once more I will shake not only the earth, but heaven too!** What is this all about? He continues: **"once more" indicates the removal of what is shaken (created things, that is), so that what can't be shaken may remain.** Peter refers to this same time when he speaks of the heavens and the earth being on fire, melting and being remolded into new heavens and earth in which righteousness is at home (II Peter 3). It is the future coming of Christ when the creation will be shaken so that all sin and its works will be removed. In verses 28 and 29 comes the victorious conclusion: **Therefore, let us be thankful that we have received an unshakable empire, and let us serve God in a manner that pleases Him with reverence and awe. Our God is a consuming fire!** Rather than fear, rejoice—and be thankful. That is the upshot of the final discussion of this chapter. Why would anyone want to return to that which was fearful, and that which could only be shaken and consumed? Hold fast to the unshakable kingdom of God.

Whenever a dispirited counselee needs refreshment, read him the picture of the heavenly Mount Zion—*his* homeland! Explain what it is all about. Show him that the writer drew this picture in order to encourage dispirited saints like him. But also warn him that if he rejects this, including the **better message** of the **blood** of **Jesus**, he is walking on very thin ice.

What a chapter! Like so many in this wondrous Book, it ends with the reader exhausted at the magnitude of the concepts that are set forth. It is not wrong to overwhelm others by the glorious salvation that they have in Christ. Perhaps the church is so effete today is because there is so little realization of the wonders and glories of the life to come. The majority of the books published today focus on this life and all that there is for us now. While it is certainly true that God has much for the believer today, it is nothing when compared with what awaits him in the world to come. Because so little is preached or spoken in counseling sessions about heaven and the joys of it, people who have lost health, property, loved ones, money, prestige, etc., find little that intrigues them in this life. Show them what God has planned for them in the world to come; that will enable them to live joyfully, *by faith*, here and now.

Chapter 13

1 Brotherly love must be maintained.

2 Don't forget to show hospitality to strangers, because by doing so some have entertained angels without realizing it.

At last we come to the final chapter of the Book of Hebrews. Perhaps it is the most magnificent of all final chapters. At any rate, it is full of help and instruction for the biblical counselor. There is a potpourri of items considered in it, beginning with a concern to see that **brotherly love** be **maintained.** When people are in the midst of confusion, some saying one thing and some saying another, as it seems was the situation among the Hebrews of the church addressed, there is bound to be strife. Consequently, it is likely that **brotherly love** will suffer. That is why it is important to stress the need to **maintain** it. Presumably, it had not all been sapped by the contention and confusion. Don't let it be! That is the message of verse 1.

And **hospitality**. Now there is an important matter. Among persecuted outcasts it was essential to meet the needs of those who had been severely deprived of their homes and their possessions (cf. 10:32-34). And traveling Christians (especially missionaries; see II & III John) needed places to lodge and provisions to help them travel to the next town. All this was involved in hospitality. It did not mean the polite sort of thing we nowadays call hospitality but rather, a sacrificial giving of whatever it was that another brother or sister in the faith needed. No wonder then that hospitality is the next thought after mentioning **brotherly love.** Have your counselees think long and hard about what **brotherly love** and **hospitality** mean in their situations. Have them write out examples of the ways in which they have shown both to other believers over the last quarter of a year. Chances are that they will not come up with much (if anything). And what they do come up with may be so meager that it is hardly worth mentioning. Many of your counselees' problems stem from a self-centered approach to life. They rarely think to do anything for another. Having looked over a slim list of instances of these two matters, you might remark to the one who offered them (perhaps somewhat shamefacedly), "Perhaps this is one reason why you find your life such a mess. The person who never reaches out to another is the person who becomes miserable. Make a new list of some ways that you might begin to show

3 Remember prisoners as if you were in prison with them and those who are ill-treated, as persons who also have bodies.

---

love and hospitality this week. Bring it in, we'll discuss it and how well you did in following it."

Now the writer himself appends an incentive for hospitality. He says that by showing hospitality, **some have entertained angels without realizing it**. He refers, of course, to the story of Lot. The point is not that you might also entertain angels; the point is that God blesses those who show hospitality. And it is possible that you will be blessed in ways that you never anticipated. Thus a counselee, reluctant to open his home and his purse to others, ought to be warned about the possible blessings that he is missing. Niggardly attitudes on the part of Christians—people who have received so much by grace—surely are inconsistent with the goodness of God. No wonder many counselees are miserable, unhappy persons; they refrain from all those practices that bring happiness into life. Then they blame others; and sometimes, they even blame God!

In a time of persecution, many would be thrown into prison (cf. Acts 8:3). In those days, those who were imprisoned had to receive help from friends without, who brought medicine, food, clothing to them. The state didn't provide luxuries at the taxpayer's expense as it does today. In fact, as I indicated, even many *necessities* had to be provided by families and friends (cf. II Timothy 1:16-18; 4:9-13). It was a hard thing to survive prison with its filth and disease. Remember, how Paul used the illustration of gangrene while writing from prison? Well, he was probably looking at a gangrenous person imprisoned with him. And, prisoners often were beaten prior to incarceration (cf. Acts 16:22,23,33). Here the writer of Hebrews mentions the fact than many were **ill-treated** and reminds the readers that, along with prisoners, they too **are persons who have bodies**. Prisoners are subject to all the physical ills and ailments that they are. Thinking of that ought to impel them to visit and care for fellow-believers who have been cast into prison. All of the injunctions thus far have been aimed at getting the reader to reach out beyond himself to other Christians (love your brothers, show hospitality to them, and visit them when they are in need in prison in order to meet those needs). These sorts of commands (not only the specific commands, however—a counselee isn't to wait until a friend is thrown into prison to do good and help him meet some bodily affliction!) are precisely what many counselees who are so wrapped up in themselves need to hear and obey. When you are able to

4 Marriage must be honored by everybody, and the marriage bed must be unpolluted; God will judge immoral people and adulterers.

---

persuade such a counselee to get serious about doing good to his brothers and sisters in Christ, and he actually begins to do so, you will soon notice a change in him for good. But, he must not do it *in order to* reap benefits for himself. He must do it first, to please God and second, out of compassion for others. What he receives in return is a by-product.

Celibacy is not preferable to or holier than **marriage**. Because of some medieval notions that seem to persist in the church, there is the idea that there is something tainted about marriage because of sexual relations which are a part of the obligations of marriage. That is not so. In Genesis 2:18, the rule is set forth: **It is not good for the man to be alone**. I Corinthians 7 mentions an exception—when there is a time of violent persecution such as the Neronian onslaught against the church that Paul was predicting. Along with Jesus' words in Matthew 19, Paul also mentions that there are some extraordinary persons whom God gifts with the gift of singleness in order to perform certain tasks in His church. But these are the exceptions; not the rule. That is why **Marriage must be honored by everybody** [or in every respect]. No asceticism is to be allowed in the teaching of the church. There is no place for a group whose members think they are holier than the rest because they refrain from marriage. **Everybody** is to honor marriage. If there were anything tainted about the sexual act in marriage then it would not have been possible for the Scriptures to speak of the *marriage* of the spotless, undefiled Lamb of God (Revelation 19:7) or to represent the relationship of Christ to His church under the figure of marriage (Ephesians 5). Every inkling of asceticism in your counselee, therefore, ought to be stamped out.

Rather, since it is holy, and the sexual act within the proper confines of marriage is right and righteous, **the marriage bed must be unpolluted.** That is true not only because that which is holy ought to be maintained without spot or blemish, free from adultery, but also because the writer warns **God will judge immoral people and adulterers.** Clearly, in our day little attention is paid to this fact even among many Christians. It is time to say something about the fact that God is not going to overlook adultery. While it is possible for adultery to be forgiven (as all other sins except the one against the Holy Spirit) nevertheless, that fact must never be used to make light of sin or to excuse it. God hates adultery. It destroys people and their children and makes light of the holy relationship between

5 Your lifestyle must be free from the love of money; be satisfied with what you have. He Himself has said, **I will never leave you or desert you.**

Himself and His people which is often spoken of in terms of marriage. Be careful, therefore, to strike the proper note of balance between the heinousness of adultery (plenty of which you will encounter in serious counseling) on the one hand, and the mercy and grace of God in forgiving truly repentant adulterers on the other. That balance (found in the Bible itself) is essential for every counselor. The tendency will be to be overly harsh or to be overly lenient. Neither represents the attitude of Christ toward sinners. He never excused sin but, rather, dealt with it for what it is. On the other hand, it was not the repentant sinners of whom He spoke most scathingly, but of the self-righteous religious leaders. Read much on the subject biblically, and you (with Him) will soon be able to strike the right note.

Again, as in Paul's discussion of money in I Timothy 6, the writer here says **Your lifestyle must be free from the love of money; be satisfied with what you have.** Note that it is not money that is wrong. It is the ***love of money*** from which one must refrain. When God blesses any Christian with money, then it is to be both enjoyed (I Timothy 6:17) and used for the blessing of others (I Timothy 6:18). It is not money that is wrong, but the desire to have money—the *love* of money. Contentment (which does not mean a lack of effort to do better at one's work—an excuse sometimes made to cover carelessness or laziness) is to be maintained at all times: **be satisfied with what you have**. Contentment may reach to poverty or to riches, and to everything in between (cf. Philippians 4:11,12).

These exhortations are all very important to counselors. Those who counsel much will use them often. The pages on which you find verses 1-7 will soon become worn from much use. If one has little, to what may he turn for help? Obviously, the Old Testament quotation at the end of verse 5 is intended to bring comfort and encouragement. He must take heart that God has not abandoned him: **I will never leave you or desert you**, He promises. If God has not forsaken him, a counselee may not rightly complain about his state of affairs. God knows what is best for him and will make sure that he is not neglected in receiving it.

The term translated **lifestyle** refers to the turn of one's life, his disposition in making decisions, etc. While one may acquire good things (God often blesses His own with wealth) rightly in God's providence, he may never live for them. He may not *determine* as the goal of life to acquire

6 So we may say with complete confidence,
The Lord is my Helper,
I won't be afraid.
What can man do to me?
7 Remember your leaders who spoke God's message to you; take a look at the results of their behavior and imitate their faith.

---

and enjoy money and what it can buy. He must glorify God and *enjoy Him* regardless of the wealth he acquires—or the lack of it. God must be his riches! Again, there is balance here that must be conveyed to the counselee (perhaps it is best worked out in the passages in I Timothy 6 to which I have referred; see the entire section for additional help, along with comments on it). Many counselees have become extremists. As a result they swing from one wrong extreme to its opposite. Your task is to help them to understand, and to live in the biblical center. To fix one's hope on God rather than on wealth will bring about balance. But always look for extremes as you counsel. Many times the problems a counselee has are due to these unbiblical extremes or—at the very least—are exacerbated by them.

Speaking in a persecution context, he urges **complete confidence** (a key word in Hebrews) in God's help. For fearful counselees, verse 6 is just the ticket: **The Lord is my Helper, I won't be afraid. What can man do to me?** That is a brief section of Scripture that it might be wise to get fearful counselees to memorize and to repeat to themselves whenever they begin to become afraid of what others are doing. Surely, man can do nothing to any of us that is not a part of the Lord's good providence. With that fact why should we be afraid of men? It is God Who guides our lives and protects us. Nothing comes into a believer's life that is greater than the Lord to repel or to see him through victoriously. Even death has been overcome. The believer is able to go victoriously to his death free from its sting (cf. I Corinthians 15:54-57).

Verse 7 (see also v. 17) is important. Today, it is only in rare cases where the **leaders** (elders) of a congregation become models for the flock. Yet that is how it ought to be. There are two problems behind this lack: first, many congregations do not heed the qualifications for leaders found in Titus and I Timothy. So churches ordain those whose lives are not exemplary. Second, members of the congregation would rather model their lives after entertainers on TV, in the movies or in sports. They are the real role models of our youth—tragically! Both problems must be reme-

8 Jesus Christ is the same yesterday, today and forever.
9 Don't be carried away by all sorts of strange teachings. It is a fine thing for the heart to be strengthened by help; foods won't do it. They haven't benefited those who have wandered after them.

---

died. When they are remedied, the verse before us becomes operable.

The **leaders who spoke God's message** we do not know by name, but they were the officers of the church; in particular, the teaching elders (cf. I Timothy 5:17). And the word translated **results** may imply that they have died. So if true, one may see what results their faithful lives have left in their wake. It is not enough to look at those who have long since lived for Christ at another time and place (as useful as that can be). There will always be those who object: "Sure, I can understand how the heroes of faith mentioned in Hebrews 11 were able to serve faithfully to the end, but what about today—things are so different?" Since differences are not really all that great the argument is specious. However, to show that it can be done in the time and place in which one is living it is also good to have *contemporary* examples to which to point. The living elders, or those who have just died (so that the *entire* outcome of their faith with its results may be seen) ought to be persons of this sort. Call on counselees to find help in meeting their problems through **imitating** the **faith** of people like this. Here are the *best* role models for them. "But," people often object, "they were **leaders**; I'm just a simple layman. I don't pretend to any sort of special ability or holiness." In response tell them, "There is nothing about them that is extraordinary. What they did (presuming that their lives are those you'd *want* a counselee to imitate) is exactly what you also may achieve. How can I say that? Because anything worthwhile in their lives, ultimately, was brought about by Jesus Christ; and He is **the same yesterday** (as when He helped those mentioned in chapter 11), **today** (as he has helped the **leaders** of your congregation) and **forever** (He will help you tomorrow, and so long as you need His help)." That is the import of verse 8, which (at first) might seem irrelevant.

In verse 9, there is a further exhortation (one immediately follows another in rapid fire fashion): **Don't be carried away by all sorts of strange teachings.** A Christian counselee who is having trouble is often a sucker for heresy and various other kinds of false doctrine. He is not making it in his life, so he is on the search for something that will solve his problems. He will often open himself wide to almost any kind of weird teaching if it promises relief. He may become like those who run to medical quacks when ordinary medicine seems unable to heal. The problem, however, is not with Biblical remedies for his spiritual ills. While *medical* answers for *physical* illnesses may be lacking, the *Bible* is sufficient to meet every *spiritual* need that a counselee may have. The problem is with him—whether he realizes it or not. Help him to see this and to ferret out the failure. He may have *misunderstood* the biblical solution and, as a result, have taken a wrong turn. He may have done the right thing *wrongly*. He didn't do it long enough or thoroughly enough or in the right manner. Perhaps his *attitude* was wrong. On the other hand, he may have diluted the biblical solution by *mixing* it with non-biblical ones. Often counselees run around to various people, getting all sorts of advice—some from this counselor and some from that one, some from a friend, some from a pastor, etc. The final product is **strange teaching**.

That there would be **all sorts of strange teachings** vying for your counselee's attention and allegiance should not surprise you. The entire New Testament warns about the problem. Counselors therefore must ever be alert to the possibility that their counselees are being influenced by those who ply such trades. Truth is one; error takes many forms. That is understandable. The devil need not be consistent since, from the beginning, he has been a liar. Warn your counselee not to go running around seeking answers of various sorts. Either he remains with you and seeks to follow the Scriptures, or you will cease to counsel him. Don't allow failure to occur as the result of this running around after various so-called solutions, sampling each, getting more and more confused, and then blaming you, the Bible or God for the failure. Any counselor who knowingly allows his counselee to seek solutions from the Bible *and something else* is a fool. That is the message from verse 9[a] for the Christian counselor!

Notice what these **strange teachings** do—they **carry [one] away.** That is to say, they carry him away from Jesus Who is the **same**. He will not alter His teaching from age to age, from place to place. Jesus has the **same** power, mediated through the **same teachings** in every era and every land. What is **strange teaching?** Teaching that is out of accord with the rock-firm teaching of Jesus Christ. What He promised the fathers, the dead leaders, and others, He promises your counselee. What He did for them, He will do for your counselees. What they had to believe, your counselees also must believe. He is the **same**. Anything, then, that removes your counselee from the teachings of Jesus which are the same throughout the ages and throughout the world is a **strange teaching.** That is to say, Jesus' teachings are the standard over against which all teaching

10 We have an altar from which those who serve the tabernacle have no right to eat.
11 The bodies of those animals whose blood is brought into the Holy of Holies by the high priest as a sacrifice for sins are burned outside the camp.

---

must be evaluated. Anything that turns one aside from the teachings of Jesus is to be rejected out of hand.

There are always ascetics (and nutrition nuts) out there who propound doctrines connected with the sorts of food that one may or may not eat. These Hebrew converts had come out of a food-conscious background (kosher food), so they were highly susceptible to influence from doctrines having to do with abstaining from (or participating in) the consumption of categories of food. As Paul did in Romans 14:17 (q.v.), the writer of Hebrews says that it is God's **help** (grace) **that strengthens the heart**; **foods won't do it**. They are barking up the wrong tree if they devote themselves to such solutions to their problems. That their hearts needed firming up in faith is correct, but what they need is more of the **help** that comes from the application of God's truth to their hearts by the Holy Spirit of grace. To **wander after** any **strange teachings** about food would be of no more **benefit** to them than it had been to those who had been sucked in by such **teaching** (v. 9). It is not wrong to talk about false views that will nor **benefit** your counselees; and to warn against them. Indeed, it might be valuable to mention how others who have been attracted to specific teachings that are out of accord with those of Jesus have **not benefited** by them. "If his psychological approach is supposed to be so helpful, then why are John and Mary still going to that counselor after two years?" Or, "How is it that after all his money ran out, they dismissed Bill and he seems no better than before he went?" To evaluate the **benefit** (or lack thereof) if some approach to problem solving, as over against the results of the faith of one's true **leaders** may be useful. It is not an ethical no-no to do such a thing or the writer would not do so here. It is God's ethics that Christian counselors must follow. And part of the ethical code of the Bible involves exposing fakes, false teachers and frauds.

Our **altar** is a nonphysical one. And those who are involved in the now outmoded sacrifices of the temple have **no right to** partake of it (v. 10). Just as the bodies of the sacrifices were dragged outside the camp (in the wilderness) to be burned after sacrificing them (v. 11), Jesus, the last Sacrifice of all, was crucified outside the city of Jerusalem (no crucifixion could occur within the walls of the holy city). Being thus set apart, He has

12 That is why Jesus suffered outside the gate—so that He might set apart
His people by His own blood.
13 Because of this, we must go forth to Him, outside the camp, bearing
His reproach.
14 Here we don't have a city that will remain; rather, we seek the one that
is going to come.
15 So then, through Him we must continually offer a sacrifice of praise to
God, that is, the fruit of our lips, which confess His name.

---

set apart His people by His blood (v. 12). As those who have placed their faith in Him, believers are to leave the camp behind and **go forth to Him, bearing His reproach** (v. 13). The **city** that we leave behind means nothing to us any more. We have departed through the **gate** by which they led Jesus away to His death on the cross. We recognize that Jerusalem (or any present earthly city) is but temporary—it won't **remain** (v. 14). Rather, the city that concerns us is **the one that is going to come** (cf. ch.11; 12:22). We no longer have anything to do with earthly cities, altars or sacrifices. They were all but types and shadows of the reality which we have found in Christ. So what is our sacrifice today? Verse 15 tells us: **So then, through Him, we must continually offer a sacrifice of praise to God, that is, the fruit of our lips, which confess His name.** The **sacrifices** that we offer **continually** are sacrifices of song and prayer, as from the very same **lips** that **confess** that Jesus is Lord and Savior we **praise** Him for sending His Son into the world to save sinners like us (v. 15). There is here a complete repudiation of all material worship in favor of worship in Spirit and in truth (cf. John 4:24). Acceptance of any legalistic practices connected with physical aspects of worship are to be dismissed out of hand as you deal with counselees. Some have been taught ideas about clothing, hair styles, types of musical scores that may or may not be used, etc. Sometimes they may become so concerned about such things that they are driven to the point of distraction and utter frustration as the list of items to be observed (or avoided) grows and grows. Concentration on these things can consume one's time and energy, so that the true sacrifices of which verse 15 speaks are virtually ignored. In such cases, try to move the counselee from the emphasis on the material, the tangible and the visible to those items that are of true value in the eyes of God. The kind of worshippers for which He is **looking to worship Him** (John 4:24) know what is important; they worship as the writer of Hebrews prescribes in verses 15 and 16.

Consider verse 16 which amplifies what true, spiritual worship is

16 Don't forget to do good and to share; it is such sacrifices as these that please God.
17 Obey your leaders and submit to them. They are keeping watch over your lives as men who will have to give an account. Obey so that they may do this with joy and not as a burden, since that wouldn't be to your advantage.

---

like: **Don't forget to do good and share; it is such sacrifices as these that please God.** How utterly different from the material, physical, earthly thinking of so many today! Counselors will do well to focus the thinking of counselees on these things, rather than to become embroiled in whether or not a given practice is right or wrong. Many times the "weightier matters" are lost in the shuffle. Here is what pleases God. It is not the earthly and the physical rightness or wrongness of certain practices that is of importance, but rather, the way in which one conducts his life before others and in the sight of God.

According to these two verses, worship is not something done in a Sunday service; it is a way of serving God by living as He orders. It is a matter of **doing good and sharing** what one has with other Christians in need. Often, the great concern over rituals and other materialistic matters having to do with worship as a gathering of the saints, is but a cover-up for failure to praise God and show love to one's neighbor by doing good to him and sharing what you have to alleviate his want. Be sure to inquire about the love one shows to God and his neighbor (the two emphases of these two verses) whenever the counselee raises grave concern about materialistic matters of worship.

The matter of **leadership** once more emerges (in vv. 17,24). The writer is not usurping their place as leaders of the flock that God has put under their shepherdly care. Rather he urges the reader to **Obey your leaders and submit to them.** That believers should do so today as well goes without saying. Indeed, so much so does it "go without saying" that it has *gone without saying*—it seems that no one is *saying* it any more! How seldom does the authority of the church have any meaning. Yet it is important to hear this injunction afresh. Why should counselees be urged to **obey** and **submit** to their **leaders**? First, and foremost, God says so. That should be sufficient. But in grace to weak believers like us, He explains: **They are keeping watch over your lives as men who will have to give an account. Obey so that they may do this with joy and not as a burden, since that wouldn't be to your advantage.** Why? You must

18 Pray for us. We are convinced that we have a clear conscience; we want to behave well in everything.

---

obey and submit because some day those who attempted to mold your life by their teaching and counseling will be able to report that they were successful. That would be a **joy** for both them and for you. On the other hand, if they are continually **burdened** by your resistance to truth due to your sinful rebellion against the authority of God invested in them, that would not be a pleasure to them when they report on your life as a believer, nor would it **be to your advantage.** Their report would be negative, and you would have to answer to God for it. Today, counselees hardly even know that there is authority vested in the leaders of the church. The fact must be retaught. And pastoral counselors must exercise that authority when counseling. They may, with profit, refer to this verse to enforce the biblical injunctions that they urge the counselee to follow.

Authority is not authoritarianism. The latter unnecessarily asserts itself. Moreover, it makes up its own standards, rather then depending on those set forth in the Bible. The demand to submit and obey the whims of a counselor is ***not*** what the verse is talking about. It is referring to those things that are undoubtedly the understanding of the eldership of a congregation. No one elder may *command* counselees to do what the rest have not agreed that the Bible teaches. He may suggest, urge or persuade, but not *command* so as to demand obedience and submission. Opinions, and what all the leaders agree is a biblical truth one must obey, ought to be distinguished. Your ability to command obedience is limited by what the Scriptures say directly or what the elders in the church believe to be the good and necessary application of general biblical principles.

In verse 18 we reach the winding down of the epistle. The writer urges: **Pray for us.** That is something every counselor may assign as homework. It does not weaken your position with your counselee to ask him to do so. Indeed, it ought to strengthen it by showing him that you are dependent on the Lord for help in the counseling sessions that will follow. Moreover, if he fails to pray, and things don't go as they ought, he knows one reason for the failure must be laid at his doorstep. In other words, he assumes responsibility for the counseling rather than laying all the responsibility on you. From the outset, he sees that his part in the success of counseling is to bring the Lord into the picture through prayer and that if he does so, he must go to the Lord in a proper manner. That may require repentance and/or humility on his part.

19 I urge you even more to do this so that I may be restored to you sooner.

20 Now the God of peace, Who brought again from the dead our Lord Jesus, the great Shepherd of the sheep, by the blood of the eternal covenant,

---

The writer is convinced that his own **conscience is clear;** that he **wants to behave well in everything—**(v. 18). That is to say, he wants to do all the right things toward them. He wants them to know that all his exhortations, warnings, explanations, encouragement is aboveboard. He has no hidden agenda. What they have read is what they get. He is straightforward and honest. He is not writing for any subtle, unmentioned purpose. Not a bad point to make with counselees. Of course, one must be sure that when he says so, he is telling the truth. Counselors may have hidden agendas. Be sure your conscience is clear whenever you counsel.

Also pray that **I may be restored to you sooner.** He wants to come to see them. Obviously letters are not as efficient as the personal contact of the writer with those to whom he writes. He is anxious to come to forestall whatever his letter does not in the possible drift of some (or many) back into Judaism. Pray that I can come sooner.

Now in verses 20 and 21 we arrive at that magnificent and extremely valuable benediction we so often use in church services—but which so few take the time to analyze. It is full of rich content. Listen to it: He addresses God as **the God of Peace.** Counselees seek peace—of various sorts. All true peace comes from God. He is the sole Source of *shalom,* the Hebrew word for peace. It meant not only cessation of hostilities, but all the positive, good things that one can picture in terms of tranquillity and prosperity. Its symbol was "every man under his own vine and fig tree." That says it all. It is this blessing (figuratively, if not literally) that flows from God as its Fountain.

This God also is the One Who **brought again from the dead our Lord Jesus**. That is to say, He has power to do things. If counselees doubt it, but think Freud or Rogers' systems can do more for them than Christian counseling, remind them of the fact. Ask, "Could Jung or Skinner bring anyone from the dead?"

And **by the blood of the eternal covenant** (that is, by the **blood** of Jesus by which the **eternal covenant** was established—see I Corinthians 11:25). He has become **the great Shepherd of the sheep**. He is the one who does all the things that Psalm 23 ascribes to Him as Shepherd, and

21 equip you with every good thing for doing His will, producing in us what pleases Him, through Jesus Christ, to Whom be glory forever and ever. Amen.

22 I urge you, brothers, put up with my word of encouragement; I have written you only a short letter.

He possesses all the characteristics of the good shepherd detailed in John 10. In dealing with uncertain counselees, who wonder whether Christian counseling can cut it, remind them that it is in Christian counseling alone that this shepherding activity of the Lord Jesus is manifested. Then read the Psalm and the Johanine passages, ticking off all the things that a shepherd does for his sheep. It is important to see that since the Lord is the Shepherd of the sheep, the sheep may truthfully say "I shall not lack." What more could one want?

Now in verse 21, what the writer affirms is most important: **he wishes for Jesus Christ to equip** His people **with every good thing for doing His will.** Don't miss that! The sufficiency that is affirmed in it is crucial. Jesus is the One Who **equips** His people to **do His will.** Such equipping will not be found anywhere else. The Bible contains the equipment necessary to do what God requires of us (cf. II Timothy 3:16,17). And don't fail to note that when Jesus equips, He provides **every good thing** that is needed to do God's **will.** There is no need to supplement what He provides in the Bible or what He provides by His Spirit empowering one to understand and fulfill that will as it is expressed therein. Where is eclecticism in light of verse 21?

He **produces in us what pleases Him**. That is the goal of counseling, isn't it? Don't we want to see counselees developing within them those desires and abilities to please God as well as the understanding of what it is that does so? Well, here we see how that takes place—whenever it does. It is God Who does it in us (cf. Philippians 2:13). And it is all **through Jesus Christ, to Whom be glory forever and ever.** To which he lends his assent: **Amen.** Do *you*? Do the practices of your counseling, in addition to the words from your lips, all utter a loud **Amen?**

By our standards, Hebrews is anything but **a short letter** (v. 22). But the writer believed it to be such. He reiterates the purpose of the letter: it is a **word of encouragement.** Sometimes when warning (such as that which we encountered in chapters 6 and 10) is given, people think that you are doing anything but **encouraging.** Moreover, they fail to understand that strong rebuke of the sort found in the latter part of chapter 5 is

23 You should understand that our brother Timothy has been released, with whom I shall see you if he comes soon.
24 Greet all your leaders, and all the saints. Those from Italy greet you.
25 May help be with all of you. Amen.

---

also a means of encouragement. They see only the positive elements of encouragement as such. This is a failure of modern thinking. Counselors, who want to encourage, need to understand the full breadth of encouragement that is set forth in this letter. It is true that a positive note is struck almost always after the word of rebuke or warning. But that doesn't lessen the fact that negative comments, handled rightly, also may lend **encouragement**.

He wants them to **put up with** his words, recognizing that they are not all easy words to accept. But understanding their necessity, and applying them to their situation, they would find them easy to put up with because his words would lead them into the paths of righteousness both for God's Name's sake and for their benefit. There is much for both the counselor and the counselee to **put up with** in the counseling process. All is certainly not sweetness and light. Sin must be exposed, repented of and dealt with. Problems must be faced and painful situations probed. Hard things must be done to bring about forgiveness and reconciliation. Discipline must be exercised in order to replace sinful patterns with righteous ones. Counselees must **put up with** rebuke and warning and counselors with the failure of counselees to listen to or to appropriate their counsel. If counseling is to be described adequately, the words **put up with** probably would appear prominently in the description.

Finally, a note about **Timothy's release** from prison (in Rome?), his possible appearance with the writer on his next visit to the church, and a greeting to the **leaders.** And there also must be words of greeting from the **saints in Italy as well.** As all the writers of the New Testament did, here the writer is helping to cement relationships between the Christians of various congregations; something every counselor also must be zealous to do.

It has been a long journey through this **short letter.** If you want to characterize the letter as a whole, you might say that it sketches the portrait of a doubting, swaying "Christian" who may become a deserter. It is a plea to him to turn back. The methods used to persuade him to do so are varied and many. They have been observed as we have stopped on our journey to look at each of them. They should all be found in the counselor's bag, and he should become skillful in the use of each. There is no more valuable Book to which to turn to forestall the defection of a professed Christian from the faith. Keep that in mind the next time you meet the problem in counseling. And of course, there is so much more. The study of this Book has proved a great blessing to me; I hope you have found it so too.

Introduction to I PETER

For some time I had said in pastors' conferences, "I suspect that there are many of you here who know more about what psychologists say concerning suffering than you know about what Peter says in his first epistle." Then I began to reflect: "How much do you know about I Peter, Adams?" And apart from the normal elements every biblical scholar knows, I concluded, "You really don't know very much, do you?" So I sat down and began an in-depth study of this magnificent treatise on how to handle unjust suffering.

That study led me to write a simple book on I Peter for preachers entitled *Trust and Obey*. Those two words summed up, I thought, the thrust of the Book: in suffering you entrust yourself to a faithful Creator and you go on obeying, doing good, regardless of what others do or say (see I Peter 4:19). This helpful letter, I concluded at length, is packed full of essential information not only for preaching but also for counseling. But what I said in *Trust and Obey* was geared mostly to preaching (not that the two are far removed from each other; they are two aspects of the same ministry of the Word—one public, the other private). Here I approach the book afresh from the perspective of Christian counseling. And as I have once more delved into the depths of Peter's work, I am all the more impressed with its practical usefulness. If I Peter could be helpful in preaching, it can be doubly so in counseling.

CHAPTER 1

1 Peter, an apostle of Jesus Christ, to those who are scattered about as refugees in Pontus, Galatia, Cappadocia, Asia and Bithynia,

---

Peter was not Simon's original name. He was renamed "Peter" (meaning "Rock") by the Lord Jesus Himself (John 1:42). His intention in doing so was to turn the weak, impetuous, vacillating man into a faithful, solid apostle. And as one can see from the content of this letter, that is precisely what Jesus did. The name Peter in itself is an encouragement to counselors, and ought to become the same to their counselees. If Peter, as we see him in the gospels, could be transformed by Christ into the Peter who wrote this letter, there is hope for every Christian, regardless of his foibles or weaknesses. Let us turn to it then with every confidence that there is help to be found.

As I said in the brief introduction, I Peter is a treatise on suffering and how to endure it. Many counselees suffer. Often, however, they suffer not only from what others have unjustly done to them but because of their own actions in which they bring suffering upon themselves. While Peter mentions the latter (2:19ff.; 3:17), his thrust is upon how to deal with suffering that comes upon one *unjustly*—especially because he has become a Christian and is living for Christ. Nevertheless, *repentant* believers who have brought about their own misery, can learn—even then—much about how to deal with suffering.

Throughout his letter, Peter speaks of elements of Christianity as **valuable** (KJ "Precious"). Because of his denial of his Lord, Peter came close to losing all he had. In his repentance (cf. John 21) he came to appreciate how valuable his Savior is and those things that he had in Him. The repetition of the word valuable is not incidental. It is central to what Peter is saying. His point in encouraging refugees is that what they have now in Christ is far more valuable than what they left behind. That point is important for counselors to emphasize to counselees who have been forced to leave jobs, homes, friends, etc., because of their newfound faith. Whatever it may be, nothing can compare in value with what one receives when he trusts Jesus Christ as his Savior.

The letter has all the appearance of a general epistle, written to many Jewish-Christian churches in order to encourage believers not to forget the precious elements of their faith in times of trouble. It is by remembering these (Peter was the man who forgot—until he heard the cock crow) that they will be able to remain steadfast and true.

He is an **apostle**. An apostle was "one sent off" by another on a mission for him. The term signifies both the work to be done and its representative character. The Greek *apostello* and the Latin *mitto*, from which the word "missionary" is derived, are exact equivalents. The twelve apostles were the first missionaries of the church. They were missionaries *extraordinaire*, possessing great authority, power and ability provided in grace by their Lord to found the church (cf. Ephesians 2:20; John 20:21-23). Along with non-apostolic men, called "prophets," unlike later missionaries, apostles were the recipients of revelation (Ephesians 3:5). In a lesser sense, Epaphroditus was "sent off" by the church at Philippi on a mission of mercy to Paul. He was an apostle, but not in the sense of the "twelve" (a special designation: cf., Mark 6:7; Luke 8:1; 9:1, etc.) whose task was to found the church and leave for all time a deposit of revelatory truth (Jude 3; II Timothy 1:12-14; 2:2) from which the church might be guided in all its activities. Today we possess what none had at the time Peter wrote: a full and completed New Testament canon with all that is necessary for us to know in order to minister faithfully. Because what they had was incomplete (the canon was still under composition), direct revelation was a necessity. Now it no longer is.

Peter was chosen by the Lord to be the apostle to the Jews (cf. Galatians 2:7,8). And it was to them that he writes. Persecution, present and imminent, was what these Jews, **scattered** about the Mediterranean world were facing. He is concerned to **strengthen** them (as His Lord had required him to: Luke 22:31,32) by his epistle so that they will be able to endure.

Jewish Christians were **scattered** throughout the Roman world. Those to whom Peter writes, in particular, seem to have been living in five of the provinces of the Roman empire. The word "scattered" was a term used of those who, like seed as it was broadcast by the sower, were "sown" in various regions. The term was first used in this way by Jews of the dispersion. Here, Peter, writing to converted Jews, uses the very familiar word to make his point.

While remaining adamant about those terms that are already technical or semi-technical in the New Testament, the Christian counselor should not hesitate to use other nontechnical terms (like this one) that communicate. Some today have gone too far, decrying any use of words like "counsel" or "problem," etc., as if to be totally biblical, one may not use them. Well, if Peter doesn't hesitate to use a word that communicates to his readers because of their background, so long as it does not distort biblical truth, you can too. I am not talking about psychological jargon, which, when used communicates all the wrong things. But you can become so "pure" in your language that you communicate only to a small, esoteric group who are already convinced of what you say; soon you find yourself preaching to the choir.

The word had already been used in Acts 8:4 to refer to those Christians who were **scattered** by persecution as they fled Jerusalem. In God's providence that scattering had resulted in widespread dissemination of the gospel. While that initial scattering drove them to Judea and Samaria, Peter is probably speaking of subsequent scatterings as well. From Acts and the epistles of Paul, we see that wherever Christians mixed with unconverted Jews there was persecution.

The word **refugees** is an important one. It immediately speaks of displaced persons who, enduring sufferings, are exposed to all the exigencies of living in a foreign land without normal rights and privileges. The fact that Peter considers his readers refugees indicates that they were in trouble because of their adherence to the Christian faith; they are refugees from their Palestinian homeland. Today, where there is war or famine, etc., we see on TV streams of refugees leaving for what they hope (but rarely find) to be better conditions elsewhere. Picture those to whom Peter writes that way. These Christians, to whom Peter writes, in addition to the indignities and outrages commonly inflicted on refugees, in general, were suffering because of their faith.

In every Bible-believing congregation, there are Christians who have had to leave jobs, perhaps congregations and even communities for the sake of their convictions. People like that are in mind as Peter writes. True, they are not scattered about as refugees in the same sense as those in Peter's day. Yet much of the same spirit and many similar problems may be found among such people. Dislodged from their foundations, uprooted because of job changes, etc., from what they thought was security, they need your ministry. Many have difficulties that are akin to those experienced by Peter's readers. Therefore, I Peter is a valuable source of help for them.

But the literal use of the word **refugees** does not preclude its less literal denotation. Peter, himself, seems to play on the connotations of this word in 2:11 and 12. Here the earthly state is considered transient as over against the heavenly one. The Christian is a resident alien, living for a while, here and there, while bound on his journey to the heavenly homeland.

2 who are chosen according to the foreknowledge of God the Father, that by the Spirit's sanctification you may obey and be sprinkled by the blood of Jesus Christ. May help and peace to you be increased!

It is important to understand that Peter, writing in these terms, communicates with those who (doubtless) thought of themselves in exactly that way. He thereby makes known to them the fact that he understands their plight. What he has to say is not the word of some idealistic novice; it is the mature thought of one who, from the outset, makes it clear that he recognizes where they are coming from. It is a message from one who himself has suffered and will continue to do so. Often, in dealing with counselees, it is wise to take a minute or two to let them know that you, too, understand what they are experiencing. Dropping a word in passing that indicates that fact (as Peter does here) is usually more effective than coming right out and saying so. Even the existence of previously prepared and printed handouts that pertain to problems people have tends to give confidence of this sort.

Verse two, in structure as well as in thought, is intimately conjoined with verse one. Suffering refugees, scattered from their earthly homes, are here declared to be God's **eternally chosen people.** From eternity past they have been **foreknown by God the Father** as a select group, especially dear to Him. This designation of God as Father, whenever it appears in the Bible, is a warm and strong one. It speaks of provision, care, protection, disciplined training, etc. That is exactly what displaced persons need to know—they have not been forsaken by their heavenly Father. Wherever they might go, He would be there to help and provide. The persecution they experience is not a manifestation of His anger, but is calculated to bless them and the elect worldwide.

By transcending the immediate, Peter brings the eternal dimension to bear upon their plight: they were **chosen according to the foreknowledge of God the Father**. He knew and chose them from all eternity **according to** His own **wise** decision. And He knew (not by looking into the future to discover it, but because He had planned it) who they would be and what would transpire in their lives. All that was taking place was according to His **foreknowledge** (i.e., according to what God knew would happen since it was His purpose to bring it to pass). Nothing about their present situation was a surprise to God. Everything is right on schedule, coming to pass as He determined it would.

How important it is to understand that God controls the present from the past. These believers are thereby assured that all will work out well. God the Father chose them to suffer in order to glorify His Son. That is the crux of the matter. And that is the crux of the matter for the counselee who complains that he "can't understand why he must suffer so much, so long and so painfully." He has forgotten the eternal dimension of his life. He is a part of God's great plan to demonstrate His grace, mercy and wrath (see my book, *The Grand Demonstration*). Until and unless he grasps the meaning of it all—that there is a larger dimension to his life than what he is momentarily confronting—he will fail to bring suffering into the proper perspective. Help him to do so. If, however, you also fail to understand God's eternal ways with men, you will be of little help and may only further confuse the counselee.

Part of the scattering, in God's providence, was to spread the gospel across the known world. As they went from Palestine to various places, they took the gospel message with them. Those who were faithful started little churches. Local citizens were converted and enlarged their congregations. In this way too, God was working out His plan. Has God uprooted a counselee from a place, a job, a church? Then He is moving in his life. That is something to get excited about. Let him take advantage of the fact.

These refugees had received the most important gift in history: they were forgiven and cleansed of their sin **by the blood of Jesus Christ sprinkled on them.** And that resulted in their **sanctification**. To be sanctified means to be set apart by God's Spirit as one who belongs to Him. God chose them, called them and set them apart from others for His own use. The word sanctification here is not used in its theological sense (as the *process* of more and more being set apart from sin to righteousness) but in a more definitive sense that views the Christian as set apart from the world to God. How wonderful to know that one has been set apart to God by the blood of Jesus Christ! But that also looks toward something else—obedience (**that...you may obey**).

Many are baffled over the purpose and plan of God certain from all eternity, yet requiring human responsibility. As you can see, Peter does not fail to couple the two into an inseparable whole. The elect (chosen ones) are only fulfilling the plan of God as He has determined it, it is true. But God planned not only the ends; He also planned the means. And the means that He adopted is to bring about His purposes (exactly as He planned them), not through automatons, but through the choices and decisions made by responsible human beings. Peter often blends predetermination and human responsibility (cf. Acts 2:23; 4:27,28). Through (and

3 Let us praise the God and Father of our Lord Jesus Christ, Who according to His great mercy regenerated us to a living hope through the resurrection of Jesus Christ from the dead,

---

not apart from) their actions, the predetermined results would occur. Human responsibility, itself, is part of the divine plan. Christians are called on to obey. Never let a counselee throw out that old line, "If it's all planned anyway, it hardly matters what I do." Your counselee was saved **to obey** (see also Ephesians 2:9,10). While the eternal choosing of God should assure the counselee that nothing is out of God's control, the flip side of that truth—his responsibility to obey—in every way keeps him where he belongs: on the hook.

Already up front Peter has called these suffering Christians to obedience. Suffering, like the eternal purpose of God, does not let anyone off the hook. Indeed, one of the things Peter will emphasize throughout is that suffering all the more requires obedience. Since he will say more about this later, I shall simply mention the fact here. But it is a fundamental principle to be gleaned from the book that one of the ways in which God expects one to suffer rightly is by continuing to do what is right in His eyes. Unlike the sniveling drivel palmed off by many counselors, the response to suffering that God (through Peter) requires is robust.

Help (grace) and **peace** is precisely what every suffering counselee needs. He will receive it from the Lord, not generate it on his own. And all Christians already have, to some extent, both of these qualities. Mainly, when suffering comes, they need to be **increased**. One of the values of suffering, therefore, is the joy of experiencing greater blessings from God. Most Christians do not think of suffering as Peter did. They need to be brought back to square one, made to rethink the purposes of suffering and how to face it. They must rid themselves of a purely horizontal, self-centered view of suffering; help them to bring the vertical God-centered view of Peter into full focus.

In these initial verses of the letter, Peter is setting forth the resources, the knowledge and the hope necessary to endure suffering in a way that is pleasing and honoring to God. To suffering refugees, in the midst of trials and difficulties of every sort, here is the goal that Peter sets forth: **Let us praise the God and Father of our Lord Jesus Christ** (v. 3). That is the objective for counselors—to help suffering saints to come to the place where they praise God in the midst of suffering. But to help them to avoid the complaining, whining, self-pitying response that so many make when

4 for an incorruptible, unspotted and unfading inheritance that has been kept in the heavens for you

---

(even the slightest sort of) suffering comes their way is often a major task. What counsel will you give in order to help bring this off? Well, the same sort of counsel that Peter gives; that's what. First, all that he has said in verses 1 and 2 are aimed at helping the suffering saint to focus his thinking on the larger picture. He is not the center of the universe; God is. And as Peter indicates, this moment in time when one suffers is a piece of the grand puzzle of God's scheme of things, a darker piece that gives contrast to that which is bright and cheerful. By the eternal plan he is involved in something bigger than himself; and some day he will look on the completed puzzle with awe and joy. Believing and understanding that, why would anyone complain?

But there is more. Suffering saints should ever keep in mind that which lies ahead in the future for them. Peter gives us a glimpse of what that is. The **Father regenerated us to a living hope** of **an inheritance that is reserved** for us, His children. This inheritance is certainly not by right, but by the **mercy** of God. Compassion is one thing; it is important and felt by one for another. But mercy is greater; it is compassion with feet. It is compassion in action. It is compassion that does something about the plight of the one toward whom that compassion is felt. Out of His mercy (and that of His Son, **the Lord Jesus Christ**) God the Father has prepared a heavenly, eternal inheritance for His children. It is that inheritance that he now describes in order to generate **hope** among those who had little to hope for in this world.

What is this hope and what is it like? Well, to begin with it is **a living hope.** What does that mean? It means that the hope (which in Scripture means "expectation," an "anticipation" of something that is certain, because it is based on the promises of God, but has not yet occurred) a Christian has is **vital**. It has impact on daily living now That is the kind of hope Peter has in mind. But he goes on: the inheritance we expect is **incorruptible, unspotted and unfading**. That is to say, nothing can go wrong with it. All of the things that can happen to destroy an earthly inheritance are incapable of doing harm to the heavenly one. Indeed, as he amplifies: it is **kept in the heavens** for them. God Himself is protecting it. Obviously then the inheritance is secure.

"But," says someone, "What of the heir? Can't something go wrong with him?" No. He also is **guarded by God's power through faith for**

5 who are guarded by God's power through faith for a salvation that is ready to be revealed in the last time.

---

salvation. Nothing can go wrong with the heir because the power of God enables him to persevere in faith to the end—until salvation is completed. There is no power greater than God's (cf. Paul's way of putting this in Romans 8:38,39). Therefore *he* also is secure.

Upon what is this promised inheritance based? As Peter says in verse 3, it is based on Christ's **resurrection from the dead**. If He died and rose again; so will we. If He entered into His inheritance so shall we (Romans 8:17). We are fellow-heirs with Christ. Our inheritance, therefore, is as certain to come to us as His was to come to Him. And we were enabled to enter into this hope by **regeneration**. Regeneration is the act of God by which He gives life to dead souls to enable them to understand and believe. This He did for His own so that they could have a vital hope while suffering in this world. They were given life to believe that they would be saved from eternal hell and for **a salvation ready to be revealed in the last time**. One is saved from the penalty of his sins when he believes (he is justified by faith). He is being saved from the power of sin throughout his life as a believer (that is sanctification). He will be saved from the very presence of sin in the future at death or the coming of Christ (that is known as glorification). It is all of this, but particularly the last of the three aspects of **salvation**, of which Peter is speaking in verse 5.

Refugees know first hand that the things of this world do not last. That there is only uncertainty connected with an earthly inheritance. So these words, together with a careful explanation of the characteristics of the eternal inheritance, is of great importance to them. As indeed it should be to your counselees who have lost everything in a financial transaction that has gone sour, when the body deteriorates beyond the ability of physicians to repair it or when they lose a child in a tragic automobile collision with a drunken driver. This inheritance is indestructible and secure.

If a person wants to become a Nouthetic Counselor but says that he isn't sure about the doctrine of the perseverance of the saints, how can he counsel? Obviously this is but one of the many passages that teach that truth. Is he qualified? How could he be? He surely does not have a vital hope; he must lack the security that hope generates and, therefore, he has little to offer saints who have lost everything in this world. The best he can offer is a hope-so hope which, when carefully examined, becomes a

6 You should be glad about this even if now you may have to be sad because of many kinds of trials

hope-against-hope. If one wants to be saved, according to the doctrine of uncertainty espoused by many, he must persevere to the end by his own determination to do so. Knowing the human heart, with all its traitorous inclinations, on that basis how could anyone expect to be saved? The inheritance may be secured in the heavens, but the heir is not preserved through God-supplied faith (cf. Ephesians 2:8). He must "keep himself saved." Here Peter says that this faith leading to the reception of the God-preserved inheritance (salvation) is **kept** till the **last time** when it will be fully revealed in all of its majestic splendor. At that time, the suffering will cease, its complete meaning will be revealed and its purpose will have been achieved. Can one who is uncertain about all of this counsel effectively? Not if there are those who want an explanation for suffering and a clear picture of the denouement of all things. To what does he point them, if he does not believe in the perseverance of the saints by the power of God? To an uncertain salvation partly dependent on what God has done and partly dependent on what the believer does? The chain always breaks at its weak link; is no stronger than that one link. Salvation, if dependent on both God and man in any ultimate sense, has a link so weak that there is no hope. Peter does not focus on what the believer must do, but on what God has already done. His concern is not subjective, self-oriented; he points to the objective work of Christ and what He has achieved for the Christian. There is no hope in subjectivism (which is the inevitable result of the doctrine of the insecurity of the saints). There is no hope in one's self. All hope, to be vital, must be in the work of God—from start (regeneration) to finish (glorification). To help those who have lost much, it is necessary, then, to be able to hold up a certain hope—as Peter does. There is no place for fudging here. Peter doesn't; neither should you.

We turn now to a remarkable statement: **You should be glad about this even if now you may have to be sad because of many kinds of trials** (v. 6). How can one be **glad** when he is **sad**? Aren't these contrary one to another? These are the sorts of questions you will receive in counseling all the time. It is of importance, then, to pursue the matter a bit. Peter doesn't say be glad *that* you are sad. The Scriptures nowhere teach any such thing. The miseries that are the consequence of sin are always recognized in Scripture as such—miseries. Even here, it is apparent that sin (yours or that of others) leads to sadness. Peter has no hesitation in speaking of Christians rightly being sad. After all, Jesus cried (out loud) at the grave of Lazarus, his friend. The consequences of sin sadden.

Well, then, what does Peter mean? He is saying that as the Christian contemplates all that he anticipates in the future [**this**] he should rejoice, though now the trials he endures bring sadness. How would a hope-so future bring any such thing? Romans 8:18-25 neatly parallels the word of Peter. Gladness can coexist beside sadness. A mother may be glad that her son is moving from town to take a good position in a fine company, but at the same time, she will be saddened to lose him. The idea here is not that of Christians becoming grinning sufferers who go around saying "praise the Lord anyway." The **many kinds of trials** that occur bring real sadness (that at times may be excruciating) which it is never wrong to properly express. But contemplating his hope of a future in heaven that is quite different at the same time brings one gladness.

One difficulty in our day is that the evangelical church has become so this-worldly, not only in adopting the values of those around it, but (as a result) rarely speaking about the world to come, that there is little emphasis on the inheritance of the saints. There is need, therefore, for the counselor to revitalize that hope in the mind of the counselee who has lost all hope. He does so by having him contemplate anew what it was he was saved from, but (especially) what he was saved *to*.

But this rejoicing in hope is not merely a privilege; the counselee is required to be glad in the midst of **trials** of every sort (there are no exceptions). "But, pastor, you don't know my problem. If you only had to contend with _____________..." is what you hear all the time. The response? It is clear: "In any sort of trial, you may be glad if you have fixed your hope on the inheritance that is yours in heaven." How often do you point your counselee to the heavenly home, and all that is his, ready to be revealed? If you do in a superficial manner, offhandedly, no wonder it doesn't help. But if you spell it out for him—as Peter does—he can get something of a grasp on what it will be like. He can rightly contrast it with the temporary trials he is suffering.

There is nothing in the passage about being glad that one is persecuted, tried or otherwise misused. That is not the idea. There are two things to make clear to your counselee: in trials 1) he should be glad for the opportunity to demonstrate the vitality of his hope in Christ; 2) the trial should remind him all the more of the glorious hope that is ready and waiting for him in the heavens.

In verse 7, **the testing of one's faith**, moreover, is a **valuable** thing, says Peter. More so than **perishable gold, which is tested by fire**. What

7 so that the testing of your faith, much more valuable than perishable gold (yet it is tested by fire), may be found to praise and glorify and honor Jesus Christ at His revelation.
8 You haven't seen Him, but you love Him, you don't now look on Him but you believe on Him, and you rejoice with inexpressible and glorious delight,
9 receiving that which is the purpose of your faith—the salvation of your souls.

---

does that mean? Well, it must have something to do with that about which the rest of the verse speaks: **that it may be found to praise and glorify and honor Jesus Christ at His revelation**. But what is the connection between the two? Simply this: as gold is tested by fire, in order to eliminate all the impurities from it, so too Peter wishes for his readers to have faith that at Christ's coming will shine brightly free from all worldly admixture. If gold, though less important, is tested to bring out its true value, so much more is this true of genuine faith in Christ. Trials purify; that is another reason to be glad when trials come. One's faith is tested as to its genuineness and, when found to be so, is strengthened by it. That is an important insight into trial and testing. Every counselee needs to hear it. But of greatest importance, you should make clear, is the fact that this purifying process is not primarily for his sake, but so his faith may shine to the glory of Christ at **His revelation**. On that day when He returns, He will be revealed for all that He is—the great God and Savior (cf. Titus 2:13). His return is *His* day, and only secondarily the day of the counselee. Too many Christians have been taught only to look forward to what they receive at the coming of Christ. That is sad. The Day of the Lord is the day of His revelation. He will be given all praise and honor and glory in that day. And you will bask and rejoice in the glory that is shown to be His. That, in substance, is what verse 8 has to say. **You've never seen Jesus**, even though you **love** and **believe** in Him. But now in the midst of trials, **rejoice with inexpressible and glorious delight** as you know that you will in the day of His return.

The remarkable event will also mark the time when you will enter into the fullness of **salvation** (v. 9)—a secondary reason for rejoicing. After all, that is **the purpose of** your faith. In that day your souls will be saved. In Scripture, the **soul** is the spirit thought of *in relationship to* the body, not apart of it. So, this looks forward to the time when a new body in a thoroughly purified soul will be the substance of your **salvation**.

In verse 10 Peter observes that it is a genuine privilege to know about

10 It was concerning this salvation that the prophets who prophesied about the grace that would be yours searched and sought,

---

the **salvation** of which he speaks. Even the Old Testament **prophets**, who were writing about it, failed to understand with any fullness **what** it was about which they were writing or **when** it would take place (cf. Daniel 12:8). They knew that there were **sufferings** that the Messiah would undergo (e.g., Isaiah 53; Psalm 22) and that there were **glories that would follow**, but to put it all together was difficult. So they **searched** [the Scriptures] and **sought** out answers. They knew a great outpouring of **grace** would take place and, presumably, discovered answers to some things they wanted to know, but there was much that did not come clear until Jesus actually came, died, rose and ascended to the heavenly throne, and received all power in heaven and earth, as the God-man. Note carefully, that they did not write on their own: it was **the Spirit of Christ in them** (that is, the Spirit that testified about Christ; cf., Revelation 1:2) Who empowered them to prophesy in word and in writing.

The inspiration of the Scriptures could not be more clearly taught (though since Peter does not expressly teach it here but only alludes to it, the doctrine is all the more established as something that the early church took for granted)! Now if inspired prophets searched the Scriptures for information and understanding of God's ways with men so, surely, should we. One problem that many counselees have is their failure to search the Bible, seeking out answers to their questions (cf. Acts 17:11; Daniel 12:4[b]). Many have tried and failed—and given up. Perhaps that is because they do not know how to do so. In order to help counselees (and others) to learn how to use the Scriptures in a practical way I have written a book, *What to do on Thursday.* In this book I set forth a method that you can recommend to your counselees In addition, there is a workbook entitled *Four Weeks with God and your Neighbor* that is designed to encourage counselees to begin studying the Bible along with counseling. It is important to have counselees pray and study their Bibles regularly. That is why I have made these books available. But whether you use these or not, by all means *get your counselee studying the Word regularly* as early in counseling as possible. Not only is it right to do so, and not only is it beneficial for him, but it will help immensely in counseling. As a background for all you do in counseling, if a counselee is regularly studying and praying, he will be thinking about God every day. That is important to all that you will say and do in sessions themselves. So check out the present practices of

11 trying to find out to what or what period the Spirit of Christ in them pointed when He testified beforehand about the sufferings of Christ and the glories that would follow them.
12 To them it was revealed that they were serving not themselves but you in these things that now have been declared to you through those who, by the Holy Spirit sent from heaven, announced the good news to you, things that the angels desire to look into.

---

your counselees in this regard and if you find there is a serious lack here (evidenced either in spotty study and prayer or in not knowing how to get anything out of it) then help him to set up a disciplined practice right away. Be sure that you monitor him by asking in every session thereafter how it is going. Don't get sidetracked on a discussion of the material he is studying, but just be sure that regular, daily study is going on.

To assign such prayer and study early in counseling is an extremely important matter; you want the counselee to recognize that it is God with Whom he has to deal, not with you. You are but an agent to serve him in his quest to please God. And when all is said and done, it is a desire to please God (rather than lesser motives) that you want to see drive him. Just as it is Christ Who will be the prime focus of His future revelation, and not himself, so it should be primarily Christ he seeks to please in changing his lifestyle rather than receiving the benefits that will accrue to him by doing so. If you do nothing more than help him to put Christ first in all things, you will have achieved the principal thing. Whenever anyone truly desires to please Him, he will soon discover the right ways to do so as he searches the Scriptures.

The prophets were told by **revelation** from God that **they were serving others** who were not yet born, rather than **themselves**, as they prophesied about things so wonderful that **angels** wanted to know about them (v. 12). There is no other way to know about salvation than through divine revelation. But all this was **declared** through the apostles and New Testament prophets (cf. Ephesians 2:20) to those of us who are living after the death and resurrection of Christ. The **Holy Spirit**, precisely as Jesus had predicted, after His ascension came and enabled them to remember and write those things that were needed to understand and propagate the gospel message and all that it entails for those who believe it (v. 12; see John 14:26,16:13). Searching the Bible also will help your counselee to recognize how privileged he is to know all about things that prophets and angels did not fully understand. That in itself ought to do something for his zeal to please God. All through these studies I have been trying to

13 Therefore, buckling the belts of your minds for action, keeping levelheaded, set your hope entirely on the grace that will be brought to you at the revelation of Jesus Christ.

---

make it crystal clear to you that the principal thing is to help your counselee get a tighter grasp on what God is like and how he must relate to Him. I repeat, it is God with Whom he has to do! Get that across in any sort of meaningful way and the other aspects of counseling (in which specific matters must be dealt with specifically) will proceed smoothly; fail to do so and you will discover that counseling is not only a chore but it will stumble along and eventually peter out.

The great point in these passages is to give encouragement to suffering saints. To do so, in order for them to persevere, they need to understand that what they are standing for is eminently worthwhile and that, at the end of the struggle in which they are engaged, everything will turn out well.

Now in verse 13, Peter comes to a conclusion, and (in the name of God) issues an important command: **Therefore** (i.e., on the basis of all that you have learned in the previous verses) **buckling up the belts of your minds for action, keeping levelheaded, set your hope on the grace that will be brought to you at the revelation of Jesus Christ**. This verse needs to be stamped indelibly on the heart of every hopeless counselee. Not only does it point him back to all that we have been looking at in verses 1 through 12, but it tells him what impact those words should have on him. There is an aorist imperative used here that means "once and for all set your hope." That is to say, come to a conclusion yourself that this is what to do in trial, and then do it.

In this verse what the counselee receives at Christ's revelation comes to the fore. When at His coming He will bring the blessings and riches of total sanctification (glorification) along with the privilege and wonder of seeing Him in all His splendor and remaining with Him forever in a new body unaffected by the ravages of sin. Here, N.B., **hope** is commanded. If a counselee fails to gain hope he does not adequately appreciate what Peter has been writing up to this point. You may have to go over the verses yourself, interpreting and applying them to him in his concrete situation.

He must be **levelheaded in suffering, Peter says. That means, sober in his thoughts and decisions. He must not take the trial lightly, he may not fall apart under testing. He must be able to control his thoughts, his actions and his tongue. There is mental work to do at**

such times. That means he must do as Peter says—buckle the belt of his mind for action. In those days, whenever one was about to go into battle or to do some strenuous work, he would pull up the folds of his robe and tuck them under his belt. So the expression buckle up (lit., "gird your loins") came to mean, *prepare for strenuous action.* It is almost an exact parallel to our *buckle up* or *roll up your sleeves.* But here, don't miss the fact that it is the **mind** that must be prepared for action. In suffering, one must not be passive. He is to think, think clearly and biblically. He is to remember all that Peter is saying, to go over and over it in his mind until he realizes something of the greatness of what Christ has done for him. That will engender hope.

Because to have hope in suffering is commanded, and because the means by which one may grow hopeful even in the midst of pain are plainly explained, counselees who fail to become hopeful are responsible for that failure. Never let them blame you if you have rightly explained everything to them, and (especially) never let them blame God. You must place the onus where it belongs—those who lack hope after hearing all that God has done and will do, either are unsaved and the message is falling on deaf ears, or (if believers) have become so wrapped up in self-pity and the things of this world that they *will* not hear. Either way, dealing with the problems that they have presented (unless it is the problem of a lack of hope) will be fruitless until this complicating problem has been solved. One's attitude must be right so that his thinking can be sober and clear.

And note also, that one must **set his hope *entirely*** on God's **grace** that is coming at the revelation of Christ. Every trial calls for exacting biblical analysis. Until one has analyzed his situation in light of the grace of God (spelled out in the Bible) he will not withstand pressures that are exerted against him and he certainly will not have answers to give to those who ask about his faith (3:15). Anything that distracts from **levelheaded thinking** in trial (e.g., allowing emotion to control thinking, attitudes and actions) must be excluded. Levelheadedness is straight thinking. One guided by emotions, rather than the Word of God rightly applied to his situation, will not think straight. His head will be knocked off balance by emotion; he will not be **levelheaded**. A self-focus, beyond that which is normal in suffering, will distract. What is beyond normal for the Christian? Anything that breaks this exclusive mindset of which Peter writes, or diverts one from biblical thought as the controlling factor in all that he does. If the prophecy of the Old Testament motivated prophets and angels, surely we, who have so much more truth revealed, ought all the more be motivated by it.

It is important to emphasize the word **entirely** (v. 13). Hope that is divided is unacceptable to God. He wants (and insists on) hope centered exclusively on Himself and His promises. Part of the problem that a counselee may have is precisely that—he has placed his hope on God and on people or systems that have nothing to do with the Scriptures. Counselors who encourage this eclectic approach are sure to harm their counselees. The word *teleios* translated "entirely" means "in every part" or "in every way." It is not that you can trust God to do some things but must trust others to do the rest; God must be the sole One to whom a persecuted, suffering saint looks. One will denude the Bible's promises by diluting them with an admixture of man's ideas and supposed solutions to problems. If there ever were a section that excludes eclecticism, it is this one.

The word translated **mind** in this verse is *dianoia,* a term that refers to thinking through questions to reach answers; coming to an understanding of something (here the situation in which one finds himself). Ask your counselee, "what is the first thing you do when suffering comes?" By his reply you will discover that he may whine, he may fall apart, he may go out and invite others to a pity party, he may become angry or he may begin to doubt his faith, etc. But it is likely that he will not respond with anything approximating Peter's command: "I buckle up the folds of my mind to do some important biblical thinking. What I want to do is to assess the circumstances from a biblical perspective and make sure that I am thinking straight." That is probably the last thing you'd hear from the average counselee. As a result, part of your task in many (most?) cases is to help counselees think straight. Here is another poster for the wall of your counseling room:

WHEN TRIALS COME
BUCKLE UP YOUR MIND FOR ACTION

(I Pet. 1:13)

I can guarantee you that it will get inquiries. In Eastern religions and New Age thinking (much of which is based on Hinduism) the **mind** is bypassed. Christianity is different. Wherever the true Christian faith has gone, it has stressed education and learning. That is because it is a religion in which one must bring his mind to everything he does. And he is to be able to use it well so that he can think God's thoughts after Him and apply the Scriptures to various circumstances of life. Be sure to make it clear to counselees who appear overwhelmed emotionally that you can begin counseling only when they stop whimpering and start thinking.

Turning now to verses 14 through 16, Peter writes, **As children who**

14 As children who are under obedience, don't shape your lives by the desires that you used to follow in your ignorance.

---

are under obedience, don't shape your lives by the desires that you used to follow in your ignorance. Instead, as the One Who called you is holy, you yourselves must become holy in all your behavior. I say this because it is written "You must be holy because I am holy" (cf. Leviticus 11:44,45; 19:2; 2:17). Notice that Peter also uses the basic put off/put on format that you find articulated in the letters of the apostle Paul. Verse 14 sets forth the negative and verse 15 the positive, while verse 16 presents the biblical basis for the injunctions given in those verses. Here is a good way to present change to counselees: first what is wrong and must be abandoned, then what right action, belief or thought must replace it, and finally, the biblical reason(s) for the above.

Looking at the way Peter puts it, you might ask a counselee, "What do you think **shapes your lif**e?" Clearly that is God's concern in this place. Nine times out of ten, if you probe deeply enough, you will find that it is **desire**. If anything is true of our present day culture it is that people act upon their desires. They not only do so, but do so unashamedly. They have been taught by a generation of psychologists and psychiatrists that this is the right thing to do. Here God, through Peter says it is not! Freud, in siding with what he called the *id* over against the *superego*, launched this desire-oriented and desire-motivated trend upon which modern society is sailing. All advertising, it seems, is also based on the appeal to human desire. But it is an unseaworthy ship. Let's take a closer look at those three verses.

First Peter speaks to his readers **as children under obedience**. What does he intend to say by those words? Well, for one thing, he is contrasting the obedience-oriented life to the feeling-driven one. This point must be clarified for many counselees. They have no concept about the importance of **obedience**. Yet, if one is a child of God, he is expected to obey his heavenly Father. If he fails to **shape his life** by the commands of God, living a commandment-oriented life rather than a feeling-oriented one, he will turn out to be a disobedient child. Before becoming a Christian, Peter says, one naturally followed his desires and **shaped** his lifestyle accordingly. But having been saved by the Lord Jesus Christ, he needs to **shape up**. Among other things, that means he must learn to obey Christ *as Lord.* He can no longer be driven by desire. The standard by which he lives and makes decisions is *not what he desires, but what God requires*. The words

15 Instead, as the One Who called you is holy, you yourselves must become holy in all your behavior.
16 I say this because it is written: **You must be holy because I am holy.**

---

of Christ in calling disciples, reported in various places, all make it clear that one must take up his cross daily, putting his own **desires** to death on it, by denying (lit., "saying no to") self and following (instead) the commands of Christ (Luke 9:23; see also Matthew 28:20).

There is no doubt about it—this is a major issue in counseling. "But," objects one counselee, "if I have no desire to do something God requires, won't I be a hypocrite if I obey? I know God abhors hypocrites!" Ah, counselees have been so brainwashed that they actually think and say such things. It is not hypocrisy to obey God against your own desires (otherwise Christ's call to discipleship would have been meaningless); no, it is simple obedience (about which you hear so little these days that people don't even know what it means). Obedience is what the writer of Hebrews ascribes to Christ when speaking of Him going to the cross (against all his feelings and desires: Hebrews 5:7,8). The only desire that you need is a desire to please God; if this fundamental desire is present, then all your other competing desires (to avoid pain and suffering, for instance) can be countered. Jesus desired to please God and to save a people; consequently, He bore the cross in spite of the fact that He loathed becoming a curse. This issue must be understood thoroughly by all who seek to serve and live faithfully for Him.

It is **ignorance** of the truth about God, man and the universe that leads people to follow desire rather than the commands found in the Scriptures. When an unbeliever, one walks in ignorance (v. 14^{b}); that is to be expected. But believers have been enlightened, the scales have fallen from their eyes. The veil has been lifted. They are no longer in ignorance. They know the basic facts that are necessary to be obedient children. So Peter says, as God is **holy** (set apart from sin to righteousness), He has **called** your counselee likewise to be holy (v. 15) in **all** his **behavior**. In other words, his lifestyle should set him apart from the unbeliever. If he speaks, thinks and acts like the world around, he is sinning. He should march to the beat of a different drummer. That is precisely what God has said about His set apart people from the beginning (cf. Leviticus 19:2; 11:44,45 to which Peter refers in v. 16). And so long as you pray the Lord's prayer, and every other prayer in which you refer to God as Father, you are to act like His children: "You must be holy *because I am holy.*"

17 If you call Him Father Who impartially judges each one by his deeds, then be deeply concerned about how you behave during your residence as aliens,

---

Like Father, like son. God doesn't have favorites either; every child of His is on the very same footing with Him. He will not prefer one over another: He **impartially judges each one by his deeds**. And because Christians must uphold the family name, **they must be deeply concerned about how they behave during** [their] **residence as aliens**. God cares about how His children **behave**; their behavior reflects on His Name (cf. Matthew 5:16). He expects behavior that will cause others to honor and glorify Him. When a counselee digs in his heels at obeying a biblical command, saying, "If I refuse to do this, I wouldn't be hurting anyone but myself, will I?" you can powerfully reply, "Yes, indeed; you will be smearing the Name of your heavenly Father in the mud!" Because of this fact, every counselee must be helped to develop **a deep concern** about his **behavior**. It is as if he were a resident alien in a foreign land representing the country of which he is a citizen; he brings honor or disgrace on it by his actions. He is a citizen of heaven (Philippians 3:20). It is necessary, therefore, for counselors to reiterate over and over again these facts to counselees. They are not on their own; they are God's children who represent Him and the heavenly country of which they are citizens.

The word translated **behave** is actually a word that has to do with one's manner of life, lifestyle or habitual walk. It speaks, therefore, of his regular, on-going, daily words and actions, not merely one-time acts. The other term of importance is **aliens**. Literally it means "one who lives beside." That is exactly what I have been trying to say: your counselee lives beside others (at home, at work, at school, etc.) who will tend to judge God and Christianity by what they see in his daily lifestyle. No wonder Peter says **be deeply concerned** about it.

What Peter has called for in the verses under consideration is unique behavior from God's children that reflects favorably on their heavenly Father. Such behavior can be developed in your counselee only by helping him shape his life through obedience to God's Word rather than by allowing him to be driven by his desires. The words in the previous two sentences, looking back on this remarkable section of I Peter, in a nutshell summarize what counseling is all about. Reread them if you went over them quickly.

But frequently counselees will protest, "That may be all well and

18 knowing that you weren't set free from the useless behavior patterns that were passed down from your forefathers, by the payment of a corruptible ransom like silver or gold,

---

good for others, but you don't know what sort of background I come from. I just can't shake it off; it influences me all the time. If you came out of the sort of home and society that I did, you'd understand why it is impossible for me to change." Your response? Something like this: "I have good news for you—you *can* change. How do I know? Because God says so. Look with me at I Peter 1:18." And counselor, translated accurately (as it is in the text above) you have one of the most potent verses in the Bible for confronting and destroying the false (yet prevalent) notion that "I am what I am because of my past, and I can't do anything about it." Some actually believe such nonsense; others use it as an excuse. Either way, the passage is dynamite.

Note what Peter says: **You were set free from the useless behavior patterns that were passed down from your forefathers.** How important to know that fact! Set free! How wonderful. "But I can't change..." O yes you can. If you are a true child of God, you have been **set free** from your past. You don't have to go on living as you once did according to the habits you imbibed at home from the members of your family or in your past associations with others. These worthless or futile ways that you developed are changeable. If they are not, Christianity is a fraud. The very premise on which it is founded is that people can change to become more and more like the One Who saved them. If there has been little or no change, or if their is a protest that change is not possible, you must take the time to sweep away all such ideas and see to it that the counselee comes to accept the truth that is presented in this verse. Until he believes radical change is possible, a counselee will settle for minimal advances in Christian living. What this verse says, in contrast, is that there is no pattern that one developed from imitating others in childhood to which he is enslaved. He has been **set free** by the death of Christ from such bondage. He does not say that it happens automatically; no just the opposite. That is why he explains and exhorts—to convince your counselee that it is possible and to urge him to act accordingly. Peter will never go along with the idea that "I'm stuck with what others did to me."

This remarkably important fact is the result of the death and shed blood of Jesus Christ, not the result of some physical, monetary payment (vv. 18,19). Like the **unblemished lambs** of the temple that were sacri-

19 but with Christ's valuable blood, shed like the blood of a spotless and unblemished lamb.
20 He was foreknown, indeed, before the foundation of a world, but at these last times He made His appearance for your sake

---

ficed, Christ's blood was shed and His life was given in the place of guilty sinners who, as a result, were not only justified but enabled to live in a way that is pleasing to God and a witness to those around them. What was paid to free Christians from the tyranny of their past was not some **corruptible** sum of money but the **valuable blood of Christ**. In other words, the counselee who thinks that he should receive something of worth and value should look again at what he has already received from God as a free gift of His grace.

Awareness of sinful behavior patterns is the first step to ridding one's self of them. One of the principal tasks of a counselor is to help counselees who may, for the most part, be unaware of their sinful ways to begin to recognize them. For instance, a counselor, after hearing over several sessions the repeated nasty remarks that a counselee makes concerning her mother-in-law may have to say something like this: "Matilda, I've jotted down several quotes of things you've said about your mother-in-law. Let me read them to you [he does]. Now, totally apart from what she may be like, do you think that the things you have said about her ought to be said by a Christian? How do you think that God wants you to respond?" And if by that he gets nowhere, he may have to continue: "Well, let me read Romans 12:14 for you to see if that throws some light on the subject!"

Verse 20 makes it clear that the coming of Christ to save us and make it possible for us to throw off the shackles of the past was no afterthought. Nor was it some emergency ploy of a befuddled, frustrated God. Christ's death was planned **from the foundation of a** (any) **world**, either this one in which we live or any other God may have created. In other words, it was part of an eternal plan by which God determined to demonstrate His mercy, love and power by these things. And **at these last days** of the Old Testament era (and the beginning of the new) the long-awaited plan became a reality. Both those to whom Peter is writing and we who live at this even later date, are greatly privileged to be living at such a time. That is his point. When counselees fail to notice, make it clear what a great privilege is theirs.

And according to verse 21, this salvation is for all those who have **believed** the truths about Jesus Christ, Who was **raised from the dead**

21 who through Him have believed in God, Who raised Him from the
dead and gave Him glory, so that your faith and hope are in God.
22 Having cleansed yourselves by obedience to the truth you can have
brotherly affection without pretense; so love one another intensively from
the heart,
23 having been regenerated not by perishable seed, but by that which is
imperishable—God's living and continuing Word.

---

and seated in **glory** at the Father's right hand. In Christ, therefore, humanity is now glorified in heaven. And that is a firstfruit of what God will do for all who are His own. As Peter will make clear later on, that glory awaits all who believe.

Because Christ has been glorified, it is possible to have a living **hope**; He is proof of what lies ahead for all. By **faith** in that message, a counselee also is given hope for his own eternity. Again, focusing on what God has planned for His own, in contrast to what they have lost by trusting Christ, is the way to handle suffering and loss. What we now possess and the inheritance of glory that awaits us in heaven are so valuable that they cannot be compared with the few trials we are required to suffer in this life for His Name's sake (v. 21).

Verse 22 does not teach salvation by works. Peter does not say that it is by obedience to the law. The way that Peter often uses the word **obedience** (when coupled with modifiers like the words **the truth** used here) is to indicate the idea of obeying the call to faith (cf. 2:8; 3:1). It is obeying the command to believe that he has in mind (cf. Acts 17:30). The root behind the term of obedience used here is "to listen to," "to give heed to." One obeys by heeding. Peter rejoices over the **cleansing** from sin that has taken place in the life of the true child of God (he speaks of that same cleansing in Acts 15:9). Now, since cleansing has occurred it is possible **to love** brothers and sisters in Christ genuinely (**without pretense**). Don't ever let a counselee tell you that he simply can't love another Christian. Peter assures us that the contrary is true. Christ has made it possible to love others, genuinely, **intensively** and wholeheartedly (v. 22)! This sort of affection for other Christians is one that extends itself, reaches out to help and care for them.

This transformation is the work of God in the life of those He **regenerates** (gives life to believe and live according to His truth). And this occurred through **God's Word** which, unlikeother **seeds** that **perish, continues and lives** on. This comment about the seed and what it produces reminds him of the more common usage of the word and takes his mind

24 Do this because
all flesh is like grass and all its glory is like a flower of grass:
The grass withered and the flower fell off,
25 **but the Lord's Word remains forever.**
Now, this is the Word that was announced to you as good news.

---

back to Isaiah 40:6-8, in which the transient nature of human life is contrasted with God's enduring Word. The words **all flesh** are a Hebraism for "every person." And the perishable nature of human life since the fall is aptly portrayed as **grass, the flower of which** quickly fades and passes away. So Peter indicates, they should not get caught up in the temporal—the eternal **Word** is about eternal realities. They are what is truly important. The troubles of this life are related only to the temporary nature of things here and now. It is a temptation of those who suffer to get caught up in the immediate. It is so painful; it is so real. But to do so is a sure way to fail God. Christians must not view pain and suffering as the unbeliever does. Peter stands firmly against pagan thinking and for a new way to view and handle suffering. What does he say? When in suffering, show brotherly affection and loving care for others. That is what makes Christian suffering unique. The Christian grows more like Christ in suffering. Counselor, it is your task to make this plain and to help your counselees to experience it as a reality.

CHAPTER 2

1 Therefore, having put off all malice, and all pretense and hypocritical ways, and envious attitudes, and all evil speaking about others,

---

Chapter headings were not a part of the original writings of the Bible. They were added hundreds of years later for convenience. They are not inspired and, indeed, give evidence in many cases of careless or uninformed thinking. That chapter 2 should begin with the word **therefore** is only one more instance of this problem. The flow of thought from the last chapter is continued into the second. This word signals the approach of a conclusion in the form of an exhortation reached from what has been said before. If dispersed Jewish Christians have left behind all those things they enjoyed in Palestine because of their faith in Christ, only to enter into things that are far more valuable, that fact should affect their lives positively. We have encountered that conclusion before (vv. 13-17). Yet there we were given few specifics. Here (vv. 1-3) Peter sets forth ways in which the suffering believer should act. He mentions first attitudes and behaviors that ought to be abandoned and then those that ought to be adopted.

We encounter at the outset the familiar **put off** scenario. What he encourages his readers to abandon is all malice, all imposture, hypocritical ways, envy and evil speaking about others. The words mean the following:

malice: badness, viciousness, the desire to harm others;
imposture: guile, trickery, lit., catching with bait;
hypocritical ways: misrepresenting true intentions, attitudes, etc.;
envy: displeasure over another's good fortune;
evil speaking about others: especially behind their backs.

The word **all** appended to several of these items in Peter's put off list means "every sort of." In *no way* may one justify *any* such attitudes or postures. Peter has made it clear that the Christian is capable of putting off old behavior patterns (cf. 1:18) and how to do so; there is, then, no excuse for failure. Counselees, confronted with attitudes that match any, some or all of those listed, must not be allowed to beg off for *any* reason.

Counselors should familiarize themselves with the items on the list because they are encountered frequently in counseling. They also ought to be able to explain what each means. Having done so, they will be able to show a counselee that he is exhibiting precisely those things that the Bible forbids. It might be well to read over the notes you take concerning coun-

2 like newborn babies, crave pure milk from the Word so that by it you may grow toward salvation,

---

selees (especially the direct quotes that you copied down) to discover whether they disclose any of these attitudes. Then at a later session, you would be able to confront the counselee with evidence of traits that violate this command to put them off. Much that you will have to alter in counseling stems from one or more of these negative qualities.

You will often experience these attitudes in the counseling session itself. "I don't think my brother, after all he has done to me, deserves to have three cars and a boat." Or you might hear another say, "I want to get even, and I will, if it takes me the rest of my life." Or perhaps, this: "I think I can figure out a way to induce her to do what I have been wanting her to do. I'll just make her think that..." Using the list just given, can you put a biblical label on each? Then having labeled it, do you know what to do about it? Moreover, how would you use the list to confront a counselee about his sinful attitude? Think these things through before you find yourself in the actual situation where you need to deal with attitudes like these. Then you will be prepared and not so likely to stumble over your own feet. In order to change, counselees who have been indulging their sinful desires in these ways, must be convicted of sin and come to repentance over their sinful ways. Only then can you begin to encourage the positive, biblical attitudes that must replace the negative, sinful ones.

What, specifically, does Peter say must be done? He writes, **like newborn babies, crave unadulterated (pure) milk of the Word**. What does that mean? The word **crave** is a strong one. It is like that desire which causes a baby to cry its lungs out for **milk** (cf. Psalm 42:1 in the LXX). It is not proper to substitute adulterated milk for the real thing. **Pure milk** is milk that has not been thinned down by the addition of water or some other substance. Here, the milk for which one ought to long is the unadulterated milk of God's **Word**. One tires of pointing it out, but the text again and again makes it clear that there is something other than God's Word that many substitute for it and that this must not be. Again, in order to overcome those sins listed above, one should yearn to find out what God has said about them in the Word and how to replace them. He did not say to turn to the philosophers (the psychologists of his day) or anywhere else. And the phrasing of his comments makes it abundantly plain that an admixture of the two is also unacceptable. What one needs is biblical sustenance *in its purest form*. The alternatives to those forbidden

3 since **you have tasted that the Lord is good.**

---

attitudes are found only in Scripture, which also explains how they may be put on. There must be a change of one's eating habits! We eat too much spiritual junk food.

Over the years the evil one has employed two basic ways in which to weaken the church: murder and mixture. While the former sometimes has been successful (think of the destruction of the church in North Africa by the Muslims) the latter has been preeminently so. This mixture of error with truth, this dependence on God's Word *plus something else* has destroyed many lives and weakened the impact of the church. Counselors should never contribute to this by the advice they give, the referrals they make or the solutions to which they direct counselees. Admixture can be discovered only as the Bereans demonstrated—by searching the Scriptures (cf. Acts 7:11). Urge your counselees to make the Bible their standard of faith and life. The use of milk as a figure of speech in this place does not correspond to its use in I Corinthians 3:1 or Hebrews 5:12 since here it does not convey spiritual immaturity. There is no condemnation here for desiring milk; rather it is strongly encouraged. What will the nourishing milk of the Word do for your counselee?

Bible milk will enable him **to grow toward salvation**. If counselees need anything, it is usually spiritual growth. And counseling ought always be a time for growth. If you see it only as a time when people rectify past wrongs in order to establish conditions that formerly existed, your view of counseling is sadly limited. Counseling is one element in the process of sanctification (that, of course, is why you must not try to counsel unbelievers; they need evangelism). Many counselees have but a very immature faith and lifestyle. Growth is desperately needed. In times of suffering and need, one must be able to endure, to stand and withstand the pressures all around. He will find that hardiness that he needs to do so, Peter says, only in God's Word, which he needs to imbibe full strength. To get a good **taste** of biblical milk means to understand how **good** it is (Psalm 34:8). The problem is that much of the way the truth of the Bible is presented is so thin and insipid that counselees never get a good **taste** of the real thing so that, with the Psalmist, they may cry out **"the Lord is good."** Watered down teaching, psychologically oriented drinks, superficial Bible study methods and pale preaching fail to give the true taste of pure milk that will make one cry out like a baby for more. Don't be a con-

4 As you come to Him, a living Stone (on the one hand rejected by men, but on the other hand, to God choice and valuable),
5 like living stones, you yourselves are being built into a spiritual house for a holy priesthood to offer spiritual sacrifices acceptable to God through Jesus Christ.
6 Scripture says:

> **See, I am laying in Zion a choice Stone, a valuable Cornerstone; and whoever believes on Him will never be put to shame.**

---

tributor to that sort of thing. Present the Scriptures in full strength to your counselees. Of course, to do so, you must learn how to study the Bible in depth for yourself. Take a course in hermeneutics (if you don't know what that is, you obviously need it), a couple in theology and (when possible) even New Testament Greek. Then you will begin to be able to nourish your counselees as you ought to.

In verses 4 through 8 Peter speaks of God's **temple**, likening believers (and even Jesus) to **stones** in it. Jesus is **the living Stone** (v. 4), **the choice and valuable one rejected by men**, but Who has become the **Cornerstone**. And He is also a Stone over which those who are **disobedient to the Word stumble and trip**. There is much in what Peter is writing, as he exposits Psalm 118:22, that you should know. Peter writes to those who have tasted that the Lord is good, and have come to Christ as the **living Ston**e. For Peter, nothing about Christianity is dead: the hope that we have is a *living* hope (cf. 1:3) and the reason is that we serve a *living* Stone about Whom we can read in a *living* Word (cf. 1:23). To him, it is the past that is dead; the present is alive—fresh and vibrant. Those you counsel often come weary and defeated. To them there seems little in their faith that they could describe in such terms. One of your tasks is to help restore the **first love** (Revelation 2:4) from which under conditions of suffering it is easy to depart if one fails to encounter that suffering God's way.

Legitimate counselees are those who have **come** to Christ the Stone by faith. They are those who have been saved by His grace. Now, Peter develops the idea of the Stone (which comes from a cluster of Old Testament passages: Genesis 49:24; Isaiah 8:14, 28:16; Psalm 34:8). A stone is usually thought of as inanimate, the epitome of that which has no life. By adding the word living, among other things, Peter makes it perfectly clear that the Stone is a Person (cf. Paul's use of "living sacrifice" in Romans 12:1). Peter is fond of speaking about Christ as the Stone (see Acts 4:11).

7 So to believers He is of value, but to unbelievers **the very Stone that the builders disapproved of has become the Head of the corner,**

We have **come** to Christ as the foundation for our lives. The Jews (the poor **builders** of v. 7) **rejected** the One Who has to His followers become the Stone from which the rest of the building is oriented—the **cornerstone**. But for them He has become a cause for stumbling. The picture is of a stone cast aside in the process of building. On the construction site where it has been left after throwing it aside, grass has grown up on all sides. As they work, the builders continually find themselves stumbling over this stone which they cast aside and now lies in their way. Christ is like that—as they go on attempting to build for God in their own way, they stumble over the One Who should be the very cornerstone of the building. They find, to their dismay, that they can never quite rid themselves of this Stone that they have rejected. He has become a Stone of stumbling (see Paul's discussion of Israel's stumbling so as to be rejected by God: Romans 11:9-11).

To God, the Stone is v**aluable, choice** (v. 4); He is His unique Son. And it is He Who has made it possible for believers to become **stones** along with Himself in the temple of God (here called **a spiritual house**). These refugees of the New Testament dispersion had left behind in Palestine the **temple, the priesthood and the sacrifices**. They wondered, perhaps, "How can we serve God under such conditions?" But Peter assures them that they have a better temple, a better priesthood and better sacrifices. **They themselves** are the house (temple) in which the Spirit of God dwells; it is, therefore, a **spiritual** temple. They themselves are a **holy priesthood** (the priesthood of all believers comes from this passage) who are privileged to offer up **spiritual** (Spirit-motivated) **sacrifices** of themselves (Romans 12:1), their prayers and praise (Hebrews 13:15,16) and their service for Christ. The old has passed away; it was but a type and shadow of the new, which is the reality of which the old was but a figure.

Many counselees fail to realize what a privilege is theirs to live in this era. The types and shadows have gone; the reality is theirs. Their worship is spiritual; not carnal. Some think of the commandments of God as arduous; describe for them what Old Testament temple worship was like—what they have been delivered from. They never had it so good! One of the major problems that counselees have is a lack of appreciation for what God has done for them. And it is precisely that—a proper appreciation of God's lavish blessings—that Peter is attempting to convey to

8 and, **a Stone to stumble over, a Rock to trip over**. They stumble, as indeed they were appointed to, because they are disobedient to the Word.
9 But you have become **a chosen race, a kingly priesthood, a holy nation, a people who belong to Someone**, so that you may declare the virtues of the One Who called you out of darkness into His amazing light.

---

his reader. He knows that, once fully recognized, one could never think of abandoning them. Moreover, once acknowledged, these blessings—here and hereafter—will serve to strengthen him to meet any and every test.

Believers, who stand with their Savior, Peter notes (quoting the Old Testament; v. 7) **will never be put to shame**. This is a biblical expression that means one will [ultimately] be vindicated in the great Day of the Lord. The word **never** is the strongest Greek negative Peter could have used: *ou me*. In spite of how things look during persecution, with Christ Himself rejected, trials and difficulties abounding, Jesus will *never* let them down. Those who stumble are not His own; they are the builders who rejected Him and who are **appointed** to do so because they refused to believe the Word (v. 8). The word **appointed** was used in drawing up official documents like bonds and wills. Something was "laid, set, ordained, appointed" as such (it is used of **laying** the cornerstone in **Zion**; v. 6). God's eternal purpose (appointment) is carried out through responsible human action (disobedience). Those in power may well reject the Stone, but those who come to Him will find that He will keep them and never let them down. That is the thrust of Peter's comments. Heartening words they are for defeated Christians.

Though the Jewish builders rejected Christ, the Cornerstone, that did not stop God Himself from laying His choice and valuable Stone in Zion. In spite of them, He built His church (cf. Matthew 16:18). Jesus predicted all of this in a very instructive parable found in Matthew 21:42,43). Referring to Hosea 2:23, Peter makes it clear that there is a new **race**, a new **priesthood**, a new and **holy nation** and **a people who belong to God** who have superseded the old and who are now appointed **to declare the virtues of God Who called them forth from darkness into His amazing light** (v. 9). This powerful verse must be understood. God is not only finished with the old order of things having to do with the temple worship, He is finished with the old Israel as well. All that was once attributed to the Jewish nation is here attributed to the new Israel—the Church of Christ. This formation of a people of God was a matter of grace; as in the choice of Israel of old, so too, it is by **mercy** alone that the new Israel has

10 At one time you were **not a people**, but now **are God's people**; you were **without mercy**, but now you have **been shown mercy**.

---

been established as **God's people** (v. 10; cf. Deuteronomy 7:6-8). The Christian church is a nation within nations. And its task, as such, is **to declare Christ's virtues** to the nations.

It is that last point that must be emphasized in counseling. Ask counselees. "Why do you think that God saved you anyway? Why did He make you part of His church? Primarily for your benefit?" The answer ought to be "Certainly not. I was saved to declare His virtue—the wonders of His amazing light." Seldom do you get a reply that approximates that one. Counselees are so often caught up in their own troubles that they forget the prime reason for their salvation. Into the midst of counseling, when it is appropriate, be sure to drop this note. Too often, Christians selfishly take their salvation for granted—almost as if God was obligated to save them. No! He did so out of mercy. Now it is the part of every believer to become the witness in life and word to God's great goodness that his salvation deserves. He is part of **a people who belong to Someone** (God); he is not on his own. There is security in this, but there is also obligation. As **God's people**, each one has the obligation to witness. How can a counselee, defeated, angry, self-centered, etc., even begin to do so? It is his own self-orientation, rather than the orientation that says, "I belong to God," that is keeping him from it. He must be brought to his senses, to recognize that he (like Israel of old) is failing in his purpose and must quickly do something about it.

The summons from **darkness** (ignorance, sin and death) to the **amazing light** (truth, righteousness and life) is a **call** that ought to bring to one's heart and lips again and again expressions of the **amazing** nature of what God has done. If you have lost the wonder and thrill of it all, or that is the condition of your counselee, then read and read again all that Peter says in order to comprehend it so that you too may be spellbound over the salvation that is yours. It is in such a setting and atmosphere that counseling should be carried on. One must not grovel along with moaning counselees in the **darkness** to which many seem to persist in returning; he must lift them to new and greater heights than they have ever known. Isn't that what Peter is doing for his dejected, suffering readers? Well, then so should you. But if you don't have it in you either, you'd better refresh you own understanding of the salvation that is yours. Counseling, to be effective, must proceed in the spirit of wonder and amazement.

11 Dear friends, as resident aliens and refugees, I urge you to keep at a safe distance from the fleshly desires that are poised against your soul like an expeditionary force,
12 having good behavior among the Gentiles, so that while they slander you as wrongdoers, by observing your fine deeds they may glorify God on the day of inspection.

Now, the theme of the **behavior** of the believer as the **resident alien** in a foreign land becomes dominant. Christians live in a community that practices much that they reject and that fails to uphold the principles and practices to which God calls them. Community life is often hostile to Christians, and at best, anything but supportive of God's ways. Because their lives are different, because they refuse to indulge in many of the activities of those around them and because their lifestyles often expose the sin in others by contrast, they are frequently **slandered** (cf. v. 12). Peter has just spoken of the evangelistic purpose for which God has called His people (v. 9); it is both by words and behavior that they must carry on that work. God's virtues (excellencies) ought not only be on the lips of His children, but ought also to be exhibited in their lives. Because of the importance of what is said in verses 11 and 12, one might even say that what follows in the remainder of the letter is the outworking of that teaching. A resident alien is not so much on the move as he is one who, having left his homeland, has settled in a foreign community. Often aliens were licensed as such and paid a small tax for the privilege of living there. Because they were *officially* registered as aliens, they were always on the spot. Peter's readers were Christian Jews who were literally aliens in foreign places. But they were also **aliens** to the world order dominated by Satan. They would clearly understand the allusion to this fact as he wrote about it. Just as they must maintain **good behavior** in what were often hostile surroundings because of their status as aliens, so too, being aliens from the world itself, they would find much that was unacceptable to their status as pilgrims and strangers in this world.

In order to maintain a lifestyle that was both pleasing to Christ and appealing to unbelievers they would have to deal with the problems in their lives. These, as Peter frequently makes clear, are not only the **mockings and slanders** of those who opposed them, but (of greater importance) the **fleshly desires** within that they must overcome. Having done so, they could readily stand up against the onslaughts of those who attack from without. The problems raised by the world would pose no serious difficulty if **the fleshly (bodily) desires poised against their souls like**

an expeditionary force were defeated. God is not against desires, *per se*. It is those desires that grow out of a body that has been given over to sin of which he is speaking. These persist as habitual dispositions that were developed from the sinful natures with which we were born. We now have new natures, regenerated and enabled by the Spirit of God to pursue new, righteous habits. Yet we often revert to past ways. For more on the problem of the body wrongly habituated and the war that must be fought against it see comments on Romans 6, 7 and 8. Every counselee has the problem of giving in to the fleshly desires that he developed before he became a Christian. He must be made to understand thoroughly that battles within have a great bearing on the results of battles fought without. He must win the war within (see my book of that very title, *Winning The War Within).* These desires are encamped over against his soul. They are ready to do battle and take him captive once more.

How is he to deal with them? Peter says, **keep at a safe distance from them**. In other words, be conscious of the problems that you have and take every measure to avoid indulging sinful desires. Your behavior must be excellent among the **heathen** (Gentiles). When they see you indulging sinful desires (and they will see; Peter speaks of them **observing** you), they will be turned away from the Lord by it. But if they **observe your fine deeds, they may glorify God in the day of inspection** (v. 12). How does one **distance** himself from these habitual desires? By putting on their biblical alternatives in order to replace them. If, instead of cursing those who curse you (as it is your fleshly and ingrained habit to do), you bless those who do so, and learn to do that over a period of time so that it becomes a new habitual response replacing the old one, you will have, in that area, learned to keep your distance from them. But when there is no effort on the part of the counselee to learn the new way that will inevitably lead to drifting into the hands of the enemy over and over again. Pretty soon, he will give up on future attempts, and simply surrender to the enemy. That, he must not do for God's sake.

Putting on the **fine deeds** that are the opposite of the fleshly desires that he must overcome will cause the **Gentiles** (the unsaved persons around you) to **glorify God** (cf. Matthew 5:16). In the face of **slander**, in which others unjustly call you wrongdoers (in the early days Christians were even called cannibals, a slander that grew out of a misunderstanding of the Lord's supper), you will be able to persist in your ways because you will have developed the patterns of response that your Lord requires of you. If, however, you fail to do so, you will find it difficult (if not impossible) to withstand the slander. Counselees frequently encounter slander.

13 Be submissive to every human authority for the Lord's sake, whether to the emperor, who is supreme,

---

Peter does not say "sue 'em!" as many do today. No. He says live down the slander by your good deeds. That is the same advice every counselee also must be given. What do you tell counselees about the problem? Do you give different advice; advice that accords with their fleshly desires? Think this through so that you will be prepared to do what God requires. To sum up: behave well among the unsaved, not indulging in fleshly desires, but doing deeds that are so fine (deeds done with finesse) that even those who are inclined to slander, instead, may glorify God. Then they will have a good witness about you in the great Day of the Lord when He comes to inspect your works.

One final word: your behavior is **observed**. Counselees may say, "Nobody cares about what I do." But they are wrong. Somebody, at some time in some way is observing. And what he sees leads him either toward or away from God. No one lives for himself. Much is riding on the Christian's behavior. Tell that to counselees.

Now Peter begins to take up some specific areas in which it is important for the believing alien to manifest exemplary behavior. His first is before the government (vv. 13-17). His exhortation? **Be submissive.** Some counselees have difficulty with the government (the IRS, etc.). As a counselor, you must be sure not to advise that which is against the law: believers are to **submit to every human authority for the Lord's sake**. It reflects negatively on the Lord's Name when a Christian refuses to do so. Keep this in mind whenever you advise in this area. It is true that the government does not always do what it should, wastes taxpayer's money and backs unholy causes. That however was true in Peter's day as well. Yet, he urges his readers to submit. The only exception to this rule is when the government requires Christians to do something God has forbidden.

There is no exception to the kinds of authorities to which believers are told to submit: Peter writes **Be submissive to every human authority**. How is that? Because everyone who holds authority, holds it from God. True authority comes from no other source (John 19:10,11). When a Christian obeys the government, he obeys God. This authority extends to **the emperor**, or lesser magistrates **sent by him** to exercise his will. Even local, city and state officials are to be honored and obeyed as they exercise God's authority. Notice what it is that the authority is to do: **to take vengeance on evildoers and to praise those who do right**. That they often fail to follow these tasks as God has outlined them (as they did then) is no

14 or to governors who are sent by him to take vengeance on evildoers and to praise those who do well.
15 This is God's will: that by doing good you may muzzle the ignorant talk of foolish persons.
16 As free persons, and not as those who use freedom as a cover-up for evil, live rather as God's slaves.

---

excuse for Christians to fail in their part. They must submit even to an emperor like Nero. Accept no complaints against the government. In the end, these often turn out to be complaints against God, and His providence. Encourage counselees to pay their taxes, even when exorbitant. Urge them to pray for rulers and to help them to perform their duties in any way that they can. Poor stewardship on the part of a counselee can never be excused by saying that it is the fault of governmental taxing and spending. The Christian is to live properly under whatever regime he finds himself. The faults of others can never be passed off as an excuse for one's own failure. Emphasize this point along with the injunction to be submissive.

Christians may call Herod a "fox," as Christ did (Luke 13:32) *if the designation truly characterizes his actions.* That means that it is not necessarily wrong to call Clinton (who is president as I write) "slick Willie." Yet, as a soldier, a Christian has no other recourse but to go to Haiti on orders from him as commander-in-chief. He may think that this is unwise, etc., but he is to submit. The Bible distinguishes the ruler as a person from the ruler as an authority. God's authority, vested in these lesser authorities, must always be respected. For more on this matter, see comments on Romans 13:1-6.

Submission is **God's will** (v. 15). **By doing good** in this way Christians are to **muzzle the ignorant talk of foolish persons**. A **fool** in Scripture is one who speaks beyond or contrary to his own knowledge. Certainly such persons abound and often give grief to your counselees. Here is how to tell your counselee to treat fools. *Demonstrate* the foolishness of their ravings by your conduct. When a Christian is truly submissive, he makes it clear that those who rail against him are speaking **ignorantly**; that their talk is but the talk of **fools**. When he answers a fool according to his own folly (that is, in kind) he shows himself also to be a fool.

Verse 16 offers an interesting insight on the Christian's status. He is **free,** says Peter. What does he mean by that? Actually every Christian is free (exempt: cf. Matthew 17:24-27, especially v. 26) from all earthly

17 Honor all sorts of men, love the brotherhood, fear God and honor the emperor.

---

government with its laws and regulations. He is a citizen of the Kingdom of Heaven. Peter brings up this point in order to anticipate and counter the specious argument that many might make: "if free, then we don't need to submit to any earthly government." That notion, however, is decidedly wrong. Christians have not been set free from **all** authority. Actually, they have become **God's slaves**. And it is He Who orders them to submit for His sake. Freedom is not anarchy; it is freedom to live as we were designed to live—according to the laws and ordinances of God. It is freedom to do good. We submit to rulers, then, because of our basic submission to God.

This Christian freedom (on which some counselees wrongly rely as justification for their evil deeds) is no license to sin. It must not be used as a cloak **to cover up** sinful acts (cf. Jude 4). As Jude says, those who do are persons who follow their own desires rather than God's will. What this freedom boils down to is that the Christian serves God, not man. That is why he is submissive to rulers: God told him to be. Be alert to the cover up of some who plead Christian freedom to justify their actions.

Now concluding this section, Peter says, **honor all sorts of men, love the brotherhood, fear God and honor the emperor**. To honor someone is to show proper regard wherever it is due. It doesn't matter who the person is; whenever it is due him, the Christian must honor him. He also must **love the brotherhood** (that is, true Christians of all sorts, wherever they may be found—with all their idiosyncrasies). And while he is **to fear God**, he is only **to honor the emperor**. **Fear of God** (awe and respect for Him) is the one fear that drives out all others—even the fear of rulers and evil emperors. Fearful Christians must be urged to center their fear on God and not on men; it is God alone with whom they must really contend in such situations. Human beings can do no more than kill the body, as Jesus said. God casts both body and soul into Gehenna (Matthew 10:28). The aorist imperative is used, meaning "Decide to honor all sorts of men." It is something that one has to set his mind to do; otherwise he will drift with the crowd that doesn't. You can see that Peter is calling for the highest standard of behavior; counselors may do no less.

The final section in this chapter (vv. 18-25) has to do with **household servants** though, at the end, his words broaden out to everyone. It is with these words that we have the pleasure of concluding our study of the chapter. And they are greatly instructive for all of us with reference to our

18 Household servants, submit yourselves to your masters, showing full respect, not only to those who are good and lenient but also to those who are cruel.

---

labor and work. Almost every second counselee (along with whatever else may be a problem for him) seems to be having trouble with his work. These words, therefore, should be of great significance for Christian counselors. We want to underscore every statement Peter makes; all are applicable to some counseling problem or another.

Remember, submission *under trial and persecution* is the theme that runs through this Book. After considering submission to a government that is not necessarily the best, he takes up submission under the authority of a slave **master** who, likewise, may not be any better. And in the next chapter he will consider the plight of the Christian wife of an unbelieving husband.

As an inducement for slaves to submit to unreasonable masters, at the end he sets forth the greatest of all examples of submission in trial—that of Christ Who, also, was treated unjustly (cf. vv. 21-25). When counselees chafe under unjust treatment at work, it is not too powerful a reminder to bring this example to bear upon their situation.

In verse 18 **Household servants** are probably addressed as an instance of the most demeaning and difficult of all working relationships. On slavery in general, see John T. Demarest's comments on this verse in his commentary on I Peter. The **master** mentioned here is the word *despot*, a term with a somewhat different denotation than its current usage in our language which describes one with absolute power over another—even the power of life and death. Because many despots misused their power, the modern idea came into being. So Peter has set forth the most extreme setting in which a Christian may find himself. Counselees may describe their bosses in similar terms, but you can be sure that they do not labor under conditions anywhere near as difficult. "If these slaves could do as God requires under those extreme conditions," you may argue, "surely you, who labor in circumstances not nearly so bad can do so too." That is a powerful way in which to use the passage. The submission to a despot by household servants was to include **full respect**. Again, the authority that he exercised was from God. And while the man may not have merited respect at all, because of the kind of person he was, yet, respect was to be shown to him in his position as master. The same is to be true of those for whom your counselees work. And as Peter says, this respect is to extend to masters of all sorts—**not only to those who are**

19 One finds favor if, out of conscience toward God, he bears up under pain when suffering unjustly.
20 Indeed, what credit is coming to you if when you are beaten for sinning you endure it? But if you endure suffering for doing good, this finds favor with God.

---

good and lenient, but also to those who are cruel (harsh, unjust). There is no difference in the source of the authority that the latter exercises than that exercised by the former. It is God's authority in both cases, so the same respect is to be given in both cases.

The point is further elucidated: **One finds favor [with God] if, out of conscience toward God, he bears up under pain when suffering unjustly**. That is hard, but it is precisely the word many counselees need to hear—with reference to unjust treatment at work or elsewhere. The matter boils down to this: do you or do you not seek God's favor?

There must be an internal motive that drives one to submit under extreme pressures. That internal power is a **conscience** that says, "I must do right because I wish to please God." The word conscience comes from two Greek words meaning "to know with." It is the process of evaluating one's own behavior, thoughts and attitudes. Along with these factors, one judges, "My attitude is right/wrong; my act in this matter is right/wrong before God, etc." but it must be a conscience that is rightly informed by Scripture. One does not come into the world with a fully formed conscience. Conscience is not a black box or organ of the human being that is filled with dos or don'ts. It is a capacity God has given us to enable us to remind ourselves whenever we are violating the principles that we accept as right. It is based on a standard. It rests and doesn't activate bad feeling when we evaluate ourselves as having done well before God. A slave (or businessman for that matter) can work enthusiastically (even joyously) under bad conditions because he is working to please God. No one may excuse his poor work or sinful behavior at work by blaming it on the treatment that he receives. If he works properly, he works for God and not for men (his conscience is **toward God**).

There is **no credit coming** if he bears up well under self-inflicted treatment as the result of his **sin** (v. 20). Peter makes it clear that he is talking about enduring severe treatment that one does not bring on himself. But God is pleased, and the counselee finds favor with Him, when he bears up well (doesn't curse, threaten, etc.) under unjust treatment. And particularly when he has been **doing good**. That's the one you hear about all the time: "Here I am busting my gut to try to do all I can for that blan-

21 In fact, you were called to this, since Christ Himself suffered in your
place, leaving behind a pattern for you to copy so that you might follow in
His steps:
22 **He committed no sin, nor was deceit found in His mouth.**
23 When He was insulted, He returned no insults; when He suffered, He
made no threats, but entrusted Himself to the One Who does judge righteously.
24 He Himself bore our sins in His body on the tree, so that by dying to
sins we might live to righteousness ("By His wounds you were healed").
25 You were wandering like sheep, but now you have turned back to the
Shepherd and Overseer of your souls.

---

kety blank and it seems that the more I succeed the worse he treats me." Counselee, that's what Peter means when he speaks of **doing good** (v. 20). What if the boss fails to acknowledge his good work? God does. That is all that ought to count. (cf. Colossians 3:22-25; Ephesians 6:5-7). There is no room in all that Peter says for self-pity. Here is the passage for you to use in dealing with this problem.

The solution to the problem of unjust suffering is to continue to do good. The most powerful way to overcome evil is to persist in doing good in a respectful and cheerful manner (cf. Romans 12:21). Christ, Himself, left **a pattern** for handling unjust treatment that involved excruciating suffering. And those who follow Him are called to **copy** this pattern. The word copy is a term used of the writings that children used to trace in learning words and writing. God's children are to trace in their lives the pattern Jesus left for them. Here is what He, Whose **steps** we must follow did: **1) He committed no sin; 2) no deceit was found in His mouth; 3) He returned no insults; 4) He made no threats; 5) He entrusted Himself to God, believing He would treat Him righteously.** That is the pattern, pure and simple. There is no doubt then about how Christians must deal with problems at the workplace.

Widening out a bit now he expatiates on the treatment of Christ and its purpose in the economy of God (vv. 24,25). He **bore our sin**. He was hung on the cursed **tree**. He made it possible thereby for us to **live rightly** even at the workplace. Like **wandering sheep**, not knowing where to turn, He brought us to repentance and **turned us** toward Himself as He became the **Shepherd and Overseer of our souls.** We shall have more to say of this in chapter 5. This has been an instructive chapter. Perhaps most of all, in observing the way in which Christ handled unjust suffering and what He was able to bring out of it, Peter provides the greatest help for counselors dealing with problems of this sort.

CHAPTER 3

1 In the same say, wives, submit yourselves to your own husbands, so that even if some of them disobey the Word they may be won without a word through the behavior of their wives,

---

I don't need to say again that the discussion in chapter 3 is a continuation of that which we considered in chapter 2. Once more we are faced with the arbitrary division of a unified section into chapters. The words **In the same way** (or likewise) show this to be true. These words refer to the way that one should submit to rulers who are not always fair and just and to slave masters who may be cruel. Now Peter takes up a third authority/submission relationship in which there may be ill treatment of the Christian. The words **In the same way** may also refer to Peter's closing remarks in chapter 2 that demonstrate the pattern that Christ left to follow, a pattern that would apply to all three of these situations.

The problem here is one that is encountered regularly in Christian counseling. In verses 1 through 6 Peter deals with the problem of a Christian wife who is the spouse of an unsaved husband who may (or may not) treat her badly. The passage is not intended to encourage or even allow for believers to marry unbelievers. But as frequently happens today, two unsaved persons are already married when one becomes a Christian. What does the wife do in her submission status in marriage? That is Peter's concern.

In answering the question in the last sentence, Peter does not dodge the issues. Rather, he meets them head on. And what he says is practical to the nth degree. The advice that he gives is applicable, he says, **even if some** [husbands] **disobey the Word** (that phrase, as we have seen, in Peter's terminology, is the equivalent of saying, "even if some of them are unsaved"). So, what he has to say applies to the wives not only of harsh Christian husbands but also of non-Christian husbands who treat their wives poorly. The fundamental difference (not dealt with here) is that Christian husbands who persist in sinful treatment of their wives may, in some cases, be subject to church discipline. There is, of course, no possibility of disciplining non-Christian husbands.

Peter is concerned about two things: how the wife may please God, and how (if He wills) she may be used to win her husband to Christ. Both require the same behavior. While Peter gives no absolute assurance that if she does as he instructs her husband will come to faith in Christ, if she is to be an agent in bringing him to faith in Christ it will be through the sort of behavior he outlines in these six verses. Yet he does hold that objective out as a possibility: **that they may be won**. But let us understand up front, whether or not he comes to faith, the Christian wife is to obey what God says. More important than winning her husband (as important as that may be) is obeying God. So then, let us examine carefully what Peter tells wives.

First he commands, **wives submit to your own husbands**. That their **own husbands** are specifically mentioned makes it clear that they do not bear the same relationship to anyone else. Indeed, for a wife to submit to the wishes of another man would, in many cases, be a betrayal of her own husband. The objective is set forth: **that they may be won**. Notice, in this she is active. Submission does not mean that the wife remains passive, taking abuse from her husband; to the contrary, a plan for winning him is set forth *in which she must play an active part*. She is to attempt to **win** him. Many wives remain passive, join in pity parties with those who will participate, and the most active thing they do is ask for prayer at the weekly prayer meeting of their churches. God calls on them to do more than this. He wants them to take the offensive: attack their husbands and take them captive for Christ.

How can going to war against an unsaved husband be squared with the command to submit? First, to **submit** is often misunderstood. Such a war is not contrary to the original purpose for which God created the woman: to be her husband's **helper** in ways that approximate him (Genesis 2:18). God's commands never contradict one another. The word helper is not qualified, except to say that the help she gives ought to approximate (or fit) her husband. What help does more so than attempting to win him to Christ? Surely that is the greatest help she can offer him; and it perfectly corresponds to his need. "But you said attack; how could that be consistent with submission?" you ask. Well, let's consider that for a bit.

When you attack another to bring him to Christ, the bullets are kindness, the bombs are love. This warfare is just the opposite of that in which some wives engage. They consistently nag and plead with husbands to become Christians, or verbally complain about the values that drive unsaved husbands. Consequently, they do not win them; they succeed only in further alienating them. Such tactics are forbidden in this passage. Peter writes: **that they may be won without a word** (the King James translation hopelessly obfuscates the passage by erroneously translating "without *the* word"). What did Peter mean by this? Not that they could

2 by observing your respectful, pure behavior.

---

ever be won apart from the message of the Word (the gospel that can be found only in Scripture); certainly not that. Well, what then? Simply this: without a word *from the wife*. To preach at their husbands day after day, will not win them. To turn up the volume on the Christian radio station when he comes home is only another way of disobeying this commandment, as (also) is the pile of gospel tracts strewn about the family room and the evangelistic booklets he must move in order to sit down. Though this is a somewhat facetious picture that I am drawing (however, not so in every case), you get the idea. You are not to nag your husband with the gospel. You may present the way of salvation when he is ready to receive it and not before.

But what may God use to bring Him to Himself? Note what Peter contrasts with the wife's nagging: **they will be won through the *behavior* of their wives**. What makes evangelistic conditions a reality is not talking about one's faith but living it. And there is no place more difficult (or more important) in which to do it than before an unsaved spouse. But that is what God requires.

How does the wife wage the war of love designed to please God and possibly win her husband? Peter says, they will be won **by observing your respectful, pure behavior**. These are some of the missiles necessary to blast away the defenses your husband has reared up against the gospel. When you are submissive, you are engaging in warfare. Submission consists of two elements: **respect** (v. 2) and **obedience** (v. 6). You may have lost respect for the man because of his sinful lifestyle and the way that he treats you. But you must respect him for the God-given authority he possesses. It is respect for *God* that you show when you respect your husband's role as head of the home (see comments on Ephesians 5). Respect is the manner in which obedience is carried out. One must not do so with grunts and complaints, or with anger manifest in every facial muscle. No, the obedience must be as **pure** (unmixed) as is her lifestyle in relation to other men. But from where does the strength to be like that come? Peter will go on to explain.

But first, note the significant word **observe**. The Christian wife is on exhibition all of the time. What she does and says will be noticed. It will be difficult for her husband to forget that cutting sarcasm, that temper tantrum, those frozen hours in which she refused to speak. All those things

3 Your adornment must consist not of outward things such as the braiding of hair, and putting on of gold jewelry or clothing yourselves with robes;
4 rather, beautify the hidden person of your heart with the incorruptible quality of a gentle and quiet spirit, which is of great value before God.

---

will hinder the presentation of the gospel to him you can be sure. But contrariwise, he will also observe the kindnesses, the thoughtful actions, the endearing word and the willingness to submit when he knows that she would rather not. There is no question about what he observes being important in laying a platform for winning him to Christ. Counselor, talk to wives about these matters. Go into them in some depth. Spend time exegeting the passage, giving examples, explaining her role in the war to win her husband. Time spent in describing the wrong/right behaviors is well spent. Indeed, you might go so far as to have her write out the behaviors in which she will engage during the week to come so that they may be evaluated at the next counseling session. When you do so, you may want to spend time showing her how she might have done better in some ways and commending her for those things that she rightly did. Here, if she has a hard time catching on, it might even be helpful to role play her part for her.

Some wives think that they can win their husbands by their **outward adornment**, by dressing up and looking sexy. That is a fallacy. To win a husband, it is not outward adornment that will do the job (v. 3); that can soon grow old (as the wife herself will!). While not letting herself go so that she becomes dowdy, she should concentrate her efforts on **beautifying the inner perso**n. That is what will give the strength that we mentioned earlier, and that is what will enable her to submit during what often may be miserable conditions.

What, specifically, must be present in the inner life in order to fight the war successfully? Peter lists this as of supreme importance: **the incorruptible quality of a gentle and quiet spirit which is of great value before God.** Husbands (and God) are impressed by wives who cultivate these qualities. When one has them within, her behavior without will be positively affected. These qualities, unlike **jewelry**, fine **clothes** or the latest **hairstyle** (complete with the spun gold threads that many women used in that day) or the like, are lasting, incorruptible. And every woman may have them regardless of the money she may or may not possess.

Now let's take a closer look at this inner quality with which women

5 Indeed, in this way also holy women of the past who put their hope in God beautified themselves, submitting to their own husbands,

---

are to beautify themselves. Peter calls it a gentle and quiet spirit. Nagging, shouting, trouble-making and the like are excluded. I remember visiting a woman in my first pastorate years ago. She was the wife of an unsaved husband. It was summer, and the windows were open. I could hear her shouting at her husband a block away! That is the sort of thing that Peter condemns. Anything that causes unnecessary trouble is to be avoided. She is to be gentle in her words and actions and she must attempt to lead a quiet life that causes the least amount of stir in the home. Ask your counselee to measure her life in these terms. There is the crux of the matter.

Peter emphasizes the fact that behavior of the sort he is advocating is not impossible—**holy women of the past who put their hope in God beautified themselves, submitting to their husbands**. When a counselee says, "That's impossible," you may counter with this verse. If they could, so could you. "Well, then, how did they do it?" The part of the verse just quoted tells you how: **they put their hope in God. They beautified themselves** (inwardly) **by putting their hope in God**. That is the open secret of their success. Instead of fearing that she will be without food because of the foolish ways in which her unsaved husband wastes money, she must **hope in God** to provide. Instead of arguing and fighting with him about the ways in which he fails to discipline her children, she does what she is obligated to do and puts her trust and hope in God to overcome any deficiencies. In other words, we could set up matters this way: *Instead of* ________________________ [you fill in the blank], she puts her hope in God. Instead of the fretting, hand-wringing, frustration, anger and tears that may have accompanied sinful behavior on the part of her husband in the past, she now entrusts herself and her family to God, placing hope not in herself, her husband or anyone else, but in God alone. That is how **holy women** in Old Testament times became the women they turned out to be. And as one example of what he means, Peter refers to **Sarah who obeyed Abraham** and **showed respect for him** as head of her home **by calling him Lord**. Note, it is not the poor example she was in some things to which Peter refers but only to those excellencies in her relationship with her husband.

Now comes the clincher: **You will become her children** (a Hebraism for being like another) **by doing good and fearing no intimidation**. This part of verse 6 presupposes possible persecution on the part of the

6 as, for example, when Sarah obeyed Abraham, calling him lord. And you will have become her children by doing good and fearing no intimidation.

---

husband. But what is she to do under such circumstances? Continue to **do good** (i.e., what God requires of her), not ceasing because of **fear** growing out of some type of **intimidation**. Threats should not cause her to become discouraged so that she loses hope in God or ceases to do the good things God requires of her. Her response to intimidation ought always be increased hope in God and increased effort to do His will.

In essence Peter is saying that threats, etc., should never be used as an excuse to lose faith and hope or to slacken in one's efforts to please God. There is no place in all of this for the wife to say, "Well, but if you had a husband like mine..." or "I'd do what God wants, and my hope would fly high if only my husband were to..." No, she should hope and do good regardless of what her husband does or doesn't do. Her responses do not depend on his actions. Most wives who do good will have little to fear (cf. v. 13), but even if they do, they should not fear and should continue to do good (cf. v. 14).

So submission is not passive but active; it is waging war for the soul of another. Make sure that counselees understand this fact. Many, when they hear the word **submit** think of themselves as being ground under the heel of their husbands. Nothing could be further from the picture Peter gives to us. But remember, submission is not a tactic; it is a manifestation of the right inward attitudes mentioned in verses 3 and 4. And it is not a gimmick to win an unsaved husband. It is inner beauty and good deeds that grow out of trust and hope in God that leave fear behind. Women who have the wrong agenda must first be shown that to submit demands a change in outlook and attitudes. And this is a fruit of repentance. You must be sure that their agenda is the same as God's as you begin to counsel. If it isn't you must take the time to renegotiate those agendas along biblical lines.

One woman who, week after week at prayer meeting, pled and begged the group to pray for her husband's salvation, and for her to be able to put up with his behavior, was furious when he was saved. She had lost her status before her congregation as the suffering wife of an unsaved man. Her interest was not truly in **winning** her husband; she wanted sympathy for herself. Be as sure as you can from discussing the idea of winning that your counselee really wants to win him.

7 Husbands, likewise live with your wives in an understanding way, showing respect for the woman as you would for a fragile vase, and as joint heirs of the grace of life, so that your prayers may not be interrupted.

Now we turn to a very powerful verse directed to husbands. It is brief, but it is chocked full of admonition. Peter writes: **Husbands, likewise live with your wives in an understanding way** (lit., according to knowledge). That succinct statement covers volumes. Ask, "John, do you **understand** Joan?" He may reply "No, I wish I could!" or, reiterating that harmful cliché, "You know pastor, no man can ever understand a woman." In response, you might say, "Perhaps more than one woman is too much for you to understand, but God has commanded you to understand one—*your* woman." Then read him this verse. No wonder so many husbands have difficulty relating to their wives: they live with them according to ignorance rather than according to knowledge (i.e., **in an understanding way**).

How does one go about understanding a woman? How does he go about understanding (gaining knowledge about) anything? You are talking to John. You ask him, John, you are a salesman, aren't you? He replies, "I sure am; and a mighty good one too." Fine. Tell me, John if you hear about a hot prospect across town, what do you do? Do you rush over as soon as possible and barge in on his secretary and say "I'd like to speak to your boss; sorry I don't know his name." "Of course not, pastor. You certainly don't know anything about selling." Well then, what would you do? "I'd research him. I'd find out his name. How many children he has. Whether he likes to play golf or—wait a minute, Pastor. You mean that I should research my wife the way I would a prospective customer?" Why not? "Yeah, but research my *wife*? I don't know..." Have you got a better idea? "No, but—Oh, well, I guess if I must, I must. But tell me how to go about it. I know how to research a client, but a wife—?" Sure, I'll give you an idea or two, but you being the salesman you are won't need much more than a hint. Here are a couple of ways: first, watch her. When you see her pick up a piece of Noritake china at Belks department store, make a mental note of that. If as you go to leave she takes one more detour to the china department and looks longingly at the same plate again, underscore your mental note—she likes it. Then if you can afford it, on her next birthday give it to her. Secondly, why not simply ask her about those things you don't understand? Make out a list that is well thought through and ask her to fill in those items about which you need help. And... "O.K.,

O.K., I've got the idea, pastor. Is there anything else?" Sure, but we must start there. What you are interested in, as Peter says, is gaining knowledge about her that you now don't have.

And the verse continues, **showing respect for the woman as you would for a weaker vessel** (or, better still, a fragile vase). If you owned a piece of Waterford crystal, you wouldn't chunk it into the sink or plunk it down on a table. How would you treat it? "With care." Right. So you see, John, as you would **respect** the valuable piece of crystal, so too should you show respect for your wife. That means you shouldn't treat her like your galvanized garbage can, the way some men treat their wives. No, you are to be gentle and care for her as you would respect a fragile vase—Ming Dynasty!

"I get it, pastor. I hope there's no more." Oh, but there is. You are **joint heirs of the grace of life**. That probably doesn't mean that you jointly bring living beings (children) into this world as some think. Rather, it seems to mean that, as Peter said in his opening words of this letter, since you are both Christians, you are both going to heaven and are joint heirs of the heavenly inheritance that nothing can defile. The idea seems to be that you will both enjoy the same things for all eternity, so why not begin now? And he caps it off with the warning, if you don't begin to understand her and show her the respect God requires, **your prayers may be interrupted**. So often counselors who want to help a husband and wife who have trouble relating to each other will say, "Let's pray about it." But God says NO! It is not yet time to pray. "If you don't talk to your wife as you should, then I don't want to hear what you say. You get things straightened out between you and then you can talk to Me." It's something like a father, whose son has been seriously misbehaving and now wants the keys to the car and a $20 bill to boot, saying "Don't even talk to me about such things until you settle the other matter first." I could go on to speak at length about how much prayer is ineffective (check out the passages in James for a start), but there is no place here for that. Just this one note: The dynamic here is the same as the one in the Lord's prayer that is expanded in the appendix to that prayer.

When Peter says **Finally**, he is not like preachers who have several conclusions to their sermons. The finally refers to the section on authority/submission areas. In these concluding words he sums up the things he has been urging throughout that section. There is a summary call for unity and mutual concern that is appropriate to what has gone before. And what he says has to do with **all [of you]**. No one is left out. It is appropriate to Christians in authority as well as those (especially in view) who are in a

8 Finally, all of you, be of one mind, compassionate, full of brotherly love, tenderhearted, humble minded,

---

submission context where those over them are unjust, harsh or cruel. It is crucial, especially in times of persecution, to be united; there is difficulty enough confronting the enemy without internecine battles among themselves. That is why he calls them to **be of one mind**. An army divided will lose. It might also be of profit to consider Philippians 2:1-3 in conjunction with verse 8.

There are five exhortations in all: **1.) Be of one mind; 2.) Be compassionate; 3.) Be full of brotherly love; 4.) Be tenderhearted 5.) Be humbleminded**. Wherever you encounter disunity—in a home, in a church, between two individuals—you will discover that the lack of one or more of these elements is to blame. It is good policy to check these off with a counselee, probing deeply enough to learn which, if any of them, will need to be pursued. Unity, **being of one mind**, comes when two conditions are present: a willingness to put others first (as Philippians 2 makes abundantly clear} and when Christians are willing to have their ideas and prejudices countermanded by the words of Scripture. As a young seminary student in 1945, not having yet attended college (as was possible at The Reformed Episcopal Seminary in those days), having been saved only earlier that very year, like every other student I was brought before the faculty on my first day. The chairman of the faculty, Dr. George Handy Wailes, asked me the standard question, as he did (individually) to every incoming student: "Are you willing to test every question by the Scriptures?" In the fifty years that followed, to do so has been my avowed goal. Others may laugh and jeer at the question asked, but I can tell you, it has been a guideline for my entire ministry that I have never regretted answering in the affirmative. The sincere answer to Dr. Wailes' question is the second element in the search for unity. Of course, being willing to admit that you don't know and desiring to change whenever you recognize that your interpretations of the Bible are faulty are essential to a positive answer.

Be **compassionate**. Literally, "sympathetic." Compassion is not merely an attitude (as we often think of sympathy today); it is an attitude issuing in *acts* of compassion. The compassionate Christian weeps with those who weep and rejoices with those who rejoice. But he also does what he can to help in every adverse situation.

When one is **full of brotherly love** he shows it. By the way he relates to other Christians in contrast to non-Christians you know that he regards them as a part of the family. He exhibits a willingness to go out of his way for a brother or sister that normally would characterize the way one acts only toward close relatives. He knows that his affinity to other believers is closer than that of members of his family who are not Christians. When counselees argue and fight and call one another names, etc., it is not at all out of place for a counselor to say, "Do you think that is any way to talk to your brother in Christ?" Emphasizing the spiritual family relationship, and how it should lead to affection (the word for love here) is a powerful deterrent to bad treatment of another who belongs to the household of faith.

Be tenderhearted. The term denotes a warm, tender attitude. It is the term of choice for warm emotion. It is easy to become callous. It is also easy to crawl into your own cave, forgetting everyone else. Taking an interest in others, being sure they understand their brothers' difficulties, will help cultivate the tenderheartedness that God wants to see in your counselees. How many today even know of the problems other Christians are facing? With our spread out cities, and people coming from distances, they may see each other only on Sunday, and then as people who sit in the pew in front. Christians, even with their very busy schedules, must take the time to get to know one another *as human beings*, not merely as "that guy who always seems to bring up crazy questions in the Bible class." Helping your counselees to see the importance of getting to know the other members of the family will make a real difference in the matter of tenderheartedness.

Be humbleminded. I have already said something about this when discussing unity. One of the characteristics of a humbleminded person is his willingness to admit he is wrong—when he truly is. He doesn't bluff his way through, making excuses. He refrains from boasting and bragging. He has more concern about proving his brother correct than in proving himself so. The American penchant for being #1 (it can be seen on book titles and on TV at the end of a football game) is hardly conducive to humble-mindedness. Much of that spirit has bled over into the ranks of sincere Christians who think it is correct to constantly put themselves forward as superior to others. These virtues are part and parcel of what every counselor regularly discusses with various counselees. Because as a rule no one else does, it is incumbent upon him to do so.

Verse 9 reiterates a principle that occurs all over the New Testament (including remarks by Peter earlier in the letter; see also Romans 12:17; I Thessalonians 5:15). The Christian's response to evildoing is to return

9 not returning evil for evil or insult for insult, but on the contrary, blessing others, since you were called to do this so that you may inherit a blessing:
10 **He who would love life and see good days must keep his tongue from evil and his lips from speaking deceitful words.**
11 **Let him turn away from evil and let him do good. Let him seek peace and pursue it.**

---

good for evil. This is so contrary to sinful human nature that it must be emphasized again and again. Don't fail to do so in counseling. Revenge is God's business and is never allowed to individuals. Should one be surprised by this fact? Certainly not; they **were called to** this. They were called to bless others and, ultimately (as a result) to **inherit a blessing**. How do we know so? Quoting Psalm 34:12-17, Peter refers to the Old Testament basis for this statement.

The support is found in these words: **He who would love life and see good days must keep his tongue from evil and his lips from speaking deceitful words. Let him turn away from evil and let him do good. Let him seek peace and pursue it. The Lord's eyes are on the righteous and His ears are open to his prayer. But the Lord's face is against those who do evil.** What a powerful statement of God's relationship to the believer who is doing His will! To **see (experience) good days** and live a prosperous **life** (materially or spiritually), the Psalmist says, he **must *do* good**. God sees and hears everything Christians do and say, and He blesses them. But the opposite is the lot of evildoers. Notice the emphasis on **the tongue and the lips**. With James, who has much to say on the matter, he emphasizes the need for speech control. The believer must learn to manage his mouth. How frequently must a counselor say something to a counselee about the use of his tongue. The sarcasm, the bitterness spewed forth, the biting, venomous comments made by one believer to another are often so out of accord with Psalm 34 that the person who indulges in them can't expect to know the **good days** of which God speaks. Nasty words hurt and sting. They cause all sorts of unnecessary turmoil. No wonder then, that (instead of acidic words) Peter quotes Scripture that urges us to **seek peace and pursue it.** How appropriate to many of the quarrels and contentions between Christians these words are! The Christian counselor who fails to remember and use them in circumstances to which they apply is missing a prime tool in his kit. Even in counseling sessions, some counselees will tell you of evil plans they are hatching for getting even with others, and in your presence, others will

12 **The Lord's eyes are on the righteous**
and His ears are open to their prayer.
But the Lord's face is against those who are doing evil.

---

lambaste someone seated beside them with words that should never come to mind, let alone be spoken. Whenever you hear such things, you can say something like this, "Well, from what I hear, it sounds like you are having hard times. You don't seem to be enjoying life and there are few good days." In response you may receive the following: "You can say that again!" Your reply? This: "Let me read something for you, 'He who would love life and see good days...etc.'" If he is a true Christian, you will find that this convicting word from God will have a strong positive effect on him. Try it; you'll like it.

The other statement to note is the command to **seek peace and pursue it**. Some people enjoy controversy. They can't wait to find something wrong in another. There are people like this who spend all their lives stirring up trouble. They know and care nothing, it seems, about love covering a multitude of sins. It is important to show them the intensity with which this command is issued. Not only does God want you to ***seek*** **peace** (a strong enough idea: to zealously look for it), but also **to *pursue* it** (a word used for hunting, tracking down a quarry). Periodically a person phones me who, it seems, always is embroiled in a new conflict, largely of his making. Moreover, if and when he isn't, he keeps someone else's pot boiling. He throws gasoline on glowing embers. He is a spiritual arsonist; he wants to see a conflagration. That is the opposite of that with which God wants the Christian to fill his life. He is to be a fireman, not an arsonist. He is to cultivate those things that make for peace. In short, he is to be a peacemaker. How far some counselees have strayed from Christ's words about "blessed are the peacemakers!" Coupling those words with those quoted from the Psalm makes it possible to mount a very strong case for peace counseling. Many problems cannot be solved until the atmosphere of hostility has been dissipated. Making peace is precisely what is lacking. To find peace, intensive efforts (seeking it zealously; pursuing it like a hunter after his prey) must be made. Settle for nothing less.

We have heard much about abuse in recent times. Peter has a word or two to say about the matter (vv. 13-17). Probably they are not what your counselee wants to hear (they may not even be what you want to tell him). But they must be followed. The first verse presents no problem, and often is the key to understanding the rest: **And who will harm you if you**

13 And who will harm you if you become enthusiasts for good?
14 Yet, even if you should suffer because of righteousness, you must be happy. In fact, you must not even fear their threat, nor be upset.

---

become enthusiasts for good? That is always a good place to begin discussing abuse. Ordinarily there will be no **harm** done if, instead of egging another on, he **enthusiastically** endeavors to **do good** to him. And indeed, in counseling where one claims to have been abused by another, time and time again probing will uncover the fact that the one abused was virtually asking for trouble, not that that excuses the abuser. But it certainly makes it clear that in many (probably most) cases, abusive behavior could have been forestalled by doing good to the other person. That important fact is so clearly stated in verse 17 that it is incumbent on you to point it out.

But this forceful reminder is followed by the (rare) exception to the rule set down in verse 17. Peter realistically says, **Yet, even if you should suffer because of righteousness, you must be happy.** That is part of the emphasis that many counselees don't want to hear. They'd rather be miserable, whining and complaining about how they have been treated. Notice that the suffering in view is not something you brought on yourself—it is suffering for **righteousness**. We have already talked about how a Christian can be glad when he suffers for doing good. There is no need to reiterate. But then, Peter continues: **In fact, you must not even fear their threat, nor be upset**. No wonder many thousands of Christians over the years have endured persecution with joy in their hearts and words of victory on their lips! They had been reading I Peter. Their consciences were clear; they knew that they had done nothing to bring the waves of persecution and suffering on themselves. So they could rejoice over suffering for Christ's sake. Can the wife of an unsaved husband who loves to annoy her about her faith do so? You'd better believe it. Can she, even if he **threatens** and occasionally pushes her around? Certainly. And Peter says that she can do so without **fear or being upset**! Is that a big order? Certainly, but not beyond the ability of those whom God enables to do so. Those who achieve this tranquillity in suffering are the ones who continue to **do good and entrust themselves into the hands of a faithful Creator** (cf. 4:19b).

To fear their fear (v. 14, in its literal translation from Isaiah 8:11-13) means **to fear their threat.** Here Peter may have been thinking with deep regret about his three denials in face of danger. He knew how fear could lead to the denial of His Lord. Never again would he do so; and he wants

15 Instead, in your hearts, sanctify Christ as Lord, always ready to defend the hope that is in you to everybody who asks you.
16 But do so with gentleness and respect. Have a good conscience so that when you are slandered, those who speak insultingly about your good behavior in Christ may be put to shame.

---

others to be able to avoid experiencing the remorse that he felt. Here was a man who knew what he was talking about. And at the end of his life (according to tradition) he was crucified upside down.

How does one go about avoiding fear from those who question your faith? Verses 15 and 16 tell you. Peter says, **Sanctify Christ as Lord in your hearts**. That is an unusual directive. What does it mean? When others **slander**, making false accusations, when they **speak insultingly about you**, it is possible **to put them to shame** (v. 16). It is sanctifying Christ as Lord in your heart that makes this possible. To **sanctify** Christ in the heart is to set Him apart from all other persons and allegiances. It is to remove all doubts from the heart, while at the same time avowing Him as your **Lord.** If He is Lord, He is in control. If He is good, everything that is happening to you is for your good (cf., Romans 8:28). Then why fear? Christ knows all about the threat or abuse. He cares for you. What is happening is not meaningless, but serves some good end (even if you can't see it now). Christ will uphold you in the trial if you continue to do His will and trust in Him. *He is the only One to think about at such a time; all else is set aside, making Him your All-in-all.* But this must be genuine; it must be a matter of the **heart.** Christ is the One whose directions you must follow in trial; He, you recognize in your **heart**, is ***Lord***.

And when persecuted or otherwise abused, you must **be prepared always to give a defense of the hope within you to any one who asks you**. And if you bear up under trial and suffering, it is likely that some will ask. You must be able to **give reasons** for this hope. The word **defense** is a court term. Every individual had to be ready to defend himself at a trial; he could not call on a lawyer. Peter is saying "If you are put on trial for your faith (literally or figuratively) be ready to state your case convincingly." That doesn't mean that every Christian must have studied apologetics. But he should have a well-thought-through response. For instance, he should be well-grounded in the Old Testament prophecies so that he can show their fulfillment in Christ. He ought to be able to articulate the gospel. And he ought to be able to give a personal testimony to his own faith.

17 So you see, it is better to suffer for doing good, if God's plan has so determined, than to suffer for doing evil.

And as a part of the defense, he should not act haughty or superior; he should give the defense **with meekness and respect**. The gentleness (meekness) and respect he shows indicates that he is not an upstart or troublemaker. He does not show contempt or anger. He avoids all antagonism and strife. The defense he gives must be firm, with no wavering; but it also ought to be gentle and respectful. There is a nice balance here that many counselees find difficult to maintain. Your job is to teach him what Peter says and how to follow it.

I have already spoken about conscience. Having the **good conscience** about which Peter writes in verse 16, means to have one that does not condemn you. Such a conscience leads to boldness and confidence. The way to maintain a good conscience is to continue in good **behavior**. That will give the lie to the slander that is directed to him. Probe your counselee to find out whether he believes his conscience is clear. If not, about what does it accuse him?

Why is it that suffering comes the way of faithful saints anyway? Never by chance; certainly not because matters have gotten out of hand for God. No. **God** Himself is behind the trial, working out His **plans**. The counselee must believe this if he is to come through the trial successfully. You must believe it to help him do so. Trial has an eternal purpose. It is part of the outworking of the glorious plan of redemption in which God is manifesting His power and His mercy to the universe. To know that God is behind the suffering and that evil men are unwittingly carrying out His plan is to bring meaning and purpose into it. It is the ultimate reason why one can endure; why he can rejoice in suffering. If that is so, then clearly **it is better to suffer for doing good than to suffer for doing evil**. And by the way, quoting this last statement in situations to which it pertains is a forceful way to make the point to a counselee. It sets before him a choice. And it includes a directive designed to make him think twice about his actions.

We come now to a very interesting section—verses 18 through 22.[1] You must follow closely or you may become confused. Peter has been

---

1. I do not intend to discuss the theory that Christ went to hell to preach to the unsaved to give them a second chance. That theory is against all truly Christian theology.

18 Christ also died for sins fully and finally, a righteous One on behalf of
unrighteous ones, that He might lead you to God, being put to death in the
flesh but made alive by the Spirit,
19 by Whom also He went and preached to the spirits who are in prison
20 because they disobeyed His Word at that time when God's patience
was waiting in the days of Noah, while he was building an ark in which a
few persons (eight, to be exact) were saved by water.

---

talking about suffering for Christ's sake. He now reverts to a further discussion of Christ's sufferings (v. 18). In the following verses he moves on to how Christ's death relates to those who are **disobedient** to the gospel (vv. 19,20). As an example and a warning, he refers to the population of the world prior to the flood. They failed to listen to Noah's preaching (II Peter 2:5) and ended up in the **prison** of hell.

Now let's tackle the problems. Peter's concern is to show the advantages of **suffering for doing good** *in contrast to* **suffering for doing evil** (v. 17). The consequences of each are not only temporal but eternal. Those **disobedient to God's Word end up in prison** in the unseen world. That is what happened to those who failed to listen to Noah. Those who suffer as Christ did, on the other hand, in Him will be **raised above all their enemies a**s (in Him) they are **led to God**. He was **put to death** physically (**in the flesh**) but was **made alive by the Spirit** (not in the spirit). That it is the Holy Spirit Who is in view is made clear from the next verse. It was **by this Spirit** at work in Noah that **Christ**, long ago, went and preached to those who are **now disembodied spirits in prison,** who **at that time** (that is in Noah's day) disobeyed God's Word. As a consequence of their unbelief they not only were destroyed in the flood, but were sent to hell. That it was in Noah's day that Christ preached by the Spirit is clear from the fact that God is said to have patiently waited ***in the days of Noah***.

Through the water eight persons (souls) were saved from the flood. It was by means of water that they were saved from destruction. To this salvation by water Peter says **baptism** corresponds. How is that? In what way does baptism correspond to the salvation of the eight persons in the ark? First note Peter's careful qualification: "it isn't water (outward) baptism of which I am speaking": **not that which removes the grime from one's skin** but something inward. He was referring to an inward change that brings about **a good conscience** (freed from the guilt of sin) because it has **approval after inquiry** (that is, it is genuine). The baptism that saves is Spirit baptism, not water baptism which is but an outward

21 As a counterpart to the water, baptism now saves you (not by the removal of grime from the flesh but by the approval of a good conscience before God through inquiry) by the resurrection of Christ,
22 Who has gone into heaven and is at the right hand of God, over angels, and authorities, and powers who have been made subject to Him.

---

symbol and expression of the inner reality. At regeneration, God baptizes His children with the Holy Spirit, thus bringing salvation to them. Baptismal regeneration confuses rather than distinguishes water baptism from Spirit baptism.

But how does Spirit baptism save? **By the resurrection of Christ** (v. 21). Spirit baptism puts a person "into" Christ (I Corinthians 12:13; Romans 6:3). When merged with Christ we become united to Him in such a way that all that He ever did in His life is attributed to us as if we had done it. We are crucified with Him, raised with Him, seated in the heavenlies with Him, etc. Peter is saying that Spirit baptism saved us by Christ's resurrection just as water in the flood saved the eight on board the ark by buoying them up above the destruction. By Spirit baptism, union with Christ, we too **are raised above angels, authorities and powers in the resurrection** that lifted Him to heaven. Those who persecute you are the losers, not the victors, just as the eight were in the flood. They can exert no final power over you; you are in principle, in Him, raised to the right hand of God.

CHAPTER 4

1 Therefore, since Christ has suffered in the flesh, arm yourselves also with that thought, because whoever has suffered in the flesh has come to a parting of the ways with sin.
2 As a result, it is now possible to live the remainder of your time in the flesh no longer following human desires, but following God's will.

In chapter 4, we continue what was begun in the previous chapter with the conclusion **Therefore, since Christ has suffered in the flesh, arm yourselves also with that thought, because whoever has suffered in the flesh has come to a parting of the ways with sin.** What Peter now teaches grows out of what he had just been saying in chapter 3. Indeed, the transition is smooth. To understand this is the key to understanding verses 1 through 6. Peter has been discussing Spirit **baptism**. We saw that the believer is introduced into Christ (remember the word *baptizo* means to merge, to put things together, to join) by Spirit baptism. Union with Christ by this baptism (see comments on I Corinthians 12:13; Galatians 3:27) leads to an identification of the believer with Christ (cf. Romans 6; Colossians 2) that attributes to the believer the entire life of Christ as if he had lived it. As Christ has gone into the heavenlies and is at the right hand of God, so is the believer considered to be there in Him. In chapter 4 Peter points to the resurrection as the basis for a new life. By identification with Him, he says, we are counted to have **suffered in the flesh** with Christ. **Arming ourselves with that thought will help us to part ways with sin**. What Peter says here corresponds closely to what Paul teaches about dying to sin and living in newness of life in Romans 6. Picking up the thread begun in 3:18 (interrupted by illustrational and explanatory material) Peter continues: Christ's death means that He has died for sin **fully and finally.** He never again has to deal with sin. He is done with it once and for all. When he returns it will be apart from sin to complete our salvation (Hebrews 4:15). So like Him, those who have been identified with Him have also **come to a parting of the ways with sin**.

As Paul says in Romans 6 when speaking of the new life in Christ, **it is now possible to live the remainder of your time in the flesh no longer following human desires, but following the will of God**. That is a marvelous truth to be emphasized time and again throughout the course of counseling. In theory, if there were no obstacles within or without, it would be possible to live a perfect life. That no one does is not God's

3 (You have spent enough time in the past furthering the Gentiles' purposes, living for licentiousness, lust, drunkenness, wild partying, drinking bouts, and forbidden idolatries.)

---

fault; we are creatures of habit who drag much of the old life into the new one; this hinders us from availing ourselves of all that God has provided for us in Christ.

Peter speaks often of the problem of following **desires**. It is a common difficulty. And in our feeling-oriented age the problem is magnified. Counselor, you will discover that many of your counselee's problems have to do with this very thing. Help your counselees to distinguish desire-oriented living from commandment-oriented living. Here you see like Paul, Peter is saying, in effect, be (in daily life) what you are (in heavenly reckoning). He uses a military figure of speech: **arm yourselves with this though**t. As he indicated in 1:13, the difficulty with desire is that it must be *fought.* The Christian has all he needs to defeat habitual, sinful desire. But he can win the battles only if he goes forth to war against these desires with the thought in his mind that he has **come to a parting of the ways with sin**. He is to **arm himself with that thought**. Biblical thinking is a weapon to be used in the warfare with sin. God's empire is promoted by use of the sword of the Spirit (cf. Revelation 19:5). Because you are now freed from the sinful ways of the past, and have parted ways with sin, you can defeat those desires that still want control of your living. You *can* follow in Christ's steps. As you do battle with sinful desires, remember that. If instead, your counselee thinks defeat, he will make minimal, halfhearted efforts to defeat the foe. But if he keeps in the forefront of his thinking the fact that he is adequately armed against the fiery darts of the devil by the knowledge that he has parted ways with sin, he will put forth the effort to win. Emphasize over and over that **it is possible** to win. Most counselees, after so many failures have lost hope; they no longer believe that they can win—if they ever did.

What is the alternative to following sinful desires? **Following the will of God** (v. 2). Even under the most severe trials, says Peter, the believer need not sin if he does. Victory will not be easy, but it is possible. It must be fought for as every other battle is. Prior to coming to Christ, the Christian **had spent enough time furthering the purposes of the heathen** (v. 3). So, **the remainder of his time in the flesh** (that is, so long as he lives in this life) he must follow God's will. Serving sin and furthering the purposes of the unbelieving world must come to an end. One second in sin's service is too long! Don't go along with counselees who are reluctant to deal with the sin in their lives. Sometimes they will tell you, "I just don't think I am ready to change yet." Oh? You should respond; then you disagree with God (read verse 3). You see, He says you have already spent enough time furthering the purposes of the pagans (Gentiles). How much longer do you think God wants you to take to end this sort of behavior? People are surprised when they are confronted with direct answers from the Word of God. Whenever possible, use the Scriptures to confront wrong responses by counselees. Then it will soon become apparent to them that it is not you that they have to contend with, but it is God with Whom they are dealing in counseling. I have mentioned this fact before, but as you can see here that understanding occurs only when counselees are brought face to face with **God's will**. Put it pointedly to the resistant counselee: Whose **will** do you intend to **follow**—yours or God's?

Since many do not see that they have been furthering pagan purposes, you may have to make that point clearer. First you can remind them that whoever doesn't **gather** (that is, positively promotes Christ's purposes) **scatters** (Matthew 12:30). But in case it is not yet clear, Peter gives some obvious examples of furthering the purposes of the Gentiles. In verse 3 there are six samples of what he is talking about. Let's consider them.

Licentiousness includes any and every sort of public indecency. It may refer to sexual immorality of a shocking sort (cf. I Corinthians 5:1). In our day, little shocks the world around. But many things that the world accepts (homosexuality, lewd movies and videos) ought to still shock the Christian.

Lust is the word usually translated "desire," but here in a list of this sort it refers to all wrong desires, longings, feelings or wishes pursued to satisfaction. It is the desire fulfilled (not wrong desires entertained in the mind but these if not rejected are wrong too).

Drunkenness refers either to the habitual drunkard's lifestyle or the whole complex of sinful activities that frequently accompany a period of drunkenness (or both).

Wild partying. Today people have turned the word party into a verb. They have no hesitation to say "Do you want to party?" and by that mean what Peter here forbids. He is talking about public or private revels. The term originally meant "festal gatherings," but because these gatherings so often turned into wild parties (cf. Mardi Gras) it came to have a negative connotation.

Drinking bouts are parties that have getting drunk as their purpose.

4 But when you do so, it surprises others that you won't run with them in the same ruinous excesses, and they insult you.
5 But they will have to give an account to the One Who is ready to judge the living and the dead.

These often ended in drunken orgies.

Forbidden idolatries were abominable acts carried out in conjunction with pagan religious rites and ceremonies.

Sinful purposes of pagans are furthered when Christians participate in such activities. God's will is found only in the Bible. It must be followed to further His purposes. It is possible to leave the destructive, sinful living that is exemplified by these items on Peter's list and to follow the will of God as, for instance, it is expressed in the list of positive virtues found in II Peter 1:4-9.

But when a counselee refuses to participate in these forbidden activities that may lead to trouble (v. 4) It **surprises** others that you won't **run with them in the same ruinous excesses, and they insult you**. We even use a similar expression today: "to run with the crowd." Christians must run with other believers, not with the crowd. The believer's refusal will be an unwelcome **surprise** to pagans who, in any number of ways, will let him know so. They will **insult** him, mock him, call him a goody two shoes. Why does this happen? Because, unlike the Christian, they have no power to refrain from these **excesses**. And they get upset because the Christian's refusal is tantamount to a condemnation of their behavior (which down deep they know is wrong) even when he has not uttered a single word of the sort. Warn counselees who are struggling with problems like these of the reaction of others when they refuse to participate. Forewarned is forearmed. That is why Peter makes it clear to his readers.

In verse 5, Peter says that it is not the Christian's prerogative to condemn pagans (cf. I Corinthians 5:12,13); Christ will **judge** them. When they stand before Him, **they will have to give an account** of their activities. He is ready (has no hesitation about doing so) to judge both those who are alive and those who have died. That is to say, *all*. It is not only Peter's hearers who have heard the **good news; dead** believers also have. Martyrs may or may not be in view here. Though they were **judged in the flesh** (by unbelievers) **like man** (according to human standards) they now **live** (with Christ) **like God** (a holy, perfect spirit life; cf. 1:15,16; Hebrews 12:23) in harmony with His standards. They did not enter into this fullness of **life** while they remained **in the flesh**, but now—**in the**

6 Now this is the reason why the good news was announced to the dead that (on the one hand) they might be judged in the flesh like man, but (on the other) that they might live like God in the spirit.

7 The end of all things is near; therefore, be sound-minded and level-headed, given to prayer.

---

spirit—death (martyrdom?) has led to a life like God's (cf. Revelation 20:4; II Timothy 2:11). They now live and reign with Christ.

We now come to verses 7 through 11. When Peter says that **the end of all things is at hand**, was he wrong? Obviously, the second coming and the end of the world didn't take place. What then is he talking about? First, he is assuring his readers that the state of affairs that he has just described, where unbelievers were judging Christians according to human standards and persecuting them, will not continue. Peter encourages them to persevere during the limited time of trial.

I Peter was written before 70 AD, when the destruction of Jerusalem took place. The letter probably was sent sometime around 63/64 AD. The persecution and martyrdom of these (largely) Jewish Christians had been experiencing came primarily from unconverted Jews. Indeed, his readers had found refuge among Gentiles as resident aliens. It is true that Gentiles also had begun to insult and slander them. This was the beginning of a new wave of persecution that would sweep across the Mediterranean world about which Peter will have something to say in the next section (vv. 12ff.). Here he refers to the severe trials that came upon Christians who fled Palestine under attack from their unconverted neighbors. The **time for the end** of Jewish persecution **was near**. That is what Peter had in mind. In six or seven years the overthrow of the Jewish nation would occur. This was predicted in the Olivet Discourse and in Revelation. Titus and Vespasian would destroy the old order once and for all. **All things** having to do with the Old Testament system would cease functioning. The **end** was truly **near**.

With this encouragement, Peter urges his readers to remain calm. These trials would soon come to an end. There would be an intermission in suffering. But in the meantime he urges, **Be sound-minded, level-headed and given to prayer.** This is an important matter. God never allows His children to suffer beyond their ability to endure it (if they do so God's way). And He promises that it will come to an end (cf. I Corinthians 10:13). Trials will end. With those promises in mind you can reassure counselees. Have these items near the top of your counseling bag so you

8 Above all, love each other intensively because love covers a multitude of sins.
9 Be hospitable to one another without grumbling.

---

can easily find them for frequent use.

Stress to the counselee that emotion must not take over in times of persecution and suffering. The emphasis in verse 7, as you can see from the words used, is on the intellect (**sound-mindedness and levelheadedness** are in view). One must keep a clear head, think deeply, rightly understand and rationally apply the truths of God's Word to his situation. Otherwise, if he follows his feelings (the great danger) he will fail to follow **God's will**. It is possible by heeding Peter's exhortation, to remain calm and cool even during intense suffering. Relief is close—just around the corner; God has so promised. Always figure that into the equation. And in the interim, prayer will sustain you and enable you to bear the pain and sorrow (cf. Matthew 26:41).

Next (v. 8) Peter wants his readers to consider **love** at the top of their list: **Above all, love each other intensively** (or extensively). It is always important to show love to brothers and sisters in the faith but this is especially so in times of persecution. Mutual love, manifested in many kinds of thoughtful actions toward one another, will help to sustain those in trouble. Few things discourage more in times of suffering than the failure of others to come to assistance. Love should be extensive; they loved it is true, but they should stretch that love to the limits in seeking to help one another. Indeed, that love should extend to the point of **covering one another's sins**. **Covering** sins means not allowing offenses to come between brothers. It does not mean ignoring them. God allows no grudges or resentment. One must cover sins in such a way that they never bother him any more. If some sin keeps throwing the covers off, then you must confront the brother and bring the matter to a successful conclusion. God does not allow for unreconciled relationships. Nor does covering sins mean never offering help to another who is stuck in some trespass out of which he is not extricating himself (cf. Galatians 6:1ff.). These matters, including this verse (which is a quotation from Proverbs 10:12) are of crucial importance in counseling.

Moving on to verse 9 another issue comes to the front: **hospitality**. In times of suffering and persecution it is incumbent upon believers to be hospitable. Many lack food, lodging, etc. But of course, when you consider the inconvenience, the financial outlay, the extra work and the loss

10 As each has received a gift, he should use it in serving the rest of you, so that you might be good stewards of God's variegated grace.

---

of privacy that hospitality may involve, it is easy to resent others who need it. Peter realizes that this can be a source of contention, so he says be hospitable **without grumbling**. Hospitality offered in love never results in grumbling. Of course, no one should be allowed to take advantage of another's hospitality. Counselors may find it necessary to sort out legitimate from illegitimate requests for hospitality. **Love** is **above all** because it affects all. One covers sins, is hospitable etc., because he gives of himself to others. Some counselees are grumblers. They grumble especially at putting themselves out for others. Good counseling will forestall grumbling. And even today when there is no persecution, when families are breaking up, children must be cared for. There can be grumbling about the extra load that these things may cause one to carry. Frequently these sorts of exigencies are faced by persons in counseling. The verse applies.

God's **gifts** to the members of His church are of various sorts; Peter calls them **variegated**. No one has them all. They were given to the members individually, but not for them individually. They were given to be **used in serving the rest** of the members. In that way, one becomes a **good steward of God's grace**. Each counselee has gifts. They may not yet have been *discovered*, not very highly *developed* and certainly (in many cases) not *deployed* in the church. A steward doesn't own that which he has stewardship over; it is owned by another. The Christian is to be a **good steward of the grace of God** in granting gifts to His church. He has no right to hug them tightly to himself. He must use them for the mutual benefit of other Christians. Your counselee may be quite deficient in his use of these gifts. Actually in whole or in part, he may be hampering his own spiritual growth because of this deficiency. It may be your task to enable him to discover, develop and deploy his gifts. One fails to **love** others as he should until he willingly does so. He may be depressed, lonely, angry or have a host of other problems that could be cleared up by learning how **to serve the rest** of the church.

As examples of what he is talking about, Peter shows how to use the gifts of **speaking** and of **serving**. They exemplify the two offices in the church (the teaching elder and the deacon). How does one use these gifts rightly? He must do so humbly; neither pushing himself forward nor taking glory for himself. It is only by God's **strength** that he can function rightly. And He is willing to **supply** it. The use of the gifts must **glorify**

> 11 When someone speaks, let him speak God's messages; when someone serves, let him serve by the strength that God supplies, so that in everything God may be glorified through Jesus Christ, to Whom be glory and might forever and ever. Amen.
> **12** Dear friends, don't be surprised at the fiery ordeal that is coming upon you to test you, as though something strange were happening to you;

God, not the one using them. And note, whenever one speaks to the church, he must be sure to **speak God's messages**. He must keep the wisdom of the world (that Paul calls foolishness) out of the pulpit. Counselors take heed; the same is true of counseling. Your **strength** to do effective counseling comes from God. It is He that must be **glorified** in every aspect of it, and when you speak as a counselor, seeking to help another by the use of your gifts, you must **speak God's messages** to your counselees without admixture.

Thinking of the glory that is due God causes Peter to break out into a doxology: **so that in everything God may be glorified through Jesus Christ to Whom be glory and might forever and ever. Amen.** God is glorified in His Son Jesus Christ, Who redeemed us. To the Father, Son and Spirit (Who strengthens) **belong glory and might forever**. The **Amen** ("Yes, let it be so") adds emphasis.

The last section of the chapter is found in verses 12 through 19. Peter has just spoken about God's **glory** in a magnificent doxology. He now develops the idea of **glory** in conjunction with the announcement of yet more severe trials and persecutions that lie just ahead. In these verses he comes back to it again and again. It is as though no matter how bad things get, the glory of God that He possesses and that He gives so outshines everything else, that suffering pales into insignificance. To use that argument is a large task, counselor. How much do you know about God's glory and the glory that awaits you and your counselees? Probably far too little, if you are willing to admit it. It might be better, therefore, simply to read and reread these verses to the counselee as necessary rather than to spend much time trying to explain them. It is easy to muddy the canvas. Don't fall for that temptation.

Well, what does Peter teach in this final section of the chapter? He looked forward to the day in which the full glory of Christ will be revealed and when, with Him, Christians would share in that glory. As a matter of fact, he even declares that it is possible for them as faithful martyrs and confessors to enter into that glory, in part, in this life. That is the

13 rather, insofar as you share in Christ's sufferings, be glad, that at the revelation of His glory you may be very glad.

---

substance of his argument. From the way that he writes, you can tell that Peter is excited about the glory of Christ (remember, with James and John he had briefly seen something of that glory on the Mount of Transfiguration and longed to see it again in all its fullness and permanence).

Now as to **the fiery ordeal that is coming to test** his readers, Peter says there is no need to **be surprised as though something strange were happening** to them. He is here predicting a second wave of persecution, an **ordeal** more **fiery** than the first. He is thinking of the Roman persecution. He does not apologize for the problems that the church will have. To the contrary, he speaks of **glory**. He does not see the suffering so much as he sees the glory it will bring to God's people. Never speak weakly about the trouble in which a counselee may find himself when he did not bring it on himself. Actually, you ought to forewarn them that such trouble is common and, in whatever form it appears, it is but that which is inevitable in this world of sin. The problem, as Peter sees it, is not the trouble; it is the view that one takes of it and how he handles it. When placed in proper juxtaposition to the glory of God trouble seems not so dark as it did before. And eventually, as one views trouble from this biblical perspective, it begins to fade more and more until at last it can hardly be seen at all. That is Peter's purpose in the words we are examining. And it can be yours too, as you endeavor to help a suffering saint bear up under his load.

Relief from Jewish persecution is but a breathing space. More and greater suffering lay ahead. As indeed it may in the life of a counselee. He should not consider this **strange**. He should be fully acquainted with the fact that in this world, all who live godly lives shall suffer tribulation. And from another angle, he must see clearly that persecution is nothing less than **sharing in the sufferings of Christ** (v. 13). Not that Christians in any way enter into Christ's redemptive work; certainly that is not in view. What He did on the cross was full and final—nothing could ever be added to it. Nor need it. As part of His body they would suffer because the world hates Him (John 15:18,19; 17:14). Bearing His Name brings Christians into close identification to Him. Since it is no longer possible for them to get at Him, the next best way to release that pent up hatred for Christ is to attack His church (for an example of this, read Revelation 12:5,13). Until a counselee understands and adopts this view, he will continue to think it is strange that he must suffer for Christ's sake. The complaints, the self-

14 If you are reproached because of Christ's name, you are happy, because the Spirit of glory and of God rests on you.
15 Now, let none of you suffer because he is a murderer, or thief, or criminal or even as a meddler,
16 but if anybody suffers because he is a Christian, let him not be ashamed, but let him glorify God in that Name.

---

pity, the whining, the doubts that so often accompany suffering are evidence that those who indulge in such things do not understand Peter's view of suffering. They consider suffering something **strange** (or that should be alien to believers). Your task is to acquaint them with the facts. Your task is to relate suffering to the glory of God.

If you are **glad** to suffer for Christ (v. 13), recognizing sufferings for what they are (that which unbelievers want to afflict on Christ), you will be able to handle suffering well. Suffering doesn't bring happiness. The joy comes from recognizing that He has so treated you that He has allowed you to stand in His place to receive the persecution with which others would like to afflict Him. And it is a joy to realize that you can suffer for the One Who suffered the cross for you. Peter adds, if you **gladly suffer** for Him now, at Christ's **revelation** when His glory as God will be made Known to all (cf. 1:7), you will not only be **glad**, but **very glad.** And if you have **shared in His sufferings now, you will share in His glory then**. That bright prospect ought to bring gladness to a counselee's heart during times of testing.

The **test** to which Peter refers, is not so much in the **fiery ordeal** itself as it is in the heart of the believer. Not that the test is not severe (after all, he doesn't call it ***a fiery ordeal*** for nothing). But what I mean is that it can become the most excruciating experience possible, or it can be a time of faithfulness and gladness for the believer depending on how he views it and responds to the trial. Tell your counselee that. After all, that is what Peter is getting at. Coming through the test successfully will not only strengthen him but, of greater importance, will honor His Lord.

As the **Spirit of glory and of God rested** on Jesus (cf. Matthew 5:11) so too will He descend in power, imparting strength and wisdom to those who stand firm in trial. The Spirit Whose purpose is to glorify the Son (John 15:26) will glorify Him through you. But as Peter observes in verse 15, if one suffers because of his own sin (as **a murderer, a thief, a criminal or even as a meddler**) he fails to glorify God; that is not the sort of suffering that he is talking about. But if he suffers **because he is a**

17 I say this because it is time for judgment to begin with God's household; and if it starts with us, how will it end with those who disobey God's
good news?
18 And, **if the righteous man is scarcely saved, where will the ungodly
and sinner appear?**
19 So then, let those who suffer according to God's will do good and
entrust themselves to a faithful Creator.

Christian he must not be ashamed (v. 16), he must stand tall for the **Name** of Christ that he bears. Peter tacks on the word **meddler** at the end of verse 15 presumably to make it plain that he is speaking of *all* sin that brings grief to the one sinning; not just of the more obvious sins.

Now in verse 16 Peter warns about being **ashamed** of bearing the Name of Christ (found in the title **Christian** by which he identifies believers). The bitterness and remorse he felt at being ashamed in his threefold denial surely must have motivated him to write these words. He did not want his readers to experience anything like that. Nor do you want your counselee to know the sting of having backed off from persecution or suffering out of shame.

Peter urges these things because, as he says, **judgment** is coming. This judgment **begins with God's household** (the church). The judgment in view is judgment in this life. God's eternal judgment will follow in time. And if God sorts out those of His children who are firm from those who cave in under suffering (the sifting power of persecution is strong), then how will those who **disobey the good news** (unbelievers) fare? Supporting this idea, he quotes Proverbs 11:31 (LXX; cf. Luke 23:31). Those who are **righteous are scarcely saved**. What then of **sinners and ungodly persons**?

Finally Peter closes this discussion with a summary statement that I used elsewhere as a title for the entire book: **Let those who suffer according to the will of God do good and entrust themselves to a faithful Creator**. That title would be *Trust and Obey*. These two things summarize all he has said about how to handle persecution and suffering. **Entrust yourself to God and continue to do good**. That is it in a sentence. If God is a **faithful Creator** He Who has power to create and to sustain His universe, in Whose hands is all that transpires, will faithfully fulfill all His promises to His own because He is able to do so and because He is true and faithful. The suffering saint need not fear. Instead, he is to concentrate on doing good. He must not allow suffering to curtail that. He will glorify God only by doing so. Here is trenchant material that any counselor who recognizes its force will want to use.

Chapter 5

1 Therefore I urge the elders among you, as a fellow elder and witness of Christ's sufferings and as a sharer of the glory that is going to be revealed,

---

How one shepherds God's flock is of concern to the Holy Spirit. And this is of special importance in times of trouble and trial. An ordered, well-trained, healthy flock can withstand much. The opposite also is true. Speaking of the fiery ordeal that was about to overtake the churches in the Roman world raises the matter of sufficient care for the sheep. They would need shepherds who could care for them during this brief, but intensive, persecution. While it is certainly of great advantage to be able to meet times of testing as a part of such a body, with shepherds bringing the various forms of help that are requisite to meet those tests, it is also clear that sheep need good shepherds at all times—even in those that are most tranquil. And as one thinks of the responsibilities of a shepherd in caring for ignorant, wandering, helpless sheep, he realizes that a large part of that shepherding activity will be counseling. While the public ministry of the Word is of great value in shepherding activities, the individual peculiarities of each sheep must be addressed. That, of course, means the need to deal with each sheep personally, i.e., to *counsel* him. Too often we hear of "the primacy of preaching." Such an emphasis is unbiblical. What the New Testament advocates is the primacy of the *ministry* (service) *of the Word* (Acts 6:4). This *service* of the *Word* (the word is taken from the *service of food*) incorporated much counseling as well as preaching. Listen to Paul speak to the Ephesian elders about his pastoral ministry among them over an extended period: "for three years, night and day, I didn't stop counseling each one of you with tears" (Acts 20:31). Clearly then, such activity was a large part of his ministry. It is unfortunate that some famous preachers in huge churches who cannot hope to effectively counsel their congregations, and so concentrate on preaching, are usually the ones who write the books advocating preaching over all else. Obviously they are speaking out of their own pulpit work rather than conveying the teaching of the Bible on the subject. Often, many of their people suffer greatly from the lack of a sufficiently personal ministry. Counseling is a major part of the work of shepherds—both those elders who rule and those who also teach.

To highlight this matter Peter writes to **the elders among** them. It is instructive that in doing so Peter refers to himself as **a fellow elder**. This designation is intended to remind them of his sympathetic understanding of the concerns, difficulties, temptations and tasks of the eldership. That same sort of relationship to other pastors is why I, as a pastor and counselor, have taken it upon myself to write these commentaries. I think that not only have I something to contribute, but that "something" is of a sort that may speak to counselors in many of the situations in which they find themselves laboring since I too am a fellow-elder in the Church of Jesus Christ.

Peter wants these elders to carry out their duties to the full. How few do is deplorable. Too many elders think of the position as an honorary post with little or nothing to do apart from officiating at ceremonial functions. Others see the eldership solely as a debating and decision-making body. Fundamentally, however, the elder is to *care for the sheep* that Christ has committed to him. If he fails in this task (and there is no excuse for not knowing what his task is—the Bible is explicit on the matter) the flock will suffer and Christ will be dishonored. The word **elder** means "old man." It has to do with the qualification of the individual chosen to this work: he must be *mature* in the faith. The word *bishop* ("overseer") is a term used for the same individual (cf. Acts 20; Titus 1). It refers to the *work* of the elder—overseeing the flock as a shepherd oversees his flock (remember the shepherds "keeping watch over their flocks by night"). These elders would play a vital part in holding the flock together by instructing and strengthening them, when the test came. Their care, or lack of it, would make the difference. Some Christians would deny their faith; others would overcome the enemy. The work of the elders in helping in times of trial would be of the highest importance.

Peter was an apostle, but all apostles were also elders. The apostleship included all of the lesser offices as well. But Peter emphasizes his solidarity with the elders in the churches to which he writes rather than his superior office as an apostle. He is appealing to them as one of themselves. That is something for a counselor to remember: he must not assert his authority unless it is necessary to do so. It is better to come alongside people on an equal plane with them. That of course can be overdone. Some counselors refuse to exert the authority resident in the office of elder at all. That is a serious mistake. But there are others who never descend from the high and lofty perch upon which they have placed themselves. That is equally serious. Peter will have something to say about this matter in his words to these elders.

2 to shepherd God's flock among you, exercising shepherdly care over it; not out of obligation but willingly, as God would have you do it; not out of eagerness to make a personal profit, but out of eagerness to serve;

Elder is the fundamental office in Christ's church. It originated back in Old Testament times as early as the Church was organized. While other offices—priests, Levites, judges, kings, scribes—came and went, the eldership continued concurrently alongside of them right into New Testament times. This organized group of men were what gave stability and continuity to the people of God under all sorts of circumstances. God, through Peter, here outlines both the duties of the eldership and the perils of wrongly exercising them, so that these Christians might have the help they needed to weather the onslaughts of persecution that would soon come their way.

Peter also appeals to the elders by reminding them that though he was one of them, and thereby familiar with their task, he was also an apostolic witness of the death and resurrection of Jesus Christ, and on the Mount of Transfiguration was one of the privileged three who **shared** in **the glory** that all will eventually experience (v. 1). Not only did he know about the eldership, he knew all about apostolic witness and work as well. He mentioned these facts, doubtless, in order to let them know of his competence to instruct them. When counseling others, it is well for you to state your qualifications. How has God and His church recognized you? Are you too an elder who has been ordained to the office by the Church? There are all sorts of persons hanging out shingles as full-time counselors who have no warrant, no authority and no ministerial experience to commend them. Nor has Christ's church set them apart to this work. They should either cease what they are doing or seek the proper credentials from the church. I am not talking about informal counseling (something every Christian is entitled and obligated to do—simply because he is a Christian). What I have in mind is those many who take it upon themselves to do full-time counseling and even take it upon themselves to instruct pastors and elders. This unruly system of things must come to an end. Denominations that come to this conviction someday must set standards for pastoral counselors in their membership that have to do with their competence as elders of the Church.

What is it that Peter urges the elders to do? Simply this: **Shepherd God's flock among you, looking after it** (v. 2). That is the fundamental task to which they are called. Doubtless Peter's fondness for shepherdly imagery is not only very appropriate (Christ Himself used the imagery; John 10), but he remembered the words of Christ directed to him (John 21). What was said in that last chapter of the Book of John is apropos to every elder. Careful examination of the words in which Christ restored Peter indicate that the prime task he was to perform was caring for sheep, including the lambs of the flock. In assuming that responsibility, it is clear that, like Paul, one must regularly counsel those over whom he has the oversight. Those whose congregations are too large to exercise this care should seriously contemplate breaking up the large body into several smaller ones in which the ministry of the Word in counseling can be carried on as it was in larger Christian communities like Ephesus.

There are three leadership problems that face the shepherds of God's flock. In verses 2 and 3, Peter sketches them together with the solution to each:

Servile Service. Peter says that the ministry of shepherdly rule must not be done **out of obligation but willingly, as God would have you do it.** That is an essential element in good care for the flock. One who takes on himself the task of shepherdly rule must engage in that rule not because he has been pushed into it by people or by financial need, but because he is anxious to serve Christ and His church. That is how God wants the elder to minister. And since counseling is so very much a part of the work, it is certain that God would have one counsel in the same way. There are people who take up counseling because they have failed in the pastoral ministry and know little else to do. The counseling task, as an aspect of the elder's responsibility, should never be considered a lesser aspect than the rest. If he failed as an elder in other respects, or if he was unqualified for the eldership in some way, neither is he qualified to do counseling. Counseling is one of the more onerous aspects of the elder's role. Of course, he has his share of true joy in seeing the Word of God transform lives as it is applied to them. But those who fail or are unqualified for preaching, administration and other duties connected with the eldership, are thereby unqualified for full-time counseling as well.

Some are crowbarred into the office. They have no inclination and probably no gifts for serving as elders. Yet wives, friends, preachers and others beg and cajole until they acquiesce. Peter's words condemn any such motive for entering the eldership. And those who are in it under those conditions ought to admit it, withdraw and take their rightful places in the church. If you are one who fits that bill take heed to my words. You will never be happy as an elder, you will serve poorly and you will harm Christ's church. It is no shame for you to demit the eldership if you are not qualified; rather, it is a commendable act. But it *is* a shame to go on as you are.

Probably what Peter has mostly in mind is the person who has lost his sense of mission and calling. He is an elder, and ought to be. Yet slowly but surely, he has drifted into serving out of duty rather than out of a sense of ministry. The first love for the work [here we will speak of counseling alone] of ministry to people in need has disappeared. The ministry has grown old and he has grown cold. There is no willingness to serve. He does so only because he is an elder and is expected to show up for meetings. Long ago, if he ever truly had it, his zeal for counseling hurting or straying members of the flock flagged. He hasn't counseled anyone for months—possibly years! Conceivably, if he wasn't properly instructed in his duties as a counselor, he never did. Few things can make the eldership a burden rather than a ministry to which one willingly applies himself, then the failure to engage individuals in face to face encounters on a regular basis. The work of the eldership is preeminently that of caring for the flock. The thing that, in many instances, will enliven his zeal once more is to begin engaging in the regular practice of counseling.

Financial gain, according to Peter is another poor motive for pursuing the tasks of the eldership. How one would make money by doing so in his time may be vague to us, but surely, it should be neither vague nor uncertain to anyone today. The lavish sums that one can accrue by hanging out his shingle are almost unbelievable. There are people who extract $40,000 or more from one counselee over a period of a few months. There are entire organizations that have been erected that lure Christians into their clutches and bleed them dry financially, then when the counselee has run out of money discard them like so much trash. These things ought not be. That is why I have opted for counseling free rather than for a fee. While the laborer is worthy of his hire, serious efforts to come to grips with what is a fair hire must be made. And those who counsel as part of their pastoral ministry should have no problem: it *is* a part of that ministry; so they should engage in it simply as a part of the ministry for which the *church* pays them regularly. **Personal profit** as a goal to be attained by taking advantage of the sorrows and sins of God's people is forbidden by Peter. Rather, the motive for ministry (that, in God's providence, may result in financial gain *as a by-product*) must always be **eagerness to serve.** If that eagerness to help members of the church by counseling them is not present, you can be sure that it will not be long before it is replaced by some other motive, often— if possible to realize it—by a desire to pile

3 not by lording it over those allotted to your charge, but by becoming models for the flock.

---

up lucrative sums of money from the work. After all, counseling is not easy. Something must motivate one to engage in it. If it is not eagerness to serve God by serving His church, then all too often, as Peter points out, the motive is financial. One may not be fully aware of the subtle shift that often occurs. He begins as Peter says, with an eagerness to serve, to help strengthen the church by helping its members overcome problems to the honor and glory of God. But over time, as he becomes more experienced at it, and the initial luster tarnishes, or as he becomes a "professional" counselor, he becomes more and more concerned about the personal profit that he can make from the work. Counselor, examine yourself in the light of Peter's [i.e., the Holy Spirit's] admonition.

Misuse of position and authority is Peter's third concern. There is a respect that adheres to the office of elder of which Paul speaks in I Thessalonians 5:12-14. And incidentally, it is in that passage in which Paul speaks of **thinking quite highly** of the elders who **labor** among the flock that he elaborates on **their work** in terms of their counseling activities (see especially vv. 12,14). Peter puts it *clearly* (which was one of his finest traits): **not by lording it over those allotted to your charge, but by becoming models to the flock.** The good shepherd doesn't drive the sheep; he leads them. They follow when he leads them well. They will trust a shepherd that does so, because they know that he has their well-being at heart. And they will be blessed. They may foolishly follow a wicked, slothful or ambitious shepherd too—but to their peril. Yet, those in dire need, who seek help desperately, may not always find it possible to discern the good from the bad. That is why the church in ordaining shepherds to care for the **charge** given to them must take great care in placing the proper persons in that office. And they must continually check them out to be sure that they are not abusing their moral and official authority—especially in counseling.

It is not the task of the shepherd to settle all questions for his counselees. For example, it is not his prerogative to determine who should marry whom; he must not tell counselees to take or leave a certain job (unless the wedding involves marrying an unbeliever or taking the job will cause one to engage in illegal or immoral work. That is to say, unless the contemplated act is a clear violation of the Word of God.). Rather, he must so strengthen the counselee by the instruction, consideration and

4 Then, when the chief Shepherd appears, you will receive the glorious crown that will never fade.

---

application of biblical principles to his situation that he is enabled to make good decisions for himself. But there is more. Rather than order counselees around in all sorts of ways (**lording it over** them) he is to model righteous behavior before them. But if he is a professional counselor, he will find it difficult to do this. A counselor of the sort Peter is describing—an elder of the church counseling a member of his flock—has ample opportunity to become an example of the very things he expects of them. They repeatedly encounter one another outside of the counseling room. Both consciously and unconsciously, if he is growing and showing it, a counselor will become the sort of person that a counselee seeks out and wishes to model his life after (on this see also Hebrews 13:7). How tragic it is for those who have failed in their lives and have been ousted from the ministry for immorality, etc., to think that as a result, they can guide others. Yet many end up hanging out the shingle. When you want to learn how to play the piano you don't turn to one who has failed at it; you turn to one who is a success.

There is a reward to faithful shepherds (v. 4). At His coming Christ (Whom Peter styles the chief Shepherd) will present a glorious crown to him. Presenting the *stephanos (*a crown made out of parsley, myrtle, etc. that was awarded the winner of an Olympic game) was a way of saying that one would receive a reward. And, unlike the *stephanos* of the successful Greek athlete, the reward that the good shepherd receives from the chief Shepherd is unfading. It is an eternal reward. That statement, made to all faithful shepherds (an important aspect of whose task is to care for the flock by shepherd-like counsel), is calculated to encourage. Every counselor experiences times of discouragement. You have worked long and hard with a counselee who seems to show promise only to have him back off from his gains. The counselor knows that some who are angry with others, or the world in general, may take out their anger on him. He recognizes that after hours of strenuous effort and inconveniencing himself for a counselee, he may walk away without even a word of thanks. All are not like that, naturally. Many do change, do express gratitude; some even become lifelong friends. But there are also plenty of the first sort. Yet the counselor should not expect his reward from the counselee; it is coming from His Lord. In serving the members of His church, he serves Him. He, therefore, is the One that the counselor must always keep in

5 Likewise, younger men, submit yourselves to your elders. All of you tie on the apron of humility toward one another, because God opposes the proud but helps the humble.

---

mind. His prime motive must be an ever-growing desire to be faithful to his Lord. If he keeps that objective in view he will not be disappointed. Indeed, the 4th verse ought to carry him through the difficult times that counselors inevitably encounter.

Thinking of elders, Peter now turns to the younger men in the congregation and urges them to **submit** to their elders. It is often hard for them to do so. The hot blood of youth may run so strongly that younger members of the congregation find it hard to move as slowly and deliberately as their elders. They want changes *now*. But though it is possible for the elders to become too conservative in their thinking and acting and decision-making, the younger members may fail to recognize that careful, cautious judgment is often required. That is why they must submit. They should respect the judgment of their elders, and be willing to learn from them. It is also true that the elders must listen to the voice of youth which, at times, may bring freshness and insight into their deliberations. Submission does not require silence. The youth of the church may rightly offer opinions and suggestions to their elders—*so long as these are offered in a submissive manner*. Many counseling situations involve the relationship of the young to their elders—and sometimes, to those officially designated to the office of elder. Counselors, accordingly, ought to emphasize these important relationships to each in turn. And in doing so, they ought to continue exhorting as in the verses that follow.

It is the manner of humility to which Peter now addresses himself (v. 5): **All of you [young men and everyone else in the congregation] tie on the apron of humility toward one another, because "God opposes the proud but helps the humble."** In vivid language he urges everyone to tie securely on himself an **apron of humility**. To what does he refer? This apron was part of the slave's attire. The slave, in his humble station, becomes a striking example of how one Christian ought to serve another. Clearly there are many opportunities for a biblical counselor to refer to verses 5 and 6. A lack of humility is precisely what gets in the way of much counseling. Many won't even come for counseling out of pride (the opposite of humility). Their self-esteem is so high that they would rather have things go from bad to worse than admit it before another person. There are people who will go to counselors other than those appointed by

6 Humble yourselves, therefore, under the mighty hand of God, that at the proper season He may raise you up.

God to care for them as elders in their church simply because they "don't want to be embarrassed." Fierce pride is a hard rock on which much counseling (and potentially needed counseling) is broken.

But then, even when eventually (usually far too late) pride is overcome by the enormity of the problem, people who do come for counseling put up all sorts of objections (even to clear requirements of the Bible) out of pride. The failure to repent of his sins and the willingness to bow before the Word of God (not the counselor) is typical of many a counselee. Until one is willing to don the **apron** that represents **humility** (i.e., be willing to relate humbly to God and others) it is virtually impossible to get anywhere in counseling. Why is that? Because **God opposes the proud but helps the humble.** Where can counseling go if God is opposed to it? How can a counselor succeed unless through his ministry God Himself **helps** his counselee?

There are times then, when you will run smack up against the wall of pride that a counselee has erected between himself and God and/or others. It is clear to you (and to him) that his refusal to move in a biblical direction is due to nothing short of pride. At that point what can you do? Since it is the Scriptures that "convict" a person of his sin (cf. II Timothy 3:16,17), use them, asking God to bless their use in tearing down the wall. Indeed, to what better Scripture than that in verse 5 could you turn? Tell your counselee: "It is not I you are opposing in this matter. You admit that God wants you to confess your sin and seek forgiveness from Tom. Well, there is only one thing standing between you and obedience: pride. And so long as you hide behind that thick wall of pride you have erected, you can be sure that your stance is in opposition to God. You have reared up that wall against *Him*. Do you think you can get away with that? Do you think that you can come up with some other solution to your problem than the one that you admit God wants you to take? In the final analysis, you must recognize that we can get nowhere because, in return, God Himself is opposing you in this matter! God is powerful, His **Hand** is **mighty** (v. 6), too mighty for you to resist and, at the same time, the hand you need to help you. Why allow pride to estrange you from the very One whose help you so desperately need?"

That kind of counseling, when called for (and it isn't always), is what God uses to break down barriers that (otherwise) will go on making coun-

7 Throw all your worry on Him, because your affairs matter to Him.

---

seling ineffective. Are you up to it? If you haven't yet the courage to say such things, then at least turn to the passage we have been looking at and, having read it to your counselee, ask "Can you think of any other reason why counseling isn't getting anywhere? If God is in opposition to you because of your pride, then you must repent and humble yourself under His mighty hand. If that is the problem, and you don't, you may expect Him to humble you Himself. It is better for you to judge yourself than to wait until God must step in and do it for you" (cf. I Corinthians 11:31,32).

Those who humble themselves under God's hand, in time will feel the gentle pressure of that massive **hand** raising them up (6^b). And it is precisely that which your counselee needs—the hand of God, through the Word that you minister, raising him up out of the problem just as it has raised him from his knees. But make it clear, this will happen only **at the proper season**. When is that? Whenever God deems it **proper**. In His time. It may be that God will strengthen through allowing a trial to continue for a season. In His wise providence, He may recognize that for the sake of others who are concerned in the circumstances it is necessary for your counselee to continue in need for a time. But through it all, that mighty hand can—and will—sustain, if the counselee humbly submits himself to God and others. One aspect of humility is admitting that one does not have the answers. Another is admitting that he does not have the strength. Still another is a willingness to receive instruction and power from Another. These are the elements that you must seek to install in the heart and life of the proud counselee. Without them, counseling will come to a screeching halt.

One application of these aspects of humility in counseling is learning to trust God enough to cast one's cares (worries) **on Him** rather than to bear them himself. **Worry** is a sin because it shows lack of faith in a loving Father (cf. Matthew 6) and because God commands us not to worry (Philippians 4). Here, instead of worry God says you can roll off that burden, give it to Him and He will carry it for you. That is a wonderful promise for the counselee; one that you must not fail to mention in the foregoing discussion with the proud person. If he will humbly admit he has no solution to the problems he faces, but that God does, and he is willing by prayer and obedience to Scripture to throw his problems God's way instead of continuing to carry them himself, he may expect genuine

8 Be levelheaded and wide awake; your opponent the devil prowls around like a roaring lion searching for somebody to devour.
9 Resist him, standing firm in the faith, knowing that your brotherhood throughout the world fully experiences the same kinds of sufferings.

---

help. There is not only rebuke and warning in the passage; there is wonderful hope and promise as well. It is always God's way to offer both to his erring children; so it must be your way in counseling that you may not wrongly represent God by emphasizing one side of His nature to the detriment of the other. Because God is all that He is, you must always represent Him as a God of anger and discipline as well as a God of mercy and grace.

Peter continues: **Be levelheaded and wide awake; your opponent the devil prowls around like a roaring lion searching for somebody to devour.** This is Peter's final warning. While the devil would be behind the Roman persecution, that might not be his most effective attack. Indeed, for some it may be but diversionary. Instead, Peter here refers to those less obvious attacks of the evil one (vv. 8,9). Because he exhorts the counselee to be **levelheaded and wide awake** it is clear that he may be seduced unwittingly by the devil. Otherwise, why the exhortation? Christians, asleep to the wiles of the devil, will fall easy prey to him, as Peter (literally) did. Sexual infidelity, divisiveness, envy and the like, strike down more Christians than the Roman sword ever did. Though valiant out on the open battlefield, the very same Christian soldier may be brought low by the devil's sniper behind the lines. How does one avoid defeat? What can you tell your counselees about the matter?

Just what Peter does: "In humility, casting your cares on God, wide awake to the fact that the enemy strolls about seeking to destroy you, **resist him.** But how? By **standing firm in the faith, knowing that your brotherhood throughout the world fully experiences the same kind of sufferings.** You must never think that you alone suffer as you do. Others, many of whom have found the help of God offered in the Scriptures more than sufficient to enable them to **stand** and not collapse under trial, have successfully resisted the evil one's attempts to weaken them and cause them to doubt or deny the **faith**. But if others have been able to withstand, so can you—that is Peter's point. It is very much like that precious promise in I Corinthians 10:13. Bad doctrine, or even lack of truth, opens one to the attacks of the evil one. It is your task to inform counselees where they lack essential truths in order to bolster and fortify them against the

10 Now the God of all help, Who has called you to His eternal glory in Christ, after you have suffered a little, will equip, support, strengthen and firmly establish you.
11 To Him be power forever and ever. Amen.
12 I wrote briefly to you through Silvanus, whom I count a faithful brother, urging and testifying that this is God's true grace. Stand firm in it!

---

devil's attacks. You can be sure that on his prowls whenever he sees a counselee willing to change and mean business with the Lord that he attacks most strenuously. So tell your counselee, "be wide awake. The more you conform to the Lord's ways the more you are likely to be attacked. Don't let the attack come as a surprise; expect it and be prepared to meet it." How easy it is for one suffering to doubt and (even) deny the providential care of God. Don't let that happen to your counselees because of your negligence in applying the truths contained in this passage to his situation.

Now look at Peter's final words of encouragement to his suffering readers (vv. 10,11). How does God help the humble? How does God strengthen His saints? Peter writes that after they **have suffered a little,** God will **equip** (for resistance in battle) by His Word and Spirit, will **support** by His church and Word, will **strengthen** (so that we may successfully fight) by His promises and will **establish** (uncertainties are turned to sureties; doubts into convictions) humble believers; He confirms their faith.

What more could one want? He is **the God of all help** (grace, in contexts like this, means help) **Who has called** His people **to eternal glory.** Having done so, will He abandon them on the path to it? Of course not. But notice, God is **the God of all help**; He will not share that title with the psychologists! There is no true help elsewhere. The help that others offer is but short-lived. In the long run, if God does not supply help, anything else (no matter how successful it may seem at the moment) in time will fall apart. One who puts his trust in the help of men (unaided by Scripture) leans on a broken reed. For all that God is, Peter praises Him (v. 11). When your counselee gains that outlook on suffering, he will be well on his way toward a solution to his problems.

Closing words. Doubtless this postscript was penned by Peter himself though, as he says, Silvanus (cf. II Corinthians 1:9) was the amanuensis who actually performed the task of writing the bulk of the letter. He is a faithful brother who urges and testifies the same things about God's true

13 She who is at Babylon, elected with you, greets you along with my son Mark.
14 Greet one another with an affectionate kiss. Peace to all who are in Christ.

---

grace and help. One parting shot about this grace (help)—**Stand firm in it!** (v. 12). The church of Rome (Babylon was the code name for Rome: Revelation 14:8; 16:19; 18:2) sends greetings to their brothers. They too are subjects of God's sovereign **election**. And Mark, who worked with Peter, sends his greetings too. Keep on showing love for one another, the kind of love that is symbolized by the holy **kiss** that it was the practice of Christians to give one another. May God grant peace to all of you who are **in Christ**.

Long, meaty, sometimes difficult to interpret, sometimes easy enough to interpret but hard to put into practice, I Peter must ever remain in the eyes of true biblical counselors one of the most potent sources of help. Turn often to it in your counseling room, read it again and again in your study, evoking ever new truths and nuances from its pages. You will not go wrong in counseling by putting much emphasis on what Peter says. It is ***par excellence*** an incomparable help for counselors.

Introduction to II PETER

No one doubts that there is a significant relationship between II Peter and the epistle of Jude. That is a given. Which author depended on which, however, is hotly debated. I do not intend to enter into the pros and cons of that issue, since it often becomes intricate, and at times absurd. Because I am convinced of the common sense view, I merely intend to state it and to give my fundamental reasons for doing so. In my opinion there is no reason for believing that Peter depended on Jude and incorporated much of his material into his second letter. On the other hand, there is every reason to believe the opposite to be true. That Jude depended on Peter seems clear for two major reasons: A lesser person normally depends on a greater one. Peter was an apostle; Jude was not. But the greatest strength in this viewpoint is the fact that Peter's words refer to something that will happen in the future (he predicts, warns and in doing so uses the future tense) whereas Jude writes in the present tense about the fulfillment of Peter's predictions. When we come to Jude, which is identified closely with much in II Peter (especially materials in chapter 2), I shall have something more to say about the matter.

Is it important for counselors to know that Jude says that what Peter predicted is actually occurring? It certainly is. If Peter merely predicted, warned and exhorted we would have far less information about the persons who brought in heresy. As it is, between the two, we not only have more information concerning these persons, but additional material about other matters. And one letter helps to interpret the other. "But why is that important to counselors?" For many reasons. One is that we have the opportunity to see what can happen when Christians fail to heed the warnings of Scripture—how both they and their congregations suffer for it. The latter part of Jude has much to say about the different conditions of counselees who are adversely affected and what to do to help each sort. So as we proceed, keep in mind the warnings in II Peter that, if they had been followed, would have made the writing of Jude unnecessary. In God's providence, of course, we are happy to have the Epistle of Jude for all that it does to inform and instruct us, but surely, the sad situation which occasioned it need never have happened. If you can keep that in mind as you think about II Peter, you may be able to pass on advice that will keep some of your counselees from falling into the traps that Peter discusses.

CHAPTER 1

1 Simon Peter, a slave and apostle of Jesus Christ, to those whose lot it is to have received a faith just as valuable as ours by the righteousness of our God and Savior, Jesus Christ.

There are some key words found in this letter (you also encounter them in Peter's first letter). They are "**remind, remember; valuable; glory, glorious; knowledge; desire; flesh**." Peter was the man who forgot (Christ warned him about denying Him before the cock crowed). He doesn't want his readers to forget the truths and warnings that they have received previously. That is why he says little that they have not heard before, but simply emphasizes and reemphasizes important matters that he wants them to **remember** after he has died. Presumably, from what we read in Jude, it seems that Peter, like (at least some of) his readers, failed to **remember**. Dire consequences followed. Pointing out this dynamic may be of value to you in certain counseling contexts. Whenever you want others to remember something of importance to their welfare and for the good of the church, retell the story of Peter and the subsequent story of his readers. Even though Peter goes to lengths to help the reader to understand, the same old temptation to let down one's guard, to forget his warnings (even when vivid examples are forthcoming) is strong. Remember that yourself and, knowing the sinful propensity of people, underscore as clearly as possible the need to remember.

Peter is so taken with the priceless nature of every aspect of the Christian faith (as well as with the Lord Himself) that he cannot help repeating the word **valuable.** To him, no matter what he has given up to follow Christ, it is worth doing so because what he has left behind, in comparison to what he has now attained, is nothing. All that he has now received, he reiterates is extremely valuable to him. He has not really left anything; he has gone toward something of such greater worth that all else pales into insignificance.

Glory and glorious are terms that also occur in both of Peter's epistles. Of course, writing to suffering Christians to help them withstand persecution of various sorts (the import of his first letter), it is important to stress how the Christian life transcends the vile, murky existence of unconverted persons in the world. It is, in contrast, glorious. And that glory experienced now in such a minuscule way will some day at death be transformed into a burst of effulgence that will blind them with joy and thrill them to the core of their being. Peter, who saw something of the eternal glory of Christ on the Mount of Transfiguration, was as a result qualified to speak about that glory. Here he sets the glory of God over against the slime of human sin. It almost seems that Peter is drawn toward his experience of glory every time he thinks of Jesus.

Knowledge is basic to all that the believer does. If he does not know Christ as he should or the truths of the faith, his life will, thereby, suffer. Peter is concerned to impart knowledge to his readers. But what he has to say, though known by many of them, is not old hat. He reminds them of the valuable, glorious truths to which they, in times of trial and temptation, must ever return for sustenance and aid.

Desire, often accompanied by the word **flesh**, is the enemy of the soul. It is the one with whom the believer must struggle for the rest of his life. Peter wants to help his readers to win those battles. Fleshly desire is a product of the body habituated by a sinful nature. The nature with which one was born trains the members of the body (including the brain) to respond in sinful ways. Now, although as a Christian one receives a new nature that is oriented toward righteousness, it is those habit patterns that he must fight. **Flesh** *means the body wrongly habituated.* These patterns now vie with one's good intentions. The desires that are sinful are hard to shake because the body desires to continue in its old, well-grooved ways. It takes effort and time to consciously alter those patterns into ways that please God and that, thereby, set up new, righteous desires to replace the old. Having said these things in a preliminary way, let us now turn to the letter itself.

Peter identifies himself as **a slave and apostle of Jesus Christ**. Both his service, done in humility, and the authority that he has received from the Lord, are balanced in this greeting. How difficult it sometimes is to balance humble service with rightly used authority! The counselor, like others who must struggle with the problem, must ever work toward striking the proper balance. When one of these elements outweighs the other nothing but trouble (and often tragedy) results. Humility in serving, out of Scriptural balance, leads to servile, sloppy, uninformed, and often obsequious behavior. Authority, untempered by humility and a desire to serve, leads to austere, cold uninterested attitudes and actions. Counselors must strike the proper balance as Peter does.

He writes **to those whose lot it is to have received a faith just as valuable as ours**. Just because he was an apostle and had been taught directly by the Lord, Peter did not think that his faith was better than that

2 May help and peace increasingly be yours by a full knowledge of God and Jesus our Lord.

---

of the most simple believer in the congregation(s) to which he wrote. Just because he had seen something of the glory of the Mount, he did not consider his faith superior to others in Christ. How is that? The readers faith, he says, stems from precisely the same source as his own: their lot as one of Christ's own depends not on themselves, nor on their experience, but on **the righteousness of God** in Christ. That righteousness is the gift of God, received by simple **faith** (which, itself, is also a gift from Him).

Counselors, who have attained something of a trusted position in Christ's church, may never forget that all that they are and all that they have achieved, is through the grace of God. Any success that has been theirs is the result of the Spirit working through them by means of His Word which they minister. How easy it is for a successful counselor to think otherwise. He can begin to take credit away from the Spirit, Who does the only effectual counseling that is ever done. If and when he does, you can be sure that it will adversely affect his counseling. In times when you are tempted to think more highly of yourself than you ought to, remember you are a **slave**. Think like one: the slave has no will of his own; he must do the will of his master. The slave has been bought with a price; so he belongs to another.

In verse 2 Peter wishes for **grace (help) and peace to be granted to his readers by means of a full knowledge of God and Jesus our Lord**. That is interesting and most instructive. Here is a clear example of 1) the relationship between doctrine and life; 2) the fact that revelation is the means of conveying grace and peace. Coming to know God and (perhaps "even") Jesus Christ more fully means that grace and peace will be **increasingly** conveyed to those who attain more and more to this **knowledge.** Though the point is made again and again in the Bible in a variety of ways, it is of use to mention it once more: Scriptural revelation about God as He is made known in His Son Jesus Christ the Word is what enables a counselee to receive increasingly more help (grace) and the peace to carry him through the difficulties he must face. It is safe to say that if counseling consisted of nothing more or less than conveying and receiving more and more of that full knowledge of God that is revealed in the Scriptures, *understood in terms of His relationship to the counselee and his problems, that would be all that is needed.* And in one sense, that is what biblical counseling really is all about. In all that we do in counsel-

3 Since His divine power has given us everything for life and godliness through the full knowledge of the One Who called us by His own glory and might
4 (through which He has given to us valuable, indeed, the greatest promises of all, in order that through these you might become partakers of a divine nature, having escaped from the corruption that is in the world because of desire),

---

ing, both the goal *and* the method is to come to know God better. That knowledge consists of intellectually understood truth ministered from the Word in the power of the Holy Spirit that is applied experientially to the life of the believer.

And that is also the impact of verse 3 in which Peter writes: **Since His divine power has given us everything for life and godliness through the full knowledge of the One Who called us by His own glory and might.** For believers to come into the possession and enjoyment of eternal **life** (so as to begin to realize it in this world) required **divine power**. Nothing short of the manifestation and application of God's **power** could regenerate and justify guilty and corrupt sinners. And nothing short of the same **power** released through the **full knowledge** of God granted in the Bible could produce godliness. But that is precisely what God, in His great mercy, has provided. ***Everything*** necessary for life and godliness (a life that is properly related to God) has been **given.** And there is no doubt about this fact because it has been given through the **full knowledge** (revelation) of that **One Who called us by His own glory and might**. When God effectively called Christians to become His children He provided all they would ever need in terms of vital information to live the godly life that He requires of them. That is important for an understanding of the doctrine of the sufficiency of the Bible in counseling. God possessed the glory to do so in a wonderful manner that would bring honor to His Name, but also in a powerful way that raised Christ from the dead and gave newness of life to those who were spiritually dead. Believers are **called by His glory and might.** There are too many today who, in the name of scholarship, etc., think that the Scriptures do not give us a full enough understanding of man and God and how man's every counseling problem may be solved. They think that the Bible contains something less than the **full knowledge** of which Peter speaks. They see what it can do as feeble rather than mighty and powerful. They think it reveals something far less than the glory of a complete, sufficient salvation. Of course they do not say such things in those words, but their com-

5 for this reason, make every effort to supplement your faith with virtue, and virtue with knowledge,
6 and knowledge with self-control, and self-control with endurance, and endurance with godliness,
7 and godliness with brotherly kindness and brotherly kindness with love.
8 When these things are yours, and abound, they will keep you from becoming either inactive or unfruitful with respect to the full knowledge of our Lord Jesus Christ.
9 This I say because the one who lacks these things is blind, nearsighted, having forgotten the cleansing of his past sins.
10 On the contrary, therefore, brothers, earnestly endeavor to assure yourselves of your calling and election, because you will never go wrong by doing these things.
11 In this way, entrance into the eternal empire of our Lord and Savior Jesus Christ will be richly provided for you.

---

ments and the actions by which they declare the need for more than the Bible has to offer, speak for themselves.

Yet in spite of the eclectic integrationists, Peter goes on to claim that God has **given us** (again he makes it clear that the gracious act of God is behind it all) not only **valuable**, but the **greatest promises of all**. In the face of such claims (vv. 3,4) how can so-called "Bible-believing" counselors tell us that more material outside the Scriptures is necessary to live the life God has required of us, and that these data are very valuable—indeed, essential to solve many counseling problems—i.e., more valuable than the promises of Scripture regarding these matters? If the thought were not so pitiful, one would like to laugh.

Indeed, not only has God given us valuable, full knowledge that makes it possible to live a life of godliness, He has even changed the believer's nature. No longer does he depend on a nature oriented away from God and toward sin; now with that change he possesses a nature that enables him to love God and his neighbor. This nature, the renewal of the image of God, is called a **divine nature** because no human being could give it to man. It is *divinely* given. The new nature of which believers have become **partakers** (v. 4) enables them to know truth as they could not otherwise and to live according to it. So God has granted not only a revelation that makes it possible to know everything pertaining to life and godliness, but in addition, a change of nature that enables one to comply with the provisions of that revelation. What more could you ask for?

12 Therefore, I shall not neglect to remind you continually about these
things even though you are established in the truth about which I am now
writing.
13 I think it is right as long as I am in this tent to stir you up by reminding
you,
14 knowing that the time when I shall lay aside my tent is near, as our
Lord Jesus Christ made clear to me.
15 But I also shall do everything I can to make it possible for you to
remember these things after my departure.
16 Now we didn't follow cleverly invented myths when we made known
to you the power and presence of our Lord Jesus Christ; quite to the contrary, we were eyewitnesses of this majesty.
17 He received from God the Father honor and glory when such a voice
as this was brought to Him by the majestic glory: "This is My dearly loved
Son, toward Whom I am well disposed."
18 Now we heard this voice that was brought from heaven when we were
with Him in the holy mountain.
19 So we have all the more assurance in the prophetic word, to which you
will do well to pay attention, as to a lamp shining in a dismal place until
the day dawns and the morning star rises in your hearts.
20 But you must know, first of all, that no scriptural prophecy ever originated as a private solution to someone's problem,
21 since no prophecy was ever brought forth by human will, but men who
were carried along by the Holy Spirit spoke from God.

When counselees wonder whether the Bible sufficiently offers what is needed to meet his problems, remind him of these important opening words of II Peter.

Chapter 2

1 But there were also false prophets among the people just as there will be false teachers among you, who secretly will bring in destructive, divisive dogmas, even denying the Master Who bought them, bringing swift destruction upon themselves.

In the spirit of Matthew 24:5,11 and 24, Peter warns against false prophets in this chapter. He is concerned because he knows that sooner or later they will appear. In Acts 20 Paul similarly predicted that the problem would be one the church would face. There is no avoiding the difficulty. It would be nice if you could always screen out such people so that they could not get a toehold in the congregation, but it is not possible. Why? Because we cannot read others' hearts, they **will bring in** their false ideas **secretly**. Since it is not always possible to exclude such persons, what must we do? The answer is found in Titus 3:10; Romans 16:17. In these passages we are explicitly told to have nothing to do with them if, after one or two nouthetic confrontations, it becomes clear that they are not teachable. Church discipline must be in place in order to remove them before a little leaven leavens the whole lump.

False teachers do not come into a congregation advertising their wares. No, they seem to be in agreement with the doctrines of the church—and may even falsely claim that they are. Yet, little by little they insinuate their views until they have a substantial following which they will pull away from the church if they fail to take it over. That is why Peter uses the word **secretly** and why he calls their teachings **destructive and divisive**. They divide congregations, families and confuse individuals. The leadership of a church may not allow this to happen. Counselors who care about their flocks will stand clearly against any divisiveness of this sort. In their counseling of such persons, they will soon cut off further counseling if they find that they are unteachable. Not only will they warn the counselees of the seriousness of their activities in attempting to divide Christ's church, but will speak to them about the doubts that this activity cast upon their salvation. Peter says persons of this stamp **will bring swift destruction upon themselves**. That is as strong a warning as he could give. As a counselor, you must do no less. It is difficult to tell a person that if he refuses to repent of his divisiveness, he will likely go to hell (what Peter's words mean), but sometimes it is necessary.

The people that Peter is writing about are not merely those who may

2 Many will follow their immoral ways, and because of them the true Way will be maligned.

---

differ on the interpretation of a verse or two, but whose interpretations become so important to them that they must have everyone else believe their way or they will split the church! And the teaching that they offer is teaching like that of the false teachers who were **among the people** who **denied the Master Who bought them**. It may sound at first like this is saying people who were bought by Christ may be lost. But that isn't what Peter is saying. He is saying that the people who were **saved out of Egypt** (as *a people*; cf. Jude 5) were redeemed *as a people* from *Egypt*. These false teachers are like those unsaved teachers *among the people* of Israel who denied God back in the period of the wilderness wandering.

As in all of the Scriptures, Peter goes on to point out that false teaching leads to false living (v. 2). And he warns that because they appeal to the lust of the flesh, **many will follow their immoral ways**. It is not a defeat that such persons enter the church secretly, nor is it the fault of the church that they are successful in drawing away followers to themselves *if the congregation, aware and alert to the problem, deals with it in a biblical fashion.* Peter acknowledges that defection *will* occur. You will not always be able to avoid it. You will have false teachers among you and you will lose people to them. But it surely is the fault of a church and of any counselor who is involved (and ought to know better because he is dealing all the time with people) if this happens because a congregation fails to do what the Bible teaches about such persons. It is his task to be able to discover the signs of insidious teaching going on in stealthy ways, and to confront those engaged in it. Too often even the best of counselors are loath to confront those who are at work spreading their errors among the members of the congregation until it is too late and something *must* be done.

Certainly it is difficult at times to do this. People will plead with you "to give them a little more time." While that is what you must do with confused persons who just haven't come all the way that they should, that is not what you should do with **divisive persons**. That "little more time" that you graciously give may be the very factor that leads to the destruction of your church. Divisive persons are not gracious in the way that they treat your people, and you are not gracious to them either if you allow teachers like this to have a free hand among the members of your church. A good shepherd protects the flock from the wolf in sheep's clothing.

3 Because of greed they will get money out of you with their fabricated stories. Their long-standing judgment doesn't linger and their destruction doesn't slumber.

And don't be surprised if, having dealt with these false teachers biblically they turn on you and **malign the true Way** (the historic biblical faith). Be prepared for this too; and don't let it shatter you. Counselors often find that they must deal with the wreckage of families and persons who have gone through a church fight. More often than not the fight is the result of false teaching. Regardless of the reason, however, they will find people coming into counseling who tell you "I can't believe what so-and-so said about me." It is your place to tell him that this should be no surprise at all. It is what the Bible says all over. Read this passage. Then also, read the words of Jesus in Matthew 5:11. Help them see that standing for the truth in a world like ours that has been defiled by sin and its results only means that truth will be maligned, and that those who maintain it will, themselves, be maligned along with it. They should rejoice that, like their Savior, they too may suffer for the truth.

On the other hand, counselors, working with the fallout from a church fight may find themselves involved with the perpetrators of the split. If they can bring them to repentance—something that sometimes happens—it will then fall to them to help reintroduce the offenders into the congregation through repentance and works that are worthy of it. He may find (like the persons who were wary about the apostle Paul when they heard that he had been converted) he must help the offended members of the congregation to receive and restore repentant offenders. But the seeking of forgiveness all around by those who have offended is the beginning. Proper willingness on the part of the remaining members who were not a party to the split may result only from successful counseling. Feelings often run high. Often harsh words are spoken. People do things that they would not think of doing under any other circumstances. They do not want the same problem to occur all over again (they may be like a spouse who returns in repentance only to find his wife hesitant to take him back). But this is a counseling opportunity, *par excellence.* Do not dance around the edges of it; plow in, work with all parties involved to bring about reconciliation. If forgiveness and reconciliation is possible anywhere, it ought to be in the church of the Lord Jesus Christ.

It is fascinating to imagine how they went about doing it, but Peter warns, **they will get money out of you with their fabricated stories.**

4 I say this because if God didn't spare the angels who sinned but consigned them to the dark pits of Tartarus to be kept for judgment,

---

Greed motivates them. And wherever greed is present, people will come up with some scam or other. There are always new angles. Teachers have advocated investing seed money, promising great returns that never seem to come. (In such cases, the greed may be on *both* sides of the transaction!) All the while, they are feathering their own nest. People—often poor people—are bled dry by such false teachers who, with bankrolls that we would gasp at, beg for more. They ride around in a Rolls Royce while imploring people who drive beat up old Chevys to "give sacrificially." Watch out for people who continually talk about money.

They **fabricate stories**. That is to say, they get money out of people by lying. Faith healers have been caught in such lies, as well as others who tell of their "needs" when they have more than anyone could want. God says that scams like this are nothing new. There has been a long-standing policy of God with reference to those who operate them: **judgment**, the judgment of God. And though they are allowed to continue for a time, judgment will come: **it will not linger and their destruction does not slumber.** It is not the place of the Christian counselor (or the church) to exercise judgment on them, beyond applying church discipline; it is his place to warn and help. God will deal with them in His time, which, from His viewpoint will not be long (remember, Peter is the one who in this letter explains that for God a thousand years are like only one day for us). He has planned from of old to do so.

Now Peter gives clear examples of the judgment of God that in times past came upon those who similarly resisted Him. In verse 4, he begins by citing the judgment of **the angels who sinned**. He says that **God did not spare** them. That is an important insight into God's ways with His creatures. If God didn't spare angels, why should a "counselee" suppose that, like some old doddering grandfather, He would spare him? There is a very strong warning here. Too many persons have a soft view of God. While God is very merciful, He will show none to those who **deny** His Son. If people think that somehow or other they will be spared apart from repentance and faith in the Lord Jesus Christ, they are sadly mistaken. And you must tell them so. It is cruel to allow people to mistakenly fall into the hands of the living God without warning them. A few lines above I included the word counselee inside quotation marks. That is because an unsaved person cannot be considered a counselee in the true sense of the

5 and didn't spare the old world, but preserved Noah, a preacher of righteousness, as one of eight, when He brought a flood upon a godless world,
6 and condemned the cities of Sodom and Gomorrah, burning them to ashes, thereby setting them forth as an example of what is going to happen to the ungodly,

---

word. He cannot change in ways that will please God (Romans 8:8), and God has not put you or me in the business of changing people in any other way. Therefore, to accept an unsaved person for counseling (rather than to evangelize him) is to deceive him and to blunt the warning.

Rather than spare the angels who left their own status as servants of God, **He consigned them to the dark pits of Tartarus**. By the time New Testament writers used the word, Tartarus had come to mean the same thing as a part of "hades"—"the unseen world." Tartarus is the Greek way of saying *Gehenna* (the Hebrew word for hell, which, along with paradise is a part of the unseen world). Jude adds that they are in chains awaiting the final judgment. Peter's way of putting it is that, like persons cast into deep pits which were used as cells for prisoners (cf. Joseph's experience), the angels who sinned (now known as demons), **are kept for judgment.** These strong words ought to give many a vacillating counselee, caught up in false teaching, more than a moment's pause. In such circumstances, you ought to learn that it is only by the strongest warnings possible (Peter uses them for that purpose) that some Christians are kept from turning aside from the true Way (the New Testament name for the Christian faith).

In verse 5, Peter mentions the flood. His point in doing so is to show that God did not **spare the old world.** This fact is mentioned to convince those who doubt His willingness to **destroy**. Let people know that God *does* bring men and women into judgment and destroys them. On the occasion of the flood only 8 persons including Noah, **a preacher of righteousness**, were saved **when He brought a flood upon a godless world.** Let no one mistake these words—millions of people perished. If someone you are counseling doubts the willingness of God to destroy people, let him think again about the flood! And let those who are tempted to follow these false teachers, dragging their spouses and children into a grave situation, take heed.

And God also **condemned the cities of Sodom and Gomorrah, burning them to ashes** in order to set them forth **as an example of what is going to happen to the ungodly.** When the fire and burning sulfur fell, God was not only wiping out those whose lifestyle was a stench in His

7 and if He rescued righteous Lot, who was sick and tired of the immoral behavior of lawless men
8 (that righteous man, by seeing and hearing their lawless deeds day in and day out as he lived among them, tortured his righteous soul),
9 then the Lord knows how to rescue godly men out of trial and how to keep the unjust for Judgment Day when they will be punished—

---

holy nostrils, but He was establishing for all time a strikingly fearful example of His just judgment on sinners. And remember, in light of these facts, it does no good to mouth that weak and false platitude that "God hates sin but loves the sinner"; God doesn't send sin to hell—He sends sinners! God didn't destroy the sin of Sodom; He destroyed the Sodomites. And in verse 6, the burning up of the inhabitants of the cities of the plain (he most clearly explains) is **an example of what is going to happen to the ungodly.** Don't for one second waver from the full presentation of the facts. There *is* a lake of fire for all who reject the true Way of life.

Thinking of the few who escaped the destruction of Sodom, Peter mentions Lot (vv. 7-9). Dragged out of the city reluctantly, by angels, Lot became an example of how the Lord saves those who trust Him. Three times Lot is called **righteous**. Why? Probably because his behavior was so poor that, though a believer, you would hardly think of him as such. Peter has to tell you over and over that the righteousness of God had been attributed to Him by faith in the coming Messiah. Lot, he says, vexed himself day by day as he saw the vile behavior of his associates. Yet, in order to obtain a life of ease, he compromised and chose a place where wickedness reigned. As a result, he himself was miserable all the while he lived in Sodom (vv. 7,8), and he lost his sons-in-law and even his wife who looked back longingly at the city in disobedience to God.

What a powerful example God has provided counselors who deal with Christians who readily drift into compromise! The story of Lot is the story of many. Christians who never intended to be one with the world do so because, like him, they "pitch their tents" toward it. The call of the Christian counselor to all such is "Don't do it! Be careful where you pitch your tent!" When he sees a modern day Lot who has already moved into the city, he must cry out "Lot, come out! Come out! Come out!"

The Lord not only **knows how to rescue godly men out of trial,** today, often using counselors as His angels (the word means "messengers"), but He also knows **how to keep the unjust for the judgment Day**

10 especially those who are following the polluted desire of the flesh and despise ruling authority.

---

when they will be punished. It is a terrifying passage that is laid before us. No wonder Peter urged his readers to make their calling and election sure!

And if judgment is due to the whole, it especially awaits those false teachers who are **trailing along (following) the polluted desire of the flesh and despise ruling authority.** Here is a further revealing description of the coming false teachers. Reading Jude, and realizing that they did appear and that people fell for their line, you wonder how they could have done so! After all, these are fearful, forceful warnings. Yet today you will discover Christians who will follow anyone who attempts to justify an immoral life (**the polluted desire of the flesh).** Some counselees grasp at any and all excuses for leading an immoral life. To fulfill their sexual desire is uppermost. Everything is interpreted in terms of its relationship to sex. Their conversation is full of sexual innuendos. They cannot keep their eyes off filthy magazines, TV and videos. They wallow in the pollution of the immoral life. There is strong warning here for them. Tell them to take heed—God does not think lightly of such a lifestyle. AIDS is clearly a consequence of this way of life. There is no excuse that He will accept. It cannot be justified. But of course the good news is that *it can be forgiven if one truly repents!* Make these facts known to your counselees.

That is what these teachers were like. They were no leaders at all, but merely followers of fleshly desire. They would be captured by their own lusts; why should one who has been saved and freed from sin's captivity emulate them? Pity them? Yes. Preach to them as Noah did? Yes. Follow along with them as they trail along after sin? No! A thousand times no. That is the counsel you must give.

Notice the interrelationship between false teaching, filthy living and destruction that runs through this section. Peter wants to bring them into such close juxtaposition in order to frighten off those who will be tempted to succumb. But it is no scare tactic. He is stating unequivocal truth. God *will* judge. And every counselor must have in his little black bag the nasty tasting medicine that Peter here ladles out. If people will not hear the lighter, pleasanter wooings of the Word, they must hear the shrieks of souls suffering eternally in hell.

Counselor, are you prepared to deal with people as Peter did? Not everyone, of course, needs such warnings about his behavior. But all too many do who have not heard them. Ours is a day in which the hard truths of the Bible are neglected. Peter didn't take sadistic delight in writing these things; nor should you. It was because people needed to be **stirred** that he reminded them of the awful facts which they already knew, but about which they were coming to think in a merely academic and sanitized way. He wanted to bring home the reality of the stories because they were forecasts of the coming judgment of God. Indeed, he would have been utterly cruel not to warn them, as some are who think they are loving by avoiding these harsher truths of the Word. In truth, *they* are the ones who are cruel; they are like those who seeing a man about to step off a cliff accidentally, say nothing.

Another characteristic of these false teachers is their **lawlessness** (v. 7), spoken of in the verse we are considering as **despising ruling authorities.** They want no other ruler over their lives but desire. No rules, no laws over *them*—all of that to them is "legalism." They want to live like those in the period of the judges when "every person did that which was right in his own eyes." They reject all authority. They want to follow their own feelings and their appetites. People who live by feelings and call these "the promptings of God" walk perilously close to the line. They leave themselves wide open to such teaching. The first thing you know, they are getting messages that tell them it is OK to do what God, in the Bible, has forbidden. Bad doctrine leads to bad living. Such teachers become their own standard, their own God.

Counselors must warn severely against any who tell counselees that God will not hold them to biblical standards. They must be utterly suspicious of any who want to twist those passages in which immorality is condemned, to say something else.

The elders of the church, the government, or any **ruling authority** you may mention (including parental authority, which is a choice target for the libertines of our day) constitute a threat to their way of life. So they despise them. And in any number of ways they make that loathing of authority known. There is a difference between law and legalism; between authority and authoritarianism. They fail to distinguish the legitimate from the illegitimate. Law is what God sets forth in His Word; legalism is man's additions to or substitutions for it. Authority is the right exercise of legitimately delegated rule; authoritarianism is the unauthorized assumption of authority to one's self or the improper use of rightly given rule. As a counselor you must be able to point out to those who have been hoodwinked by slogans and assertions that do not hold water; distinctions that make all the difference. You can be sure that teachers like those men-

Bold, impudent! They don't tremble when they insult glorious beings,
11 while angels, greater in might and power, don't bring an insulting accusation against them before the Lord.

---

tioned here are astute at confusing things for them.

Warn your counselees against anyone who is antiestablishment, if his attitude amounts to an excuse for sin. The two are often intricately bound together. These teachers will tell you that (biblical) authority is too narrow, that it is an unnecessary restriction on freedom, that because some authority is corrupt (and there are always those they can point to) one may safely disregard it. Those who buy into this teaching soon find themselves not only disregarding rightful authority but also **despising** it. Take heed to this dynamic, counselor, and whenever you see it intruding into the life of a counselee, stamp it out firmly with Peter's clear teaching.

These teachers who hanker after **pollution** Peter calls **bold, impudent!** That further characterizes them. But their **boldness** is not the holy boldness of the apostles that is mentioned through the Book of Acts. A different word is used here, which in this place signifies brazen, headstrong action. They speak and act beyond their ability to deliver. Their impudence goes to the extreme of insulting glorious beings—whether they are earthly or heavenly. They think nothing of the glory and honor that is due to them because of their positions in the providence of God.

When you listen to some faith-healers "rebuke the devil" (as they call it) they sound as if they had all the authority in heaven and earth to do so. Yet **angels, greater in might and power, do not bring an insulting accusation against them before the Lord** (this is further explained in Jude, which we shall discuss when we comment on the verses in that letter that pertain to it). These very things that false teachers do for showmanship is but one more identifying mark that should provide astute counselors with evidence that they are not all they are cracked up to be. Never neglect, or allow your duped counselee to neglect, such clear signals. They put on a show of power that they simply do not have. The false teacher wants to back up his words with the claim of power; but when called on to demonstrate it, like the prophets of Baal, he cannot produce. As Jude puts it he is a **waterless cloud** (full of promise, but it does not deliver). Watch out for anyone who speaks ill of heavenly as well as earthly authorities—even of Satan himself. If these teachers were ever to find themselves in a genuine contest with such beings, the greater might and power of the angels (even those that are fallen) would, in short order,

12 These persons, however, speaking insultingly about matters of which they are ignorant, like irrational animals, naturally born to be captured and destroyed, will be destroyed with the same destruction, suffering harm as wages for doing wrong.

---

become apparent. These teachers talk big, but their power and authority are nil.

Now when they do these things, they do not go unnoticed; they do them **before the Lord**. He sees, and in the judgment will repay. Their **fabricated stories**, by which they pry money loose from their spellbound devotees, may be about their so-called battles with "spiritual forces in high places." They often refer to this as "spiritual warfare." All such claims, when carried on in a manner inconsistent with this passage (and the parallel one in Jude) must either be challenged or ignored. It is the counselor's task, whenever dealing with problems stemming from teachers of this sort to oppose their error as Peter did. He made no bones about it, but spoke plainly in order to warn. Their showmanship must be exposed for what it is—a scam designed to extract money from well-meaning, but frightfully gullible Christians. A counselor with biblical convictions will not only be outraged at what this does to counselees and other members of Christ's church, but he will be angry (especially) over how it brings disgrace to God since it is done in His Name.

That they do not know what they are talking about is clear from verse 12: **These persons, however, [speak] insultingly about matters of which they are ignorant.** When confronted with truth and an intelligent, believing presentation of scriptural truth their errors are readily exposed and easily refuted. Counselor, can you do that? Are you willing to?

Whenever the teachers are confronted in this manner, watch them retreat into "experience," their favorite castle. They will not do biblical exposition. They retreat into experience for two reasons: they do not know much about the Bible (though they may claim otherwise, they are **ignorant** of those things that count) and they think they are safe (since they believe experience is irrefutable: "who can argue with what I claim is my experience?"). But neither is. If experience conflicts with the Bible it is to be rejected (cf. Deuteronomy 13 and comments on I John 4). That brings us back to the Bible; where we should have been at the beginning (and where they do not want to go). Moreover, it is easily noted that the claims of "experiences" by false teachers are worthless. Mormons, Christian Scientists, the magicians of Egypt and others all appeal to experience. If the argument is to be made from experience, then who is to say whose experience is to be believed. After all, various experiences contradict each other. Once more, we are brought back to Scripture to determine which experience, if any, is the correct one. And do you remember Peter's important observation in the first chapter of this letter? His experience on the Mount of Transfiguration—as great as it was—did not measure up to the **more sure prophetic Word** from God found in the Bible alone. Apart from God's infallible, inerrant Word, then, there is no standard. The subjective appeal to experience leaves us in a quandary.

Now not only are these teachers **ignorant**, they are like **irrational animals, naturally born to be captured and destroyed.** And Peter goes on to say, **they will be destroyed with the same destruction, suffering harm as wages for doing wrong.** As Paul put it, "The wages of sin is death." These people are servants of their own appetites, desires and sinful inclinations. They do not look beyond themselves and their own advantage—just like animals. And as animals are captured and destroyed, God will destroy them for their animallike lifestyle. Animalized man is a shame. It is a disgrace because it casts a reflection on the goodness of God Who created man in His own image. Irrationality is not fitting to that image. But the image was marred by the fall and (apart from Christ) left people with no other option than to act in a more-or-less animalized fashion. That, indeed, is what B.F. Skinner, along with a host of his followers, see only too clearly is the way many live. But in their own sin, they wish to standardize life on that level. Watson's and Skinner's behaviorism is hereby condemned as an ungodly and heinous view that leads men to destruction.

God says that these teachers, because they lead others astray, will receive their just desserts: **destruction and the suffering of harm** for the harm they afflict on others. That is their wages. I know that this is heavy material through which you are wading, counselor. It is nothing like the sweetness and light teaching of the Los Angeles-Dallas-Chicago-Colorado Springs sort of counseling instruction that many of you may have been taught. Chances are that in all your training at one or another of those centers of eclecticism you never considered the matter of the confrontation of unbelief, error and false teaching as a part of your counseling work. But if that is so, what will you do when you must counsel a Christian snared in error? Think that through. You will get nowhere until you learn to thoroughly expose and refute the errors that stand in the way of change in their lives.

And that means that you must be able to set these errors to rest with-

13 They consider a day's luxurious living a pleasure! They are spots and stains, enjoying their deceitful ways while they eat together with you.

---

out getting sidetracked, the way Jesus did when speaking with the woman at the well, then quickly go on with your agenda as He did (cf. John 4:19ff.). That often requires some fancy footwork; but studying the way Jesus counseled will help you learn how to develop it.

Further information concerning these errorists follows: **They consider a day's luxurious living a pleasure!** They focus on the ephemeral. The Superbowl is so important to them that they would mortgage the farm to attend. They sell the day to buy the hour. They think only of the immediate; whatever brings pleasure at the time is what they do. They think nothing of the consequences of their actions. As a result, they continually get themselves into trouble here and they will be in trouble with God for all eternity. Many counselees have opted for that sort of living without anyone teaching them to do so. You will deal with them regularly. Personal pleasure can never be the reason for a Christian's action. Yet if you could lasso a dozen persons on the street and ask them what is really important to them, if they answered truly they'd say they are living for pleasure. There is no reason to argue the point. Simply compare the salaries of a movie star or sports "hero" with that of a preacher, or even a physician. Where the money goes is where the interest lies. There is no refuting that! The pursuit of personal pleasure and amusements designed to produce it is the religion of the day. As you sketch this for any reasonable Christian he ought to be able to see it. And being ephemeral, there is no future in it.

To the contrary, the Christian must live to please God. In doing so, he will find lasting (everlasting) joy as he enters into the **pleasures at God's right hand**. These are **forever more**. Help counselees see the difference, so as to make the right choices now. Point to Hebrews 11:24-26 as a prime example of this difference in living.

When you get together for Christian fellowship at a meal, like **spots and stains** on the tablecloth, the conversation and actions of these false teachers mar and blot the evening. They deceive those around them into thinking their way is superior. They ply their trade on such occasions and seize them as an opportunity to speak with various members of the church. They insinuate their leaven into the fellowship and do much harm thereby. Get rid of them! Discipline them out of the church; forbid them entrance into your times of fellowship. You cannot fellowship with evil-

14 They have eyes for nothing but an adulteress, eyes that continually look for sin. They seduce unstable persons; having hearts trained in greed, they are under a curse!

---

doers who **deny** our Lord Jesus Christ.

And all the while, they are **enjoying their deceitful ways while they eat together with you.** Perhaps that is the most heinous aspect of all. They hawk pleasure through fleshly gratification, but they know that the enjoyment is only temporary. Yet they lie about the fact and drag others down with them into the slime pits of human degradation. Paul referred to the same attitude in Romans 11:32. How rotten this is: to pretend that there is satisfaction in licentiousness in order to deceive others. It is exemplified in people with AIDS who knowingly inflict death on others through it. In Ephesians 4:17-19, the failure of a pleasure-centered life is set forth in graphic detail. Sensuality cannot bring satisfaction; only glorifying God and *enjoying Him forever* can do that.

Verse 14 plainly tags them as sensualists. Peter writes: **They have eyes for nothing but an adulteress, eyes that unceasingly look for sin. They seduce unstable persons; having hearts trained in greed, they are under a curse!** What a bevy of revealing verses there is in this second chapter of II Peter. Having heard what he said last, one wonders what more he could say. Yet verse after verse, relentlessly Peter finds more and more characteristics by which one may detect these false teachers and may expose their errors to those who may be tempted to swallow their tripe. The passage is damning!

Note, especially, that the **heart** may be **trained.** That is an important piece of information. Many people think that only the body is subject to habitual training. That is not so. Indeed, the heart is what motivates the body. Heart, in the Bible, does not mean emotion (that is "bowels") but the inner you—including thinking, feeling, decision-making, motivating desires, etc. When a heart is trained by the sinful nature with which we are all born, then it must be retrained after conversion since the habitual patterns that we developed prior to salvation are carried into the new life. See my book, *Winning The War Within,* along with comments on Romans 6 and 7 in this series, for more information on this issue and help in going about making necessary changes through counseling.

As you look at the description of these persons that Peter draws, are some of you wondering where Peter's concern for their self-esteem may be? Obviously, he cared nothing about building them up in their sense of self-worth. And remember, these words are not Peter's alone; as he wrote he was carried along by the Holy Spirit. The idea that everyone, simply by virtue of his humanity, is of infinite worth and should have high self-esteem can be seen in all its foolishness in the light of how Peter (God) speaks of these persons. The trouble is that they have too high a sense of self-worth. They think the world revolves around them—or, at least, *should*. The world is their oyster; it owes them pleasure at all costs—even at the cost of the destruction of many lives in addition to their own.

One of those very serious costs mentioned in verse 14 is their goal of turning members of the congregation into **adulteresses.** Along with their concern to elicit money from the unwary, they also solicit favors from **unstable women whom they seduce.** Perhaps that is one way in which they become blots on love feasts. They may use these holy occasions for plying their unholy purposes. One thing is certain; they are always on the lookout for such opportunities. They **unceasingly look for sin.** They have become expert in doing so. Their **hearts are trained in greed.** This greedy lust for more and more sinful pleasure is obviously the result of their failure to find it. They continually search for that which they deceitfully promise others: lasting pleasure. And they do this even when they know that they are full of hot air. They know nothing of the true Source of real, lasting pleasure; so they go on seeking it in sin.

They are under God's wrath; they are **cursed** by Him. That is, never having trusted the Savior, Who bore the curse for His people's sin, they remain under that curse as do all unsaved people. But it seems that Peter's words go beyond that; he says that they are under a special, perhaps we should say double, curse. That idea is in harmony with James 3:1. Compare this list of **wages** (v. 12) with the passage in James to see how serious a matter it is to lead God's people astray by teaching falsehood.

As a counselor you must teach. There is no way to avoid it, if you are doing biblical counseling. But you must be ever learning, studying your Bible so that you may become proficient in using it not only to counsel, but to confute false teaching. You do not need to spend time engrossed in the writings of the pagan psychologists and counselors who are favored by so many in the church over the Word of God. Now, I know they would not say that this is so, of course, but so often it is true. Ask, and answer this question: How much time do you spend learning what God says in the Bible as over against reading books of pagans and the eclectic Christian writers? Here's another: Count the volumes on your shelves devoted to psychology and counseling over against the commentaries, Bible Dictionaries and other helps intended to enable you to better understand the

15 Leaving the straight road, they have gone astray, following the way of Balaam, Bosor's son, who loved the wages of wrongdoing.
16 But he received a rebuke for this very kind of transgression: a beast of burden, that couldn't speak, addressing him with a human voice, put an end to the prophet's madness.
17 These persons are waterless springs and fogs driven by a hurricane, for whom the gloomy darkness has been reserved.

Bible. You may be surprised at what you find. And if you are a preacher, who may have a number of commentaries, etc., ask the question this way: how often do I use these rather than counseling books (including mine) to discover how to help someone in counseling? Go on; I dare you to do it. Then repent if the answer brings conviction. And begin to do works fitting that repentance.

Peter is not through yet! In verses 15 and 16 he compares these teachers to **Balaam** who left **the straight road because he loved the money he was promised for doing harm** to God's people. These teachers are similar to him. But God did not ignore him either. Rather, **he received a rebuke for this very kind of transgression: a beast of burden, that couldn't speak, addressing him with a human voice, put an end to the prophet's madness.** How utterly frustrating and embarrassing that was! Here was a prophet, in touch with God, who sold out to His enemy and had to be rebuked by a lowly donkey. God will embarrass these men (and all like them) as well. Their madness will not prevail. People who will do almost anything for money (even to the point of defying God) will be put to shame. Ask your counselees if they also want to stand beside such persons when, in God's timing, His rebuke comes.

Can Peter say more? You'd better believe it! They are **waterless springs, fogs driven by a hurricane.** What does that mean? Simply that they have nothing to offer after all their promises. The thirsty man goes to the spring to drink, but it has dried up. The fog seems so substantial; but a blast of wind instantly drives it away. Like a **fog** they have no staying power. They are unstable; there is nothing to them. Like the ephemeral that they enjoy, they themselves are the very quintessence of it.

Like the angels that sinned, God has reserved a place for them at death: **gloomy darkness** that, unlike the fog, will be driven away by nothing but the final judgment. Ask your counselee if he wants to follow persons like this when he knows where they are headed. They may continue to tell their fabricated stories, which Peter says are really nothing more than **impressive-sounding claptrap**, but God will not give them the time

18 Through uttering impressive-sounding claptrap, by an appeal to fleshly desires and to impure practices, they bait a trap for persons who have barely escaped from those who live in error,
19 promising them freedom while they themselves are slaves of corruption (one is a slave of whatever has defeated him).
20 Indeed, if having escaped from the contaminations of the world by a full knowledge of our Lord and Savior Jesus Christ, they are entangled again and defeated by them, the last situation has become worse then the first.

---

of day. They are hollow, having no substance. What these people do by fabrications is **appeal to fleshly desires and impure practices.** Moreover, they **bait a trap for persons who have barely escaped from those who live in error, promising them freedom while they themselves are slaves of corruption.** Look out for the one who promises freedom that is not, at the same time, slavery to God. Their actions, as we saw earlier, are deliberate. Here they are described as **baiting traps** for unsuspecting new converts (those who have just **barely escaped** this very sort of corruption into which they would like them to return). They promise freedom to others though they cannot obtain it themselves. They are not free; they are **slaves of corruption.** How does Peter know this? The same way you can. By recognizing that **one is a slave of whatever has defeated him**. Like slaves taken in war, these teachers have been defeated by sin and corruption. Counselors must become even more dedicated to freeing their counselees than these men are to enslaving them. I wonder how often you inquire into the beliefs of your counselees and as to where they obtained them. I have known counselees who had been strongly influenced by cults. Usually they have been enticed by the **promises** they have been given. These promises are like waterless springs; they do not produce that which one seeks. Point this out. Use Peter's imagery; it is vivid. Ask if they have found the promised freedom. If so, why are they sitting there in front of you with problems they have not been able to resolve by following the false teaching? Come down as hard on error as Peter does. Why? Because you, like Peter, have a trust given to you by God. You are a shepherd who must protect the flock from wolves in sheep's clothing.

These teachers, having heard all there is to know about the gospel (**a full knowledge of our Lord and Savior Jesus Christ**) and **having escaped from the contamination of the world** by associating with a Christian congregation, because their profession of faith was not genuine, went back to their former state. They are **entangled again** and defeated

21 It would have been better for them not to have fully known the Way of righteousness than, having had such a full knowledge, to have turned back, forsaking the holy commandment that was delivered to them.
22 The true proverb applies to them: "**The dog turned back to his own vomit** and the washed hog to its wallowing in the mud."

---

by sin and corruption. And their **last situation has become worse than the first** (for parallels to this see Matthew 12:45; Luke 11:26; Hebrews 6,10). **It would have been better for them not to have known the Way of righteousness than, having had such a full knowledge, to have turned back, forsaking the holy commandment that was delivered to them.** The verse reminds one of the saying of Christ in Luke 17:1,2. Here are people fully informed about the way of salvation, who associated with Christians as if they too were believers, had benefited from this association, but had turned back to their former ways *because* they did not really belong. They are an example of the **true proverb** that says **The dog turned back to his own vomit and the washed hog to its wallowing in the mud.** They turned back because they never were sheep; all the while they were hogs and dogs.

Whew! We have finally come to the conclusion of the section. What follows, however, will not be much milder. Indeed, there looms ahead a picture of the final judgment mentioned throughout this chapter. This judgment that will come upon persons like them and others who mock the faith, will be devastating. There are warnings remaining and interesting material, some of which is not found elsewhere. Christian counselors should find chapter 3 of special help (among other things) in allaying doubts about God's promises and in encouraging spiritual growth.

CHAPTER 3

1 Dear friends, this is now the second letter I am writing to you; in both of them I have been trying to stir up your sincere minds by reminders
2 of the words that were spoken beforehand by the holy prophets and of the commandment from the Lord and Savior given to you by your apostles.
3 First, you should know this, that during the last of the days scoffers, who live according to their own desires, will come

---

Peter explains why he has written as he has in the previous chapters and why he will say even more of the same in this **second letter** of his. He says, **in both of them I have been trying to stir up your sincere minds by reminders.** We have already said much about the importance of reminding counselees of what the **holy prophets...the Lord and Savior...**and the **apostles** wrote (vv. 1,2). He speaks here about the **commandment from the Lord and Savior**. In verse 21 of the previous chapter, he mentioned this same commandment, calling it **holy**. I have waited until this place to comment on it. Peter was speaking of predictions by the Old Testament prophets, a commandment given by the Lord Jesus which was then passed down to them by *their* apostles (the ones who brought the gospel to them or labored among them). The most likely interpretation of this is Christ's command, repeated in verses 4,11,23 and 26 of Matthew 24 regarding false prophets and false Christs. They were neither to believe these false teachers nor to follow their directions. They were to **watch out that nobody mislead** them (Matthew 24:4); that seems to be the basic command of which the rest are explanatory and which emphasize the extent of the problem that they will encounter. As we know, Paul was careful to warn of false teachers (Acts 20), and surely Peter does so here. Presumably, whoever the apostles were of whom he speaks they gave the same warnings. It seems that not only did Christ anticipate this problem of false teaching into which these teachers fell (2:21), but the entire New Testament is evidence that they came—one after another in great profusion. Ever since, the church has been plagued with false prophets and teachers. And that is true today no less than at any other time. Wouldn't it be tragic if counselors, who genuinely wish to serve Christ in their efforts to help others, also neglected to heed Christ's commandment? Peter anticipates the advent of **scoffers** who, like the teachers mentioned in chapter 2 **live according to their own desires** (fundamentally, everyone who fails to live according to the commandments of

4 saying, "What has happened to the promise of His coming? From the days that the fathers fell asleep, everything remains as it was from the beginning of creation."
5 They want to forget the fact that long ago heavens existed and an earth was formed out of water and through water by the Word of God

---

the Lord Jesus, lives a desire-driven life). These scoffers will come after the **fathers** die (Peter gently says, **fell asleep**). This accords with Paul's use of the term in I Thessalonians 4, and seems to have been a lovely euphemism in the early church for death. It referred, of course, to the body; not to the personality which lived on awaiting the resurrection of the body. Peter may have been speaking of the **end of the days** that constituted the forty years prior to the full end of the Old Testament era, if this letter was written before 70 AD as it seems to have been. Or he may have been talking about the end of the era in which we now live. Certainly, he does go on to describe the final end of this order of things in the remainder of the chapter and speaks of the second coming of Christ. It is perhaps instructive that Jude mentions nothing of this prophecy being fulfilled.

What is it that they taunt the Christian with? That the promise of Christ's **coming** has been delayed (v. 4). Nothing has happened for so long, they say; **everything remains as it was from the beginning of creation**. Of course that is a lie; they "conveniently" **forget** facts that contradict the assertion (v. 5). That is an all-too-frequent ploy employed by counselees who don't like to face reality. Notice how Peter contradicts the false assertion with a recital of the facts and a comment on the manner in which they make it: **They want to forget**. That is, they find it helpful to their false accusation against God (it is no less than that) to simply ignore the bald fact of the flood. He does not allow scoffers to make points based on the erroneous interpretation of history that they advocate. Rather, he says that so obvious an omission leading to so serious an error can be no less than a studied, willful ignoring of the facts. There are times when counselees, wanting to avoid or pass over important facts that contradict their assertions, must also be brought up short by the counselor.

The flood had interrupted the course of human history in a very dramatic manner (so dramatic that it is one of the major events in the history of the world). To assert that **From the days that the fathers fell asleep, everything remains as it was from the beginning of creation,** is an egregious lie. The **fathers** means Old Testament characters known to all

6 (it was by a deluge of water that He destroyed the world of that time);
7 but by the same Word, the present heavens and earth are stored up for
fire, kept for Judgment Day and the destruction of ungodly men.

Jewish readers (the most likely referents) not to New Testament fathers (those who were prominent at the beginning of the New Testament Church but nowhere else called **fathers**. The point of the scoffers is that since the promise of the second coming of Christ was made nothing has happened any more startling than those events that have occurred since creation. This statement purposely ignores that outstanding event that we call the flood.

Interestingly, Peter's refutation of their assertion (with which he arms his readers against the scoffers he expected them to encounter) is not merely that. It is not only a clear refutation, but he uses it also as an example by which to introduce the facts about the second coming that they **want** to deny. In making the refutation and developing it into a foreshadowing example of the coming that was yet to take place, Peter gives enough detail to make his analogy complete. He says that **long ago heavens existed and an earth was formed out of water and through water by the Word of God**. That statement is very difficult to interpret and probably has nearly as many interpretations as there are interpreters. What it alludes to, however, seems clear enough. The original watery chaos out of which the earth was formed is first mentioned. This happened through God's Word at the beginning. Then later, the flood occurred through the waters that fell on the earth and that were spewed forth by the fountains of the deep. Now all that happened by the Word of God. The **promise** that they scorn is simply another instance of the **same Word.** Peter has done two things by this reference.

The very Word by which **the heavens existed** is the **Word** that promised the second coming—and the **Judgment Day**. At that time **ungodly men** will be destroyed just as the old world of Noah's day was. Only this time judgment will be by **fire** rather than by water (v. 7). The heavens and the earth are **stored up** for the judgment. Why should the heavens require judgment? Clearly, Peter didn't understand what we understand today. We know that sinful persons have been traveling in space and depositing junk throughout the solar system. Wherever sinful man goes whatever he touches must be renewed. For all we know of the future, there will be sinful occupants of the various planets at the time of the coming of Christ. At least we know that they are even now spending

8 But don't forget this one fact, dear friends, that one day with the Lord is like a thousand years, and a thousand years are like one day.
9 The Lord is not delaying His promise in the sense that some think of delay, but He is patiently waiting for you, not wanting any of you to be destroyed, but every one to come to repentance.
10 But the Lord's Day will come—as a thief—in which the heavens will pass away with a shrieking sound and the earth, and all her works, will be laid bare.

---

time in space stations.

Is God delaying the fulfillment of His promise? In verse 8, Peter makes a very significant point: time has no meaning for God. As the ever-existent One, a **day for the Lord is like a thousand years, and a thousand years is like one day.** Time is a matter of creation; for God it means nothing. He knows the beginning from the end. He does not exist in time. All, for Him, is an eternal now. Because this is true, it is foolish to speak of God **delaying His promise**. According to I Peter 4:5 He is ready to judge. Why, then, has the promise not been fulfilled? Peter's answer is that God is **patiently waiting** for the sake of Christians, **not wanting any of you** [His elect people] **to be destroyed, but every one** [of you for whom He patiently waits] **to come to repentance.** God will not have Christ's death frustrated. Everyone for whom Christ died will come to repentance. Judgment will not come till all of them have been redeemed. If God will not allow His timetable to be upset by the mockery of scorners, why should you care about their jibes. All too soon they will be faced with the errors of their ways and the tragedy of the judgment that awaits them. Christian counselors must not lose patience either. What God has planned *will come to pass*. And it will take place—just as the **repentance** of the elect will—by the ministry of the Word. Their task is to be faithful; God's task is to activate their ministry in those for whom He has ordained it. Scorners who mock because the ministry of the Word in counseling is not always effective must be told that the Word of God has not failed; it is only the counselee who has.

But the Lord's Day will come, says Peter. And then those who mocked will see that the Lord did not delay the fulfillment of His promise **as some think of delay**. No, it was a planned program on His part, and until the timetable ran out, no scornful jibe of men could make even a dent in it. When it comes, it will come **as a thief.** That is to say, suddenly it will take these scorners (and all those who are unsaved) by surprise (a thief does not announce his coming). **The heavens will pass away with a**

11 Since, therefore, all these things are to be dissolved, what sort of people ought you to be in holy behavior and godliness,

---

shrieking noise and the earth, all her works, will be laid bare. What is Peter saying? There will be a great conflagration in which the very **heavens,** from which the water fell in the days of Noah, **will pass away**. It will be a frightful time in which unimaginable sounds will be heard. And the earth, with all the tainted **works** of sinful human beings will be exposed for what they are.

Since this is true, Peter points out (in v. 11), and since the heavens and the earth are to be dissolved, you ought to ask yourself the question **what sort of people** ought we to be **in holy behavior and godliness?** The things of this world are not lasting. Why be so taken up by them (an excellent question to ask counselees all caught up in some problem that involves property, etc., that will be **dissolved**)? The focus, instead, should be on **holy behavior and godliness. Holy** behavior is behavior that is different (set apart) from ordinary behavior. The Christian's life should exhibit decision-making, acting, speaking and thinking that is unlike that behavior that is taking place all around him. Not that the Christian seeks to be different; no, exactly not that. But his behavior will naturally be different because his behavior tends toward **godliness**. Godliness is living that is oriented toward God because it is regulated by His Word. A counselee must aim toward living the godly life. But he should remember that the more godly he becomes the stranger he will look in the eyes of others (even of some Christians who may question or resent it). But it is God whom he must seek to please. After all, the judgment is coming when all these problems with others will be **laid bare.** Then it will be seen who is right and who is wrong. What others do or say here is really very unimportant—that is Peter's point. Why? Because those matters that often seem so important at the minute will pale into insignificance when the earth is **dissolved** and all the things that men do are **laid bare.** When that happens, only those things that are holy and godly will be of any lasting value. So Peter urges, concentrate your efforts on these. What a good and relevant word this is for counselees who are all worked up about those things that they will find of no significance at the judgment. It is sometimes fruitful to read verses 10 and 11 to such a counselee and to ask, "Now, how important will that issue be when the earth is dissolved?" If nothing else, that ought to set him back on his heels, causing him to consider his set of values.

12 as you anticipate and hurry the coming of God's Day, because of which the heavens catching fire will be dissolved and the elements burning intensely will melt?
13 But according to His promise, we anticipate new heavens and a new earth freshly made, in which righteousness will be at home.

The thing to do is to **anticipate**, and thus [in your thinking—you couldn't affect the actual event itself] **hurry the coming of God's Day**. That is to say, you can hurry it along in its effects on your behavior by anticipating. You can act as if it were actually occurring right now—or, at least, tomorrow. Let its coming influence how you act today. Hurry it along in the decisions you make; take it into consideration as if it were happening now in the words you speak. Live as if it were the most present event that you have to face. Of course, it truly is. In his own way, Peter is saying the same thing as John (cf. I John 3:3). Use the facts of the second coming of Christ as they relate to the coming judgment to call recalcitrant counselees to a reappraisal of their values and lifestyles. That is how Peter applies the teaching.

Peter wishes to make the scene vivid (as you should do too) so as to impress the nature of the event upon his readers. He says that at **the coming of God's Day...the heavens catching fire will be dissolved and the elements burning intensely will melt.** This can be nothing other than the purging of all that is sinful and all the effects of sin in the present heavens and earth. This having taken place, God will make of the molten mass **a new heavens and earth...in which righteousness will be at home.** That is also something that we should **anticipate.** Anticipation of the negative (the dissolution of all things) is important, but anticipation of the **freshly made new heavens and earth** is even more so. How vital it is for believers to look for this perfect state of things! Keeping one's eyes on this future state, he can endure all that the present world has to throw at him. It was for no lesser hope that the martyrs of old and those who in our day have given their lives for the truth, went to their deaths. If that could happen, how much more so could your counselees endure the paltry difficulties that they face?

Try to picture what it will be like. Turn to Revelation 21 and 22 and in conjunction with the present verses read the pertinent passages in those chapters to your counselee. Infuse into him a sense of expectancy of the wonders God has prepared for those who love Him. This will enervate him as he meets trial and difficulty. Create a burning desire in him to live

14 Therefore, dear friends, as you anticipate these events, do your best to be found in peace, spotless and blameless before Him.
15 Think of the patient waiting of our Lord as salvation, just as our dear brother Paul also wrote to you according to the wisdom that was given to him,

---

a holy and godly life as he anticipates the ultimate destruction of all that is evil and the ultimate existence of all that is good. The remaking of the heavens and the earth into a place in which righteousness dwells is also of the utmost importance. There will be no sin and none of its consequences there (see the pertinent passages in Revelation 21,22 for this as well). Focus, for him, on that—what it will mean in relation to the present problems for which he came to counseling. "Are you saying that counseling exists simply of asking others to endure in the light of eternity while doing nothing about their problems in the present?" Of course not. The Bible has much to say about how to live, make decisions, deal with people, etc., during this life. And it is essential for counselees to be instructed and encouraged to do whatever God says to do about the trials and difficulties that they are facing. But *how* they do so is altogether important. If they do so as though what happens here is their only motivation, they will not please God because they will opt for whatever is pleasing to themselves. But if they think, act and speak as people who are living for eternity they will make holy and godly decisions.

So, nearing the conclusion of the letter, Peter sums up: **Therefore, dear friends, as you anticipate these events, do your best to be found in peace, spotless and blameless before Him.** The conclusion is: become the sort of people who are not causing trouble or, as the entire letter seems to be saying, allowing others to cause trouble for the church by their false teachings. There are counselees who, because they will not let go of a matter, or because they are intent on having their own ways, or who, by the wrong manner in which they pursue a right end, keep things stirred up in a church, a home, etc. Because they do, this concluding summary exhortation is important. There is never any excuse for being **found** at Christ's coming as a troublemaker. Nor is there ever any excuse for being found full of spots and stains and full of blame for what one is when Christ returns. Many believers may be embarrassed in that day.

And if you must think of the fact that God has not yet fulfilled His promise of Christ's coming, think of it this way: the **patient waiting of the Lord** means **salvation** to those who have not yet come to Christ. He

16 as he does also in all his letters when in them he speaks about these events. Some things in them are hard to understand, which untaught and unstable persons twist, as they do the other Scriptures, to their own destruction.
17 You, therefore, dear friends, since you know this already, be on guard so that you won't be led astray by the error of lawless persons and lose your own stability.
18 But grow by the help and the knowledge of our Lord and Savior Jesus Christ. To Him be glory both now and to the Day of eternity!

---

will not have the work of Jesus Christ frustrated (cf. v. 9)! And if God patiently waits, we may certainly infer, so ought we to do so. If God puts up with the scorn, sin and unrighteousness of men, so can we.

These last events are things that Paul also deals with in the scriptural letters that he has written, says Peter. God gave him wisdom to understand and explain these truths. And just because there are some things that he writes that are not readily understood—especially by those who don't make much of an effort to do so (those who are **untaught and unstable**)—his words are easily twisted in order to make them say what the false teachers want them to say. Again, counselors should warn against those who twist the Bible. Many counselees are the dupes of false teaching. But if they are, in the final analysis it is because they are **ignorant and unstable**. One of the goals of counseling in cases of this sort is to teach counselees what they need to know in order to help them to become firm in the faith. Sometimes you must even help them to acquire the fundamental skills of Bible study and interpretation.

But this was not new material (remember, Peter was "reminding" them). They **know this already**. But they can be **led astray by the error of lawless persons** (those who care nothing about authority and the law of God) and **lose** the stability that they had already developed. This is a very important warning that, according to what we find in the book of Jude, his readers failed to heed. That is important to know because a person may lose the truth that he has gained by being taken in by false teaching. You will find counselees whose problem is just that. When they tell you of all their studies and training, it is useless; the critical thing is who they have been listening to most recently. The opposite of this loss, and what will keep it from occurring is growth by God's **grace** mediated through His Word. This will give one a deeper knowledge of Christ, which is the means of growth. With eschatological thoughts still in mind, Peter concludes with the words **To Him be glory both now and to the day of eternity.**

CONCLUSION

II Peter is unique. In it alone do we obtain much of the material that we have about the last judgment and the eternal state. In it alone do we meet such graphic and powerful warnings. In it alone do we read of the twisting of Paul's scriptural epistles as the way in which false teachers operate. And as you have seen, there is more. Counselor, make the most of these unique features in your counseling. Don't neglect II Peter as is the tendency of many (check out the scriptural indexes of books on counseling that have such indexes and note how few refer to II Peter). It is valuable for counseling purposes.

Introduction to JAMES

Luther was wrong. James is *not* an epistle of straw! Because he was no exegete, because he was wedded to an artificial, wooden, law-gospel method of interpretation combined with a failed attempt to shake off Alexandrine allegorizing, he missed the major point of the Book. James is not a Book in which good works as such predominate; James goes behind the works he advocates to the faith that motivates them. It is the *righteousness* that Jesus said must "exceed" that of the scribes and the Pharisees with which James is concerned. Indeed, almost every point that James makes can be traced back to the Sermon on the Mount and other comments. In many ways, the Book of James can be said to be an exposition and application of Jesus' sermon. And if anything it is not *dead* works but, rather, *live* works that *demonstrate* the presence of true faith; it is those urged in the Epistle of James. While I shall not note all the correspondences with the Sermon on the Mount as we procede (that is not the purpose of this commentary), I suggest that if you are interested in doing so, it might be profitable to be on the lookout for them. To get you started, however, note the following: In James there are no less than 22 references to Christ's sermons. In some form, every one of the beatitudes is mentioned. The following correspondences should suffice to make my point: compare James 1:5 with Matthew 7:7; James 2:5 with Luke 6:20; James 3:18 with Matthew 5:9; James 4:4 with Matthew 12:39,16:4; James 5:1-6 with Luke 6:24; James 5:12 with Matthew 12:34-37. James applies the principles of Christ's sermons to current church problems. That is why it is so helpful for counseling purposes. In James, to boot, there are six allusions to the Book of Job and ten to Proverbs. While Christ is not mentioned often (perhaps because of his relationship to Jesus, James tries to avoid name-dropping) what James teaches is built entirely on His teaching. Christ is definitely *honored* in the Book.

Now, let us consider what James is. It is a piece of *wisdom* literature. While wisdom literature takes a number of literary forms (proverbs, poetry, aphorisms, etc.) in the case before us, as in all wisdom literature, the emphasis is on *principles* of action *applied* to life situations. Often a principle is illustrated by one or more concrete examples of how it applies; yet (as Paul observes when discussing salaries for Christ's ministers from a command not to muzzle oxen at work—I Corinthians 9:8-10), frequently, its full application is broader than the specific, exemplary application in which it is presented. Principles are taught in applicatory form in order to show their relevance to everyday life and how they should be applied in concrete situations. If James does anything, he does that. He shows the relevance of faith to the way you must make decisions and carry them out. Few things could be more important to the Christian counselor in his use of the Bible.

James teaches, for instance, not merely that one should pray, but *how* he should do so. It is not enough to engage in the good work of prayer; a counselee must do so with the proper motives, attitudes, etc. That is what I mean when I say that Luther was wrong. He missed James' point. He seemed to view the works James advocates in pharisaical rather than Christian terms. He must not be excused for doing this; throughout history, his untempered accusation has cast doubt in the minds of some on one of the most important Books and some of the most important teachings of the New Testament. Don't hesitate to devour and live according to the Book of James—in spite of Luther!

What is in the Book of James? The following themes are treated:

trials	planning
endurance	God's will
doubt	favoritism
wisdom	rich/poor
prayer	anger
desire	the tongue
faith/works	jealousy
sickness	quarreling/strife
slander	

Would you say that a Book dealing with such matters as these is important? Would you say that it is of special importance to a counselor? How could it be otherwise?! As I Corinthians is a Book concerned with the problems of a gentile church, so James is a Book pertaining to a Jewish church (actually churches).

Moreover, the Book is filled with brief metaphors that demonstrate how to *make* truth live. Some commentators call the Book a sermon. Rather, it seems to be pieces (or summaries) of many sermons.

Another point of interest: James largely *exhorts*. There are more than 50 imperatives in the 108 verses of this letter! James *teaches* only indirectly. In James, truth is *applied.* Here you find truth *aimed at life.* That fact also means that the Book is invaluable for counselors. It *meets* the counseling issues *head on.*

As a Book for counselors, James is unparalleled. One may turn to it for direction in dealing with so many things he encounters in the work of counseling. But as he does, he must always be sure that he uses the Book as it was intended to be used—as a volume that teaches Christian, spiritual religion, not pharisaical (or even pharisaically-tainted) works-righteousness. So remember that thought—it is *the* single most important thought you can have in mind as you approach the study of James. James takes us *inside* man. What psychologists vainly search for James reveals. He shows how sin works within, how unbelief unsettles all of life, how testings produce endurance, how we make prayer a waste, how we can become evil, obsequious judges in our hearts, how self-centeredness causes destruction and how anger can destroy righteousness.

In form, one way James frequently proceeds is as follows:

1. A question or a command, followed by
2. An explanation or exposition and application, then
3. A recapitulation.

Themes are sometimes intertwined. We shall try to single them out as best we can. Remember, however, that is how counseling problems often come to you—intertwined (for more on how to single them out, see remarks in the commentary on I Corinthians). This will mean some minimal retracing of the same ground from differing perspectives. We will work through the 17 themes listed earlier in the course of our study. But at times, since the themes reoccur, each place dealing with an aspect of it, I shall attempt to pull the threads together (as well as treat them in place) from time to time in order to discover James' theology of each subject.

What is the purpose (*telos*) of the general epistle of James? It is the same as that which ought to be the objective of every truly Christian counselor: to help his counselee become a *teleios* person. What does that mean? The fact is emphasized in 1:4; 3:2 (see also 1:17,27) where the word appears and the thought is amplified. The Greek term *teleios* means "complete, entire." It pictures that which has achieved its goals. James speaks here of one who, *in every area of life*, has begun to live and grow as he ought to. It is the person whose life (in Old Testament terms) is *tam.*

That Hebrew word *tam*, corresponding to the Greek *teleios*, is found in Job 1:1; Psalm 18:32; 37:37; 101:2, etc. In those places, the KJV translates it as "perfect." But that translation, today, is misleading. What *tam* means is similar to the import of our phrase "to have it altogether" except that the expression must be understood in a *spiritual* sense. The **complete** person **lacks nothing** from God (v. 4)

Most Christians find the pursuit of holiness difficult. It is that problem with which the Book deals. James wants to supply the help your counselee needs to meet his deficiencies so that he too will **lack nothing**. People fail to grow in some areas for various reasons. One of these is that they do not know what God requires. Another is that they do not know what it takes to meet those requirements. A third reason is that sin hinders from doing so and distorts one's understanding of God's will and what He expects one to do about sin and failure. James knows this and, in his letter, wants to help them overcome whatever it is that stands in the way. Because of this, you will discover that the Book truly is invaluable for counseling.

CHAPTER 1

1 James, a slave of God and of the Lord Jesus Christ, to the twelve tribes in the dispersion: Greetings.

We come now to the exposition and counseling applications found in the Book itself. The first topic with which James deals is the purpose he has in mind (see Introduction above). He wants Christians to be **complete, lacking nothing.** But first, note his salutation: **James, a slave of God and of the Lord Jesus Christ.** By his own example, he has exhibited from the first line the attitude that leads to *teleios* living: humility. He could have bragged about the fact that he was the brother of Jesus Christ. Or he might merely have stated the fact, since it was true. But he didn't. Rather, he called himself Jesus' **slave**. Moreover, he understood his proper relationship to Christ as a subject in His church. That is clear from his designation of Him as **the Lord,** and by his placing Him on equal terms with **God** the Father: he is equally the **slave** of *Both.*

Until a Christian acknowledges himself as a **slave**, he is incapable of living the Christian life as he should. What was a slave? A person with no inherent rights. A piece of property to be bought, sold and used. One who had no will but the will of his master. Until a believer sees himself that way, as one who (by grace) has been bought by the blood of Christ, who belongs wholly to Him and who should have no will but the will of his Lord, he will continue to **lack** the attitude that is vital to progress in spiritual growth. If James, the brother of Christ, so humbled himself, surely your counselee—with no such illustrious pedigree—can do the same! Whenever counselees boast of who they are, or insist they should be treated in special ways (or that they should not be treated as someone has treated them) ask them who they think that they are. Press the question until the right answer is given: **a slave of God and the Lord Jesus Christ.**

On the other hand, whenever one acts for His Lord, doing His will, he acts with authority. The slave of God and the Lord Jesus, when speaking His words, and accomplishing His purposes, is acting as a representative of Deity—nothing less! That must be reckoned with. *You,* as a biblical counselor, have that kind of authority and ought to be respected for the sake of the One Whom you represent, and in Whose stead you are ministering. Of course, all such authority is qualified by the word "biblical." Every counselee has the right (obligation) to evaluate whether or not what you say and ask him to do is *biblical*. When he concludes that it is, he must give due respect to such ministry. When he does not, he ought to differ cautiously, discussing respectfully what he believes to be unbiblical in the counsel given to him. After all, as an ordained officer of Christ's church, you are Christ's **slave**. He must, therefore, not reject what you advise out of hand, realizing that *he* may be the one who is wrong and that, thereby, he may be rejecting the Savior Himself.

James is writing to the Jews of **the dispersion** who have become believers. As the pastor of the church of Jerusalem, he would have a deep interest in and responsibility to them. The word **dispersion** is literally "the scattering," or "sowing." It was used of the sowing of seed. In His wise providence, God had scattered His people all around the Mediterranean world. These little colonies of Jews were the ones to whom Paul went "first." Associated with them were many "God-fearers." These were Gentiles who, while believing in Jehovah as God, nevertheless, had not become full proselytes to Judaism. They were also called "Gentiles of the Gate" (those who stood outside of the Jewish community, but looked in on it with belief). It was from both these Jews scattered around the Roman world and (especially) the God-fearing gentiles, that the converts of the early church outside of Palestine was largely gathered. As pastor of the mother church of Jerusalem, it was appropriate for James to write to them.

In verse two, James identifies himself with his readers as **brothers.** The entire Christian fold the world over was also a family. If a Christian, in that mobile New Testament age, moved (or was forced to move; cf. Acts 8:4) he could be sure to find other brothers and sisters in Christ somewhere near the place to which he went. The same is true today. The church is one grand family. It is difficult for others who move to find friends; the Christian has relatives (unknown, but nevertheless, true) everywhere. That is a comforting and reassuring fact. If you are counseling a Christian who has just recently taken up residence in your area, but who has not yet looked up his "relatives," urge him to make himself known to some of them and to unite with the nearest vital branch of the heavenly family! No one can go very long in this world of sin and temptation apart from the care and the discipline of God's family. Many of the problems that your counselees have stem from failure to become active participants in family life. Either they stayed away from the family for a considerable period of time in which they learned bad patterns of living that they still carry over to the present or they are currently absenting themselves. Stress the importance of heeding the remarks by the writer to

2 My brothers, consider it nothing but joy when you fall into trials of various sorts,
3 knowing that the testing of your faith works endurance.
4 Let endurance have its full effect, that you may be complete and entire, lacking in nothing.

---

the Hebrews (Hebrews 10:24,5). The Jews had spoken of one another as **brothers,** but they were thinking of Israel after the flesh—a hereditary thing. Our family relationship depends not on birth but on the second birth.

In beginning to show how to become complete, James surprises his readers by urging them to **consider it entirely a happy situation [or pure joy] when you fall into trials of various sorts.** Suffering as many of them were, they might think otherwise. When a counselee finishes explaining what problems drove him to you, how often have you responded, "Great! That is reason for nothing but joy, happiness and thanksgiving!"? Chances are, you've never said anything of the sort. But that is exactly what James is doing. Since he does, it might be worthwhile considering whether you might not do something similar. In order to understand, let's see what James had in mind. He says that these **various trials test** their **faith**. That is why they should be happy about them. Does that make sense to you? Well, let's see where James is going with this. The **testing of faith**, he says, **works endurance.** And **endurance** must be allowed to **have its full effect** (vv. 2-4). That **full effect** is to make the sufferer **complete** [*teleios*] **and entire, lacking in nothing.** In other words, it is through trial and suffering that one becomes *teleios.* The term that I have translated **entire** is *holokleros* which refers to something "with every part intact." It is something that "has all its parts." That is, it has complete integrity. This phrase, **complete and entire,** was a common phrase with double impact that was used in order to stress the idea of *entirety*. That this is James' thought is even more strongly emphasized by the negative appendage, **lacking in nothing.**

Well, then, plainly it is not your part to moan and groan with those counselees who come doing so. While never denying or minimizing the severity of a problem in a counselee's life, you must even more strongly emphasize the reason why trials come: to **complete** what is **lacking** in him. Trials are what make one *tam* (frequently translated by *teleio*s in the Septuagint). And if that is so (as James says that it is), then one ought to consider circumstances in which he finds himself **enduring tests of his**

faith nothing short of joy.

"Wow! That's tough," you say. Well, yes—and no. It is difficult even for redeemed sinners to acquiesce in the loving ways of God. Rather, they want to rebel, question or complain. But none of those responses to trials help. That is why there is a "no" as well as a "yes" in the above answer. The "no" means that it is easier (much easier) on himself for him to recognize and appreciate trials as gifts from God sent to strengthen and complete his faith than it is to add his own misery and complaining to the trial. The attitude in which one **endures** suffering has a lot to do with how well he endures.

And beyond that, he does not want to short circuit the benefits of trials and testings. They must be allowed to **have** their **full effect** (v. 4). It is only when one endures *to the end* that the **full effect** of that endurance is realized in his life. Enduring enables one to benefit **fully** from the experience. If, however, he breaks down (usually because he fails to recognize God's loving purpose in sending the test) rather than endures, giving in to his feelings and to the pressures of the situation, he will be less **complete and entire** than he might otherwise have become. It is like someone who runs a race almost to the finish line, at which time he has a good chance of winning, only to quit before he reaches it because of the pain and exertion involved. James is here setting forth a philosophy of pain and suffering that every successful counselor understands and knows how to introduce into the counseling session.

Work on doing so. A counselee tells you of the enormity of his suffering. Rather than inanely saying "I feel your pain," which does no one any good, say, "Yes, I am sure that it is difficult. But let me help you explore what benefits you can reap from it. And as you recognize some of these, perhaps you will not only be able to endure the suffering better, but you may even be able to **consider** your problem **entirely a happy** one." When you counsel that way, people will be helped now and later on. *Now*, in the sense that a good attitude makes endurance easier; *later,* in the sense that **happy endurance** of suffering builds one up and **completes** him. This emphasis, hitting his readers right in the face at the beginning of the letter, is of extreme importance. If it were not fundamental to all else that he is about to say, it is doubtful that James would have said it up front so abruptly.

Notice the word **consider** found in verse 2. There is no command to *feel* **happy,** but to **consider** stressful **situations** entirely happy ones. What does that mean? Well, it has to do with how you look at and evaluate them. If you bring the goodness of God, molding you into a *teleios* person by trial, into the picture, by properly considering what this means, you will be able to **consider** it unmixed joy. Your happiness over the event will grow out of your reasoned evaluation of it. The primary idea in the word **consider** is to "lead." The secondary usage of the word is to "consider, count, regard." Here is how that comes about: to **consider,** in this passage, means "to lead one's self to think." In other words, what is required when in trial is hard thinking. What so often happens, instead, is reckless emotionalism. "When in trouble," tell your counselee, "stop, think and learn." It will take a deliberate act on his part to wrench himself out of the cesspool of self-pity. Self-pity only adds to one's misery. It is a process of self-exaltation in which one thinks that he deserves something better than what he got. If he thinks of grace and, in addition, thinks of the **trial** as an act of God's grace toward him, by which he is being placed in a condition where **endurance** in an entirely happy manner (unmarred by complaining) will help complete his Christian experience, he will be able to obey this divine directive. *But he must **think***. Instead, as I said, the sinful tendency is to *emote*. The difference between these two responses to trouble makes all the difference in the outcome.

Counselor, you have a whale of a lot of teaching (and coaching) to do to encourage counselees to think this way of their trials. But if you don't, what will you say to a person who is persecuted at work for his faith? How will you help a husband who has been financially scalped by his unsaved wife in a divorce suit? What will you do for an abused person? Will you focus on the counselee, and his feelings, as the world does? Then you will only help him to continue and enlarge his misery. If you do, you will help him to build a life centered around the wrongs done to him, so that he goes on throughout his days thinking of himself as an "abused person." NO! If you would truly help counselees, you will focus on the fact that, no matter how severe the trial, *God is in the picture*. That, you see, is what James is trying to get across to him. God means this testing as a means of building him up in his faith.

What is the **effect** of **endurance?** The **effect** is to fill in whatever is lacking. James is not any more definite than that because the **lacks** differ with the persons involved. So too, do the **trials**; they are of **various sorts.** These trials, you may assure your counselee, are not fortuitous, but are adapted to his particular lacks for which at this time God is providing remedies. God supplies His children with what they truly need (not always what they want or think that they need). And He often (not always) does so through their enduring specific difficulties adapted in a vital and individualized way.

The tests, then, are a blessing intended to meet wants in the character of the counselee. Above all else, enable him to see this. Otherwise he may wish to cut the process short *before* realizing the benefits involved in it. **Endurance** must **have its full effect** on him! Part of your task as a counselor is to help him to understand this and learn how to endure and reap the benefits of the trial that are best suited to him.

So what is the counselor's task? Since almost all counselees visit counselors because they are unsuccessfully facing trouble, you must 1) help them to develop a biblical attitude toward trouble; 2) show them that God sends trials to develop endurance; 3) help them to continue to allow endurance to have its intended effect.

Before leaving this matter behind, I should like to make a few more observations. While one is to **consider it an entirely happy situation** when he falls into various sorts of trials, there is an important distinction always to be kept in view. Never tell the counselee that he is to rejoice over pain, rather, that he must rejoice over the effects that **enduring** it will produce. That distinction, I say, is vital. Masochism is not Christian. And counselors must never become sadists. It is the **effects** of pain *rightly handled* that should be applauded. And the principal one, in addition to all the rest—whatever they may be in any individual's situation— is that the counselee has served his Lord well and lived through it for him.

The word translated **testing**, as I shall show later on, is a neutral term that could also be translated **temptation**, depending on its context. Every test is (from the devil's point of view) also a temptation; every temptation is (from God's point of view) a test. It becomes one or the other depending on which way the counselee decides to go. The counselee himself is responsible for making it a test or a temptation. When a test becomes a temptation, it is because the counselee stepped through the door that the devil opened wide for him.

It is true then that the test (successfully endured) will produce benefits; it is true also that the test (unsuccessfully endured) will reduce one's effectiveness for Christ. Since the trials one must endure are **tests**, they are not meaningless events. They have value and importance. How one handles them, then, is of importance.

In verse 2, the words **fall into** are, literally, "fall among." The idea in the word is to fall *into the thick of* trials, which may surround one on all sides (cf. its use in Luke 10:30). The words **of various sorts** are the translation of one Greek word that means "many colored; variegated." Outside of the Bible it is used to describe the veins in marble and the skin of a leopard. The trials James has in mind are of various sorts: the fiery reds of

5 So if any of you lacks wisdom, let him ask God for it, since He gives to everyone unreservedly and without reproaching, and it will be given to him.

---

persecution, the icy blues of loneliness, discouragement and rejection, the yellow-greens of sickness and death, etc.

To **endure** is, literally, "to remain under." It means to hang in there when the going gets tough. Counselees and counselors (like physicians who too quickly medicate) may tend to cut short the process of endurance. If they do so, they virtually remove all meaning and purpose from the suffering. God wants a finished product; not one that was never completed. The work of endurance is an inner issue. Successfully handling trials strengthens and teaches; it prepares for greater things to come and it enables one to understand something of the suffering of Jesus Christ for him.

In the desire to relieve pain, the process can be cut short, as I have said. This may be demanded by the counselee who becomes insistent on relief (when that becomes his one goal). He can lose heart before attaining the blessings that could have been his. And he can simply give in to the lures of some temptation. The counselor may focus on feeling only, or unduly. He can attempt solutions before repentance. He can settle for less than God's Word does. And he can agree to solutions that weaken rather than strengthen faith.

Encourage your counselee while he is enduring trials. The promises of God, the success of others who may become models for him and the willingness to stand by and remind are all endeavors that will help. For now, that is enough on temptation. There will be more later. But now, let us move on to the next item. In James 1:4, the writer indicates that God doesn't want the counselee to lack *anything*. But the one thing for which he stresses the need while enduring trial is **wisdom.** We must discuss this virtue.

Under trial, the one thing that your counselee will need is **wisdom**. To **consider** and thereby **endure the trial** in ways that please God and bring his own life closer to the *teleios* person he ought to be, he will need to know how to apply the fruit of biblical thinking to his situation. That takes **wisdom. Wisdom** is a word that is rarely encountered in popular writing. You can read the newspaper from cover to cover day after day and never run across it. Surely you rarely, if ever, hear it spoken by a TV newscaster. Scholars talk and write about everything else, but the word

wisdom seems to have eluded them. Doubtless, what you hear so little about exists only in small quantities! That is why there is so much difficulty in the church as well as in the world: the less **wisdom**, the more trouble.

You, as a counselor, surely need to know how to dispense **wisdom** from the Bible; your counselee needs to know how to apply wise counsel to his circumstances. If there ever were a word that characterizes what a counselor ought to be, it is the word **wise.**

James says **if wisdom is** lacking**, ask for it.** While you may have thought and talked informally about praying for wisdom, have you ever emphasized the idea of *structuring* prayer for wisdom into the counseling process? That is worth thinking about, isn't it? A carefully worded prayer for wisdom might be precisely what is needed at various points when you and your counselee find yourselves at loss for answers or direction. And in every counseling case, once having reviewed the data that the first session brings forth, would it not be proper to take time at the conclusion of the counseling hour to ask?

It is interesting to note that James doesn't say that there is a need for knowledge, information, etc.; what he flags for us is the need for **wisdom** (v. 5). All these things are necessary, it is true, but James is interested in you and your counselee living and acting according to wisdom. Wisdom is greater than all of these because it includes them all. **Wisdom** cannot be defined by the Greek term *sophia*, because into that word there is also packed all of the Old Testament understanding of wisdom. The comparable Hebrew word carries the meaning of "skill in living God's way." The "fear of the Lord is the beginning of wisdom." The essence of *teleios* living, then, is life lived scripturally in full recognition of Who God is in order to please Him. It involves biblical truth applied in biblical ways. Since **wisdom** will be defined by James, as it is in Proverbs (cf. 1:2; 4:7), as the obedient, practical way of applying God's Word to life, we see immediately that there is no place for Rogerian non-directive counseling. Rather, there is an Authority from which wisdom is gained that needs to be acknowledged and incorporated into daily living; there are no wise answers inherently in ourselves. Here, in facing trials, the essence of wisdom is to discover from the Bible what to do and how to do it.

The simple response to trials is to take God at His Word when He says, **if any of you lacks wisdom, let him ask God for it.** That is what it boils down to—believing prayer according to the commandments and encouragements of the Bible. The way to gain wisdom is simply to ask for *(aiteo)* it. How do we know it is that simple? God says that, other than faith, there are no strings attached. He will give **unreservedly and without reproaching** (v. 5[b]). The first word means "simply, liberally or unreservedly." Out of His limitless supplies, God—the only Source of true wisdom—will without skimping give you the wisdom that you need. Do you regularly pray for wisdom for solving the various counseling problems that you are called upon to deal with? Do you ask your counselees to do so? If they don't think there are wise solutions, ask them, "Do you think that God will provide only *part* of what we need?" Of course, He will not. **Everyone** who asks in Christian faith will receive *all* of the wisdom that he needs. God gives it ***unreservedly.*** That is a remarkable, wonderful promise. Make it. Then, together, pray—in faith.

The second word is translated **without reproaching.** The way that some people give, you'd rather they didn't. Their attitude in giving is not only superior, but that of one who is holier than thou. They say such things as, "Well, I wondered if you'd ever get around to asking!" or "I'm going to give you this but..." The word means "without scolding." God doesn't kick you when you are down. When you ask rightly, you will hear no reproach, just His willing, lavish response. That is good to know. There is no reason to hesitate in asking. The counselee need not fear. If he is repentant and comes in faith, he will receive what he needs (it doesn't say *desires*).

Now, note the fact that wisdom doesn't come through experience alone. Nor does the endurance produce it automatically. The wisdom your counselee needs comes as the result of asking for it. That is God's promise. It is a gift: **He *gives*** it (v. 5). That's the way Solomon got it (read I Kings 3:9-12). This whole idea is opposed to learning from experience (the movement that goes back to Dewey and that is touted so widely by Christians today). No, read also Proverbs 2:6 that says God gives it, that it comes from His mouth. Wisdom has its basis in divine *revelation.* The Book of Proverbs, for instance, was given to reveal wisdom to covenant youth. James has a similar purpose. Apostolic wisdom (I Corinthians 2:6) is now inscripturated in the Books of the New Testament. The matter of praying for this gift *in faith* will come up next under the problem of doubt and instability—prominent characteristics found among counselees.

Help your counselees to distinguish between the wisdom of God and the wisdom of the world. But that is another matter, to be taken up when we treat James 3:13-18.

So let us go on to verses 6-8. All one need do is ask, he will receive the wisdom he needs—*if* (and that if is very important): If he asks **in faith, without doubting** (v. 6[a]). Here is a complicating problem. There

6 But let him ask in faith, without doubting, because a person who doubts is like a wave of the sea that is driven and tossed by the wind.

---

are two kinds of problems encountered in counseling: original (or principal) problems and complicating problems. The latter arise in some way in or around the former. Complicating problems may arise out of faulty or sinful ways of handling original problems. They may also arise from wrong attitudes that accompany right actions. Here, the problem is that if one needs wisdom, what he must do is ask God for it and God will give it to him without reserve and without scolding him. But if he asks, doubting this promise, he cannot expect to receive the wisdom that he needs. Indeed, to doubt in prayer is to only strengthen the doubt since it leads to a self-fulfilling prediction: "See, I didn't think I would get it anyway."

A complicating problem must be dealt with before the original problem. It stands in the way. Though secondary to the other, nevertheless, it must be given priority over it since there is no way in which the original problem can be dealt with God's way until the complicating problem is removed.

You will counsel many doubting persons. Bringing it up right away, James indicates that the difficulty is one that is frequently encountered. He will return to a different aspect of the matter of doubt in 4:8-10. But for now, let it be sufficient to note that doubt may stand in the way of becoming *teleios*. Here, the person in view is called an *aner dipsuchos* (that is, a double-souled man). It is the opposite of the *teleios* man who has it all *together* (who is an *integrated* person). The man, divided in himself, mixes unbelief with faith. That sort of diluted faith, James calls **doubt.** The word used for **doubt** pictures one who can't agree with himself. He is undecided; he carries on a self-debate that causes vacillation. Many counselees are like that. Until they are shown clearly in the Scriptures what God promises them, and are willing to commit themselves entirely to that promise, **without doubting**, they will fail to receive what they ask God for.

Many counselees come divided, on the one hand, between obedient, trustful action based on God's Word and, on the other hand, acts of or continuance in sin. They are limping between two opinions (I Kings 18:21). That is, like a man with a limp, who as he walks tilts first to one then to the other side, so too, they lean first one way, then the other. The disturbance in such a person makes him **like a wave of the sea;** it **drives and tosses** him about. He is at the mercy of the various **winds** that blow.

7 That person shouldn't suppose that he will receive anything from the Lord,
8 because a double-minded man is unstable in all of his ways.

Indeed, one of our metaphors is that such a person "wavers." He is not sure of God and His promises. Often the turmoil within such a counselee is great, often overwhelming. Relief can come to him in but one way. He must humbly rest his heart and soul on the Word of God.

It is important for the counselor to remember that until he does, **that person shouldn't suppose that he will receive anything from the Lord** (v. 7). Too often, counselors move ahead in spite of that clearly-revealed fact, attempting (and consequently failing) to solve the original problem. Counselees often will urge them to do so. But the counselee must be told that he will only fail in every such attempt for lack of faith. Once again, (incidentally, contrary to Luther) note how important faith is for James. Never proceed as though success depended on counselor/counselee efforts alone. Wisdom—God's truth at work in Christian action—is *essential* for success in facing trials God's way. But wisdom is given only to those who ask—*in faith*. By the way, here is another reason why you cannot counsel an unbeliever (for a full discussion of this, see comments on I Corinthians 2): he is an UNbeliever—i.e., one without faith. Christ made the same point about faith that James does (cf. Mark 11:24). The concept is not new. Why should God give anything to those who don't expect Him to?

Again, it is possible to see that, to James, it is not just works (even the work of prayer), but the inner dynamic behind it, that is all-important. Luther was wrong. James is a man of faith. He is concerned about the inner struggles that we have in living for Christ. Indeed, it may be said that if there is to be any change at all in any counseling case, regardless of the problem(s), that change will require **faith**. All counseling must be done in the atmosphere of faith. Where there is no faith, or where **doubt** predominates, it is necessary to work on that problem before all others. In those instances where faith fails, you must help the counselee to come to a believing commitment to God's Word.

How can you tell whether there is lack of faith? One sure sign is *instability;* a **double-minded man is unstable in all his ways.** Now, that is an important insight that the world doesn't understand. The word **ways** here means "one's habitual course of conduct." Cf. Psalm 91:11; 145:17; Proverbs 3:6. If you see someone who is unstable generally (i.e., in **all his**

ways) look for double-minded doubting. It works in both directions. If someone speaks of doubts (or you discover them) you must counsel around the circle of his life, bringing God's Word to bear on every area, since doubt causes instability generally.

What is instability? Here, the meaning is "unsettledness." The doubting person is in turmoil; he vacillates. Often, he will try to hedge his bets. But God won't allow that. He is described as **a wave of the sea that is driven and tossed by the wind**; the picture is of one who is agitated, disorderly, cannot be pinned down to anything, inconsistent (now saying/doing this; now that). He trips over his own feet trying to go two ways at once.

So you can see from this instance how important it is to deal with complicating problems that stand in the way of original problems. Faith must be involved in all biblical problem-solving (read Hebrews 11:6, including the comments on that passage). Faith and order (including discipline) are essential to change that pleases God. Faith is being sure enough of God and His Word to depend and act on it.

But how do you help a doubting counselee? The interesting thing is that in 4:8-10 James tells you. He calls the doubting counselee to **repentance**! While I don't want to anticipate all that must be said there, I want you to note that God considers doubt a moral problem. It is not an academic or intellectual one. The only way to doubt God is to turn against Him and His promises in some way or other; that is a moral problem. Ultimately, all doubt turns out to be exactly that. The Bible, prayerfully used, will bring conviction that may lead to repentance (cf. II Timothy 3:16). Repentance involves confession of sin and the seeking of forgiveness from God. That is the negative side. The positive side is to read prayerfully those promises that one has been doubting over and over again until growingly faith replaces doubt in the heart: faith comes by hearing, and hearing by the Word of God (Romans 10). If there are problems in the understanding of the promise, then the counselor can help clarify. But in order for you as a counselor to build faith in your counselee, you must explain the promises of God, *and* call on him to believe. We shall have more to say about the problem when we study the fourth chapter. There are things that get in the way, pleasures that cloud one to the reality of the promises of God. But that must wait until we reach that place.

Instability because of lack of faith is one of the causes of other problems that counselees present. Yet, few counselors investigate the matter in these terms. Few unstable persons, therefore, are helped. Probably, many counselors have turned away from the investigation of this probable cause

9 Now let the brother in lowly circumstances boast about his high circumstances,

---

because of the cavalier manner in which some scripturally-unsophisticated and foolish believers throw around statements like, "All you need is more faith." While, in certain cases, this evaluation may be on target, their use of faith as a panacea for *everything* is deplorable. People like this give the truth taught here in James a bad name. In reaction, many counselors are turned off and rarely pursue the problem of **doubt** as often as they should. It is also possible to become too sophisticated.

When a person is unstable in some one area, a counselor ought to have in the back of his mind that it is possible that he may have a *general* problem of instability. Probing for this diagnosis of the problem, therefore, is in order (but be careful not to "invent" instability where it doesn't exist!). If, through probing him (and any other person who knows him well), you discover that the difficulty *is general*, then look for doubt at the base. Good counseling notes biblical connections like those mentioned here between doubt and instability (not neglecting the emphasis on the pervasive nature of the effects of doubt: **in all his ways**). Observations like these give great insight into the functioning of human lives. Is James straw-like?

Much more will be said about prayer at a later point, especially about how a great deal of prayer is wasted (another great insight given mainly in the Book of James). But now we turn to verses 9 through 11. In addition to what we encounter here, there is more about money in 2:1-7; 5:1-6, which we shall consider at those places. Incidentally, for a more systematic treatment of this and the other seventeen matters in the Book of James mentioned in the Introduction, see my book, *A Thirst for Wholeness.*

One key problem of counselees is trials that arise over finances. Husbands and wives fight over finances; many worry themselves into a frazzle over their lack, etc. While James doesn't speak the last word on financial issues (see I Timothy 6 for the basic biblical principles involved), what he says is important for counseling. James is concerned about *how Christians view* their financial conditions. What do your counselees think of poverty and of riches? The answer to that question is the background for all counseling about the matter.

Verses 5 through 8 are somewhat parenthetical; James picks up where he left off in verse 4 about trials, now setting forth one of the major tests that many have—their attitudes toward poverty and riches. His con-

10 and the rich one about his humble circumstances (because like a flower of the grass he will pass away—

---

cern is for counselees to understand that *both the rich and the poor are alike in God's sight.* There is no advantage to either condition so far as God is concerned. Poverty is no evil and riches are no advantage (cf. Philippians 4:11,12). God says, **Let the brother in lowly circumstances boast about his high circumstances, and the rich one about his humble circumstances.** Then, in the rest of verse 10 and 11, he explains why this is a reasonable view of things. What is the fundamental attitude toward one's financial condition about which James says this? It is important for you to understand since, as a counselor, you will find it difficult (but necessary) to explain this viewpoint to counselees who do not understand and often are extremely resistant to it.

If he sees poverty as the world does, the counselee will feel angry, envious and dissatisfied. He will think his condition is "unfair." Or, he may even attempt to justify sinful behavior because of it. All such attitudes are taboo for the Christian. Rather, he must develop God's perspective on poverty: he must **boast about his high circumstances.** Unlike those around him who know nothing of salvation, he truly has riches about which he can boast. These are the riches he has now, and some day will enter into even more fully, in Christ. There is a play on the words: literally, the **lowly brother** should boast about his **heights.** He is the child of a King—no, the child of the King of kings—with a kingly inheritance promised to him (cf. James 2:5). That is truly something to boast about. Right now, in this world, he also has access to the throne of grace. Available to him are spiritual benefits so numerous that it took the longest sentence in the New Testament to list them (found in the first chapter of the Book of Ephesians in the original). He may boast about His Lord and all that he does for him. That is the true attitude toward poverty.

But what of the rich? He is to boast **about his humble circumstances.** What does James mean by that? Just this: the rich brother [note, incidentally, there can be such; cf. I Timothy 6:17ff.] should direct his thinking toward the poverty of those who have nothing more than material wealth. It is nothing in comparison to the riches one has in Christ Jesus. All come to the cross as spiritual beggars saying, "nothing in my hand I bring." His circumstances are truly **humble** before God. Verses 10^{b} and 11 tell it all: He is rich in this world for only a short time. **Like the flower of the grass he will pass away—the sun rises with its scorching heat**

11 the sun rises with its scorching heat and dries the grass and its flower drops off and the beauty of its appearance is destroyed); so too the rich man in his pursuits will fade away.

---

and dries the grass and its flower drops off and the beauty of its appearance is destroyed [that's what the sirocco—like the Santa Annas in California—coming off the desert in Palestine does]. His point? **So too the rich man in his pursuits will fade away** (reread the story of Lazarus and the rich man who had nothing more). When the rich dies, he can take nothing with him. If he had nothing more, he is truly poor; if he has Christ and all there is to come, present riches are dimmed and diminished by the promise of the heavenly ones. The rich man who is rich only in the things of this world may be "dead rich" today; tomorrow *dead*!

Your task, before dealing with the many aspects of finances necessary to good stewardship, is to lead counselees into an understanding and acceptance of this biblical point of view. Otherwise, all the planning, budgeting, etc., in which you may engage will mean little; his major problem, one that will adversely affect all else that you do, will remain untouched. That problem is a wrong perspective on wealth. The words **let the brother...**are in the form of a command issued to him through someone else. They mean "You should command the brother." The phrase also indicates the necessity for him to acquire an attitude of boasting about God's provisions for him. Anyone who can truly boast about the good things God is doing (and will do) in his life cannot complain. Getting a biblical perspective on wealth is essential therefore. Remember, the movement of thought to achieve in the mind of the counselee is a transfer of focus from material poverty/riches to spiritual riches. Ideas about money that are found in the standard textbooks written by unbelievers will not do. If *you* do not make the points that James is making, the chances are that the counselee will never hear them elsewhere. Be sure, then, to check out the counselee's world-view with reference to wealth before attempting to help him in specific ways.

There are dangers in not proceeding in that manner which we shall encounter in 5:1-8, but we will leave that to when we begin to do an exposition of the chapter.

Moving on to verses 12 through 16, then, we take up the question of temptation, how it works and what God says to do about it. Few things could be of greater importance to counseling. The ordinary counselee, if not already tempted to sin in various ways when he comes for counseling,

12 Happy is the one who endures trial, because when he has been approved by testing he will receive the winner's crown of life that He promised to those who love Him.

---

may, during the course of the sessions, consider taking seeming solutions to his problem that are nothing less than a violation of the commandments of God. You must not only know all about temptation; you must be able to recognize what is (and what is not) a commandment of God that may be transgressed.

The matter of **testing** and **trial** is still before James. The one who **endures trial** and **has been approved by testing will receive the winner's crown of life that He promised to those who love Him** (v. 12). Here is additional information concerning trials and their relationship to temptation. James holds forth the incentive to **endure**: the **crown of life.** At the end of the race, he will receive the **crown** that is given to the **winner** of the race. The **crown of life** is the reward of eternal **life** that is awarded when life's race is over (cf. Revelation 2:10). The word *stephanos* (from which the name Stephen comes) was often used instead of the term "reward." It is the prize that is given to all those who **endure** to the end. They are **approved by testing.** The word behind these three words (it takes three English words to say what this one Greek word says) was used of assaying metals. A coin was put through various **tests** in order to assure that it was solid. When it rang true, it was declared **approved**. Christians are also approved by means of being subjected to tests (trials). In trials, they too must ring true. That is one way of saying that their faith is real. So trials are important for counselees in order to evaluate *their* metal.

Those who **love Him** (Jesus Christ; see II Timothy 4:8) will pass the test. That is not to say that they will not from time to time fall in the course of the race; but **those who love Him** will get up, dust themselves off, and, relying more fully on His grace, continue to run the race. It is not wrong to press the point with a recalcitrant counselee: "Do you really love Christ? Doesn't His death for your sins move you to hang in there even in the face of trials and temptations?" After all, He said, "whoever endures to the end will be saved." **Endurance** is the factor by which one's genuineness is determined. The happiness that results (v. 12) from this approval and the **promise** of future **life** is what can sustain and enable him to continue to endure other (perhaps even more serious) trials in the future.

13 Let no one who is tempted say, "I am being tempted by God," because God isn't tempted by evil things and He tempts no one with them.

All of which leads to a valuable discussion of **temptation**. Verses 13-16 are crucial. As a Christian counselor you not only must become familiar with them but be able to explain them to counselees who are facing temptation. There are problems with understanding temptation; James says as much when he concluded the discussion with the words: **Don't be misled, dear brothers** (v. 16). There are various ways in which false teachers are misleading counselees today. Some teach doctrines that can be summed up in the erroneous statement "The devil made me do it." In this definitive discussion of temptation, James does not even mention the devil! After all, is there anything that the devil could "make you do" that you couldn't do on your own? That is a question to ask those who are convinced by the **misleading** idea that falling into **temptation** is something they cannot help because the devil controlled them when sinning. James, as we shall see, places the responsibility exactly where it belongs—on the counselee, not on the devil. It is possible to be **misled** by those who blame **God** for the temptations into which they fall. Since that is where James begins his discussion, let's see what he has to say about that.

James makes his point very clear: **Let no one who is tempted say, "I am being tempted by God," because God isn't tempted by evil things and He tempts no one with them** (v. 13). James is saying that to make such a charge is to impugn God. He isn't One Whose nature craves **evil things**; to charge Him with **tempting** others to sin, therefore, is to cast doubt on His character. That is a serious matter. One must not be **misled**.

Well then, what of Matthew 4:1 where the King James Version (wrongly) implies that the Holy Spirit led Jesus into the wilderness to be tempted by the devil. There is a subtle, but absolutely crucial, matter that must be understood if one is to sort out what [apparently] is a contradiction. The word translated in various places "to tempt" is also translated "to test, to try." The term itself is colorless and takes its meaning solely from the context. The same word (and word-root) was used in verses 3 and 12 of this very chapter and translated **testing and trial.**

Well, what is the upshot of this? Simply this: as I said previously, every temptation is also a test; every test [trial] is also a temptation. From God's perspective, as James has just finished saying, the experience comes in order to test one so that he may be **approved** by **enduring** it (v.

14 Instead, each one is tempted by his own desires; like a fish going after bait he is lured away and enticed.

---

12). On the other hand, that test [trial] which one *fails* to pass, somewhere along the line became a temptation to sin. If he failed, he failed by sinning. So the key thing to make plain to counselees is that the tests and trials that come his way may become temptations to sin into which he falls, or tests that bring strength, approval and happiness when he passes them. But what they turn out to be in the end depends upon his response to them. That means any (every) trial one endures has much within it that can lure him away from the proper, godly response.

Well, if it is not God or the devil upon which one can blame his failure, where should the blame be placed? Squarely on his own shoulders—as James does: **each one is tempted by his own desires; like a fish going after bait he is lured away and enticed. Then when desire is conceived it gives birth to sin, and sin, when fully matured, brings forth death** (vv. 14,15). Those are powerful words! Let's take the time to fully understand them and their implications for counseling.

In this desire-indulged, feeling-oriented age nothing could be more important than to get a grasp of the biblical information about **desire** that James presents. He says that giving in to desires when the Bible forbids it is the *source* of personal sin. Rather than focus on God or the devil, he wants you to focus on your **desires**.

Desire is not wrong, *per se.* The word *epithumia*, though mostly used of evil desire in the Bible, is sometimes used of good desires as well (cf. Luke 22:15; Philippians 1:23; I Thessalonians 2:17). When the word is used of sinful desires it is often (but not always) combined with the words "evil," or "fleshly." The word refers to any and all *cravings.* That is to say, desire is *always felt in the body.* These *arise* in two ways. The first is body-engendered desires usually referred to as appetites (hunger, thirst, sex, etc. For more on this see Moulten and Milligan). Those are natural desires. Others are body-*implanted*, implanted by the mind. These are the habitual desires, arising because one has habituated himself to indulging in them. The body is habituated so as to crave something or other. For more on this, see my book *Winning the War Within* and information in this commentary series on Romans 6, 7, 8 and Ephesians 4.

These desires are what lead to sin, says James. The desires within are the source of one's temptations. Because of this, it is vital for counselors and counselees to deal with desire in the counselee. What desires are

15 Then when desire has conceived it gives birth to sin, and sin, when fully matured, brings forth death.

---

they that he seeks to indulge by succumbing to any given temptation? That is a critical issue. If it is one of the original, body-engendered desires, then he must be taught (and must learn to practice) the biblical principle of moderation (cf. I Corinthians 6:12). If they are unnecessary, learned desires, habituated into the lifestyle of the counselee by his sinful nature, then he must be taught how to replace them with biblical patterns.

These desires, James says, **lure and entice** us just as **bait** leads a **fish** to his death. The dynamic of the matter is spelled out in terms of the conception and birth of a child. Here is how one moves from temptation (which is not in and of itself sin) to sin. Behind this figure, James presumes a depraved nature. The family line makes it clear in the passage that sin is the offspring of sinful desire.

Desire, like a harlot (or a fisherman) **lures** the counselee into her net. His desire entices your counselee to yield. When he agrees in his heart to do so, that is the intercourse that brings about **conception,** that ultimately gives **birth** to **sin** (here, meaning acts of transgression). The sin is first in the heart, then in the act. Sometimes, of course, because of fear or other outer restraints, the sin gets no farther than the heart. Nevertheless, heart-consent is sin. Finally, James says, **sin, when fully matured, brings forth death.** Paul's words in Romans 6:23 are in exact parallel: "The wages of sin is death." Sin, unforgiven, leads not only to physical, but also to spiritual death.

Now because of James' analysis you can see that there are at least three points at which the counselor may break in to cut off sin. Beginning at the end point, **death** is cut off by regeneration and faith leading to conversion. The life-course of sin is disrupted by salvation. That, of course, is bedrock. At stage two, prior to actual transgression, sin can be cut off by radical amputation: cf. Matthew 5:28ff. (See my book, *The Christian Counselor's Manual* for information on this all-important concept). Finally, sin can be cut off at the pass (avoided altogether) by understanding desire's enticing ways and refusing to go to bed with her. If James had not broken down the process into actual steps in the life-cycle of sin, there might be more confusion and less opportunity for resisting sin. But though it is easy to be deceived (even by one's own heart; cf. v. 16) there is no excuse. Self-deception need not occur when there is such clear teaching on the problem. While it is always best not to let sin occur—even

16 Don't be misled, dear brothers.

---

in the heart—it is also possible to retard its growth into actual transgression or into ultimate death.

Let's take a closer look at the avoidance of sin at the initial stage of temptation. One of the enticing lures desire uses is "You deserve it." How often do we hear this on commercials! Well, your own inner desires tell you the same thing! Tell your counselee, "**Don't be misled**, **dear brother**." Child molesters characteristically become whiners, filling themselves with self-pity, saying "I deserve better." Over a period of time they say such things as, "My wife doesn't satisfy me sexually; it is right to get that satisfaction elsewhere. I deserve it." Over and over they say such things to themselves until they begin to believe it. Knowing this makes it possible to break into this inner dynamic of sin to prevent it from taking hold.

Another enticement of desire is "You must learn to love yourself first." If you don't love yourself, we are told by the disciples of Maslow, *et al.*, then you won't be able to love God or others. That, of course, is sinful nonsense. I won't get into this subject here since I wrote an entire book on the subject of self-love in which I dealt definitively with the matter. But, for here, simply remember this—often, counselees justify *acts of sin* by the inner consent to this false proposition.

Thirdly, desire lures by calling things "needs" that are not. The great emphasis on need today is seen in the new phrase "I have a need to (for)..." People used to say, "I need a [whatever] to do [such and such]." Now, they talk about some undefined, overwhelming, inner necessity. That is all misleading rhetoric, nothing more. Substitute the word desire for the word "need" in such phrases and you will have the truth; "I have a need [*desire*] for..."

There is good reason for concluding the present discussion with the words, **Do not be misled.** That is precisely what desire does when tempting you; it misleads. That is the function of a lure. Whenever your counselee has a strong desire for something, teach him not to give in to it but, rather, to search it out. Just what is involved? What do the Scriptures say about that? The counselee must be taught to be suspicious of strong desires other than those clearly motivated by an attempt to please God. And even then, one must double-check those to be sure there is no self-deception present. A seeming desire to please God can actually be the

17 All good giving and every perfect gift is from above, coming down from the Father of lights, with Whom there is not a single change or a shadow from turning.

---

desire for praise of others, self-righteousness, etc. The key thing is for counselors to teach counselees to examine their desires with care, being sure they are thinking, deciding and acting according to the Bible and not being **misled.** In light of James' caution, it is unwise not to caution counselees as well.

Because of misleading desire within, it is helpful to know that **God** is dependable and that all that He **gives** us is **good** (vv. 17,18). Good things originate with Him, not within the desire-framework that your counselee's sinful nature constructed within him. The answer to those things that we need, therefore, is found without, not within. One should look to **God**, and not to his desires. God is the **Father of lights**. **Father**, here, as in many places in the Bible, means Originator. He is the One Who created the sun, the moon, the stars. And like them, He is dependable. He is like light, not like the shifting, **changing shadows**. That is important for your counselee to know. If he abandons his own desires, "denying self," he must know that he can trust the One Who said, instead, "Follow Me." God is trustworthy. To abandon self and follow Christ is to cast away the shadows for the light.

Gifts that God gives are **perfect** and the **giving** of them is **good.** How wonderful to know that! Things may not always *look* so; often we think that if we were providentially ordering our lives we could do a better job of it than God. However, that is never true. His way is the **good and perfect** way. Faith affirms this even when the trials seem to declare the opposite. In goodness, He is ever giving that which makes one *teleios* (**perfect**). It is not so much that the gift is complete (although that is true—God never does things in halves) as that the gift is one that is *designed* to complete. Because the **giving** is **good** (not just the gift) your counselee can be sure that God has thought through *just how, just when and in just what manner* He will give it. When God gives, He doesn't merely dump the gift into your lap; He gives it in an entirely appropriate manner. God makes no mistakes in this matter. Reassure your counselee of that fact from this verse. God is the One Who supplies that which satisfies *true* needs.

What we receive that we truly *need* is what He determines to give us. And it is never dreamed up or manufactured by us. It is truly a ***gift***. It is

18 By His own wish He gave us birth by the Word of truth that we might be a kind of first fruits of His creatures.
19 Dear brothers, know this: Every person should be swift to hear, slow to speak, slow to anger;

---

important, then, for counselees to be driven out of their desires into prayer for those things that *God desires* for them in order to make them truly complete persons.

After all, as verse18 makes plain, it is according to His **wishes** that **He gave us birth by the Word of truth** in order to make us **a kind of first fruits of His creatures.** God is the **Father** (Creator) **of Lights,** but He is our Father in the *parental* sense of the word: according to **His own wish He gave us birth**. How wonderful was this choosing of His own to become His children. Just as our salvation depends on that **wish** (will) of God, so too, does all that we receive from Him. What He gives us now is as certain, as good and as dependable as the salvation that we received from Him as a **gift**. Indeed, it is all included in that greatest of all gifts—the gift of eternal life.

Sin brings forth death (v. 15); God brings forth life (v. 18). As He recreated us through the gospel (the **Word of truth**) we became a **kind of first fruits of His creatures**. That means that as the first fruits in the Old Testament were holy and belonged to God, so too He separated us from others as His own peculiar possession (cf. Jeremiah 2:3; Revelation 14:4). Counselees must be shown the privileged position that is theirs by means of God's good giving and the complete nature of what He gives. And once more, note that the **Word of truth** is involved. All depends on the truthful message of God contained in the Bible. At every point, God drives us back to His Word; it is through the Scriptures that He works to do good for us. Never let the counselee get very far away from the declarations of God's will in the Bible.

Turning to verses 19 through 21, James deals with a problem that is ever-present in the church: **anger**. Much is said about anger elsewhere in other passages in the Bible, especially in Proverbs and in the fourth chapter of Ephesians. Here, we are concerned about James' important contribution to the subject. What he says will help you deal with angry counselees.

What is **anger**? It is a powerful emotion designed to destroy something. Every emotion God gave us is proper, in its place. That is true even of anger (cf. Mark 3:5; Psalm 7:11; Ephesians 4:26). Two words are used

20 the wrath of a man doesn't achieve the righteousness of God.

---

by James, which I have translated **anger** and **wrath.** The first is *orge,* which primarily refers to pent up emotion ready to burst (though sometimes it refers generally to any kind of anger). The other is *thumos*, a word that means anger that is loosed, poured forth, vented. Together, they speak of all wrong anger.

When is your counselee's anger justified; when is it not? That is important to understand and to convey to him. First, anger is wrong when it is aroused over the wrong things. If the reason for anger is your pride, jealousy, or some other self-focused matter, it is sinful. On this, cf. Cain's anger over God's acceptance of Abel's offering rather than his own. When someone complains that he was not acknowledged at a banquet, that he was ignored at church, etc., those are illegitimate causes for anger. Acceptable anger centers around those things that offend God rather than one's self.

The second factor in illegitimate anger is when anger is wrongly expressed by blowing up or clamming up (cf. Proverbs 29:11,20; Ephesians 4:26,31).

Such anger **doesn't achieve the righteousness of God.** As a motivating power, anger ought to tear up and destroy problems, not persons. Only God's anger and wrath may be loosed on persons. Anger that is out of accord with God's will fails to **achieve God's righteousness**. That is, it fails to bring about righteousness that pleases God. It may seem to do so (as in the killing of an abortionist) but, in the end, it will turn out that sin rather than righteousness is all that comes from it. Of course, God is not only talking about glaring sin here (murder) but of the many things that day-by-day corrupt and stir up strife. Proverbs tells us that sinful anger brings "strife" and "abounds in wrong" (Proverbs 29:22).

Here, it is the anger of an individual **man** (not mankind in general, as the original Greek indicates) about which James writes. How often will it fall to you to counsel angry persons? Probe to see how they are causing strife in their homes and in their churches. Show them that, though they may maintain that their cause is just and that they are only attempting to establish righteousness and fairness, they are actually achieving the opposite. Such anger disrupts; it creates unrighteous conditions wherever it is manifested.

James' major thrust, seen here as earlier and at places later on, is that

21 So, put off all dirtiness and evil excesses and in meekness welcome the implanted Word that is able to save your souls.

BEHAVIOR MUST FOLLOW SCRIPTURE, NOT FEELINGS. Verses 18,21 and 22 all emphasize this fact. The passage is a discussion of God's Word. God gave us our new birth by the **Word.** Note this is *gave birth*, not *conceived.* It refers to the act of the mother in bearing the child. This happened in the preaching of the gospel. Prior to birth was conception, which was the work of the Spirit in regeneration. The idea is that "since the Word is your mother, angry person, listen to her." **Be quick to hear** the Word. That is, eager to learn. **Slow to speak** in anger, as a consequence of hearing the Word. On this point, see Proverbs 14:29; 15:18. Proverbs 29:11 virtually says "count ten" before you speak. Hold back, check that anger. The Bible opposes ventilation of anger.

But, someone says, "I can't control my anger." Oh? Is that so? You are ranting and raging before another employee when you see the boss approaching. Do you go on doing so? No? What do you do? "Well, I guess you're right—I control it!" The problem is that you have not learned to control anger in certain places where you think (wrongly) you can get away with it. That is what you need to tell counselees who have trouble understanding that they can control anger. Surely, God would never have told you to do so if you could not obey, would He? He has told you the opposite. And, if you truly *read* His Word, you will learn so and be encouraged and strengthened to do it.

What God wants from every counselee is *behavior that accords with His Word.* It intrudes into our lives as if it were innate; it is **implanted** (this word is used by Galen, the Greek physician, to mean innate). Once it becomes a part of your counselee's life, the Word is as if it were something built in from the beginning. So—welcome the Word.

Acting on this principle, do those things that the Word enjoins. It is as if you had the ability to obey built in, but you are failing to exercise it. Rather than angry, become docile, subtle, easily bent and directed by the Word. Welcome it since it has become a part of your character. It will enable you to put off all dirtiness—that is, those things that soil a Christian's life before God and men. Show that counselee how his whole life is bound up in God's Word from the beginning of his new birth. Make it clear that he is already committed to the Word, and that it is to guide all his thinking and actions. He cannot escape it. The filthiness that "remains over" (as a surplus, a remnant) from the past life can be removed only by

22 Become doers of the Word and not only hearers, fooling yourselves;

---

heeding God's Word. It will enable the counselee to deal with both individual acts and with patterns of evil.

What the counselor ought to aim at is helping counselees to **become doers of the Word, and not only hearers, who** thus **fool** themselves (v. 22). That counselees *do* **fool themselves** is certain. It is important, therefore, for the counselor to understand James' discussion in verses 21 through 27 that follows. Here is his first comment on the faith/works issue.

Many counselees talk a good game. They know much, say all the right things, agree with you, but then do nothing—or go away and do as they please. This is one of the most common faults you will encounter in the counseling process. As a result, there is no change. In such cases, you should find James quite helpful. James insists that talk, insight and intellectualizing about problems will not do the trick. God is not impressed with these things. All talk must be turned into life. In verse 1:19 he had urged listening—hearing the Word—but this listening, hearing, must issue in a changed life. The story at the conclusion to the Sermon on the Mount hovers in the background of all that James writes. James' ideas about works are no more "strawy" than those of the Lord Jesus as He delivered those words.

You will counsel people who have deceived themselves. The phenomenon is common enough for James to make a point of it. Perhaps self-deception is one of the most difficult problems you will encounter. It will take clear, pointed, biblical teaching to dislodge the errors about which counselees **fool themselves**.

First, note that it is easy to **fool** yourself. One such concrete way of doing so is cited in verse 26. There are many others. The word used in verse 22 is a term that means "to deceive by false reasoning, to cheat in the reckoning (as when one is adding up figures)." These are counselees who think they are O.K. because they understand what God tells them in the Bible. They know His requirements and they know what He expects them to do. Yet they do not *follow* them; the charge here is *dead orthodoxy*. In speaking of the Jewish religious leaders, Jesus once said to follow what they say but not what they do (Matthew 23:3). This was not a thrust against orthodoxy. What God wants is both orthodoxy and orthopraxis. And to obtain both comes only by following the Word, doing what one

23 whoever is a hearer of the Word and not a doer is like a man who sees the face he was born with in a mirror—
24 he sees himself, and goes away and immediately forgets what he looked like.
25 But whoever looks into the perfect law of freedom and continues to do so, becoming not a hearer who forgets but a doer of deeds, will be made happy in the doing.

---

learns there.

To follow the Bible will solve not only the problem of anger, but all others as well. It is time to wake up counselees who think that they are safe because they can recite biblical principles and truths to you. Examine their lives. Ask them, "Given the biblical understanding that you have, tell me how it has affected your life?" Search out the ways in which they have learned (or failed to learn) to put truth into practice. You may not only have to teach them that faith without works is dead, but if they want to put feet on their knowledge, you must also help them to discover biblical ways of doing so. That the problem is widespread can be seen in the failure of the many sermons preached across the land. Think what would take place if those thousands of sermons preached to millions of Christians were put to work by all the hearers during the ensuing week! These sermons have little or no effect because of the failure of hearers to implement them.

The hypocritical counselee is foolish. He is like a man who looks into a mirror, sees himself dirty (a sinner), then goes away and immediately forgets what he saw (vv. 23,24). He treats the facts lightly. He is unconcerned; that is clear because he **forgets**. The look in the mirror is useless; the act is fruitless. He does nothing about the dirt that he sees.

Who is this man? He is the counselee who looks into the Bible (on his own or with your help), hears God's message there, and goes away without doing anything about what he has learned. The wise counselee, on the other hand, is the one who looks into God's **perfect law of freedom and continues to do so,** in order to become a doer of the Word and not a hearer only (v. 25).

There is a lot in that 25th verse. First, the word "look" in this verse means more than at first appears. It indicates that the one who does so, does it by stretching himself to see, something like a man bent over a map studying it with care. The person in mind, it is clear, is one who wants to know so that he can use his knowledge. His is no light glimpse. And as he studies the Word, he discovers that it is **perfect**. The word used here

26 Whoever thinks he is religious and doesn't bridle his tongue but swindles his own heart, his religion is worthless.
27 Clean and undefiled religion before God the Father is this: to look after orphans and widows in their affliction and to keep oneself from becoming spotted by the world.

---

means "complete." The Bible really *does* have all the answers that one needs to live a life pleasing to God. And it is a **law of freedom.** That is to say, it is the source of freedom. Those who conform to it are truly free for the first time. This is the way a counselee ought to view the use of the Bible in counseling: it will bring freedom from sin and its consequences. He must treat the Bible seriously, seriously enough to do something about what he reads therein. He must take the time to understand and figure out what to do: he will study the Bible and **continue to do so.** Change occurs.

And he discovers also that the happiness is in the doing: **he will be made happy in the doing** (v. 25). Many want to be happy before doing. They make doing depend on the right feeling. But happiness is not the goal; it is always the by-product of the change. Some wait for a change before they begin the doing. Some want the courage, the strength, the right feeling first. This is a part of the self-deception about which James warns. The blessing comes from the change, but it is found only in the doing. It is often hard to begin; but tell the counselee that though he is reluctant, once he starts on a biblical path, he will find it easier as he proceeds. Happiness *follows* obedience.

Now James offers a concrete example of self-deception (vv. 26,27). He introduces you to the counselee who **swindles his own heart.** It is foolish to swindle anyone, but particularly foolish to swindle yourself! He is the one who thinks that he is putting it over on others (and may do so for a time) but, in the end, he shortchanges only himself. How is that? Not only by the way that others treat him once he is found out—and inevitably he will be—but by the fact that he cannot swindle God! God is not mocked; He is not duped; He is not swindled. He Who sits in the heavens only laughs that laugh of pity as he views the self-deceiver thinking that he can even put it over on God! God will accept no such approach.

This man thinks that he is religious when he isn't. Here there are works, but they are only a show. They are sham works—all outward. The word *threskeia* means "participation in outward ceremonies." It refers to ritualism, pure and simple. It is the Rich Young Ruler summed up in a word. It refers to counselees who talk a good game, but that is the sum and substance of it.

Christian Counselor's Commentary

Genuine, God-accepted **religion** issues in works pleasing to God because they are done for His glory and not for the recognition that those who perform them receive. It does not matter whether the counselee seeks to receive such recognition from the counselor, from a spouse, or even from God. That is not the goal of good works according to the Savior in the Sermon on the Mount; good works have to do with bringing others to recognition of *God*. It is *He* that ought to receive the praise. The kind of works that are **clean and undefiled** by hypocrisy, inconsistency and self-centeredness usually take place in spheres that are not readily identified as *religious* by others. These are areas like helping orphans or widows when they are needy or in trouble. And it means personal purity as one keeps himself **unspotted from the world**. On this point, see Jude 23 in the commentary on that Book. I shall say more later on about the "world" when considering James' discussion of worldliness.

Chapter 2

1 My brothers, don't hold on to the faith of our glorious Lord while showing favoritism.

As we begin to consider the second chapter of James we immediately meet with a problem that has not lessened through the years: the danger of showing favoritism. I was delighted when a family joined our church after having said that they would never join any church again. When they did, the husband's comment was "I see that around here the haves and the have nots are all equal." Nothing could have been a finer commendation of our congregation. Our people are to be applauded for making this a reality to him and to others. Yet, too often, this is not the case—as his comment implied. What is the problem, how does it relate to counseling and what can be done about it?

The matter is, perhaps, every bit as important for the counselor as it is for the counselee. There is a tendency, not only among members, but also among those whom God has appointed to serve them, to pay more attention to, to make greater allowances for and (in general) to cater to those who in one way or another are more prominent. James closed the previous discussion (1:26,27) with a brief discourse on true **religion**. He had just exhorted his readers to **keep themselves unspotted from the world** as a mark of true **religion**. There was no chapter division in the original; the one discussion naturally flows into the next. As an example that may have been especially pertinent to those to whom he was writing, in 2:1-9 James takes up the **worldly** practice that has crept (galloped?) into the church—obsequious favoritism.

James makes it clear (his terms are in no way uncertain) that favoritism toward anyone is sin (cf. vv. 1,9). Obviously, he is not speaking of friendships (some seem to confuse the two). Not everyone can be equally the friend of every other Christian (though I wonder if that could be possible in eternity). There will always be levels of friendship. Jesus Himself demonstrated that. There were the multitudes, then there were the twelve with whom He was more intimate. Of the twelve, there were three, Peter, James and John, who went with Him up into the Mount of Transfiguration and into the garden during His last days on earth. But even of the three, there was the "disciple whom Jesus loved," John. That is not what James meant. Yet because they were friends on one level or another, they still

2 That means that if a man with gold rings and splendid clothes enters into your meeting, and there also enters a poor man in shabby clothes,
3 and you pay attention to the one who is wearing the splendid clothes and say, "Sit here in this good seat," and to the poor man say, "Stand there," or "Sit on the floor at my feet,"

---

ought to have been given no preferences that grew out of obsequious favoritism. True friendship has nothing of the obsequious note in it.

Favoritism is out of sync with **the faith** (cf. v. 1). Christ is our **glorious Lord**; it is He toward Whom all our favor must be shown. To kow tow to men is to put them in His place. We must not deny the **faith** by setting the power and the influence of men over the authority and the rule of Jesus Christ. In other words, to glorify men is not to glorify Him. Favoritism is a form of exchanging the glory of God for the glory of man (cf. Romans 1).

Teaching from Old Testament times on was clear on the point: **You shall neither favor the poor man nor show deference to the influential** (Leviticus 19:15). It is informative that those who (like many of the guilt-ridden liberals of our day), for whatever reason, show favoritism to those who are disadvantaged are condemned for it along with those who show deference to the rich and powerful. And study Leviticus 19:8,18 (especially). One's **neighbor** mentioned in this place, as Christ's parable of the Good Samaritan shows, includes *all.*

What is favoritism? The Hebrew words *masa panim* ("to receive the face of") perhaps paint the best picture. It is to prefer the person (face) because of some characteristic you are enamored by. James illustrates this sin with a concrete example (vv. 2,3). A rich person comes into your meeting (lit., "synagog"), he says. It is obvious that he is rich because of the clothing that he wears (salesmen still observe what kind of attire a prospective buyer wears). He has **gold rings** (a bigger deal in those days than now) and **splendid clothes** (lit., "shining clothes"). And at the same time a **poor** man (who again is judged such by his appearance) enters in **shabby clothes.** And, says James, if **you pay attention to the one who is wearing the splendid clothes and say, "Sit here in this good seat," and to the poor man say, "Stand there," or "Sit on the floor at my feet,"** you have engaged in the sin of obsequious favoritism. That is what it is all about—courting the rich and powerful *for the sake of advantage.* The poor also can be preferred in order to solicit praise for one's generosity. This is a sort of reverse favoritism we have been subject to in affirmative action programs.

4 haven't you discriminated among yourselves and become judges with evil thoughts?

This sort of **discrimination,** he points out, makes one a **judge** with **evil thoughts**. What does that mean? You are one who judges what he sees (and acts accordingly) *from ulterior motives* (that is what he means by **evil thoughts**). The one who shows favoritism has (wrongly) **judged** that the rich man is more important (the issue of judging will be raised again in 4:11). James is rightly concerned that we make no such judgments.

What is wrong with favoritism, and how does it affect the counselee and his counselor? Favoritism of some leads to the detriment of others. Let's say that your counselee is the head of a committee in his church with the responsibility of choosing those who will work with him. Rather than choose persons who are most likely to do the job well—who have the ability and the inclination to—he places those on the committee who are more influential in the community (the banker, lawyer, physician over the painter, plumber or mechanic). What is the result? The work is done poorly rather than well, thus hurting the church; those with the gifts are not given the opportunity to use them, and even the counselee is hurt since he turns in an inferior piece of work.

But of even more direct importance, take the counselor himself. He fills a slot in his schedule with the rich or powerful person rather than a poorer, weaker one. He gives him better hours, making it harder on the poorer person to come. He changes his counseling style in deference to the rich man's response; he meets at his home rather than according to his common practice of meeting in the church office. It is this sort of thing that James has in mind.

You have "hurt" the poor because you have made him wait too long, you have "hurt" the rich because you've already compromised your God-given authority in relation to him by your kow-towing (and don't you think that he doesn't notice this), and you have "hurt" Christ's work by

1. misrepresenting Christ's ways with men;

2. practicing favoritism which is contrary to and inconsistent with salvation by *grace*;

3. and, incidentally, because God is above such things, you have misrepresented *Him*.

It is a serious matter to practice favoritism. God's children and God's church must never give others the impression that God sides with those

5 Listen, my brothers: Hasn't God chosen the poor in this world, to be rich in faith and heirs of the empire that He promised to those who love Him?
6 But you have dishonored the poor man. Isn't it rich men who oppress you; isn't it they who drag you into court?
7 Isn't it they who blaspheme the good Name by which you are called?
8 If, however, you really fulfill the royal law, which according to the Scripture is, You must love your neighbor as yourself, you do well;

---

who have power, position and wealth.

And James points out, favoritism toward the influential is foolish (vv. 5-7). As Proverbs keeps on telling the reader, it is the fool who sins. All sin is foolish; all foolishness is sin. No one who follows Scripture need sin—nor be foolish! In the next three verses, James demonstrates these facts. His argument is as follows:

1. You despise those who love God and whom God often honors when He gives them riches of faith and promises for eternity (v. 5).
2. You honor those who often despise you and oppress you legally (v. 6^{b}).
3. You honor those who often are the very ones who despise God (v. 7).

You ought to be convicted of this sin, James says, if you read and apply the Bible, since it **convicts** as **transgressors** all who do (v. 9; see also, comments on II Timothy 3:16 and my book, *How to Help People Change*). Note, if you want to convict a counselee of his sin, to do so you must use the law of God. The purpose of God's law is to show us our sin and drive us to Jesus Christ.

James smoothly merges these thoughts into a vital discussion of love, law and motive (vv. 2:8-13; see also 1:25). In contrast to sinful favoritism, James says, **if...you really fulfill the royal law, which according to the Scripture is, You must love your neighbor as yourself, you do well; but if you show favoritism, you commit sin and are convicted by the law as transgressors**.

There is a tendency to call some sins something less than sin. You will run up against this problem in counseling. When you do, you must deal with it. How? In particular, how do you convince someone of sin in his life (a task at which every biblical counselor must become proficient)? We must discover the answer to that question. But on the other hand, it is important to keep in mind that something that may look like sin, as the result of investigation, may prove otherwise. The decision as to whether or not a sin has been committed often lies in the *motive behind an action.* But counselors do not know the motives of another person and are forbidden to guess at them (I Samuel 16:7). God, alone, is the Heart-Knower (Acts 1:28). So, what can you do about motives? You must instruct the *counselee* to examine his heart (cf. how Paul does this in regard to the Lord's Supper: I Corinthians 11:28,31,32).

James has discussed favoritism and how it displeases God (vv. 1-7) but now takes up an instance of what looks like favoritism and might, or might not, be according to the motive of the counselee. This is an important issue. Too frequently counselors jump to conclusions without weighing all the factors involved.

Keep in mind at all times WHAT *LOOKS LIKE SIN* MAY NOT BE. James takes up an example in which concern for a rich man may be lawful: **If, however**, instead of showing favoritism in warmly welcoming an influential unbeliever, you are **really fulfilling the royal law** (Leviticus 19:18) of love toward a **neighbor**, that's *kalos* (fine); **you do well**. The same act can be sin or love according to the motive behind it. If your purpose is truly evangelistic, for instance, or if your concern is to help (perhaps he is deaf and needs a particular seat in order to hear), if your actions grow out of genuine love for the individual, O.K. You have done **well**. Nouthetic counselors have been accused of calling everything in sight sin. That simply is not so. Much that is involved in counseling does relate to sinful activity, but not everything.

So, in such a case, what should you do? You must leave the responsibility for acting according to right motives strictly with the counselee. That is what James did. It is not your business to do more than to raise the question of motive with him, to press the importance of proper motives on him strongly and, only after a sufficient time of help, to examine the results in terms of fruit that is worthy of repentance.

James first acknowledged that an act or word that looks exactly like what he has described as sin *might not be*. And he said it to the very persons that he was warning against that sin. He raised the possibility of a proper motive as well as an improper one. Then he commended the proper motive when and where it exists. He was not giving the sinning counselee an excuse; he was acknowledging a problem that every counselor faces—he cannot look into his counselee's heart.

But then he warned, "Be sure that your motive is proper or you will be committing sin" (v. 9). Throughout, he left the responsibility for determining motives to the counselee himself. It is not your part to read hearts, counselor. I Corinthians 11:28, with which I paralleled this approach,

9 but if you show favoritism, you commit sin and are convicted by the law as transgressors.

---

doesn't say, "Let the elders examine his motives."

Then James did one more thing—without which it would be very difficult to allow matters to stand as they are. He showed the counselee how he may discern his own motives. When James quotes Leviticus 19:18, he gives the biblical basis for examining motives. He points out the biblical standard by which they must examine their motives. He makes it clear that sin is determined, and one is convicted of sin, by the Bible. It is utterly essential to make all determinations of sin by comparing the act (word, attitude) with the *biblical* injunction that relates to it. You must never allow the counselee to turn to extrabiblical lists that others have drawn up and added to the Scriptural Standard. This is the essence of pharisaical legalism. He must be warned against it. In addition, you must deflect his thinking from experience, feeling, tradition or anything else other than explicit biblical teaching.

Inferential determinations, deduced from the Scriptures, need to be examined with care to make sure that they logically derive from the Bible by good and necessary consequence. The counselor must, of course, become a casuist (in the good sense of that term). That is to say, he must learn the process of using biblical principles to determine specific courses of action, etc., in ways that are truly implied by those principles. This is tricky business, and many counselees are unable to reason this way. It is important for you, therefore, to go through any such reasoning from biblical principles step by step with him. Thereby you not only show him how you reached a biblical conclusion, but also give him a lesson about how to do so himself in days to come. There is always danger here of faulty reasoning. You must be careful. That is why you may not depend on man-made lists that have no such plain and evident course of reasoning behind them.

Explain to your counselee that sin is lawbreaking (v. 9); it is not mere alienation or some sort of bad relationship. Those may be aspects of what results from sin, but sin itself is refusing to do what God commands or doing what He forbids. It is a slap in God's face by a disobedient child who will not obey his Father.

In verses 10 and 11, James observes that **whoever keeps the whole law, but stumbles in one point, has become guilty of all**. That, he says, is because **The same One Who** gave one commandment gave all the rest

10 So whoever keeps the whole law, but stumbles in one point, has become guilty of all.
11 The same One Who said, "**Don't commit adultery,**" also said, "**Don't murder**." So if you don't commit adultery but murder, you have become a transgressor of the law.
12 Speak and act like those who are about to be judged by the law of freedom.

---

as well. The same law is broken—breaking even one commandment in the law *breaks the law*. The issue is not how *many* laws (no one breaks only one, however), but *whether* God's holy law has been broken. The same Lawgiver is offended. Break a corner of the mirror and it is proper to say "The mirror is broken." It is not a matter of how many sins one commits; to commit any makes him a **transgressor** of the law. Break any one link of a *chain* and the chain is broken. James' words are a forceful way of saying it is not the nature of the sin or the number of sins committed, but the fact of dishonoring God by sin that is critical. Don't let people say, "Oh well, what is favoritism, anyway? It's not as bad as adultery." Perhaps the social effects may not be as devastating (though they might be), but the fact of disobeying God is heinous no matter what the nature of the sin itself is. That is what the counselee must be made to see. The emphasis here (v. 11) is on God, **the One Who** commanded. All sin, in relationship to God, is alike. It is all an offense against Him done by breaking His law. Therefore, don't allow counselees to grade sins as if some were A+ and others only D- sins.

How should one act in accordance with the kingly **law of love**? He should see that in Christ there is a law of freedom, that one may **speak and act like those who are about to be judged by the law of freedom**. What does that mean? Counselees are to live as those who are to be ***judged* by** (or, lit., "through") **the law of freedom**. That is to say, as those whose sins have been forgiven by grace and mercy, and **who** are now free to love and obey. Because they have this freedom (cf. Romans 6-8), they are expected to exercise it. (Claims that they are unable to live in accordance with God's will are illegitimate). And in doing so, they should also be free from the prejudice, self-deception and bad motives about which James has been speaking.

As wretched sinners, transgressors, lawbreakers, we are not in ourselves anything. But in Christ, we have received mercy and are not held to all the lawbreaking we have done. If that is true, tell your counselee, "don't treat other believers as if it were not true of them. Let **Mercy tri-**

13 I say this because judgment will be without mercy to him who doesn't show mercy. Mercy triumphs over judgment.

---

umph over justice in all your dealings with them. Otherwise, God will treat you as you treat them" (On this cf. Matthew 5:7; 18:35)! Here, then, is a strong warning to those who judge others according to standards that have little to do with love and mercy. Use it that way, and be sure that you do not fall into the same trap as those who judge motives.

The rest of the second chapter holds together as one piece (vv. 14-26). It has to do with challenging the counselee (remember James *exhorts* throughout) to justify his claim to faith by works. He trenchantly bores in on the one who talks a good game but does not have the lifestyle to back it up. Counselees must learn to structure their lives for change that accords with biblical knowledge. The important point here for the biblical counselor is that neither insight counseling nor cognitive counseling is biblical. Both depend on knowledge imparted to or developed within the counselee, that their proponents hope will lead to a change of lifestyle. But so often it does not. And that is precisely what the counselor finds himself up against again and again. Many counselees *know* what God requires of them (they have some sort of faith) but that is as far as it goes; the knowledge just doesn't seem to make any difference in their lives. James will have none of this. With His Lord who told the story of the two houses, one of which was built on sand and the other on rock, James sees two kinds of profession of faith: one stands in adversity because it is well founded and issues in a changed life, the other does not. Remember, the Lord says that the difference was between those who hear His words and *do* them and those who do not. That is exactly what James is dealing with in the passage that we must now explore.

But first, a comparison between Paul and James is in order at this point. Look at the chart that follows:

	Genuine	Spurious
Paul	Faith	Works done to save; dead works (Heb. 6)
James	Works (Fruit of the Spirit)	Faith that is dead

14 What good is it, my brothers, if somebody says that he has faith but
doesn't have works? This sort of faith can't save him, can it?
15 If a brother or sister is naked and lacks daily food,
16 and one of you says to him, "Go in peace; be warmed and filled," but
he doesn't give him the bodily necessities to do so, what good is that?
17 So also, faith by itself, if it has no works, is dead.
18 But someone will say, "You have faith and I have works." Show me
your faith without works, and by my works I'll show you my faith.

What James calls *erga* ("works"), Paul calls the Fruit of the Spirit. Both issue from true, living faith. If you read *Fruit of the Spirit* for **works** in James 2, you will understand what he was saying. What Paul means by **works** is those that people do in order to gain favor with God; works they consider meritorious. Paul condemns works done as saving merit; James commends works done as the result and evidence of true faith. James and Paul are facing different problems. Paul was combating legalism; James antinomianism. Both believe faith produces works. James comes from the East, Paul from the West but they meet. James gets to faith through works; Paul reaches works by the route that takes him through faith.

I now wish to center our thinking on a couple of verses. First, verse 16: words don't feed and clothe; works do. The phrase **Go in peace; be warmed and filled** is still used among many who live in Palestine. It is spoken in order to get rid of people! It means, "God help you; don't expect me to do so." That is the sort of thing that James is combatting; he wants nothing of such empty talk. Christians should not, as many do today, dismiss people with a meaningless, "I'll pray about it," when there is something that they can do to alleviate another's need.

No wonder James concludes **So also, faith by itself, if it has no works, is dead** (v. 17). That kind of *seeming* faith (after all both expressions—the Palestinian, and the even more pious-sounding American one—are religious in nature) really isn't faith at all. It is only words. But they hardly express love and concern for another in need. Such "faith," James says, is **dead**. Counselors who detect in counselees no willingness to demonstrate their faith by works designed to help others may need to press the question, "Do you think that your faith is genuine? Or is it dead?" And don't settle for the kind of excuse that James says some offer: "Well, you see, my gift is faith; someone else's may be works." Many excuses have been offered in our time by persons who think that they have only one gift (a false teaching) and therefore need not exercise any others. In verse 18 James puts the kibosh on all such thinking! The only way to

19 You believe that there is one God? Fine! But the demons also believe—and shudder!
20 But are you willing to learn, you worthless person, that faith without works is barren?
21 Wasn't Abraham our father justified by works by offering up Isaac his son on the altar?
22 You see that faith worked along with his works, and faith was completed by works,
23 and the Scripture was fulfilled that says, **Abraham believed God and it was reckoned to him righteousness,** and he was called God's friend.

---

show faith is by works he says, challenging the objector to produce another.

Then comes verse19. It is a sound enough creed to **believe that there is one God**. James has no quarrel with it. But unsaved **demons** also agree to it. The demons are orthodox! The faith of the one about whom James writes is in the gospel; the dead faith of the one mentioned here is in the mere existence of one God. It is possible to talk about God in an orthodox manner, yet not know Him savingly. The kind of "faith" James condemns is **barren**; i.e., it gives birth to no truly good works (v. 20). When there is nothing but barrenness in the life of a counselee who claims to be a Christian, after all sorts of help has been extended toward him, then it is time to press II Corinthians 13:5 upon him.

In verse 21, the matter of Abraham arises. Paul uses Abraham as an example of justification by faith apart from works, citing Genesis 15:6. James is not unaware of that verse since he quotes it in verse 23 of this chapter. But it seems that he draws the opposite point from the verse and the story of Abraham. What is the explanation of this seeming contradiction? Paul uses the word **justified** to mean that Abraham was counted righteous before God. James uses the same word to indicate that Abraham's faith was **justified** (or shown to be true faith) by his works. James use of the term means "vindicated, shown to be as claimed," or words to that effect. James says that Abraham's works proved his faith to be genuine (as also Rahab's works did). When was Abraham's faith demonstrated to be genuine, vindicated? When he prepared to offer up Isaac; fifteen years after the statement made in Genesis 15:6! The offering of his only son vindicated the statement made in Genesis 15. The works *followed* the faith. They did not save him; his faith did—years before! In verse 23, when James says that the **Scripture was fulfilled**, he meant that Abraham's action proved the statement true. Calvin pointed out the fact that

24 You see that a person is justified by works and not only by faith.
25 Likewise wasn't Rahab the prostitute also justified by works when she welcomed the messengers and sent them out by a different route?
26 Just as the body without the spirit is dead, so also faith without works is dead.

"an effect can never be its own cause." The works—even here—are clearly shown to be the *effect* of long-standing saving faith.

This is complex for many, so you will probably not want to enter into a detailed explanation of the passage in counseling. Nevertheless, it contains several very pointed statements about works, which is one of the concerns of every counselor. God saved us so that we might do good works for His honor and glory. Such works are what a counselor wishes to help a counselee attain to. That is why it is important for the counselor to understand this passage and to be able to explain it (or at least use it) when dealing with those whose lives are unfruitful. Perhaps one of the most powerful statements in the entire discussion is the one with which it concludes: **Just as the body without the spirit is dead, so also faith without works is dead.** There are points about the separation of body and spirit at death to be made from this passage (against those who deny the fact) but we will not go into that here.

CHAPTER 3

1 My brothers, not many of you should become teachers, because you know that we teachers will receive stricter judgment.

One of the major emphases of this chapter is the use of speech. James will address those who think that they should become teachers, but should not. He will also talk to those who have difficulty controlling their **tongues**. These two issues, together with other material that he will introduce, make the third chapter of the Book of James one of the most important to a counselor. Since the chapter begins with erstwhile teachers, then moves to general exhortation for all believers, we shall look at the material first in the light of the counselor, then the counselee.

God is clear about it: **teacher**, you will be **judged more strictly** for what you say than non-teachers. That is His Word through James to *you*. "But," you protest, "I am not a teacher; I'm a counselor." That distinction will not do; you cannot let yourself off the hook so easily. If you are not a teacher, you are not a *biblical* counselor. Rogerians are not teachers, but neither are they counselors. Strictly speaking, in the history of the world, up until Carl Rogers, the word "counselor" meant (and should still mean) "one who advises." That is to say, a counselor is one who gives advice. Like it or not, that is what a biblical counselor is—one who advises counselees about the application of the Scriptures to their particular situations. Rogers' revisionism of counseling, in which he opposed all advice-giving, has not stood the test of time. Not only did he declare that he had failed, but prior to his death he turned to spiritism! I suppose that it is not good for men to advise one another, but is it O.K. for spirits to do so?

While I agree that other human beings are rarely those to whom a counselee should turn for advice, the Christian counselee has One Who is *superhuman* to Whom he may turn for advice in troubled times. That One is the Lord Jesus Christ Who teaches us about life and godliness in His holy Word. Because that is true, you, as a counselor, must know that Word and how to instruct counselees in its purposes, meanings and applications to their lives. You are a teacher.

The subject of teaching in counseling is large enough to warrant an entire book concerning it (see my book *Teaching to Observe*). But for now let's turn to a consideration of James' very strong warning: **My brothers, not many of you should become teachers, because you know that we**

teachers will receive stricter judgment.

It had been true both of the Old Testament prophets and of the Lord Jesus that they all took special aim at the religious teachers of their day when issuing their condemnations of a sinning people. It is no less true of New Testament teachers that God will judge them more strictly than the common man-in-the-pew Christian. That is why James issues his strong warning. But there are many who have failed to heed it. I am not talking about non-Christians; James isn't either. His remarks are addressed to his **brothers**. It is from them that he wants to see only those teachers arise whom God has called, gifted and ordained to the work.

In our day, there has been a liberation of the laity. That the older clericalism, in which the preacher did everything, was wrong is clear. Ephesians 4:11,12 has rightly been interpreted to counter any such notion. On the other hand, however, there has been an extreme reaction in which, without calling, without authorization by the church of Jesus Christ and without training, many have taken it upon themselves to instruct the church. They are able to do this through modern means of mass communication that now exist, and through the use of private funds that sometimes rival or exceed those of the church itself. The results, in some cases, have been disastrous. Not only has every sort of counseling theory been brought into the church and offered to confused people in trouble by such persons, but all sorts of heretical and erroneous interpretations of the Bible. The Scriptures have been used in an entirely cavalier fashion by those who have little or no understanding of them. That is one of the major reasons why I am spending the time to produce these commentaries. I can only underscore James' warning to any of you who think that you are prepared to counsel God's flock because you have had a counseling course or two, have a smattering of biblical knowledge or are in possession of some tapes or books by a Christian who claims to do biblical counseling. That probably is not enough.

While all Christians should counsel informally (see *Competent to Counsel*), James is speaking of those who set themselves up as full time counselors. To do something as a life calling and to do it as an informal thing now and then are two different things. The title "teacher" of which James speaks is, as I have shown, included in the title "Counselor." It is, therefore, entirely proper to apply James' warning to the Christian counselor. There are people who break into print, who speak on radio broadcasts, who conduct seminars and meetings of every sort, who, heedless of James' warning, say whatever they happen to think. They spout forth the trendy ideas of the time, only to modify their views and substitute newer

2 All of us stumble in many ways. If anybody doesn't stumble in speech, he is a perfect man, able to bridle the entire body also.

---

trends for them later on. That is not Christian teaching. Christian teaching recognizes a deposit of truth *once for all* delivered to the saints. While one may discover more and more about that deposit of truth, and may refine his views as he continues to study the Bible, he will not jump from one theory of men to another over his lifetime to keep up with the trends. If there is anything true of biblical teaching, it is its lack of trendiness!

Think of the many who are leading God's people astray today! One can only fear for the future of those who have placed themselves under the threat of God's **stricter judgment**. Surely, after giving them space to repent and change their ways, God will judge them in one way or another, thus vindicating His Word and His truth. In time then, He will deliver His people from false teachers. While all Christians will be judged for their speech (cf. Matthew 12:36,37), **teachers** will be **more strictly judged** because of the influence that their speech has on God's people. And of even greater importance, what teachers say in God's Name properly represents His views or misrepresents them. It is a very serious matter, intentionally or unintentionally, to lie about God (Jeremiah 28:15,16).

Counselors are *men of words*. The biblical term *nouthesia*, which is the word Paul uses for counseling, means (among other things) "to bring about change *by verbal means*." That is why the Scriptures are so intimately involved with counseling. It is *God's* Word that was given to bring about *God's* change. Nothing else will. If that is true, then nothing else ought to be used in its place.

So I urge you, *be sure of your calling before setting yourself up as a teacher who counsels.* Be sure that the Church has authorized you by ordaining you to the work.

We turn now to the second matter of concern: the **tongue**. Here is a problem for all to consider—counselees and counselors alike. James put it this way: **All of us stumble in many ways** (here sinless perfection views are eradicated). **If anybody doesn't stumble** (sin) in **speech, he is a perfect man, able to bridle the entire body also.** Anyone who can control the most difficult problem of all, the use of his tongue, ought to be able to control everything else. If the greater, then the lesser. Counselors are men of words; therefore, they must be able to control their words. That means that they must recognize the importance of learning when to speak, when not to speak, what to speak, how to say it and the right words in which to give voice to an idea (cf. Ephesians 6:19).

Using the right words in the right way in counseling can be all-important. The stock words of the psychotherapists of any given time have a lure. They sound good, even erudite. In truth, they are confusing; many contain little or no genuine content and, more often than not, are used to describe symptoms rather than causes. By resorting to such usage, it is possible to appear to have knowledge when one's words only mask his ignorance.

The biblical counselor will use biblical terms to describe a person's problem. Then the counselee will be able to understand the true nature of his difficulty and will be able to read what God says about it in His Word. As Christians, we are spreaders of light and truth. We care nothing about how we may sound; we want to make truth apparent to each counselee. We don't want to "snow" him with language that fails to communicate what God's Word says about him. Psychological terminology not only covers ignorance, it fails to point to God's solutions to problems.

In talking to counselees about their speech, make it clear that their speech is powerful. Lives can be upset, people's reputations can be ruined and persons may be seriously misled by their words—if not true and loving. Gossip, for instance, is a powerful tool. It can be used to destroy homes, churches or whatever organization against which it is employed. Gossip is not only a matter of telling untruths but also of telling truths that there is no need to tell. It may be true that so-and-so had a fight with what's-her-name, but is it necessary to tell anyone else about it?

It is important, then, for counselors, whenever necessary, to confront counselees about their speech. In addition to other matters, raise questions of how one is speaking to another in the counseling session, how he will address someone at work, etc. Don't allow for ungodly speech to be used without reprimand during the counseling hour. It is as important a matter to deal with as any other. Seldom, however, do counselees expect you to do so. So it is often essential to show them this passage in order to impress on them how important their habits of speech are.

Often it is not only what is said, but how it is said, that makes all the difference. One must be careful of using words and terms that make others bristle *when it is not necessary to do so.* Sometimes, to be faithful, of course, it *is* necessary. But usually there is a better way of saying something than the way that is almost certain to elicit an unfavorable response. Help counselees practice saying things in a loving, clear and truthful way. One means to use in doing so is role playing. Role play several encounters between the counselee and those to whom he must speak in a new manner.

3 Now we put bits into the mouths of horses to make them obey us, and in this way we direct their entire bodies.
4 Look too at ships: they are so large and are driven by hard winds, yet they are directed by a very small rudder to go wherever the impulse of the pilot wishes.
5 So too, the tongue is a little member, but boasts about great things; consider how large a forest can be set ablaze by a little fire.
6 And the tongue is a fire. The tongue is a world of iniquity set among our bodily members, spotting the entire body and igniting the course of nature and itself being ignited by Gehenna.
7 Now all kinds of beasts and birds, reptiles and marine life can be tamed and have been tamed by human nature,
8 but no human being anywhere is able to tame the tongue. It is a reckless evil, full of deadly poison.
9 With it we bless the Lord and Father, and with it we curse people who are made in God's likeness.
10 From the same mouth comes forth blessing and cursing. This isn't right, brothers; these things are not fitting.

You may even have to switch roles with him, taking his part, from time to time to demonstrate how it might be done.

In this passage (vv. 2-12) James uses six figures of speech to demonstrate the power of speech. How serious a matter the misuse of the **tongue** can engender. First (v. 3), he looks at the horse. The **horse** is large, the **bridle** is small. The same point is made in verse 4 where the **rudder** is small, the **ship** is large, and in verse 5, where the **spark** is small, but the **fire** spreads over a large area. The point of the first three illustrations is that one small word can have large effects and even cause great damage. The small word spoken (for ill or for good) can be powerful. That shows the importance of all speech—including the idle word, the thoughtless comment, the nasty dig, the hasty retort. Often, you will have to use these illustrations to demonstrate that "What you said may have been very little, but it only takes a small amount of the wrong thing to lead to a great amount of trouble." The **world of iniquity** of which James speaks means either "the sum total" or the place where the world has its say (one often recognizes the influence of the world in speech). The pervasiveness of the damage is also in view, as I previously observed. A **tongue** shooting forth sparks can cause a conflagration that destroys one's whole life. It is like a **fire** spreading into the whole "wheel" of life (i.e., it spreads into every area or piece of the pie).

The second set of illustrations (vv. 11,12) of the **spring**, the **fig tree**

11 A spring doesn't send forth sweet and bitter water from the same opening, does it?
12 My brothers, a fig tree can't produce olives, or a vine figs, can it? Nor can salt water produce fresh water.

---

and the **water** illustrate the inconsistency of a hateful, troublesome tongue in a true Christian. The contrasts that vie with one another are used to make this point: **bitter** vs. **sweet, fig tree** vs. olive tree (or **grapevine** vs. **figs**) and **salt** vs. **fresh water**. Hypocrisy can be spotted in speech. That is a point for the counselor to remember. Sinful speech from a sacred source is unacceptable. The two clash; they are not in sync. Double-tongued speech, like double-minded persons, are an anomaly in God's kingdom. The one or the other must go; eventually, a lack of change will reveal the insincerity of a counselee's profession of faith, or a change in his speech patterns to conform to his profession will prove his sincerity. Counselor, learn to put it to your counselee in either/or terms. James does; so should you.

Well, what can be done to help? According to 3:2, everyone has problems, and specifically, problems with his **tongue**. Is it ever possible to make progress in controlling the tongue? After all, from what he says in verse 8, James obviously thinks it very difficult to control the tongue: even though every kind of animal can be tamed, **no human being anywhere is able to tame the tongue.** Then is it worthless to try? No. This **reckless evil, full of deadly poison,** can also be tamed. But not by **human beings.** God must do so. He has the power and will give the grace (cf. 1:26) to bridle it (cf. Psalm 39:1; 141:3). But if you don't bridle (control) it, in time it will bridle (control) you. When, by His grace and power, you learn to control the tongue, which is the hardest thing in your life to control, you will be able to control the rest (cf. 2^b). Learning to do that, you will become "perfect" (**complete**). James doesn't do much about telling us how to control the tongue. But he does say **be slow to speak.** That is one of the principle elements with which to begin the learning process. When a counselee takes time to respond or to initiate speech, he is much more likely to say better things in more proper ways. The railroad crossing signs used to read "Stop, look and listen, before crossing." Perhaps the sign one should post in his mind is "Stop, listen, think before speaking that word!" You might even write this—or something comparable —on your counselee's homework sheet for the week. In addition, material in the Book of Proverbs and in Ephesians 4 is helpful.

13 Who is wise and intelligent among you? Let him show this by his good behavior, by his works done in wise meekness.

The next section runs from 3:13 to 4:3; once more we find it necessary to transgress a chapter heading. The section deals with conflict—**quarreling** and strife. That is a most appropriate topic for the Christian counselor. If you don't understand this passage and you don't know how to apply it in counseling, your counseling will be far from complete. So, we will take the time to deal with the passage in a thorough manner.

An important part of counseling is the resolution and prevention of conflict. In order to learn how to achieve these goals, it is important to understand the origin of conflict. James locates the source of conflict, as he does temptation, in **desire**. It is not desire itself that is wrong; it is desire misdirected and allowed to run wild (4:1,2). That is, unchecked, uncontrolled, unguided desire. Since we have already discussed desire previously, it is now important to see how what was learned then may be applied to a different manifestation of the same basic problem. But James does not begin with the matter of desire; he leads us to that conclusion through a prior discussion of **wisdom**.

James asks **Who is wise and intelligent among you?** In order to demonstrate true intelligence and biblical wisdom, one must do so through his **good behavior.** Like faith that can only be discerned through works, so too God's **wisdom** manifests itself through wise behavior. Wise **behavior** is **behavior** that is in accordance with God's will as it is expressed in God's Word. And these are **works done in wise meekness.** It is not only the ability to discern and follow the principles of the Bible that constitutes godly **intelligence** and wise behavior, but also the performance of these works in **meekness**. And it is works that are the outgrowth of a lifestyle. The word for **behavior** is *anastrophe*. It means *habitual* behavior, not behavior done only once in a while, or on certain occasions, but behavior that characterizes one.

Intelligence is not manifested by an attitude of superiority, even though the two are often associated with one another. A truly **wise** person, schooled in the **meekness** of Christ, is able to converse with those of the lowest intelligence in ways that are fully communicative and helpful. And *education* is not the index of **intelligence** either; certainly not of **wisdom**. Education can take place (and in these days does take place) in contexts where neither the teacher nor the student has even the slightest idea of what humility, meekness and wisdom are all about. When counselees

14 But if you have bitter jealousy and rivalry in your heart, don't boast about it and lie against the truth.

---

exhibit some of the rotted fruit of such "education" in order to excuse themselves in one way or another, it is your task as a counselor to bring them down a notch or two. These verses are pivotal in doing just that. In effect, they say that true wisdom always bows at the foot of the cross. Make it clear that in God's estimation no one is intelligent or wise who fails to translate that knowledge into an ability to grasp and apply the truths of the Scriptures that he has attained into everyday living. Here, **good** means that which accords with the will of God. So in introducing the matter of strife, conflict and quarreling, James begins with that which is the remedy to it—**good behavior** flowing from **wise** decision-making and actions done in **meekness. James** has already put the counselor in possession of the fundamental goals and the basic means for reaching them that he will need in dealing with conflict.

Now he launches into his topic: **if you have bitter jealousy and rivalry in your heart, don't boast about it and lie against the truth** (v. 14). These two items that counselors find in so many counselees not only tear people apart, but set them over against others. **Bitter jealousy** (or a *harsh zeal* for something one desires directed against another who has it) can destroy a family, a church or any relationship in which it grows. It must be cut down and rooted out. This attitude **in the heart** can lead to fierce **rivalry** (or "party spirit," when it affects others who side with the person involved). There is no place for sibling rivalry among brothers and sisters in the faith.

When you detect manifestations of these in the speech and actions of counselees, warn them that their behavior is unbecoming to a child of God, that it is neither **intelligent** nor **wise** *behavior*, and that it is the opposite of godly **meekness**. It is important to teach them to rejoice with those who rejoice. If Joe is chosen to head up a committee at church, don't envy him his position, become opposed to all he does and attempt to undermine his efforts. Rather, rejoice with him, help him, support him and assist him in any way you can—that is the sort of **good behavior** that James advocates in Christ's Name.

But what of the rest of verse 14? James says, **don't boast about it and lie against the truth**. He means, don't think that if you are able to muster a group against another out of party spirit or if you are able to thwart another in some personal manner because of your **jealousy** toward

15 This isn't the wisdom that comes down from above; rather it is earthly, sensual, demonic.

---

him, that what you have done is wise and intelligent behavior. Not on your life! It is the opposite. When you **boast** about sinful, bitter, jealous behavior as an achievement ("Well, I guess I stopped Bill in his tracks as he was attempting to do such-and-such"), and perhaps even say, "I guess the Lord was good to us for not allowing Bill to get his way," dragging God into the conflict, you **lie against the truth** says James. Nothing you do, even if it has the right end in view, is proper in the sight of God if it is done out of jealous motives. Tell counselees to examine their **hearts** (*you* can't, as I have previously made clear, because it is not your prerogative to do so). Counselees can detect bitter jealousy and rivalry or party spirit when it is there. If so, until they practice doing loving acts toward those of whom they are now jealous, and learn to rejoice with them over the good things that come their way, they will be wrong before God (Who considers all their pious talk a **lie**) and will cause trouble in the church.

James goes further; he writes: **This isn't the wisdom that comes down from above; rather it is earthy, sensual, demonic.** That is a strong statement (You have noticed, have you not, that James doesn't hesitate to call a spade a spade? That, too, is a trait a counselor must develop. He must learn to tell it like it is. He may be the only person the counselee ever encounters who will level with him about his sinful behavior). This sort of "wisdom," James says, comes from the evil one. Clearly, it does not come from God. **Earthly** wisdom is wisdom that sees no farther than this world; it has both an earthly source and a limited vision. In acting, it fails to take eternity into consideration. **Sensual** thinking and acting (which can be present in a Ph.D. as well as in anyone else) is motivated by desires and appetites. It is "soulish," operating on the level of an irrational animal. Such attitudes and motives are in accord with and promote the devil's agenda. They are encouraged by his minions. That is why they are **demonic**.

In verse 16, James records a principle vital to good counseling: **Where jealousy and self-seeking exist, there will be disruption and every worthless practice.** The principle runs both ways. When you detect what seems to be **jealousy** and **self-seeking** in a counselee, ask yourself (and your counselee) "What sort of **disruption** is there in your life and in the lives of those with whom you associate?" The presence of such **disruption**, traced back to **jealousy** and **self-seeking**, will confirm the exis-

16 Where jealousy and self-seeking exist, there will be disruption and every worthless practice.

---

tence of the latter in your counselee's life. It is one way to check your initial assessment of his problem. The other way to go is this: When you see **disruption**, look for **jealousy** and for **self-seeking**.

There is more and more **self-seeking,** and the concomitant **jealousy** that almost always flows from it, every year, it seems. You will find that these phenomena are not unusual. Why is that? Because **self-seeking** is not only part of the sinful nature with which one is born, it also has been legitimized in our society. An entire generation has been taught that self must come first. That is, of course, exactly the opposite of the Christian message which puts God and one's neighbor before one's self. But the Adler-Maslow approach has been brought even into Evangelical Christianity by the self-appointed psychologists and psychiatrists and hoodwinked pastors who now abound in the church. This is a tragedy. Little children are taught to pat themselves on the back, telling themselves how valuable, how great they are—and expecting others to believe that lie too! The self-love, self-worth teachers have spawned a host of persons who are no longer ashamed to think and say that they are so important that the world should revolve around them. When they discover that it doesn't, they not only hungrily begin to seek ways and means of glorifying and satisfying their desires, but become excessively jealous over others who have what they do not. Persons like these need to be confronted with the passage before us. They need to be told that they have been taught to believe a lie. They must be helped to understand that **jealousy and self-seeking** are opposed to God's order, and stem from the evil one alone. For details on this matter, see my book, *The Biblical View of Self-Love, Self-worth and Self-Esteem.*

The disruption, disorder and confusion in the life of the counselee and of those around him who have been affected by his problems may lead to **every sort of worthless practice.** That means that the person infected with this self-orientation will do almost anything to obtain what he seeks. You will discover all sorts of attempts on his part to gain things, power, recognition, accolades, attention or whatever from others. When you find **jealousy and self-seeking** in the life of a counselee, look for the **practices** (habits patterns) along these lines that he has developed over the years. It is not merely repentance over his self-conceit that must take place (that's where to begin, of course), but also these **practices** must be

17 But the wisdom from above is, first, pure, then peaceable, gentle, open to reason, full of mercy and good fruits, free from favoritism and hypocrisy.

---

replaced by new, biblical ones. Unless that is done in addition to instruction and subsequent repentance, you will find that he will continue to fall back into the same sins.

For what sort of practices should you look? Those that are **worthless**. That is to say, those that are good for nothing, vain, empty. They achieve no good end. When a counselee says, "I try this and I try that, but nothing seems to get me anywhere," start looking for them.

The wisdom from below is not true **wisdom**; that James makes clear. He uses the word in an ironic fashion. Indeed, it is the very opposite of wisdom. But there is a true **wisdom** that comes **from above** (v. 17). It is God-given wisdom. We have discussed this to a great extent in chapter 1 and will not repeat what was said there. In this place, however, James adds some facts that we should observe.

James describes true wisdom from God; it is not **worthless**, but rather, **is pure, peaceable, gentle, open to reason, full of mercy and good fruits, free from favoritism and hypocrisy.** That starkly contrasts with demonic "wisdom." If you had any doubt about it, you can set it to rest: these are the qualities with which the demonic wisdom must be replaced. Here is your counseling agenda for persons enmeshed in the Adler-Maslow legitimization of sinful selfishness.

Let's review them.

First, it is **pure**. That is to say, it is properly motivated action, action that puts God first. This must replace **jealousy and self-seeking** ***in the heart*** (v. 14). The need is for an inner transformation leading to the practice of **righteousness** (as these qualities are summarily called in v. 18). The counselee who wants to become what God requires of him is also **peaceable**. He is not easily provoked. He causes little stir because he is patient and has learned to put up with the shenanigans of others. He is **gentle**. This means, as someone has translated it, he is filled with "sweet reasonableness." He is **open to reasoning** by others; he is not a know-it-all. He will hear out what others have to say. There is a pliableness about him that will not compromise, but will bend as far as is biblically possible. Then comes **mercy**, a willingness to do for others what they do not deserve (he never forgets the mercy God showed to him in Jesus Christ). And after that, **good fruits**. There is plenty of evidence of the changes

18 And the fruit of righteousness is sown in peace by peacemakers.

---

that repentance and proper counseling produce. As James has just said, he disapproves of **favoritism** and is **free from** it in his own dealings with others (see previous discussion). There is no **hypocrisy** in him. What you see is what you get. You can see that these qualities will put down **disruption** and confusion; they bring people together. Indeed, that is precisely what James goes on to say.

Rather than causing disruption, the one who lives wisely is a **peacemaker.** Becoming a **peacemaker** (v. 18) is the result of the **righteous** living described in the previous verse. Wherever that sort of living is **sown**, the harvest is **peace**. And that is the crop that every counselor should be able to produce by the proper sort of counseling. If you are unable to bring about peace, then either you have not been counseling properly, the counselee has not been cooperating—or both. The presence of peace, where previously there was disruption, is a clear index of the success or failure of counseling. But *note well*, it must be the **peace** produced by **righteousness**, not a false, misleading "peace" that comes from the compromise of truth, the knuckling under of one to another, etc.

So much for chapter 3. But the chapter heading (as I previously noted) breaks into the thought of the discussion. So we will continue here through verse 3 of chapter 4. This belongs to the flow of thought we have been pursuing. **Peacemaking**, and the resultant **peace** that follows, is the goal. But instead, so often what we find is *war!* In contrast to the word **peace**, James goes on to speak of the battles and warfare in which some Christians engage with one another. There is war in the church among God's people. The fact is all-too-obvious to the world outside which, often becoming privy to it, laughs and scorns the name of Christ. To remedy this sad situation is one thing that counselors may do to uphold the honor of their Lord's Name. Doing so, and not merely considering the welfare of the counselee, should motivate every counselor to work for peace.

What James is speaking about in verses 1 through 3 is *personal* quarrels (note the words **among you**). He calls them **wars** and **fights** ("battles"). Congregations are often divided into sides; families and family friends are at odds with each other. That is the picture. They throw ammunition (usually by their tongues) at each other in an attempt to weaken the other side. They must be brought to **peace** by **peacemakers.** Your coun-

CHAPTER 4

1 Where do wars and where do fights among you come from? Isn't it from your pleasures that are warring in your bodily members?

---

selee, properly counseled, may become a **peacemaker**. That is the objective: to turn a combatant into a peacemaker.

You too, by bringing righteous living into the life of your counselees, may consider yourself a **peacemaker**. This is an activity which helps counselees, but also blesses the one who engages in it, as Jesus said in the beatitudes (again, we see the Sermon on the Mount behind James' exhortations). How wonderful to bring peace between warring factions in Christ's church! Can you think of any more rewarding activity?

As a counselor, you must get to the bottom of these quarrels. As James plumbs the depths, he reaches rock bottom: **where do wars and where do fights come from? Isn't it from your pleasures that are warring in your bodily members?** That is his God-given conclusion. It is, therefore, one to which Christian counselors may confidently turn whenever dealing with church fights. At the very bottom, after all else has been scraped off, James sees the **desire** for **pleasure** as the cause (vv. 1,2). These **desires for pleasure**, literally translated, are "soldiering" or "campaigning" in **one's bodily members**. That is, they are in full muster and are prepared to **fight** to obtain the pleasures your counselee desires. The warfare, then, begins *within*. The battle that the counselor fights is with the soldiers within. He must bring them into line and help them to serve the cause of God rather than the selfish desires of the counselee. A counselee who exhibits a way of life that is a pursuit of pleasure is one in whom, sooner or later, you will find the troops amassing to fight against his better wishes so as to mobilize him also to attack other believers. This is what Paul was talking about in Romans 7:23. The tendency for pleasure-seeking may become so habituated into our lives that, without even realizing what is happening, one calculates his every decision and move in the light of his objective. To make him aware of it and to replace it after repentance is your task. This may be your first task. Throughout the section are various insights that James gives in order to help make him aware. Many counselees have heard so much justification of sin that they don't even realize that self-seeking is sin. Use chapters 3 and 4 of James freely in order to offset this problem.

2 You desire something and don't have it. You murder and envy and still can't obtain it. You fight and you war. You don't have because you don't ask!
3 You don't receive when you do ask, since you ask wrongly—to waste it on your pleasures.

So to sum up, outer quarrels among Christians come from losing battles within. Once again (contra Luther) James takes an inside view of man. James does this, as before when dealing with temptation, to expose the dynamic at work so that you will know where to aim your efforts to rectify the situation. It is *within* that the first and foremost change must begin. One must realize his sin, confess it and seek God's forgiveness (and the forgiveness of those he has offended) and then, after reconciliation, begin to put on the new, biblical, righteous ways outlined in the Scriptures.

James shows how desire frustrated is the problem: **You desire something and don't have it** (v. 2). Desire itself is not wrong. But jealousy and envy out of frustration are sinful. You **murder** [here, probably the correct translation is "envy" rather than murder] **and are jealous and still can't obtain it.** Now in that description the desire is getting up a head of steam. It is here, in the heart, that one's sin begins. He conceives outer sin by this jealous envy of what others have that he doesn't. Finally, at the last stage, he **fights and wars** to get it. And if he had asked in prayer, the chances are that he would have obtained it. At any rate, if God did not grant his request, he would have received the best answer to his prayer—the one God wanted to give him. One that would have been satisfying and led to peace rather than to frustration. But he didn't ask! He envied; he fought for it instead! That is bad news. A counselor may point out this dynamic to his counselee. And he may show him how to cut it off at the pass. If when he discovers a strong desire for something, instead of moving to envy and jealousy, he prays, willing to have whatever answer God gives, he will more often than not **have** it, as James says, and when he doesn't get what he desires, will have something better instead. In both responses from God, the counselee will **have.**

To stop the warfare within, one must be prepared to put others first (cf. notes on Philippians 2) and pray properly (v. 3). Even when counselees pray, they often pray wrongly: **to waste it on their own pleasures**. "Never waste prayer. When you pray simply for your desires to be answered, you may waste your prayer since God may not give you what

4 Adulteresses, don't you know that friendship with the world is enmity with God? So whoever determines to be a friend of the world thereby sets himself up as an enemy of God.

---

you want. But if you pray, 'Lord, this is what I desire, but nevertheless, not my will but Yours be done,' you will always receive an answer. Then prayer will not have been wasted. You will **have** what God thinks is best for you at the moment. What could be better than that? But you must mean it." That is the sort of thing you ought to be telling counselees who are grappling with the problem exposed in these two chapters by James. Teach them to pray *rightly* according to I John 5:14.

This chapter has been one I hope you see is of significance to counselors. Use it often in your counseling and you will help many.

Since the argument of chapter 3 spilled over into chapter 4, I treated the first three verses of this chapter there. Consequently we shall begin on a new departure, as James does, with verse 4. That subject is worldliness.

Worldliness is a common counseling problem to be faced seriously by every counselor. At first it may seem not so significant. But when you read what James has to say about the matter, you can see that God does not take it lightly. Perhaps the reason for the rather casual attitude of many toward worldliness is the perversion of the problem by some who view the matter legalistically. If you tell a counselee that he is having a problem with worldliness, chances are he will conjure up pictures of lists of do's or don'ts to which he does or does not conform. But that is not worldliness according to the Scriptures.

What is worldliness? Worldliness (or its absence) is a matter of one's *orientation*. Is he oriented toward God or toward the world? It is finding guidance, meaning and satisfaction in the world rather than in God. James calls it **friendship** and **adultery** with the world.

Your counselee may be having an "affair" with the world. That is why James speaks of worldly Christians as **adulteresses**. They are married to Christ, so to have an affair with the world is adultery. James may have picked up on Christ's words about an **adulterous generation** (Matthew 12:39; 16:4). At any rate, the metaphor is one that our Lord Himself used. And of course, even before His use of it, it was an Old Testament figure of speech (see Isaiah 54:5ff.; Jeremiah 3:6-14; 20).

The context as I have shown at the conclusion of chapter 3 is prayer. How can one expect his prayers to God to succeed when he is having illicit relations with another? The believer may not run around with "Mr.

Cosmos" while traveling on this earth and still profess that she is being true to her Husband in the heavens! When you suspect worldliness as the problem in a counselee's life, ask, "Are you having an affair?" When the indignant "No!" comes back, explain what you mean. The use of such a figure of speech, strong as it is (i.e., as the Spirit inspired James to use it), is designed to get people to sit up and take notice. Many worldly persons, who would not think of betraying their spouses by having an affair with another human being, think nothing of worldly attitudes that in God's sight are equivalent to adultery. Since the figure of speech is designed to startle persons into thinking, use it for that purpose! Far too little use of metaphor and striking language and figures of speech takes place in counseling. I have noticed that whenever I do use such methods to try to awaken otherwise lethargic counselees they do respond. Often, this response is the first that I receive from them. And they frequently bring up the matter at a later date, proving that the figure has stuck with them. Sometimes they even speak about having pondered it for a while. Learn from the Bible, which does not confine itself to cold, scientific language. Learn to put things as the Lord and His disciples did—vividly in terms that strike one hard, and are memorable to him. A good time to ask the question above is when a counselee complains that God has not been answering his prayers. Why should He when he has been depending on another? Unfaithfulness begets a response from God.

Notice, in verse 4, James speaks of the counselee who **determines** to **be a friend of the world**. That is an interesting point: one does not only drift into such a relationship, he makes a choice to have an affair with the world. The term *boulethe*, used here, means "resolves, chooses or determines," in the sense of a deliberate act. The responsibility of the counselee is paramount in that word. Whenever a Christian becomes a **lover** of the **world,** while he may not have made one deliberate choice to commit spiritual adultery, he surely has made many decisions along the way that led him inevitably into the affair. If you and he were to consider the step by step process by which he became a lover of the world, you would uncover many deliberate decisions that were made in spite of the fact that they were known by him to be wrong (cf. comments on the last verse of this chapter). Just as one puts himself into a position where he may be attracted by another, just as he flirts in word and act, just as he allows himself to go along with suggestive behavior in the conduct of a relationship that may turn out to be illicit, so the same has been true of relationships that led to adultery with the world. Checking out these steps to adultery may help to put him in a place to avoid it in the future after he

5 Or do you think that it is to no purpose that the Scripture says, "The Spirit Whom God caused to dwell within us earnestly desires to oppose envy"?
6 But He gives greater help, as it says, God resists proud persons, but gives help to the humble.

---

repents and is beginning to shore up his life for the days to come.

The other responsibility term is **sets himself up** (*kathistatai*) **as an enemy of God**. The determination to become a **friend** (lit., lover) **of the world** necessarily involves a negative relationship to God. How can the Christian, when he comes to realize it, side with the enemies of God? It is unthinkable. The one who does so but never repents of his sin cannot be considered God's friend. By his actions he **sets himself up** over against God and His will and, consequently, must be considered His **enemy**.

What is the principal cause of friendship with the world? **Envy**. It is the problem of Psalm 37; it is what James has talked about in verses 1 through 3. It is the subject of verse 5: **Or do you think that it is to no purpose that the Scripture says, "the Spirit Whom God caused to dwell within us earnestly desires to oppose envy?"** Whenever a counselee decides "I want what the world offers for myself," he is in danger; he has begun flirting with the world. Envy is a form of self-centeredness. And since the entire milieu within which Christians live today (often even the church milieu) is oriented toward self-assertion and self-satisfaction, the temptation is great. Perhaps the world never had so much with which to attract the *common* man. It is possible that, as a result, America has the most worldly church of all time. There is more here in this country that the world offers, more that is available to the average person. And it is difficult to decide what is worldly and what is not. The problem is not easy to handle. But it must be faced. Counselors will not get very far if they fail to do so.

How may a counselee deal with worldliness? The **Spirit Whom God caused to dwell within** is his ally. He does not have to "go it alone." The Spirit convicts of sin and strengthens within (Ephesians 3:1; cf. also Galatians 5). How can one resist? In verse 6 we read **But He gives greater help, as it says, God resists proud persons, but gives help to the humble**. Clearly humbling one's self in repentance is the answer. Whenever one does, the **help** that God gives to resist temptation to worldliness is **greater** than all the attractions of Mr. Cosmos. Those who are **proud** and resist the counsel of God will find that God **resists** their efforts. They will

7 So, submit to God; but resist the devil and he will flee from you.
8 Draw near to God and He will draw near to you. Wash your hands, you sinners, and purify your hearts, you double-minded persons.

---

not obtain what they desire. "Why does God always seem to keep me from doing or having what I want?," and complaints of that nature, should receive a response something like this, "According to James 4:6, **God resists proud persons**; do you think that is at the bottom of your problem?" Pride gets in the way of progress in counseling. Until it is dealt with biblically, forget trying to do anything else. How can you proceed further when God has determined to **resist**? It is foolish to attempt to do so when God has set Himself against your efforts.

In verses 7 through 10, God describes the repentance that is necessary. He begins by saying, **Submit to God.** That is, stop trying to do things your own way. Forget whatever it is that you want. Submit to Him and to His will as you find it in the Bible. That is the way to **resist the devil**. It is how the Lord Jesus did it when He was tempted in the wilderness. He **submitted** to God's revealed will (and even quoted it). Urge counselees to stop their frantic attempts to obtain things, status, position, power or whatever it is that they are putting in the place of God and His will. Urge them to **submit** to Him by orienting themselves—their thinking and all their behavior—toward Him. The orientation toward the world is, at bottom, an orientation toward self: it is a desire to have all that the world offers as the means of obtaining satisfaction. Instead, one must find his satisfaction in God and what He provides—then, all these things will be added to him. But to **submit** to God is to put the Kingdom of God and His righteousness *first.*

The **devil** will **flee**; that is, temptation will cease when you repent and put God first. It was when Christ submitted to the will of God in the Scripture passages that He quoted that the devil gave up and left Him. Every counselor must learn from this fact.

What does true repentance involve? In verses 8 through 10 we read about that. It involves **sorrow**, confession of sin (acknowledgment that one's **hands** and **hearts** need **washing**) and **humbling** so that God may **exalt** him. That is how one **draws near to God** (cf. Psalm 24:4). He confesses that he needs cleansing from sin; a rapprochement with God takes place (obviously, the need for **drawing near** indicates that there has been a break in his fellowship, as there is, one way or another, in all **adulterous** relationships). Moreover, there must be a genuineness about his sorrow:

9 Be distressed, and sorrow and cry; let your laughter be turned to sorrow and your gladness to dejection.
10 Be humbled before the Lord and He will exalt you.
11 Brothers, don't speak against one another; whoever speaks against a brother or judges his brother speaks against the law and judges the law. But if you judge the law, you aren't a doer of the law but its judge.
12 There is but One Who is Lawgiver and Judge—the One Who is able to save and to destroy. But you, who are you to judge your neighbor?

---

he cleanses not only his **hands**, but also his **heart,** by seeking forgiveness from God. Again, the problem of **double-mindedness** arises (v. 8). You cannot be the lover of God and a lover of the world. God will not allow His wife to maintain another lover on the side.

When one **draws near to God** in repentance, God, in turn, **will draw near** too. That is to say, fellowship will be restored. The proper relationship with God will once again be in place. That, of course, is the problem in so much counseling. People come to get help *apart from the knowledge that they must repent first or God will not help them.* God **gives help** to the **humble**. The **humble** are those who **submit** to Him and who are willing to acknowledge their sin before Him, seeking forgiveness and cleansing. Let me warn you counselor; you will get nowhere when the problem standing in the way of solving other problems with which the counselee came is **pride**. Until your counselee **humbles** himself and is willing to come to God in that manner, he will find that God will **resist** his (and by extension *your*) every effort. True **exaltation** comes only from the Lord, and not from the world. That, in essence, is what counselees need to learn (cf. v. 10). So tell them. Make it plain that there is no hope for progress in any other way. You do a counselee a disservice if you fail to.

Moving on, we turn to James' next concern: *slander* (vv. 11,12), where we shall consider two of the most important verses in the Bible on the subject. James writes, **Brothers, don't speak against one another; whoever speaks against a brother or judges his brother speaks against the law and judges the law. But if you judge the law, you aren't a doer of the law but its judge. There is but One Who is Lawgiver and Judge—the One Who is able to save and to destroy. But you, who are you to judge your neighbor.** In these two verses slander, gossip and **speaking against** a **brother** is equated with **judging**. In parallel fashion, what is said about the one is also said about the other.

Why are these verses so important in counseling? Well, naturally, as you can understand, since there are so many who have problems with their brothers and sisters, there is the tendency to talk negatively about them behind their backs. A counselor must realize this fact, be alert for every manifestation of it and prevent it whenever it occurs. He must never do it himself in counseling sessions, never encourage others to do it and must not allow it to go on in his presence. Some, following unbiblical theories of ventilation, etc., *encourage* talking about others who are not present. Those counselors who are trying to make their counseling biblical in all respects are careful to avoid this at all costs.

A young man came in for counseling last week. His parents will come with him this week. But he wanted to come alone to "fill me in" on all of the problems that his parents have. I would not allow it. I told him that he can speak all he wants about them to their faces (politely), but that this verse tells us that we may not talk about them behind their backs (as the verb *katalaleo*, that is here used, means). So we spent the time together talking about *his* problems. I also pointed out that talking about them would be of no real benefit since they were not present to know what changes to make or to make any commitments to do so, presuming that it was necessary for them to do so. He could see this and, because he wanted to get his relationship to them straightened out in a Christian manner, readily assented.

James had just spoken about **humility**. Humility prohibits one from looking down on another. Instead, it requires him to make a hard appraisal of his own failures and sins. That is where you must place the emphasis in counseling. The word *katalaleo* means, literally, "to speak down." It is equivalent to our term "to run down another." It carries the idea of defaming others or, as Ropes puts it, "speaking harsh words about the absent" party. There are so many ways in which the prohibition can be transgressed. For instance, in data gathering one may go too far. The general principle to keep in mind is this: allow any positive comments about one who is not there, but no negative ones.

The **law** in Leviticus 19:16 tells you how to treat your **brother**. It is the law of love. When one speaks negatively about a **brother** he transgresses the **law**, and, in effect, **judges** the **law** by his disobedience to it. He virtually says, "the **law** is wrong; I do not want to obey it. I have a better way." Thus, he sets himself up not only as a **judge** (critic) of the law, but as a **lawgiver**. But to do so, he attempts to usurp God's position as **Judge** and **Lawgiver**. Slandering others, when they do not abide by our own man-made laws, again usurps God's place. God alone is Lord of a man's conscience. It is not possible for a human being, who does not know the heart of his brother, to know what motives he has for doing what

13 Come now, you who say, "Today or tomorrow we'll go to this city or that, where we'll spend a year and trade and make a profit"—

---

he does. Sometimes, if we knew the motive, we would recognize that the action which at first looked like sin was not. Moreover, we may judge too leniently. God alone knows the heart; He alone therefore is the true **Judge**. Moreover, when one speaks about another behind his back, the brother who is defamed is not there to explain motives, facts, exigencies that may have a bearing on the incident. Remember the principle in Proverbs 18:15.

And, says James, it is only the one who is able to enforce the **law** and his judgments who has any clout anyway: Only God can **save** and can **destroy**. Men cannot. A counselee must be taught to assume his rightful place *under* the **law** of God and *under* His **judgment**. He has no power, right or authority to place himself above either. With James, ask a proud counselee who revels in judging others, "**who are you to judge your neighbor** (v. 12[b])?" It is a powerful question; use it to bring conviction of sin to those who transgress the law in these ways. Once again, we see that James does not pull his punches. He is straightforward, clear and penetrating in his analyses of human problems. And he is concerned not only with outward behavior, but with the **heart**.

James concludes what later became this chapter with a discussion of planning. That, too, is an important issue for many Christians. A number of counselees fail in their Christian walk because they neglect to **plan**. Others plan in ways that do not take God's plans into consideration. Both are wrong. James teaches you how to instruct a counselee to plan in ways that acknowledge and please God.

You will often have to help counselees plan. You will be doing planning with them about business matters, marriage and family issues, and careers. Therefore, you yourself must have a biblical perspective on the issue. Here, particularly in contrast to presumptuous planning, James lays out important particulars. All planning should have behind it three important convictions.

The first inner conviction a counselee must have to plan biblically is that *life is short*. He takes to task those who fail to heed this fact: **Come now, you who say, Today or tomorrow....** There is no evading the point that James makes—your **life** is brief. He wants your counselee to think beyond the parameters of this life and not confine his plans to it the way a worldly person does. Men try to evade the fact that they must soon die.

14 you who don't know what your life will be like tomorrow! You're a
mist that appears for a short time and then vanishes.
15 Rather, you ought to say, "If the Lord wills, we'll live and we'll do this
or that."

But every birthday, every serious illness, every death of a friend or relative, every accident shouts out loudly, "You too will soon die." Shouldn't Christians take death into consideration when planning?

James makes it clear that one's life is but a **mist that appears for a short time and then vanishes** (v. 14). Why, he doesn't even know if he will awaken to ***tomorrow***. Tell him to take out the family snapshot album now and then. Old slides or movies will do as well. Now mom and dad's voices are silent. They smile at you only from a faded photo! Don't let him scoff "emotionalism!" He is the one who is ruled by emotions who thinks otherwise. He is a fool who covers the fact that life is short and stumbles on—to death!

But that is not all. A second fact must be kept in mind when planning: for human beings with their limited knowledge, *Life is unpredictable*. Human projections into the future are not very predictable (even the weather man can't be relied upon). Think back ten, five years—even one year ago. What did you think you'd be doing today? Where did you think you'd be living? What interests did you think you'd be pursuing? You could not know or predict the future. James says, **You don't know what your life will be like *tomorrow*** (v. 14)!

This fundamental unpredictable nature of life is the reason why James stresses *conditional* (or *providential*) planning. What is that? Providential or conditional planning is *planning conditioned by God's will (or providence)*. That is to say, the counselee must be willing to bring *God's* planning and input into his planning. As James puts it, he **ought to say, "If the Lord wills, we'll live and we'll do this or that."** James is not against planning for the future; his concern is for the counselee to include God in the planning. The **if** that he urges is vital. It isn't an **if** of doubt or concern but the **if** of confident reliance on God. It is the **if** of expectancy, the **if** of anticipation to see whether (and if so, how) God will blue-pencil his plans for the better. It is the willingness to make all plans a joint venture with the Lord. It is the willingness to have His way prevail over one's own plans. It is the belief that whatever God does about your plans for tomorrow will be better than what you do.

Your counselee must plan; that James is not opposed to. But he must

16 But, as it is, you boast in arrogance; all such boasting is evil.

---

be taught to plan with a holy caution and with maximum flexibility that attaches (either audibly or silently) the sincere proviso, "Nevertheless not my will but Yours be done." Even our Lord Jesus prayed that way. As the counselee (or you and he) plans, you must use the best understanding of Scripture applied to the circumstances as you are able to discern them in the most prudent, careful, biblical manner. But in spite of that, you must leave room for God's changes, corrections and substitutions as He works providentially in life and circumstances. In other words, in all your planning, and the planning that you help counselees to do, you must keep God, and His will, in mind.

So often counselees think that their decisions are like those of the Medes and Persians—final. Such thinking is subChristian. We must expect, indeed call upon, God to review and revise our best plans. It is an act of faith and trust to do so; it is an act of **boasting** that grows out of sinful **arrogance** not to (v. 16).

But there is a third consideration to be borne in mind as your counselee plans. He must be told, *Your life is feeble*. It is a child's loose milk tooth! One twist...and that's it. Since life hangs by so slender a thread, since the counselee can't really control its termination beyond doubt, it is also **arrogance** to plan like the Jewish merchant described in verse 13. He **boasts**, says James. What is **boasting**? Fundamentally it is making unwarranted assertions, claims one can't make good. Since he can't deliver on these claims—even for the next minute—it is sheer arrogance to plan *un*conditionally. All proper planning takes into consideration the fact that one's **life is a mist that appears for a short time and then vanishes.** It is done in the spirit of the old Latin abbreviation, D.V. (*deo volente*, "if the Lord wills") which originated out of this passage from James. This isn't a magic formula, to be tacked on to every statement or prayer. Rather, it is an attitude that affects the way that the counselee plans. There may be times to actually *say* it, but one ought always to *think* it. The only certainties for the future are those clearly outlined in the Scriptures—heaven, hell, etc. Remember, the counselee must understand that God does not oppose proper, biblical planning (indeed, that is what He is teaching through James' words), but only rigid, unbending, self-confident, self-assertive boastful planning. God is to be his planning Partner!

Concluding the chapter and referring back to all that he has said so

17 So then, whoever knows to do good and doesn't, for him that's sin.

---

far (and perhaps all he has said in the letter to this point), he writes, **So, then, whoever knows to do good and doesn't, for him that's sin**. It is clear that this is a timely warning. And it has aphoristic force. That is to say, it has universal application; it is an absolute. It refers not only to the matters being discussed when it is stated, but to any and all other matters that fall under its rubric. It is a fundamental principle of life. As such, counselees ought often to hear it repeated. It is essential to good counseling. Talking to a potential suicide, I recently used the statement. Because of the power of this brief, but clear and forceful, Word from God, the person in view backed off and became willing to eliminate that option. The Spirit uses His Word. Such epigrammatic utterances are extremely useful in counseling. You, as a counselor, should have your quiver full of them. They are arrows that you may use to good effect in innumerable situations. Here is one that you should not only memorize, but also know where it is located so that, if need be, you can show it to a doubting counselee. Believe it: God's Word, used effectively in the right situations, rightly interpreted and applied, is the most powerful weapon in the counselor's armory. Don't go to battle unarmed. There is no need to do so with such sharply honed instruments that God has provided for you. Remember, Scripture is more powerful than any two-edged sword, and that it penetrates into the inner being of the counselee—to his thoughts and to his intents. Here is one such piece of counseling equipment. Use it, I urge you!

CHAPTER 5

1 Come now, you who are rich. Cry and weep out loud about the distresses that are coming upon you.
2 Your riches have rotted and your clothes have been eaten by moths;
3 your gold and your silver have rusted, and their rust will stand as a testimony against you and will eat at your flesh like fire. You've hoarded
riches in the last days!

James returns to a discussion of the rich man. He begins, **Come now, you who are rich**. This phrase, used also of the merchant in the last chapter is designed to alert the person addressed that he, in particular, is in view, and that he is about to be called on the carpet for some sin that he is very likely to have fallen into. It is a warning, signaled by a call to listen to his judgment. Riches wrongly used (more often the situation than not) can bring great temptation, sin and consequent sorrow. Listen to what follows: **Cry and weep out loud about the distresses that are coming upon you**. Are all riches wrong? Is James condemning all rich persons out of hand? Certainly not. For a clear perspective on this matter, see the last chapter of the commentary on I Timothy and comments there.

Well, then, what does James have in mind in so castigating the rich? As Calvin says, this is probably a description of the unsaved rich. There is no exhortation to repentance. Why then this outburst? It is written to bring consolation to the poor who have been ground under the heel of the rich. That would explain why the words appear in a letter to Christians—James is explaining the ultimate fate of those who oppress and persecute poor believers.

Speaking in a great apostrophe (as if the rich were there in the presence of the poor who are suffering under their greedy hands) he says, "Your **riches** are not lasting: they have **rotted**, are **eaten by moths, your gold and silver have rusted**. And in the day of judgment that rust will **stand as a testimony against you**. Indeed, like the rust that destroyed your wealth, and like fire that consumes all perishable goods, your riches will **eat at your flesh!** That is to say, like your riches that will be destroyed, so too you will meet ultimate ruin."

While they seek to acquire and hold on to all they can with a grasp that will not let go, these rich persons will lose all their wealth anyway! In a **day** when they ought to be preparing for judgment, they have **hoarded riches** (v. 3). How foolish! They will not be able to take them with them.

4 See, the wages of the workmen who mowed your fields, that you kept back, shout out at you, and the complaints of the harvesters have entered into the ears of the Lord of Armies.
5 On earth you lived in luxury and extravagantly. You've fattened your hearts in a day of slaughter!
6 You've condemned, you've murdered righteous people, when they didn't resist you.

Like an animal unaware of the fact, these fat cats were being **fattened** (not for their own benefit but) for the **slaughter** of the Destruction to come (v. 5; here, judgment probably refers to that which took place in 70 AD, though with overtones of the final judgment as well). According to verse 4, God declares Himself on the side of those who have complained against such treatment from the hands of the rich. He too is against them. The **harvesters'** pleas have been heard and He is about to descend upon their oppressors with all His **armies**. The deeds of the unsaved rich are described in verses 5 and 6. For these acts they will be judged by God Himself. God is the Protector of the vulnerable; He has declared himself so (cf. Proverbs 22:22).

Rich counselees must be warned against the callous attitudes they can take toward the poor while fattening their own pocketbooks. God will countenance no such behavior. Though they may seem to be getting away with **murder** (perhaps, literally, as here noted in v. 6) they will not. This is the strongest warning in the book—a book in which there are many strong warnings. Rich brothers may never live like these rich people. Those who after exhortation and counseling refuse to repent and change their ways must be dealt with as if they are not brothers at all (they probably are not)! There is a time for a counselor to recommend that church discipline be exercised (cf. Matthew 18:15ff. and my *Handbook of Church Discipline* for details).

Doubtless, it will take courage on your part to tell the truth to rich persons who gouge the poor. You probably will not often have the opportunity, though, from time to time, the occasion will arise. I want you to note the utter fearlessness of James' words. True, he is not actually speaking to the rich, but only talking as if he were for the sake of the suffering believers to whom he is writing. Yet, if he were to face these very same people eyeball to eyeball, you can be sure that James would moderate his words and tones (if at all) only slightly. You can feel the emotion in the man as you read. Do you ever get upset enough about the effects of sin on poor, suffering saints to say something about it? Here is an opportunity

7 Wait patiently then, brothers, for the Lord's coming. Look at how the farmer waits for the valuable fruit of the land, waiting patiently for it until after it has received the early and late rains.
8 You too must wait patiently. Firm up your hearts since the Lord's coming has drawn near.

---

for you to think about your own life, your concerns for others in need, etc. How deeply you feel their misery will indicate how deeply you care. A counselor must be a caring person; and caring, here, means anger and outspokenness! Do you ever think of caring that way?

Flowing naturally from the previous discussion, James now considers the matter of **patience** in those who suffer (vv. 7-13). Most counseling situations call for **patience**; often much. Both counselors and counselees need to learn to be patient. **Patience** is two-sided. There is an *endurance* side to patience and there is a *waiting* side. True patience is the manifestation of both in harmony. The endurance side has already been discussed earlier (chapter 1); here, I shall consider the waiting side. Verse 7 is a command: God calls both counselor and counselee to **wait patiently**. This is a quality dearly to be desired for every counselee and for yourself. In the context, the threat concerning the wicked rich indicates that God will bring their oppression to an end. But here, James inculcates an attitude of patience as the sufferer waits for the end to come. God's judgment will not fail; the counselee may expect **the Lord's coming** (v. 7).

How does one **wait patiently** like the **farmer waits for the valuable fruit of the land?** How does he endure, wondering whether the **early and later rains** will come in adequate supply? James provides the answer in verse 8: **Firm up your hearts.** That is the answer. Again, James is concerned with the condition of the believer's heart (Luther, take heed!). The idea here is that rather than becoming doubtful and losing faith in the promises and concern of God, one must become stalwart, strong and trustful. His heart must be reinforced by the promises of God (e.g., here, **the Lord's coming has drawn near**). Only faith in the Word of God will enable one to become patient in the face of oppression or other suffering. That is where you must place the emphasis. That the Lord did come in judgment upon those who were persecuting poor Christians is clear. See my commentary on the Book of Revelation, *The Time is at Hand,* for details. It is easy to lose patience in times of trial and testing. But the Book of Revelation is the story of the overcoming martyrs who stood fast, even to death, because they accepted the Word of God that the time would be short.

9 Brothers, don't complain against one another lest you be judged. See,
the Judge stands at the door.
10 Brothers, take the prophets who spoke in the Name of the Lord as an
example of patient waiting while suffering hardship.
11 Take note of the fact that we call "happy" those who endure. You have
heard of the endurance of Job, and you have seen the final outcome that the
Lord brought about. The Lord has great compassion and pity.
12 But above all, my brothers, don't swear, either by heaven or by earth,
or with any other oath. Instead, let your yes be yes, and your no be no, lest
you fall under judgment.
13 Is anybody among you suffering hardship? Let him pray. Is anybody
in good spirits? Let him sing a hymn of praise.

There is encouragement here, even in the illustrations James uses: the **farmer** (v. 7), the **prophet** (v. 10) and **Job** (v. 11). All are examples of those who, because they trusted God, were able to be **patient**. What helped them all? Looking at the long term rather than the short haul helped (note vv. 7-9). Christ will come in judgment and right all wrong, just as God did in the case of **Job** when his **final outcome** proved God's blessing and goodness was upon him. God comes to set things right, but He comes in *His* time. And remembering something of the Lord's nature should help as well: **The Lord has great compassion and pity** (v. 11). God is not cold and hard; His providences all have a good outcome for His Name and the welfare of His children. To remember that is important; stress it to counselees.

And on the other hand, it is also important to remember that *losing* patience is sin. That is one thing that verse 12 teaches. One way of doing so is **swearing.** The words **Above all** are possibly a formula used when a letter is drawing to a close (Moffatt); cf. I Peter 4:8. Ropes translates it **especially**. It is more important than not **complaining against one another** (v. 9), a tendency that often is seen among those who are called to wait. This does not forbid proper swearing (cf. II Corinthians 1:23; 11:31; Galatians 1:20; also Matthew 5:33-37). It means not to irreverently call on God's name in times of distress. Swearing attempts to make some speech more truthful than others. All the Christian's speech ought to be utterly truthful; his yes should mean yes and his no, no.

Continuing the theme of **suffering hardship**, James writes: Well, **let him pray** (v. 13). That's what the martyrs did; and at length (after their cry "How long?") they were told that the time would be no more, and their vindication came. Clearly, James has a word for each situation. Suf-

14 Is anybody among you sick? Let him call for the elders of the church and let them pray for him, rubbing him with oil in the Name of the Lord,

---

fering, he says, should issue in prayer, **good spirits** (cheerfulness) in **singing a hymn of praise.** In other words, the counselee must be taught to respond to the providential circumstances that come into his life in an appropriate way. He must be taught what that appropriate way is.

Now, he turns to sickness, which brings forth an important word. What is the appropriate response to sickness? Verses 14-16 explain. This response must be taught to congregations as well as to counselees. **Is anybody among you sick? Let him call for the elders of the church**. How often have sick counselees done so? How often have you asked them whether they have? Many counselors, as well as counselees, have been utterly remiss in this matter. There is no doubt about what James says; they are to call for the elders. Before going to the physician, before going for tests, unless it is an absolute emergency, the counselee should be instructed *first* to involve the elders in an illness that debilitates him (James speaks of illnesses that necessitate bed rest: notice the elders [literally] pray *over* him, and he needs **raising up;** v. 15). The whole church (represented by the elders) is to be informed. The sick member is obliged to take the initiative. It is altogether likely that the elders may not hear about the sickness in time if he doesn't. What happens when the elders arrive?

They are to **pray for him** (v. 14). That is the first thing. Then they are to **rub him with oil in the Name of the Lord**. That is, they are to administer consecrated medicine. The word translated **rub** is not the ceremonial word for anointing, but the everyday term for rubbing down athletes or rubbing oil (with herbs) on a patient who is ill. It means "smear, rub." Herod, in his last illness, had a bath of oil (Josephus, *Wars*, 1:33:5). Hypocrites speaks of oil as "medicine." The Jews used oil as a common medical agent (cf. Mark 6:13; Luke 10:34). Early interpreters suggest that James mentions medicine in order to preclude charms, incantations, etc., which were very common. Indeed, of late, some have even turned this passage into a sort of magical ceremony. Galen calls oil "the best of all remedies for paralysis" and the Jerusalem *Talmud*, Berakoth 3:1 says, "Mingle wine and oil and rub the sick on the Sabbath." This refers to a cure for a headache! Ross says about 700 AD was when people began to wrongly consider this a ceremonial anointing. The word used here is *aleipho*, not *chrio* (from which *Christos* came). Be sure to lead your coun-

15 and the believing prayer will deliver the one who is sick, and the Lord will raise him up. And if he has committed sins, he will be forgiven.
16 So confess your sins to one another and pray for one another so that you may be healed. The petition of a righteous person has very powerful effects.

---

selees away from any sort of magical, ceremonial ideas of "anointing."

There is something for the sick person to do besides call for the elders: he is to **confess** [his] **sins** to those against whom he has sinned; if this is behind his sickness, and **if he has committed sins, he will be forgiven.** The parties involved also are to **pray for one another** (vv. 15,16). Notice, it is **believing prayer** that will make the difference. It is because of such prayer that the Lord will **raise him up**. The medicine is not incidental, however; it is through the means, not apart from it, that God will answer the prayer. One of the means is also confession of sin.

That sin is behind some sickness is clear in the Bible. Cf. I Corinthians 11:30; I John 5:16. But the Book of Job, as well as John 9:1, makes it abundantly clear that not all sickness is the result of the patient's sin. That is why James says **if** (v. 15). Because James makes the point about sin as one possibility behind illness, counselors ought to question sick persons to discover if they know whether sin is associated with the illness. That is one possibility, not the only one, however. The statement about confessing sins to **one another** does not mean to the elders, but is a general statement about what we ought to be doing all the time.

When James says the **believing prayer will raise him up**, it is clear from the participle **rubbing** that it is the prayer, not the medicine, that is the primary act. Even the medicine must be administered *in the Lord's Name*. Medicine used apart from God is used in a pagan manner. The Christian is to turn, principally, to God in illness, while not neglecting the best modern medicine.

Since the prayer is central, that theme continues in the verses that follow: **The petition of a righteous person has very powerful effects** (v. 16^{b}). Here it is the *deesis*, the prayer arising out of need or a sense of lack, that is in view. It usually implies the warmth of desire (opposed to formalistic, ritualistic prayer). When asked for earnestly, the prayer a **righteous person** like **Elijah** prays has **powerful effects.** There is no power in prayer itself; it is in the divinely ordered effects that the power is seen. Many misunderstand and think that "prayer changes things." Not so; *God* changes things!

17 Elijah was a man with the same sort of difficulties that we have, but he prayed earnestly that it might not rain, and for three years and six months it didn't rain on the earth.
18 Then he prayed again and the sky gave rain and the earth brought forth its fruit.
19 My brothers, if anybody among you errs from the truth and somebody brings him back,

---

But God works through those who in His sight, because of Jesus Christ, are **righteous**. There is no hope in an unsaved person praying unless he is praying a prayer of repentance toward God and faith in Christ as Savior. God hears only those who have been declared righteous through His Son.

Well, since Elijah is given as an example, let's look at what James says about him: Elijah was no different from any other believer. He was a **man with the same sort of difficulties that we have**. How, then, did he differ? James says, **he prayed earnestly...then he prayed again**. The form used here is a Hebraism, an intensive form: literally, "in prayer he prayed." It stresses that he really prayed with all his heart and soul. What James is teaching is that prayer should not only be offered, but that it should be offered in the proper way if it is to be offered at all. And that proper way is to pray intensely.

A **righteous person** is not only one declared righteous, but one whose lifestyle is also righteous. James is here thinking not only of justification but also of sanctification. Consider Psalm 66:18: **If I regard iniquity in my heart the Lord will not hear.** We have spoken of this problem earlier. God is not a cosmic dispensing machine into which you place a prayer coin, push the button and out comes whatever you prayed for. Precisely not that! God is a Person Who wants you to sustain a right relationship to Him. When that relationship is faulty, when there is estrangement because of sin, God will not listen to prayer. He expects prayer to be earnest and the one who prays to be living righteously. Counselees often have superstitious ideas about prayer. They think there is something about it that gets God's hearing. Not so. It is the relationship they bear to Him that does so. Clarify this matter for counselees.

James concludes his letter with an implied appeal to help one another when there is some sin interposed between a believer and God. It is the closing note to you as a counselor. Counseling is regularly (though not exclusively) involved in restoring erring Christians to their place in the church (cf. Galatians 6:1ff.; Jude 22ff.). Peter Davids thinks that this is the

20 you should know that the one who brings back a sinner from the error of his way will save his soul from death and will cover a lot of sins.

---

purpose of this book. If he is correct, our exposition of James as it relates to counseling is right in line with it.

There are many who need to be restored. The church is filled with believers who have **erred from the truth**, both deliberately and because of false teaching that they have received. To **err from the truth** includes both sin in thought and in deed.

As a counselor working with such a person, if you **bring him back, you should know that the one who brings back a sinner from the error of his way will save his soul from death and will cover a lot of sins.** The word **soul** means "him." And James is here speaking of *physical* death. He has not fully left behind the sick person who, apart from repentance, may die (I Corinthians 11 indicates that in such situations some **slept;** a beautiful Christian euphemism for death).

To **cover a lot of sins** neither means "cover up" nor refers to the sins of the counselor (as if in some meritorious manner his act freed him from sins). The Old Testament idea of the day of atonement (literally, "covering") is in view. The real reward of the counselor is not that of a bounty hunter but that of one who rejoices to see so many sins forgiven in the lives of those he is able to help bring back from the error of their ways. Cf. I Peter 4:8; Proverbs 19:12; and Psalm 32:1. In these passages, you have it all in a nutshell.

CONCLUSION

Can you think of a single other book of the New Testament that has so much to offer the Christian counselor? It is hard to do so. Each, in its own distinctive way, does contribute something new and fresh. But there is so much in James that is not even touched on or only touched on very lightly in other places. James is truly unique. It is a counselor's handbook. If you don't know it well enough to use it in counseling, then you need to go over it again and again until its main elements are firmly fixed in your mind. Until you do so, the book will not be used as fully as it ought, and counselees will not be helped as adequately as they may be. Learn all about James; learn it inside out. Remember, that is what James is all about—how that which is inside comes out in life. Don't let Luther's adumbrations fool you.

Introduction to JUDE

There is no question about the close relationship between II Peter and Jude. That Jude was dependent on II Peter is my firm conviction for reasons I mentioned in the introduction to II Peter. Here, I should like to add two more. First, it is reasonable that in a letter written in an emergency situation (Jude had not planned to write a letter of this sort, but a quite different one) the writer might readily lean on something that had already been written to the same people to remind them about what they had heard; especially when it had the endorsement of the prince of the apostles, Peter. It is highly unlikely that Peter would depend on Jude when he is writing a letter in a more relaxed situation. Why do so? Moreover, Jude refers to previous warnings that had been given to the congregation(s) to which he is writing. And to mention what I said before (which is the clincher for me) Peter predicts the coming of false teachers, describing them in chapter 2 of his second letter; Jude says that his predictions have been fulfilled. They have come. Sadly, they have been influencing persons who should have heeded Peter's warning, but (presumably) didn't. In Jude, you read of the sorry conditions of people who thought they knew better than the apostle.

It is most instructive to have two letters in which there is warning and, then later on, the fulfillment of all that was anticipated. There is much instruction in this for both counselors and counselees alike. The former may see how even the apostles were not always heard by those to whom they wrote. That should encourage counselors who, as is inevitable, find themselves in the same predicament. It happens to the best. If Peter, writing inspired material, did not succeed in convincing all of those to whom he wrote (some, perhaps the majority to whom Jude wrote did heed, as we shall see), who are you or I to think that we shall have a better track record? But the letter of Jude does not merely tell of conditions that prevailed in the church(es); in it Jude gives inspired directions about what to do about the false teachers, and those who have been influenced by them. While Peter focused on the former matter—how to identify and deal with the teachers, Jude advances a step and tells us what to do for those who have been duped by them. That fact, incidentally, is also another reason for believing Jude wrote after Peter, and not before. Such information is invaluable to the Christian counselor.

1 Jude, a slave of Jesus Christ and brother of James, to those who have been called, loved by God the Father and kept by Jesus Christ.

As we begin to study the Book of Jude in relation to Christian counseling it is important to understand that there is much that is parallel to II Peter 2. Because of this fact it will not be necessary to discuss some of the material at great length. However, the two are not identical. For instance, Jude has Peter in hand, but then writes what he finds there in his own style (in particular, he likes threes, a trait that may have been habitual in his preaching). Moreover, there is no slavish dependence on II Peter; Jude may omit, alter or add material. So where these differences exist, for the most part, it will be important to spend a bit more time on them.

At the outset, it is instructive to learn who Jude is and how he views himself. He is the **brother of James**, he tells us. But James was the brother of the Lord. Does Jude not identify himself as such because of humility? Many commentators believe so. I am thinking of someone who does just the opposite. If it were not so pitiful, it would be amusing. He identifies himself all over his stationery as what he is, stinting the use of no title or activity in which he is engaged. Moreover, in speech, when he speaks of himself (which is rather frequently) he always does so by the title "Doctor." At times, when around others, it is actually embarrassing. To avoid any of this worst of all name-dropping, Jude identifies who he is by the lesser of two possible references. There are counselees, like my acquaintance, who need to learn from this. They turn others off because in a variety of ways they want always to tell you how important they are.

There are those who believe that people do these things because they have low self-esteem. However, the opposite is true: they think they are more important than they are and they are desperately trying to tell others so. They want recognition they think that others should give them. When they fail to receive it, they give it to themselves. Their efforts are a futile attempt to boost their supposed worth in the eyes of others. There is powerful pride in this that must be combated. Keep an eye peeled for any who do such things; they need to acquire from counseling a bit of the humility that Jude presumably shows along with whatever else is necessary. However that may be, it certainly is interesting that Jude fails to make hay out of his physical relationship to the Lord Jesus Christ. Instead, he refers to himself as Jesus' **slave**.

Let's consider that appellation common to many of the letters of the New Testament. The idea, more fully expressed in Romans 6 and 7 than elsewhere, comes from the thought of the emancipation of the Christian from the slavery of sin and his subsequent entrance into slavery for Jesus Christ. This new slavery actually is true freedom. To be Christ's slave is to be bought with a price (Christ's precious blood) that leads to a willingness to do as He commands (a slave has no will of his own; his will must be the will of his Master). These facts create an insightful imagery that is instructive about what it means to be **a slave of Jesus Christ**, and what attitudes counselors must inculcate in proud individuals.

As Jude addresses his readers, he says that **have been called, loved by God the Father and kept by Jesus Christ**. Here we see the first of the many triplets that permeate the book. Through His Spirit, the Christian is *called.* There are two calls: the inner and the outer. The latter comes through the presentation of the gospel; the former through the regenerating operation of the Holy Spirit Who gives life to the dead sinner in order to enable him to believe the gospel. It is the inner call to which Jude refers in this place. Once again, it is evident that our salvation and all that goes along with it is not our doing, but is the result of the remarkable grace of God.

God expressed His **love** to His elect people by sending His Son to die for their sins. And He has continued to manifest His love toward them in a thousand different ways ever since. Surely, the entire scope of the love of God is here in view. Defeated, discouraged, disheartened counselees need to be reminded of that love. Here were believers to whom Jude was writing who needed to be reminded because some may have wondered whether God had forsaken their church(es). Jude assures them that God's love remains steadfast, even when we waver. It is a love that calls one back through repentance when he wanders. It is a love that provides for all one truly needs (I didn't say "desires"). It is a love that transcends one's ability to comprehend. God's love is steadfast and sure. That's what counselees must believe if they are to make progress in counseling.

But true Christians, despite the efforts of false teachers to upset them, will persevere. How do we know that? Because, as Jude says, they are **kept by Jesus Christ**. If He guards and protects them from their enemies, their salvation is secure. No one has power or authority greater than He. There is, therefore, no person or force that can dislodge them from His protecting care. Those whose sins have been forgiven will never face eternal punishment for them; Jesus did that on the cross. God does not exact punishment for the same sins twice. When Jesus paid the price it was paid fully for all time. Nothing can change that.

However, Christians may wander and go astray as some about whom

2 Mercy, peace and love toward you be increased.
3 Dear friends, I was making a serious effort to write to you about our common salvation when it became necessary instead to write calling on you to contend vigorously for the faith that was delivered to the saints in a full and final way.

Jude was writing did. It is then that the keeping power of Christ is displayed in large measure as He defeats their enemies, convicts them of their sins against a loving heavenly father and through repentance and sanctification restores them to a higher level of life than before. He even uses their sin (reprehensible as it is) to bring them closer to Himself. One means of doing so is through his people. That, of course, is why Jude is writing. That is one reason why you counsel.

But though they have all this, it is Jude's wish that they would receive more of the same. He writes **Mercy, peace and love toward you be increased**. Counseling is part of the process of sanctification. It has as its goal the **increase** of each of these elements at work in each counselee as they positively affect his daily living for Christ. The church needed not only **love** (there were deep differences that may have led to incriminations on the part of some) but also **mercy**. Apart from the mercy of God (His goodness and pitying care expressed toward His erring children) we all would be finished. Counselees sometimes think of God as a hard taskmaster whose judgment is ever present and ready to fall on them. That God never condones sin is true; but He is a Father Who pities his children and even in their sin shows mercy toward them. Make this all-important balance clear in counseling. Many counselees fail to make progress because of wrong notions about God. Surely this church as a whole and each individual in it needed **peace**. It was being disrupted by error and licentious living. This deadly combination is calculated by the evil one to disturb the peace of the church. And when Christians begin to fight and devour one another, that only adds to the problem. That is not to say that there are no steps to be taken to oust the false teachers with their sordid teaching and to reclaim those who have been adversely affected by it, but *how* that is done is all-important. Jude wants it to be carried on in a manner consistent with **peace**.

In verse 3, a pivotal verse, Jude reveals his purpose in writing. Actually, he had begun to write with one purpose in mind (to encourage his readers in some particulars of their **common salvation**) when, instead, **it became necessary** to write calling on them **to contend vigorously for**

the faith that was delivered to the saints in a full and final way. Scraping his original purpose, he crumpled up the papyrus roll on which he was going to write to them, pulled out a single sheet of papyrus and shot off this letter to meet the emergency that had arisen.

What had happened? It seems as if he heard of the intrusion of false teachers into the church(es) to which he was about to write. They had come in unknown, but had become a potent force for evil to which some (perhaps even many) of the members had succumbed. This brief letter, therefore, is a forceful appeal to **contend vigorously** against their teaching and for **the faith delivered to the saints in a full and final way** (the word in the original is *hapax*). The term translated **contend vigorously** means to fight so as to hold ground that the enemy is attempting to take. The gains that a church (or an individual in it) has made must not be lost. In II John 8 the same point is made with reference to individuals. False teaching can so confuse and stunt the growth of one who has gained a significant amount of knowledge and has developed a growingly Christian lifestyle that it may set him back for the rest of his life (see also I Cor. 15:33 and comments on that verse). Jude was fearful of this. The faith had been given to the **saints** in a **full and final way**. Nothing more need be added; none dare say that God had given an insufficient revelation to His people. Yet you will discover counselees who are looking for "something more." There is nothing more to be found. What they need is not something more, but more of the something that they already have in Christ. Invariably, it is those Christians who are looking for a quick fix, for some formula by which they can obtain peace and safety, who are searching for something more. That is why they are all too willing to follow anyone who promises additional truth. But the something more always turns out to be something *different*. And that is true because there is nothing more; the faith (that we are to believe and follow) has been **delivered** in a full and final way.

The word **delivered** refers to the same deposit of truth to which Paul alludes when writing to Timothy (II Timothy 2:12-14). There it is referred to as a body of truth in a form that could be passed down through the ages. It is not to be altered but entrusted to able men who would preserve and proclaim it clearly. Whether it is Jude or Paul writing, the point each makes is the same: God has deposited with His church all that is necessary for life and godliness (see II Peter 1:3). Whenever a counselee refers to "something more" than that which is a part of the deposit of **the faith** now found in the Bible alone, warn him that what he is playing around with is dangerous because, in reality, it isn't something more but some-

4 Certain persons have slipped in surreptitiously, who were previously assigned to judgment for this a long time ago; they are ungodly persons, who are twisting the grace of our God into a reason for debauchery, thus denying our only Master and Lord, Jesus Christ.

---

thing *different.* Whatever is added to the once-for-all delivered deposit of the faith always becomes more important than the truths contained in that deposit itself. You will get nowhere with him if he is confused or is taken in by this added material. You must contend vigorously against it so as to dislodge him from its icy grip. But more of that as we progress. Let it be enough to say that in contending (fighting) one is involved in warfare. But he must never stoop to the atrocities of the enemy in doing so.

It is important to see how Jude considered it **necessary** to drop what he intended to do and to get involved in the battle for the faith. If when you see a counselee affected adversely by false teaching you do not feel the necessity to do something about it there is something remiss in your ideas and attitudes toward counseling. As I said in the discussion of II Peter, many counselors have never been told that warfare against error (and those who teach it) is a part of their counseling task. I hope, however, that you will see clearly that this teaching failure is dangerous. As we come to the final few verses of Jude you are going to discover that, in Jude's view, every counselor also is a fireman. It would be nice if all we had to do was to discuss our **common salvation**, but in a world of sin, where the enemy is constantly at work, that is not possible. Jude found it so, and if you are astute to the many forces at work in the thinking of your counselees, you will too. But enough of that for now.

What can we learn about these teachers? Well, to begin with, we do not know who they were. They are simply called **certain persons**. New Testament writers do not hesitate to name names where it is possible and necessary to do so; so presumably these false teachers were not known to Jude by name. Besides, there was no reason to name them; by now the church(es) to which he writes knew who and what they were. Yet that was not always true. Originally, when they came into the membership of the church(es) they **slipped in surreptitiously**. That is to say, they were openly received, but not for what they truly were; they did not come into the church with their colors flying. They came bringing in their false doctrines in such a way that no one knew what they really believed. They represented themselves as in agreement with the congregation(s) with which they affiliated. It was only later on, when they had gained the ear of some (many?) that they trumpeted their teachings. Most error slips into the church this way. It cannot always be detected at first. That is why it is so important to know what to do about it when it finally rears its deadly head. And here, that is most clearly stated: those who remained true to **the faith must fight (contend) vigorously against it**. Those whom God calls to lead His church must heed His further **call** (v. 3) to contend just as seriously.

The words **slipped in surreptitiously** come from a root that means "to go under." I never think of this term apart from thinking of my childhood at the circus. When the policeman's back is turned, a number of kids would slip in *under* the side of the big top tent. That is the same image that Jude wants to plant in your mind—people slipping in when your back is turned. Sometimes it is our fault, because we are not vigilant enough. But frequently, it is impossible to know what they are up to until later, when they think they are firmly entrenched and begin to hawk their heretical wares.

But this is no new thing. It has been going on for millennia. Errorists have been insinuating themselves into the midst of God's people from the time when the mixed multitude came out of Egypt with the children of Israel right up to the present moment. And God's **judgment** of such persons was written **long ago**. Now it is possible that Jude is referring to what Peter had written some time before. (The words for "long ago" *can* refer to a time or an event that is not so *very* long beforehand. But either way, it is clear that God *has spoken, and has pronounced judgment on false teachers who lead His people astray*.) The reason I refer to a long distant announcement is because this view accords with Jude 14 and 15 (especially because of the use of the word **ungodly** in both places). But whichever it is, the message is the same: God has determined to bring judgment on false teachers who disturb His church.

They are **ungodly persons**, says Jude. What does that word mean? It comes from the idea of "not shrinking with awe"; it is irreverence in thought and action. They have no hesitancy about plying their nefarious trade among the people of the Almighty God. They have no qualms about leading them astray. They give no thought to what God may do; they are truly *un*godly. They concern themselves only with what they want; they simply give *no* thought to God. People like this are in contact with your counselees all the time, some within but most without the church. Either way, they have impact for which you must probe to see how potent it is. If your counselee has weaknesses, he is fair game for these ungodly persons. Counselees, remember, do not live in a vacuum. Counselors often forget that fact. Check out influences that may be leading counselees astray (and in doing so, don't fail, check to unsound influences that may come from within the church itself).

What did those who were going beyond the deposit of the **faith** teach? Well, they were clever enough to use the truths of Scripture **as the basis for** their erroneous teachings. Peter, you may recall, spoke of them as persons who would **twist** the Scriptures (II Peter 3:16). And that is precisely what these men did. They based their teaching on the biblical doctrine of **grace**. But the way in which they taught this marvelous truth ended up as an excuse for **debauchery**. Presumably, they were saying that if all is of grace (a truth we revel in) then it doesn't matter how you live. God is a gracious God who will forgive and bypass your sin regardless of what you do. So why not really live it up? It is not so much when people bring in new truths that advertise themselves as such; the gravest dangers come from those who have a new "twist" on old truths. What the Bible-believing church has believed over the centuries should never be lightly set aside. God *may* be giving new insight into His Word through contemporary teachers, but it will be rare when this happens. The advice you must give to your counselees is "be wary of it."

This false view of God's grace was such a perversion of truth that it could only have come from persons who were devoid of the Spirit. And that is precisely what Jude says about them: they **deny our only Master and Lord, Jesus Christ**. To deny Him is to deny the faith; it is to give evidence of one's reprobate state (cf. Matthew 10:33). Note that Jesus is called **Master and Lord**. That is a way of saying that He is supreme in the life of a genuine believer. Those who deny Him, of course, do not recognize Him as such; rather, to them He and His teaching are but a means to serve their own ends. To "profess Him" (falsely) is but a way of gaining entrance into the midst of the church. To affirm belief in God's grace, only to twist, warp and pervert it so as to make it teach the opposite, again is but a means to their evil ends. It is not always what people *say* they believe; it is how they interpret and spell out their understanding of doctrine that counts. And it is also what they do that separates the true from the false. Counselors, by virtue of their task of sorting things out for what they really are, must always keep this in mind. Counselees will tell you they, or those who have overwhelming influence upon them, believe the doctrines of that deposit of truth that constitutes the **faith that was delivered to the saints**. But you may not in and of itself accept their profession as "gospel." It is your job to examine exactly what they mean. More often than you might think, counselees have accepted some twisted version of

5 Now I want to remind you—although you have a full and final knowledge about it—that the Lord, having saved a people from Egypt, later destroyed those who didn't believe.

---

the truth that is getting them into trouble. It may not be as serious as the perversions offered by these false teachers, but since all doctrine is important for life, you can be sure that some harm comes to those who accept it.

Now, in line with his triple impact methodology, Jude presents three Old Testament examples of how God dealt with those whom He judged. They are a fearful lot: the people destroyed in the wilderness, the angels who sinned and Sodom and Gomorrah. It is his purpose to show that teachers like this, and those who follow them, do not get away with their sin. God knows, and in His time, He judges them. That is the reason for citing these examples. They are solemn warnings to those who read.

Notice how he begins: **Now I want to remind you—although you have a full and final knowledge about it**—What is he saying? That they needed to be reminded about these events. "But, if they knew so completely what the stories were all about, why remind?" That they knew is Jude's point. They knew (indeed, all he had to do was to refer to an example and the entire story would come to his reader's minds), but they knew *in an academic manner*. They had not related the events to what was happening in their church(es). They saw the Old Testament as an interesting record. They could have given the right answers about these events in a Bible quiz held at the temple in Jerusalem. But the events seemed not to touch their lives.

That is a problem frequently encountered in counseling. You meet people who can give you all the answers, quote all the passages, but who are living in ways directly opposed to what those passages teach. Just tonight, a homosexual wandered into our church looking for money. He claimed to be saved, could quote Bible verses and said that he was a "backslidden" believer who had been saved by the death of Christ for his sins. But backslidden for 7 years during which he was carrying on a homosexual lifestyle and had not yet repented? That is highly questionable. Look carefully at what people *do* as well as *listen* to what they say. If the two utterly contradict one another, it is likely that you have either a lying hypocrite or a totally confused person—or both.

The Israelites had been delivered (**saved**) from the bondage of Egypt as **a people**. That does not mean that every individual was saved spiritu-

6 Angels who didn't keep their own original state but left their proper dwelling place He has kept chained in gloomy darkness, awaiting the judgment of the Great Day.

---

ally. Later, in the wilderness, God **destroyed** those **who didn't believe**. These are many who "go along for the ride," as we often say. They are not really a part of whatever group it is that they accompany. The same is true of Christ's church. People like this are described in Hebrews 6:10 where it is clear that they experience many of the blessings of God's people, but are not truly part of the church. That was what had happened in Old Testament times, and that is what was happening in Jude's day. It also happens in ours. One thing that you must continuously ask yourself, if a counselee either resists direct commands of the Bible (I'm not talking about your suggested advice to him) or after every kind of attempt still fails to do as God requires, is "I wonder whether this counselee is truly a Christian? Or is he only a fellow-traveler?" After church discipline is applied to them, many you counsel will turn out to be persons who should be treated as **a heathen and a tax collector**. That there is a mixed multitude in every congregation is a given. And that doesn't always mean that the church has been negligent. People slip in unawares.

But the point of the passage is that eventually God will **destroy** them. The same is true of the **Angels who didn't keep their own original status but left their proper dwelling place**. We know very little about what occurred. What we learn here of the angels who sinned is that because they were dissatisfied with the status that God gave them (wanting something different or something more) they failed to maintain **their original state**, but **left their proper dwelling place** (presumably heaven) for some other. This brief reference (which leaves us in the dark about the details of this rebellious attitude on the part of some of the angels) was not intended to *teach* the reader. He already knew those details. It was to *remind* him about what happened to the angels: God **has kept [them] chained in gloomy darkness, awaiting the judgment of the Great Day**. Like those who didn't believe among the Israelites who were saved as a people from Egypt, so too these angels will receive judgment at the coming of Christ on the last **Day**. Jude wants his correspondents to know two things: 1) these men, like the sinning angels, will receive their punishment; 2) they are not worth following (indeed, it is dangerous to do so since they are people under God's judgment). Counselors must similarly warn counselees about false teachers with whom they have become enam-

7 In the same way Sodom and Gomorrah and the cities around them,
that in a similar manner engaged in sexual immorality and went away after
different flesh, are set forth as an example of suffering the punishment of
eternal fire.
8 In spite of this in the same way these persons also by their dreamings
pollute the flesh, set aside ruling authority and insult glorious beings.

---

ored.

And there is a third Old Testament event to which Jude directs attention: the destruction of **Sodom and Gomorrah**. Like the others who will be judged, so too were the cities of the plains. Why? Because they engaged in homosexual practices and their behavior was an abomination before the Lord. Because of their unrepentant lifestyle, they were wiped out and became **an example of suffering the punishment of eternal fire**. These examples are **set forth** in order to warn true believers about the end of those who are unbelievers.

Even though these facts are known to them, the false teachers, **by their dreamings pollute the flesh**. Doubtless, Jude here references adulterous behavior of the leaders in Israel who did such things in conjunction with false prophecies and revelations that they claimed to receive in dreams from God (see Jeremiah 23:13-29) and led the people astray. Today, so many appeal to subjective experience rather than to the objective Word of God. There are leaders who claim the Name of Christ who through dreams, or in some other way, pretend to receive new revelations from God. Yet as the prophets polluted the land of Israel by their false prophecies intended to justify their licentiousness, so do these teachers stain their **flesh** (their bodies). Is there any need to say that nothing has changed about this in our time except, perhaps, it may have gotten worse?

Watch out for persons who are antiestablishment. They are those who set aside **ruling authorities** over it. They insult **glorious beings** (possibly the angels, but also quite conceivably, more generally, all those to whom honor and respect are due). In our day it is clear that since the Scriptures have been set aside by most of the leaders of our country and even by many of the so-called leaders in the church, there is a preponderance of those who fall into this group of persons. The arrogance they display when they speak of the authority in His church is incredible. Be sure that you are not influenced by them. They parade under the banner of "scholarship," declare biblical truth "simplistic," and disguise their sensuality under such rubrics as "freedom" and "enlightenment." Be on the

9 Yet Michael, the archangel, when he disputed with the devil, arguing with him about the body of Moses, didn't dare to make an insulting accusation against him, but said, "The Lord rebuke you!"
10 But these persons insult whatever they don't understand, while by whatever they do know instinctively, like unreasoning animals, they ruin themselves.

---

lookout for them. Consider what the changing buzz words of the day may be and listen for them in their conversation. How far will such persons go?

Jude says that **these persons insult whatever they don't understand** (v. 10[b]). Their behavior is totally opposite to that of **Michael, the archangel**, who showed respect even for the authority of the prince of darkness when he **argued with him about the body of Moses**. It is not clear what this phrase refers to. One thing we do know is that it was Moses and Elijah—two persons about whom there was something unusual that had to do with their bodies when they left this world—who appeared on the Mount of Transfiguration. That Elijah was transformed without seeing death is clear; that there was a dispute over Moses' body is also clear from this passage. It would seem that at God's behest Michael came to retrieve the body of Moses when he died and that the devil objected. It is not important for us to know more or God would have revealed it to us. But the important point is that in that dispute, Michael **didn't dare to make an insulting accusation against him, but said, 'The Lord rebuke you!'** The familiarity with which a goodly number of faith-healers and others address Satan is appalling. They scream and holler at him, call him names (thereby insulting him) and act as if he had no authority they should respect. Avoid people like this. Haven't you sometimes wondered how they got on such familiar terms with the devil?

Because they are irrational people (**like unreasoning animals**) who act **instinctively**; out of the ignorance, **they insult whatever they don't understand**. Whenever something happens that he doesn't understand, my dog "insults" it by barking loudly and furiously. They are just like that. But it is a terrible insult to the God Who made them unique among His creatures in His own image for them to abandon reason for the mere stimulus-and-response instinct of animals. Behaviorism is an insult to God. Man is more than an animal, and even though His image has been marred by the fall he ought still to give some evidence of its remaining remnants in his responses. But all those who live an animalized life bring **ruin** to themselves. Whenever you see a counselee who had degraded

11 Woe to them because they took Cain's path, and for reward rushed headlong into Balaam's error and have destroyed themselves in Korah's rebellion!
12 These persons are blots on your love feasts, banqueting with you without a qualm, shepherding themselves. They are waterless clouds, swept along by winds; autumn trees that are fruitless, uprooted—doubly dead!

---

himself to the point of living like an animal, bring him up short by reading this verse to him. Don't allow him to get away with such behavior without assuring him that he is insulting the living God, who, if he fails to repent of his sin, will bring him to ruin.

In an emotional outcry at the thought of that ruin, and all that it entails, Jude shouts **Woe to them**! Their end is like that of **Cain, Balaam and Koreh**. Again, Jude reaches back for *three* Old Testament events that swirl around *three* characters who came into disfavor with God. **Cain** was both the first man born and the first murderer. Why? Because in his desire for importance (self-esteem) and approval by God, and out of envy over His acceptance of his brother's offering and the rejection of his own, he slew him. But there was more. God had warned him, but he refused to heed the warning. The same was true of **Balaam**. Because of his greed for money, he angered God Who repeatedly warned him and even used a donkey to do so. Yet he went on attempting to curse Israel to obtain money from Balak. Then there was **Koreh** who wanted the authority that belonged to Moses and Aaron. God had made him a Levite, but he wanted more. A warning from God through Moses went unheeded, and this man with 250 of Israel's most prominent men who followed him were swallowed up by the earth which opened and then closed upon them. In every case, the fact was that, whether out of a desire for greater esteem, out of greed for money or out of an attempt to gain greater power and authority, each of these men **destroyed** his own life. The false teachers, Jude says, were just like that. They too failed to heed warnings from God or His representatives. The interesting thing is that they are represented as worse than any one of these Old Testament characters—they are like all three combined! Counselor, be alert to those who will not heed warnings.

In a sweeping characterization of the false teachers, Jude now piles figure on top of figure in order to enable the reader to identify the enemy. These teachers are **blots on your love feasts**, he says. Like stains on the tablecloth that ruin the effect of it, they ruin the times when you want to have loving fellowship (see II Peter for additional information regarding

13 They are wild sea waves foaming out their shameful debris, wandering stars for whom the dark gloom has been reserved forever.

---

this). Though they knowingly set out to deceive and divide, they go on **banqueting [with you] without a qualm**. They have no reticence about the destructive activities in which they engage. It seems as if they relish causing trouble for the saints.

Moreover, they are always **shepherding themselves**. They care nothing about helping others. Their care is only for themselves; they are self-centered. You will see more and more of this among those who have grown up under the aegis of the self-love teachers. Be prepared to counter it with this passage. The simple phrase **shepherding themselves**, that speaks so powerfully of those who care only for themselves, should have a potent effect on those who need to hear it.

They are **waterless clouds, swept along by winds**. In a land in which every raindrop is important, this expression would be instantly appreciated. They promise much, but like the cloud that promises rain, yet is swept away before a drop falls, they fail to deliver on their promises. They are all talk and no action. Look out for counselees who never deliver on their homework after making promises of all sorts.

They were never believers, so like **autumn trees that are fruitless, uprooted** they are **doubly dead**! These people have none of the Spirit's fruit at the time when it ought to appear; they are uprooted and consequently dried up and withered. There is no spiritual life in them. They are dead in trespasses and sins. A vivid description of those who claim to be Christians (even Christian teachers) but who, themselves, have no life in them!

They are also like **wild sea waves foaming out their shameful debris**. Have you ever walked along the seashore smelling the stench of the dead plants and carcasses of sea creatures that litter its sands? They are like that. Wherever they have gone they have left a trail of putrefaction. It is a shame to speak of the ruined lives, the ravaged souls and the perverted minds that they have left in their wake. They make a big splash that leaves behinds only foam and filth.

And then, Jude sketches what is perhaps the most fearful picture of all. They are **wandering stars for whom the dark gloom has been reserved forever**. Those who joke about having "plenty of company in hell," fail to realize that it is going to be a state of utter loneliness. Like planets and stars, light-years away from one another thrown out into the

14 Even Enoch, the seventh from Adam, prophesied about these persons, saying:

See, the Lord is coming with ten thousand of His holy ones
15 **to execute judgment against all of them, and to convict all the ungodly of all their ungodly works that they have done in an ungodly way, and of all the hard things that ungodly sinners have spoken about Him.**

---

cold darkness of space, such persons will for all eternity wander far from the warmth and light of Christian fellowship with one another and with God. Why associate with persons headed for such a destiny? What have they to offer? What can they teach you? That is Jude's (and a faithful counselors') message.

In verse 14, Jude shows how this phenomenon of false teachers who will be judged by God is nothing new. The pattern is as old as **Enoch, the seventh from Adam**. That is going back! Just as the **way of Cain** runs back through the centuries to the very beginnings of the human race, the problem of ungodly teachers reaches back to those near beginnings as well. It can be recognized in the prophecy of that saint who **walked with God**. Where Jude obtained this information about Enoch's prediction is not known. There is an apocryphal book called I Enoch, where similar things are said. But it's highly unlikely that Jude is quoting it. It is more likely that both writers refer to some lost source. At any rate, Enoch prophesied about these **ungodly** persons (note his stress upon this adjective).

Enoch wrote: **See, the Lord is coming with ten thousand of His holy ones to execute judgment against all of them and to convict all the ungodly of all their ungodly works that they have done in an ungodly way, and of all the hard things that ungodly sinners have spoken about Him**. The judgment of which he speaks will occur on that final Day when Christ returns with his holy angels (cf. II Thessalonians 1:7ff.). It will be comprehensive. God will remember not only the **works**, and the **ways** that these works were performed, but the **words** that were spoken as well. In all of these things the prevailing characteristic is their **ungodliness**.

But what does Enoch (and Jude) mean by an **ungodly sinner**? Is it every sinner of which he speaks? Well, of course, all are ungodly. But not all have spoken against the Lord as viciously as these teachers have. They are ungodly in a way that goes beyond the ordinary ungodliness of other sinners. They are singled out for special judgment. Some will have fewer

16 These persons are grumblers, malcontents, who live according to their own desires, and their mouths speak arrogantly, flattering people to gain a favor.

---

stripes; they will have more.

"O.K.," you say, "I see that. But what is **ungodliness** as such?" It is important to understand this matter. The *asebeia* (**ungodliness**) comes from the Greek root ("godly") that pictures someone shrinking back with awe. To it is added the negative (an alpha privative) which acts like our prefix *un*. So an *un*godly person is one who is not godly because he is one who has no awe or reverence for God either in word, attitude or action. The word always involves conduct, but behind that conduct is an attitude of heart that does not "fear" God. An ungodly person is one who forgets that he must face the Creator of the universe at death. But people like these teachers are particularly flagrant in their disrespect for God. In their works, the evil ways in which they perform them, as well as in their words, they show defiance toward Him rather than awe and respect. Their judgment is sure. It was prophesied from the beginning.

Like Peter, Jude does not end there. On he goes, describing some of the evil works and words that you will find in them: **These are grumblers, malcontents, who live according to their own desires and their mouths speak arrogantly, flattering people to gain a favor**. There you are—a forceful condemnation of grumbling! How greatly needed it is for many counselees to hear what God thinks of grumbling. The grumbling may be about conditions, circumstances, or other people, but (when you boil it all down) ultimately it is against *God*. That is partly what Jude means when he says **their mouths speak arrogantly**. It is arrogant to complain in God's world about how He is ordering it. There is never any reason for grumbling. But at times, it can become insidious. Once it gets hold of one person, as he grumbles to another and then another, it soon spreads like a deadly disease among the members of a congregation. First thing you know, the dissatisfaction among the members becomes so widespread that everything that anyone does is considered wrong. Counselees are particularly prone to grumbling. Read God's view of it to them from this verse. And remind them of I Corinthians 19:19 as well (be sure to relate the preceding verses in that chapter to this verse as well).

These **malcontents, who live according to their own desires** are malcontent (never content with anything) *because* they **live according to their desires**. Desire-driven living does not satisfy. It gives pleasure but

17 But you, dear friends, remember the words that were spoken beforehand by the apostles of our Lord Jesus Christ
18 when they told you, "At the end of this period there will be scoffers who will live according to their own ungodly desires."

---

for the moment. Counselees who insist on having their desires met (usually these days the word "needs" is substituted for "desires" in order to justify living of that nature) must be told that there is no light at the end of that tunnel. Only commandment-driven living, obedience that one renders out of gratitude and love toward God, will bring lasting satisfaction. Desire-driven living becomes a never-ending quest for that which they will never find.

And in order to obtain what they desire, they will stoop to almost anything. They will even go about a congregation flattering **people to gain a favor** that they think will satisfy them in their search. Counselor, don't let them take you in with their flattery about how greatly they have profited from your counsel, etc., etc. Rather, see through this. They will have profited greatly only when their lives show it; not merely when they mouth about it to you to gain some concession from you.

Jude continues in words that indicate his love and concern for his readers: **But you, dear friends.** His words so far have been harsh; Jude didn't want the readers who had not gone over to the enemy to think that he included them in this camp. In this battle for the faith, there were friends who would stand with him, who would listen to his message and who would take up the battle for the faith. He addresses them as friends who are close to him, and for whom he had true affection and love in Christ.

But there were those, perhaps even among them, who needed the **reminder** of the words of the apostles of Jesus. They predicted the coming of **scoffers at the end of this** [the current] **period**. The time of which he speaks may refer either to 70 AD or to the second coming of Christ. If it exactly parallels II Peter 3, it refers to the latter. But Jude has a way of launching out on his own, so he might refer to the former.

The preponderance of weight falls on the second coming. This is because of the parallelism and because in both the passages Jude and Peter speak of **scoffers** (v. 18). These people will **live according to their own ungodly desires.** Enough has been said already about desire-driven living. But it is important to note how frequently the matter arises in these general epistles. A good study for you to make might be to take a concor-

19 These are the persons who cause divisions. They are soulish because they don't have the Spirit.

---

dance (or quick verse computer program) and run down the word "desire" (remember sometimes it is rendered "lust"). Every counselor ought to know what the Bible has to say about such motivation; it is the predominant power behind the sin in our culture. And not only is it appealed to by every commercial advertisement, but it is justified by most of the psychological systems of our day. To combat desire-driven living, one must always oppose it with gratitude-driven living that, out of thanksgiving to God for sending His Son to die for our sins, a Christian lives according to God's commandments. It is obedient, gratitude-motivated living that counts.

Desire, of course, is not wrong in itself. God is the One Who created man with all of his passions and parts. There is, therefore, a proper place for desire. But that is desire regulated by biblical requirements (precisely what these teachers were rejecting). Here, and in II Peter, the two writers are talking about **ungodly desires**. We have already discussed what the word **ungodly** means. In light of that discussion, we can say that these **ungodly desires** (because they are not regulated by biblical requirements) are desires for things that are against God, but that are pursued anyway regardless of the consequences. There is no fear of God in those who indulge them; they are persons who have no sense of reverence. They go on satisfying their every whim with no thought of God.

Verse 19 gets to the heart of the problem: **These are the persons who cause divisions.** Literally, Jude says "They mark off limits." Because they draw lines that the Bible doesn't they gather together people to the other side of the line and divide them from the rest of the congregation. Titus 3:10 tells you how to treat divisive persons. As the second of three characteristics, Jude says they are **sensual.** That accords with the third: **They don't have the Spirit**. All they have is their own drives, distorted opinions and twisted interpretations of the Bible. They do not have the Spirit to help them understand the Scriptures (cf. I Corinthians 2), and no matter what they do, they cannot please God (cf. Romans 8:8). It is Jude's last word about them. And we are glad that this extended description is over.

But Jude is not finished. Perhaps, apart from verse 3, the most important section now begins. Certainly, it is of great importance to the Christian counselor—or *should* be. Jude is still thinking about contending

20 But you, dear friends, by building yourselves up in your most holy
faith, through praying by the Holy Spirit,
21 keep yourselves in God's love, waiting for the mercy of our Lord Jesus
Christ that leads to eternal life.

---

for the faith, as he has throughout. But now, he considers what must be done to rescue those who have been taken captive by the enemy. Clearly, that is a function of the counselor. He writes: **But you dear friends, by building yourselves up in your most holy faith, through praying by the Holy Spirit, keep yourselves in God's love.** Here are three more exhortations. Let us consider each in the light of verse 3.

If you are going to do battle with the enemy (the false teachers who have invaded your territory and are now in the process of trying to take captives) you must have the right equipment to carry on warfare successfully. That means, in terms of spiritual warfare, you must be able to articulate your faith and demonstrate that it is biblical. You must **build yourselves up in the faith.** Perhaps one reason why Christian counselors fail to retrieve more of those who are being taken captive is because their knowledge of their faith is so weak; they may know more about Freud than about David. A soldier of Christ must be fully armed with the Bible; otherwise the enemy will cut him down in argument and those he seeks to rescue will become even more convinced of the error to which they have been attracted.

The second thing necessary for carrying on biblical warfare is **praying by the Holy Spirit**. Romans 8 explains the Holy Spirit's part in prayer. He makes our ragged prayers acceptable to the Father. So we need not hesitate to pray. For what should the soldier pray? That the Spirit will work in the hearts of those who are being led astray. If He doesn't do that sort of work, you can do nothing. Pray also for yourself that your attitudes will be good and that your memory of the Word and your use of it may be what it should be. Apart from prayer, it is all in vain.

Then the third thing is to **keep [yourself] in God's love.** It is easy to win the battle and lose the war. Your attitude in retrieving those who are going over to the enemy must not be antagonistic, but loving in every respect. You are to contend vigorously; but that does not mean becoming contentious.

These three exhortations are foundational to fighting for the **faith**. All the while you should have good expectations about the outcome: **waiting for [expecting] the mercy of our Lord Jesus Christ that leads**

22 Show mercy to doubters,
23 save others by pulling them out of the fire, and show mercy to others with caution, hating even the clothing spotted by their flesh.

---

to eternal life. There are souls at stake. And Jesus is merciful. Expect Him somehow in the battle to win some to Himself through your witness. Keep that in mind. Perhaps some of those who are taken in by the enemy are not really Christians after all; it is conceivable that through your battle for the faith they will come to believe. I remember well a contest between two Mormon elders and myself and a companion, in which two individuals came to know Christ. One of these is now a minister of the Word. So expect things to happen. Christ's mercy is wide. He can manifest Himself in this way. Remember the conversion of Paul!

There are three classes of persons who are being affected by the enemy. In the first group are the **doubters**. They need mercy. These people need to be worked with gently, quietly, carefully and in a manner that is calculated to set their doubts to rest. If you have been **building yourself up in the faith**, your merciful handling of them will pay off. If you think of yourself as a fireman, these are people who are near the fire, fascinated by it, but getting much too close to it. They are in danger. In mercy, warn them about the dangers inherent in their fascination. This letter sets them forth.

Secondly (again we are looking at triplets), Jude says **save others by pulling them out of the fire.** These people have gone too far. There is no use warning. They are *in* the fire. They are in serious danger. There is no time for gentle, considerate discussion. Jude says pull **them out of the fire**. Literally, he says "*snatch* them." Even if it takes violent action, pull them out of harm's way! You don't stand on ceremony when rescuing someone from a fire. It is not always possible to be tactful; emergency situations call for emergency measures. Too many think that to be tactful is more important than anything else. If the enemy's views must be destroyed, it is not wrong to *devastate* his position, if that is what it takes to rescue members from the conflagration that he started. After all, these teachers are spiritual arsonists.

Then there is a third group; they are *in* the fire, *on* fire. When you go into the burning house to rescue them, be careful, Jude says (cf. Gal. 6:1ff.). You, yourself, may become contaminated with the contagion of the running sores that spot their garments (the word **clothing** here is the undergarment that is closest to the body). The figure has changed to one

24 Now, to the One Who has power to keep you from falling and to present you faultless before His glorious presence with great joy,
25 to the only God our Savior be glory, majesty, might and authority through Jesus Christ our Lord, before all the ages, and now, and for all ages to come! Amen.

---

who has a loathsome disease. You must be careful about what you do so that you, too, will not become contaminated by the very same errors and, in particular, by the same sinful acts that they have bought into at the behest of the false, licentious teachers. Many counselors, because they were not careful even about how they handled the garment of one who was sinning have ended up sinning in the same way (many have become enamored with a counselee and committed adultery with her). Should one not counsel persons of the opposite sex, as some foolishly say? No. That isn't the solution. Jude presupposes that you will help them. But he cautions you about the manner in which you do so. He wants you to take special care about how you do it. If there is the slightest possible danger, ask another person to sit in on counseling.

Now comes the benediction—appropriate in every regard to the situation about which he has been writing. God has the **power to keep [them] from falling** into the clutches of the enemy. And He is the One Who can take you through all of this difficulty in such a way that on that final Day you will be **faultless**. Does that mean perfect? No, he is thinking about the present problem: He can preserve you from becoming contaminated with the enemy's filth. And rescuing you though the ministry of the Word (after all that was why Jude was writing; God's uses His appointed means), He can present you before **His glorious presence with great joy**. That is joy over having overcome the temptations of the enemy and having defeated him in the battle for other members of Christ's church. This One about Whom Jude is writing is **the only God or Savior [to whom there should] be glory, majesty, might and authority through Jesus Christ our Lord, before all ages, and now, and for all ages to come!** What a fitting conclusion. Jude focuses upon the eternal glory and power and authority of God. In Him there is all that one could wish to wage successful warfare; and God has put it all at your disposal. So there is no excuse for backing away from the battle. In Him, you have all the supplies and other resources needed. Counselor, you are in a war—do battle!

www.ingramcontent.com/pod-product-compliance
Lightning Source LLC
Chambersburg PA
CBHW062147080426
42734CB00010B/1595